The *Sams Teach Yourself in 24 Hours* Series

Sams Teach Yourself in 24 Hours books provide quick and easy answers in a proven step-by-step approach that works for you. In just 24 sessions of one hour or less, you will tackle every task you need to get the results you want. Let our experienced authors present the most accurate information to get you reliable answers—fast!

Tcl/Tk Quick Reference

The following is a concise reference to the notation used in Tcl, as well as to arithmetic operators and mathematical functions that can be used in the `expr` command. For more information, see *Tcl/Tk Reference Guide* by Paul Raines and Jeff Tranter, which can be found at `http://www.slac.stanford.edu/~raines/` `ref.html`. (Even though the *Guide* refers to Tcl/Tk version 8.0.2, most of the material is still valid for versions 8.1 and 8.2 of Tcl/Tk.)

Basic Notation Used in Tcl

Command	Description
`;` or newline	Command separator.
`\`	Command continuation.
`#`	Characters following # up to newline are treated as comments and are ignored. Think of it as a command. Use `;# my text` for inline comments.
`var`	A simple variable.
`arr(index)`	An associative array variable `arr` with the name *index*.
`arr(i,j)`	Multidimensional array variable.
`$var`	The value of variable `var`.
`[command]`	Brackets used for evaluating Tcl commands or user-defined procedures.
`\char`	Backslash substitution.
`"hello $var"`	Immediate substitution of an embedded variable.
`{hello $var}`	Prevent substitution of an embedded variable.

The expr Command Arithmetic Operators and Expressions (in Decreasing Order of Precedence)

Command	Description
`-  ~  !`	Unary minus, bitwise NOT, logical NOT
`*  /  %`	Multiply, divide, remainder
`+  -`	Add, subtract
`<<  >>`	Bitwise shift left, bitwise shift right
`<  >  <=  >=`	Boolean comparisons
`==  !=`	Boolean equals, not equals
`&`	Bitwise AND
`^`	Bitwise exclusive OR
`|`	Bitwise inclusive OR
`&&`	Logical AND
`||`	Logical OR
`x ? y : z`	If x != 0, then y, else z

Mathematical Functions

Function	Description
abs(x)	Absolute value of integer or floating-point number
acos(x)	Cosine inverse (for example, acos(-1.0)).
asin(x)	Sine inverse (for example, asin(-0.5)).
atan(x)	Inverse tangent (for example, atan(1.0)).
atan2(y,x)	Four quadrant inverse tangent. (For example, atan2(1,-1) returns an angle in the second quadr Note that the y is the first argument for atan2.)
ceil(x)	Round x to integers toward infinity (for example, ceil(1.4) is 2).
cos(x)	Cosine (for example, cos(3.1)).
cosh(x)	Hyperbolic cosine (for example, cosh(1.0)).
double(x)	Covert x to floating-point value.
exp(x)	Exponential (for example, exp(1.0)).
floor(x)	Round x to nearest integer toward minus infinity example, floor(1.4) is 1).
fmod(x)	Floating-point remainder (for example, fmod(2.5, is 0.1).
hypot(x,y)	Hypotenuse $\sqrt{}$, x^2+y^2 (for example, hypot(3,4) retu 5).
int(x)	Converts x to an integer by truncation (for exampl int(1.9) is 1).
log(x)	Natural logarithm (for example, log(10) is 2.3026)
log10(x)	Base 10 logarithm (for example, log10(100) is 2).
pow(x,y)	Returns x^y (for example, pow(2,0.5) is 1.414).
rand()	Returns a floating point number between 0 and ju less than 1. No argument is required.
round(x)	Round toward nearest integer (for example, round(1.4) is 1, whereas round(1.6) is 2).
sin(x)	Sine function (for example, sin(0.5)).
sinh(x)	Hyperbolic sine (for example, sinh(1.2)).
srand(x)	Sets the seed of random number generator (for e ple, srand([clock seconds])).
sqrt(x)	Square root (for example, sqrt(3)).
tan(x)	Tangent function (for example, tan(0.7854)).
tanh(x)	Hyperbolic tangent (for example, tanh(0.75)).

To find all the available action subcommands for a Tcl command in the interpreter, use the command name followed by an *inadmissible* string For example, string xx returns bad option "xx": must be compare, first index, ...

A similar trick can be used for Tk commands, as well. For example, .b config -state xx returns bad state "xx": must be active, disabled, c normal.

Venkat V.S.S. Sastry, Ph.D.
Lakshmi Sastry, Ph.D.

SAMS Teach Yourself Tcl/Tk in 24 Hours

SAMS

A Division of Macmillan USA
201 West 103rd St., Indianapolis, Indiana 46290 USA

Sams Teach Yourself Tcl/Tk in 24 Hours
Copyright © 2000 by Sams Publishing

International Standard Book Number: 0-672-31749-4

Library of Congress Catalog Card Number: 99-63721

Printed in the United States of America

First Printing: November 1999

01   00   99   4   3   2   1

Trademarks

Warning and Disclaimer

ASSOCIATE PUBLISHER
Bradley L. Jones

ACQUISITIONS EDITOR
Chris Webb

DEVELOPMENT EDITOR
Thomas Cirtin

MANAGING EDITOR
Lisa Wilson

PROJECT EDITOR
Dawn Pearson

COPY EDITORS
Mary Lagu
Rhonda Tinch-Mize

INDEXER
Johnna VanHoose Dinse

PROOFREADER
Megan Wade

TECHNICAL EDITOR
Ed Murphy

TEAM COORDINATOR
Meggo Barthlow

MEDIA DEVELOPER
Dave Carson

INTERIOR DESIGN
Gary Adair

COVER DESIGN
Aren Howell

COPY WRITER
Eric Borgert

PRODUCTION
Dan Harris
Cyndi Davis-Hubler

Contents at a Glance

Contents

About the Authors

Venkat V.S.S. Sastry is a lecturer in scientific computing at RMCS, Cranfield University, Shrivenham, United Kingdom. He obtained his PhD in applied mathematics from the Indian Institute of Science, Bangalore, India. His current research interests include intelligent problem solving environments, dynamic flow visualization in virtual environments, and high-performance boundary element methods. He is the coauthor of the well-received *Tcl/Tk Cookbook*. Venkat is a member of SIAM.

Lakshmi Sastry is a principal applications developer at CLRC VR Centre, Rutherford Appleton Laboratory, United Kingdom. Her research interests include intelligent user interfaces, 3D user interaction, the visualization of and interactions with computational simulations in immersive virtual environments, and experiential training simulations. She is a coauthor of the Web-based *Tcl/Tk Cookbook*. Lakshmi is a member of IEEE.

About the Technical Editor

Ed Murphy began a career in UNIX system administration at the University of New Orleans Department of Computer Science in 1992. From there he moved to University Computing where he initiated the effort to establish the university's first Web site. In this effort, Ed was introduced to two new scripting languages, Perl and Tcl/Tk, the latter of which would have a profound effect on his career. In 1996, Ed left UNO to begin working for Computerized Processes Unlimited, Inc., a system integrator in Metairie, Louisiana, which uses Tcl/Tk extensively. His technical expertise and experience teaching at UNO afforded him the opportunity to begin working in CPU's training group. While working in this group, Ed taught and authored courses dealing with Tcl/Tk and its extensions for companies all over the United States and in Europe. Ed is currently working with CPU's Marine Technology unit, which uses Tcl/Tk to provide integrated hull monitoring systems for deepwater oil and gas platforms. He has lived for the past 18 years in the New Orleans area, where he met and married Cindy, his wife of 10 years. His dog, Chance, is currently his only living heir.

Dedication

To our parents and grandparents.

To our dear daughter Priya.

— Lakshmi and Venkat

Acknowledgments

We sincerely thank Chris Webb for his unfailing support and encouragement from the start to the completion of this book. Tom Cirtin and Ed Murphy deserve our gratitude for their comments, which added great value to this book. Our thanks also go to the Macmillan USA editorial team, especially Dawn Pearson, Mary Lagu, Rhonda Tinch-Mize, and Katie Robinson for the great job they did in preparing this book.

We wish to express our warmest thanks to Dr. Joyce M. Aitchison, head of AMOR, RMCS, Cranfield University, U.K. She actively encouraged us and supported Venkat by streamlining his other commitments while he was writing this book. Our thanks also go to Dr. D.R.S. Boyd, head of CLRC VR Centre, RAL, U.K., for his support.

We would like to convey our deep sense of appreciation to Professor F. R.A. Hopgood for introducing us to computer graphics and for his support and encouragement over the past decade. We would also like to thank Professor J.K. Ousterhout for Tcl/Tk, a language that has caught the imagination of so many people around the world.

Last, but not least, we would like to express our gratitude to our daughter Priya for backing us up with great humor (and no, darling, Tcl is not your mother tongue!).

Tell Us What You Think!

As the reader of this book, *you* are our most important critic and commentator. We value your opinion and want to know what we're doing right, what we could do better, what areas you'd like to see us publish in, and any other words of wisdom you're willing to pass our way.

As an Associate Publisher for Sams, I welcome your comments. You can fax, email, or write me directly to let me know what you did or didn't like about this book—as well as what we can do to make our books stronger.

Please note that I cannot help you with technical problems related to the topic of this book, and that due to the high volume of mail I receive, I might not be able to reply to every message.

When you write, please be sure to include this book's title and authors as well as your name and phone or fax number. I will carefully review your comments and share them with the authors and editors who worked on the book.

Fax: 317-581-4770

Email: adv_prog@mcp.com

Mail: Bradley L. Jones
           Associate Publisher
           Sams Publishing
           201 West 103rd Street
           Indianapolis, IN 46290 USA

Introduction

Welcome to Teach Yourself Tcl/Tk! This book will equip you with the knowledge and confidence to start developing your own Tcl/Tk applications very quickly. It is aimed at novice programmers who want to develop interactive applications based on WIMP interfaces (windows, icons, menus and pointers) using Tcl/Tk. Tcl, the Tool Command Language, is a scripting language with a simple syntax. Tk is an associated graphical user interface development toolkit. To help you achieve your objective, this book includes lots of practical, graded examples, which not only help you to understand the concepts but can also be adopted and reused in your applications.

We do not expect you to have any previous knowledge of graphical user interface (GUI) development or even scripting languages. We assume that you are conversant with the use of a window-based desktop environment (such as Microsoft Windows) or Unix-based window environments (such as OpenWindows). You should have some familiarity with basic programming constructs such as input, output, data types, compilers, and so forth. Familiarity with one or more higher-level programming languages (such as C) and knowledge of a scripting language (sh, csh,) can be an advantage, but these are not a necessity. This book is self-contained.

The book is designed to have you programming and in Tcl/Tk almost from the beginning. If you are new to interactive GUI-based application development, it is worth reading the next two paragraphs. They describe the guiding principle behind this methodology and the steps needed for structuring such applications.

Interactive Applications for Window Environments

During the past decade, WIMP-based graphical user interfaces have become standard front-ends to all interactive 2D desktop applications. The point and click interface provides an effective mechanism to hide the finer details of an application. Because the functionality is transparent to the end-user, he can focus on the task and quickly gain familiarity in using the application. The basic idea of one main window per application enables the user to keep several applications open at the same time and effectively switch between them without loss of context.

There are many hardware platforms and many windowing environments such as the Microsoft Windows or the Unix-based OpenWindows, OSF/Motif, and so on. Whatever the application or platform, and whatever the windowing system, the basic interaction methodology of using icons, buttons, and menus with the mouse pointer is consistent and well understood.

Programming with Graphical User Interface Tools

Graphical user interface (GUI) development tools help you to develop your application's GUI. There are many such tools, and they vary in the level of support they provide for application development. However, the basic concept behind all such tools is essentially the same. Whatever tool you use, it needs to be recognized that the design and development of GUI interfaces demand considerable time and effort.

Application developers are also required to meet stringent requirements for consistent "look and feel" for their applications across a range of hardware platforms and development solutions—often within tight time schedules. In this book, we aim to cater to this need and to equip you with the ability to develop your own applications. You will be using the Tk toolkit and Tcl for cross-platform deployment. That means, after you have developed an application, it runs with minimal changes (or even no change) on PCs and workstations.

When you begin GUI toolkit programming you must decide.

- The user tasks or application functionality that needs to be supported.
- The inputs required for each application function or user task.
- The design of an interface containing the interaction objects (often referred to as widgets) such as windows, scroll-bars, menus, and so forth.
- How to interface each application functionality that you have identified to the user interface components in the GUI. This is the part that makes the application functions to be invoked when the user interacts with the GUI.

Once you have made a design decision, implement an incremental prototype, testing it at every stage. The toolkits provide an inherent event-loop. At runtime, this event-loop waits for the user's interaction (an event) with the interface objects and invokes the associated responses from the application. This process continues until the user quits the application. That is all there is to it! After you have a prototype working, you might want to change it or expand it—but that is recursive design and not a change of structure.

In our Tcl/Tk Cookbook, `http://www.itd.clrc.ac.uk/Publications/Cookbook/index.html`, the reader is encouraged to try out graded examples from the outset. It works! The success of this Teach Yourself series by Macmillan is proof in itself that working through examples is the best way to gain programming knowledge and confidence. We encourage you to read this book while sitting next to your PC or workstation. When you put the book down, start experimenting with segments of code. Please explore the set of resources we have listed in the Appendices too.

We hope you have as much fun learning and using Tcl/Tk as we have had writing this book about it.

PART I
Essential Tcl

Hour

HOUR 1

What Is Tcl/Tk?

The Tool Command Language (Tcl) is a high-level scripting language. Tk is an associated toolkit to create window-based interactive applications using Tcl. This hour introduces the basic requirements for beginning to program with Tcl/Tk. In this hour, you will learn

- How to start using Tcl
- The basic structure of window—system-based interactive applications
- How to start using the Tk toolkit

This book is filled with simple examples to illustrate programming constructs that are best understood by actually trying them out. The examples are mostly developed using Tcl/Tk 8.1 on UNIX and Windows NT platforms. Examples should work with Tcl/Tk 8.2. Wherever there are hardware platform specific differences, these are highlighted.

Understanding Tcl

Tcl, the Tool Command Language is a high-level scripting language, created by *Professor John Ousterhout*. It provides variables, arrays, lists, data-flow control loops, and procedures for application development. Tcl is cross platform; it runs on Windows, Windows NT, Macintosh, and UNIX platforms running the X Window System.

It is powerful as a high-level, rapid-prototyping scripting interface for running other programs and gluing them together. It is designed to glue modules of software into applications. You can use it with the World Wide Web and with your own applications written in C/C++. Before beginning to use Tcl, you should first understand what the term *scripting language* means in practice and the reasons for using a scripting language.

Why Use a Scripting Language?

Scripting languages provide what appears to be a direct communication interface to your computer system. The language that you are using to issue your set of commands or instructions is, or appears to be, the same language of execution used by the software interpreter front-end that you are communicating with. Compare this with issuing a set of commands in a programming language such as C, C++, or FORTRAN. The set of commands in such a language will be called *source code*. This code must be translated (that is, compiled) into a machine-readable binary code, which is then executed.

A scripting language provides a higher-level interactive application programming interface than does a compiled language, such as C/C++. It enables you to test your applications interactively, boosting rapid prototyping and learning.

Scripting languages reduce the verbosity that compiled language programming requires. At the same time, a scripting language such as Tcl enables you to develop applications using appropriately compiled languages within the scripting environment. It enables you to seamlessly access and exploit the greater performance efficiency, finer data-flow controls, and flexible data structures that compiled languages offer.

Why Tcl?

There are many popular scripting languages, such as Perl and Python. The adoption of one instead of another is often a matter of choice. It is not the purpose of this hour to argue a case. If you are considering serious application development, it is pragmatic to compare languages for their functionality, maturity, ease of learning and using, the customization possibilities, the extensibility, and equally importantly, the acceptance and usage by the user community. Tcl scores quite high on all these counts.

Apart from the vast number of applications listed in the Tcl resources Web site, you will find an increasing number of domain-specific software applications, such as the Visualization Toolkit, that use Tcl as their interactive script interface. This rich set of resources points to a strong user community and the maturity of the software, which are good reasons for using Tcl.

Another reason for using Tcl is its extendable architecture. Tcl is designed, from the outset, to be a gluing language that enables you to integrate self-contained software modules into useful applications. Integrating applications can be achieved in one of two ways. One method is to rewrite the code to create a new extended application. The more efficient method is to use a scripting language to talk to cooperating applications. A particular strength of Tcl is that it enables the gluing of applications together to create a productive development environment for programmers and users alike (see Figure 1.1).

FIGURE 1.1

Tcl supports effective communication between applications.

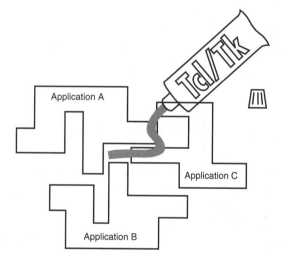

Getting Started with Tcl

You can run Tcl scripts using either one of two applications, tclsh or wish. Tcl is an interpreted language, and your commands or scripts are interpreted by the Tcl interpreter. Tcl scripts are either built-in Tcl commands or Tcl procedures written in a compiled language. The Tcl Shell, or tclsh, is a Tcl application that provides an interface to the Tcl interpreter. It is like any other command shell, such as korn, C shell, or the MS-DOS window.

Do I Have Tcl?

Use the command which tclsh at the UNIX shell prompt to find out if you have access to tclsh, if you are using a UNIX system. Check with your system administrator to eliminate the possibility that your path environment variable setup does not include the right directories.

If you are using a PC, check whether tclsh.exe exists under c:\program files\ tcl\bin. If not, try the Windows find mechanism to search for the Tcl executable tclsh*.exe. Note the use of the * after tclsh. This is used because it is likely that the executable has a version number appended to it.

If Tcl/Tk is not already installed on your system, download the source code or binary from http://www.scriptics.com and follow the installation instructions. The installation is straightforward. On PC platforms, Tcl/Tk is available as precompiled executables and dynamically linked libraries that can be installed using the self-extracting software module. You can also create shortcuts for tclsh*.exe and wish*.exe in your main menu. You can create shortcuts to the executable programs that target the directory you want the executable to run in.

Using tclsh

Tcl scripts are executed by invoking the Tcl interpreter. You can execute your Tcl scripts either interactively or directly. In the interactive mode, you start a tclsh and execute commands at the command prompt in much the same way you execute UNIX or MS-DOS commands. When a tclsh application is running, it will display its command prompt %. You can execute Tcl commands at this prompt in much the same way you use a UNIX shell or a MS-DOS prompt. You can run many tclsh and, hence, many Tcl interpreters at the same time. Tcl will automatically generate and append a numeral to show the numbers of interpreters currently running on your desktop.

In the direct execution mode, your script is contained within a disc file, typically with the filename extension .tcl. You instruct the operating system to execute this script. The operating system finds and runs the interpreter and executes the script. To do this under a UNIX system, you "source" the file whose first line is #!<YOUR_TCL_PATH>/bin/ tclsh8.1 and has its execute permission set. (You can set the execute permission by issuing the UNIX command chmod u+x <filename>.) In a Window environment, double-click on the script file icon to start the Tcl interpreter and execute the contents of the script file.

The interactive mode is often more productive for exploring commands and options while learning and testing small applications. Start up tclsh and try this with the following code in Listing 1.1.

LISTING 1.1 Using `tclsh` Interactively

```
 1: %tclsh8.1
 2: tclsh8.1> puts "Hello World!"
 3: Hello World!
 4: tclsh8.1> set tcl_version
 5: 8.1
 6: tclsh8.1> gets stdin name
 7: Lakshmi
 8: 7
 9: tclsh8.1> puts "Hello $name"
10: Hello Lakshmi
11: tclsh8.1> expr 5+4
12: 9
```

ANALYSIS In line 1, you invoke the Tcl 8.1 `tclsh` at the command line, here a UNIX shell. In line 2, try your very first Tcl command `puts`. `puts` takes a single argument, a string, and prints that string in `stdout`. The string `"Hello World!"` is printed out in line 3. In line 4, you try another useful Tcl command, `set`, which reads and writes variables. When you execute `set` (giving it a variable name, but no value), it reads and returns the current value of that variable. Here you pass the built-in variable `tcl_version` to `set` to find the current version, as in line 5.

The Tcl command `gets` reads a line from a given channel, in this case the `stdin`, as shown in line 6. When you execute this line, Tcl waits until some keyboard input is given. It reads the keyboard input until the Return key is pressed, returns all the characters, excluding the Return, and assigns it to the variable specified in the input argument. In this case, the variable is `name`. The keyed input is `read`, and the number of characters read, 7, is returned to indicate the end of this task in line 8. Check the value of `name` with executing `puts` again in line 9. The exact syntax of this command and input will be described in Hour 2, "Getting Started with Tcl."

You can see from line 10 that `name` has been given the value keyed in. In line 11, you can try the Tcl built-in command `expr` to return the value of adding *4* and *5*.

In the previous listing, we changed tclsh applications default prompt % to `tclsh8.1>` to make it stand out. The Q&A Section shows you how to alter the default prompt.

Listings 1.2 and 1.3 give the script file versions of the Tcl script in Listing 1.1 for UNIX and PC platforms.

LISTING 1.2   Executing Tcl Scripts from a File—UNIX

```
1: #!<Your_TCL_Path>/bin/tclsh8.1
2: puts "Hello World!"
3: set tcl_version
4: gets stdin name
5: puts "Hello $name"
6: expr 5+4
```

ANALYSIS   You should insert the pathname to the directory that has the `tclsh` version you
want to run. You should also change the version number accordingly. You can then
source this script file as you do with any UNIX shell script.

LISTING 1.3   Executing Tcl Scripts from a File—Non-UNIX

```
1:  puts "Hello World!"
2:  set tcl_version
3:  gets stdin name
4:  puts "Hello $name"
5:  expr 5+4
```

ANALYSIS   First, make sure that your PATHEXT variable is set to point to the directory that contains the version of the `tclsh.exe` you want to execute. Then, double click on the
script file containing the lines of Tcl commands in Listing 1.3. Alternatively, you can
create a shortcut for the `tclsh`, specifying the target where `tclsh` is installed and setting
the start in the parameter to the directory containing the previous script file. You can
either source the script, or you can use the open option from the File menu of the Tcl
Shell.

> Note that when you execute this file under any system and in any mode, the
> interpreter will await the input for the name variable.

Understanding Tk: An Overview of GUI Development

Tk is a toolkit associated with Tcl that enables you to develop *windows, icons, menus,
and pointer-based (WIMP-based)* interactive applications that can execute Tcl commands. It is beneficial to understand the structure of such WIMP-based applications so
that you can design your applications and use Tk more effectively.

The topic of *graphical user interface* (GUI) development and the details of interface development toolkits are so rich and vast that it is easy to lose an overview of the purpose and methodology of undertaking a GUI development. However, this overview is essential. Stripped to its bare bones, the two fundamental ideas to grasp are

- The structure of an interactive application in a windowing environment
- The support facilitated by a GUI toolkit to interface a user's interaction goals to the input and output requirements of the application

The Structure of Interactive Applications

In the terminology of a desktop environment, the term *display* refers to the monitor or the screen of your computer. Each application running on the desktop has a single top-level window that is uniquely identifiable with that application. The term *window* refers to a rectangular area of the screen, allocated for presenting the front end or the interface of an application to its user.

Each application communicates with the user via a special application called the Window Manager (WM). The application requests the WM to allocate screen space and special border decorations. The application informs the WM about the keyboard and mouse events that it is interested in. The WM allocates the application's requests for screen space, if possible. WM also monitors and responds to the user's interaction with each displayed window, gathering and delivering that interaction information to the appropriate application.

The communication between the window manager and the application is seamless, and most of these communications are inherently handled by the GUI toolkit automatically. So, it is very possible that you can develop full applications without ever having to give explicit directives to the window manager.

Below the top-level window of an application, you can nest as many windows as required. For instance, you might want to draw some graphics in a window and also display some text separately. Essentially, your graphical user interface is a tree structure of windows, with branch and leaf windows. All the windows below the top-level of an application are often referred to as internal or children windows of that application.

GUI Toolkit Structure: Widgets, Events, Callbacks

The primary mechanism of input control and user interaction with GUI applications is through a set of user-interface components that are called widgets. Buttons, scrollbars, and entry fields that can be used for keyboard input from the user are typical examples of widgets. In toolkits such as Tk, these user-interface components are basically internal windows that can be nested within the top level. That is, the data structure of a widget is the same as that of a window with associated attributes that determine its appearance and behavior. For this reason, the terms window and widget are used interchangeably throughout this book and everywhere in the literature.

Widgets are designed to respond to user actions created with physical input devices, such as the keyboard or mouse. These user actions are referred to as *events*. Key presses, mouse movements, and mouse button presses are typical examples of events, as are cut-and-paste and drag-and-drop.

Each widget has a set of *event handlers* or *callbacks*. In this book, we use both these terms to refer to the same mechanism. An event handler is a piece of code or script that is invoked in response to the event associated with that event handler. An event handler in Tcl, for example, is a Tcl script or a C, C++, or FORTRAN routine wrapped as a Tcl command or script.

The event handler is basically a routine or a script, an implementation of any desired functionality. For instance, the event handler of a button widget might be to invoke a Tcl script to request that a dialog window pop up. In another instance, selecting the menu button Open of a File menu might pop up a file selection widget. Still another example is the event handler of a top-level window in response to user requests to drag and resize the window. The top-level window might be the application's root/main window, or it might be an internal branch window that holds several leaf widgets. Such windows can be called container widgets.

A top-level or container widget carries out the geometry management task of its children, according to some predefined geometrical positioning algorithm, when the user changes its size or that of one of its children. The event handler for the resize event is this geometry management script.

Widget toolkits dictate a policy of *look*, how the widgets appear, and *feel*, how they behave. The Tk widgets follow the Motif toolkit look-and-feel policy, if it is applicable to the platform the toolkit is running on.

Event Loops

When a GUI-based interactive application is invoked, it initializes all its windows and widgets and their startup internal states, and then it enters into an *event loop*, waiting for the user's actions. When an interesting event happens over a window or widget, the associated callback is invoked and its results are reported.

This, in a nutshell, is the basic structure of an interactive application. The GUI development toolkit provides the predefined object components with appearance and functionality. Tk plays the same role.

Using Tk

You execute Tk scripts by using the Tk application wish. Wish is a simple program that creates a main window and then processes Tcl and Tk commands. The difference between tclsh and wish is that the Tk interpreter associated with wish knows how to interpret both Tcl commands and Tk commands that are an extension of Tcl. The Tcl interpreter associated with tclsh understands only the core Tcl commands. wish stands for *wi*ndowing *sh*ell. It provides a main or root window to create and manage the user interface components.

On UNIX platforms, the console window that you use to invoke wish provides an interface to the Tk interpreter. The following section describes how to start a console with wish on PC platforms. This will help you try Tcl/Tk commands interactively. If you want to try Tk commands interactively from standard input, invoke wish with no arguments as shown in Listing 1.4.

LISTING 1.4   Using wish Interactively

```
1: %wish81
2: % button .button -text "Press ME" -foreground red -highlightcolor blue
3: .button
4: % pack .button
```

ANALYSIS This script starts up a wish shell and then executes two simple Tk commands to create a simple button and make it appear in the window. The button has a label that reads Press Me. It has a red foreground color. When you select this Tk button widget by left-clicking with the left mouse button, the text is highlighted in blue. Notice that when you press and hold the left mouse button on the Tk button widget, this event redraws the button widget to make it appear sunken, indicating the widget's changed state (from Unselected to About to Be Selected). This behavior results from the built-in look-and-feel policy of the Tk toolkit. Figure 1.2 shows the result.

Running wish on NT Platforms

On NT platforms, wish starts up in direct execution mode because the install program sets up a single file-type for Tcl scripts (.tcl) that executes the script in the wish interpreter. As a result, you do not have a console that your scripts can use for standard I/O streams. That means you cannot pass command-line parameters to Tcl scripts, and you cannot execute scripts by their "base" name in the same way as you can executable programs.

FIGURE **1.2**

A Tk button widget.

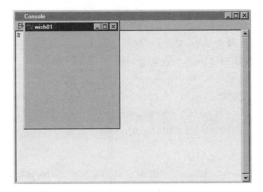

Download the registry file from `http://www-dse.doc.ic.ac.uk/~np2/software/`
`tcl-setup.html` and run it, following the instructions given. This will better integrate
Tcl/Tk scripts with the Windows NT shell. It provides a console for your `wish` shell, as
shown in Figure 1.3.

FIGURE **1.3**

A console with wish
makes I/O streams
available to the script
and enables you to
enter command-line
arguments.

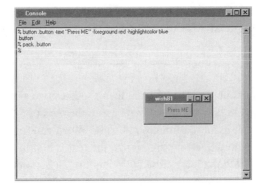

Why Use Tk?

This simple script illustrates the answer to the question "Why Tk?" It is an easy-to-learn
toolkit that hides much of the verbosity and many of the details that programs using
toolkits such as Motif require. It is cross-platform, so you can develop it on one platform
and execute the same script across different platforms. At the same time, it is flexible
and extensible, enabling you to attach your own application-specific functionality—
written either in Tcl or in other languages, such as C/C++—to your Tk-based GUI. You
can even create your own widgets using the Tk library procedures.

Just as with `tclsh`, you can mimic Listings 1.2 and 1.3 to create and execute script file versions of the script in Listing 1.4. Make sure you invoke `wish` instead of `tclsh`.

1

Summary

This hour introduced the Tool Command language Tcl and its toolkit extension Tk. You can use both these packages across different hardware and operating system environments. You use the two applications `tclsh` and `wish` to execute your Tcl and Tk scripts.

In the next hour, "Getting Started with Tcl," you will start to learn in detail the commands and the syntax of Tcl. You may very well want to revisit the section on the overall view of the structure of window-based interactive applications when you start Hour 10.

For more information, please read the following articles:

Cameron Laird and Kathryn Soraiz. "Choosing a Scripting Language—Perl, Tcl and Python: They Are Not Your Father's Scripting Languages." http://www.sunworld.com/sw01-10-1997/swol-10-scripting.html.

John Ousterhout. "Scripting: Higher Level Programming for the 21st Century." http://www.scriptics.com/people/john.ousterhout/scripting.html. (The article appeared also in the March 1998 issue of *IEEE Computer*.)

Q&A

Q How do I customize Tcl prompts?

A You can define start up and set up parameters for your `tclsh` by including these in its resource file, .tclshrc. For instance, the directive `set tcl_prompt1 {puts -nonewline "tclsh8.1>"}` in .tclshrc will produce the prompt.

Q How do I make the file extensions recognizable as executable files?

A Define the environment variable `PATHEXT`.

Q Why another shell?

A The existing shells, such as `sh`, `csh`, and so forth, are not embeddable in your C application.

Workshop

The "Quiz" section is designed to provide you with an opportunity to recall some of the important concepts introduced in this hour. These can be commands, command syntax, common mistakes, usage, and so forth. The "Exercises" section helps you consolidate the material you learned via an example of practical value. Our aim is that these two sections should reinforce the knowledge you have gained in this hour. The answers to the quiz that follows can be found in Appendix A, "Answers to Quizzes."

Quiz

Solutions to the exercises are on the CD-ROM that accompanies this book.

1. What is an interpreter?
2. What is the difference between `tclsh` and `wish`?
3. What is the default Tcl prompt?
4. How do you execute a script file directly in the interpreter?
5. What are typical events?

Exercises

1. Write a script `hello.tcl` which prints your name in the Tcl console.
2. Write a program that asks for *yourFirstName*, and prints `Hello Mr.` *yourFirstName*.
3. Write a program to display a button with a label `PressMe`, which when pressed prints `Hello World` in the console.

HOUR 2

Getting Started with Tcl

In the last hour, you have seen what Tcl and Tk are all about, and you wrote a simple script. In this hour, you look at Tcl commands in some depth, and you learn how variables are defined and subsequently used. Everything in Tcl is a string. As a result, the concepts of variable substitution and command substitution play a central role in Tcl programming.

In this hour, you will learn

- The general structure of a Tcl command
- How to define variables
- How to create variables using variable substitution
- How to create variables using command substitution
- How to compute variable names using variable and/or command substitution
- How to appreciate the difference between the two grouping mechanisms—curly braces and double quotes
- How to inquire and clear variables

What Is a Tcl Command?

A Tcl command consists of words separated by spaces. The first word is the name of the command, and the remaining words are its arguments. The arguments can be further subdivided into subcommands, options, and arguments. A tab or a newline can also separate words. The characters for space, tab, and newline are called whitespace characters because they are invisible on the screen. Any options to the command are specified with a minus sign immediately followed by the name of the option. The general structure of a Tcl command is shown in Figure 2.1.

Learn to read the documentation. Tcl commands are documented as *command* [*subcommand(s)*] [*options*] [*arguments*]. Optional arguments are identified between two question marks. For example, the documentation for the set command appears as set varName ?value?.

Every Tcl command has a return value including a null string.

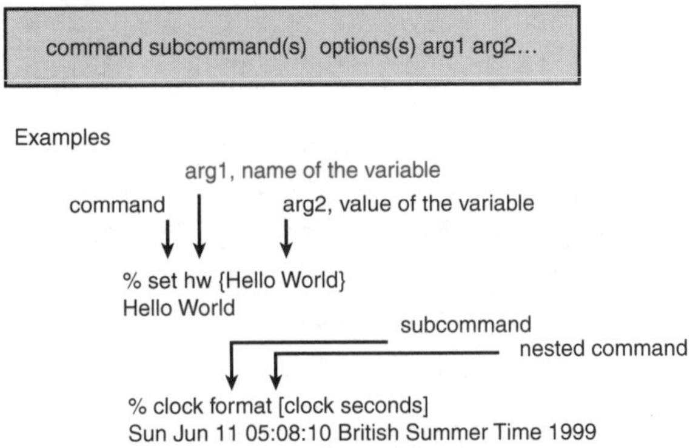

FIGURE 2.1

The general structure of a Tcl command. One or more spaces separate commands, subcommands, and arguments. Note that not all commands have subcommands.

command subcommand(s) options(s) arg1 arg2...

Examples

arg1, name of the variable

command   arg2, value of the variable

% set hw {Hello World}
Hello World

subcommand
nested command

% clock format [clock seconds]
Sun Jun 11 05:08:10 British Summer Time 1999

In Tcl, there are commands, not program statements. After you have fully grasped this distinction, you have mastered the language. More than half the syntax problems are caused by this misunderstanding and will disappear if it is eliminated. We will be reinforcing this distinction throughout this book.

Understanding Variables

Variables are the building blocks of any programming language, and Tcl is no exception. A variable holds a value. The name used for the variable can contain most of the alphanumeric characters with the exception of $ (dollar sign), [(openbracket), " (double quote), { (open brace), and } (close brace). Avoid blank, tab, and newline characters as well. These characters, shown in Table 2.1, have special meaning in Tcl/Tk, as you will see in a later section, "Variable Substitution."

TABLE 2.1 Special Characters

Character	Used for
$ (dollar)	Variable substitution
[(open bracket)	Starting command evaluation
] (close bracket)	Terminate command evaluation
{ (open brace)	Starting a group of blank separated words
} (close brace)	Closing a group of blank separated words
→ (tab)	Separating words
(space)	Separating words
⏎ (return)	Separating words within curly braces
. (period)	Separating components in a widget hierarchy
# (hash)	Starting a comment line
" (quote)	Starting a group of words with variable substitution
\ (back slash)	Escaping the special meaning of the special character

Using set to Define Variables

Variables are defined with set and cleared with unset. The basic usage of set is shown Listing 2.1:

LISTING 2.1 The set Command

```
 1: % set tickle1 Tcl/Tk
 2: Tcl/Tk
 3: % set tickle2 {Tool Command Language/Toolkit}
 4: Tool Command Language/Toolkit
 5: % set tickle3 {Tool Command Language\
 6: >                /Toolkit}
 7: Tool Command Language/Toolkit
 8: %set tickle1
 9: Tcl/Tk
10: %
```

NEW TERM   *Command continuation* is used when long commands that won't fit on one line are continued onto the next line using the character \ (backslash) as the last character followed by a return.

ANALYSIS   Variables are assigned values with `set` command. The command takes the name of the variable and its value as its arguments. Line 1 defines the value of the variable `tickle1` to be `Tcl/Tk`. When the value of the variable contains blanks, as in line 3, you need to protect them with curly braces. Note that the curly braces are used in Tcl/Tk for grouping arguments, and they are not part of the value. Accordingly, line 4 does not contain any curly braces.

When the value is too large to fit on one line, continue the command (or value) using the backslash (\) character. The continuation prompt and the text are shown in line 6. (This continuation prompt will not appear if you are using `tclsh` or `TkCon`.) `set` command can also be used to recall the value of an existing variable. Simply supply the name of the variable, and its value is returned, as shown in lines 8–9.

Here are some salient points to remember about variables:

- Inquiring the value of an undefined variable is an error.
- Variables are removed from the interpreter with the `unset` command. You can supply more than one variable name. For example, `unset a b c` will clear the three variables named a, b, c.
- The case of the variable names is significant. For example, `fileName` and `FileName` are two different variables.

A semicolon can be used to separate two commands. For example, `set a 3; set b 4` typed on the same line defines two variables—a and b.

Variable Substitution

Variables are associated with a value. The value stored in the variable is recalled by preceding the name of the variable with a dollar sign ($). Look at a simple example. You want to display the value of a variable on the screen, together with some annotation; this is illustrated in Listing 2.2.

LISTING 2.2 Simple Variable Substitution

```
1: % set Tcl {Tool Command Language}
2: Tool Command Language
3: % puts $Tcl
4: Tool Command Language
5: % puts "Tcl stands for $Tcl"
6: Tcl stands for Tool Command Language
7: % puts {Tcl stands for $Tcl}
8: Tcl stands for $Tcl
9: %
```

ANALYSIS The set command in line 1 has two arguments. The first argument is the name of the variable called Tcl in this example. The second argument to set consists of the three words—Tcl, Command, and Language. Because this argument contains space characters, you protect them using curly braces. Without the curly braces, the interpreter gets the four words—Tcl, Tool, Command, and Language; and the interpreter will complain—wrong # args: should be "set varName ?newValue?" By now, you should know the reason why. Without curly braces, there is no way of telling which word is the variable and which word is the value.

To refer to the value of the variable, you simply precede it with a dollar sign. In line 3, you use the puts command to display the value of the variable to the screen. By default, the puts command writes its output to the screen. In line 5, you want to write an annotated string to the screen (or standard output). The text for the string refers to the value of the variable Tcl. Because the puts command requires one string argument, you need to protect the embedded variables. In this line, there are blanks in the annotation text, as well as in the value of the variable. Previously, you have used the curly braces for grouping simple text. With curly braces, embedded variables are not substituted. If you want the substitution to take place, and you also want to protect the spaces, you must use the double quotes for grouping (line 5). Line 7 demonstrates what happens if we use the curly braces.

Use curly braces for grouping embedded spaces. The grouping can be either for a variable name or its value. For example, the command set {Ordinal Numbers} {First Second Third} defines a variable Ordinal Numbers that contains a blank. The variable's value contains two blanks.

Avoid using whitespace characters in the names of variables.

Use double quotes for grouping with embedded variable substitution.

Curly braces inside double quotes are harmless. For example, `set x Tickle;` `puts "This is {$x}"` prints `This is {Tickle}`.

Escaping Special Characters

The special meaning of the characters (See Table 2.1), $, {, }, [,], ", (space), (tab) and `newline` character can be suppressed by preceding them with backslash. Listing 2.3 shows a simple example.

LISTING 2.3   Suppressing the Meaning of Special Characters by Preceding Them with a Backslash

```
1: % puts "Travel Costs:      \$27.50"
2: Travel Costs:     $27.50
3: % puts "Speed :         1.25 \[m/s]"
4: Speed :        1.25 [m/s]
5: set balance 2500
6: 2500
7: %puts "Outstanding balance: \$$balance"
8: Outstanding balance: $2500
9: %
```

ANALYSIS   In line 1, you want to use the literal character dollar, $. In line 3, you escape the opening square bracket. Note that close bracket is not escaped. Without the corresponding open square bracket, a close bracket is harmless, and it is treated as part of the text. Line 7 prints the value stored in the variable `balance`. The first dollar is escaped to print the literal character, and the second dollar is for the variable substitution. Return to line 1 for a moment. What happens if you use `puts "Travel Costs: $27.50"`. You get a response such as `can't read "27": no such variable`. Tcl is trying to read the variable named `27`. Of course, there is no such variable because that is not what you meant to do. There is a lesson in this story. A variable name can contain pure numbers alone.

Everything Is a String

In Tcl everything is a string, and no arithmetic is performed automatically. Listing 2.4 illustrates a typical example.

LISTING 2.4   Everything Is a String

```
1: % set a 1
2: 1
3: % set b 2
4: 2
5: % puts "Sum of $a and $b is $a+$b"
6: Sum of 1 and 2 is 1+2
7: %
```

ANALYSIS   Lines 1–4 define two variables a and b which hold the strings 1 and 2, not decimal numbers. If we attempt to print their sum to the screen, as we do in line 6, we notice that the variables are simply substituted, and that no arithmetic is performed. Arithmetic is done by explicitly invoking the Tcl command expr. That command is introduced in Hour 3, "Working with Tcl Commands."

Command Evaluation

You have seen a simple variable substitution to define new variables demonstrated in the previous section . Often, it is useful to evaluate a simple command to manufacture the value of a variable. A Tcl command is invoked by enclosing it in square brackets as shown in Listing 2.5. Tcl commands can be nested to arbitrary depths.

Listing 2.5   Defining Variables Using Command Evaluation

```
1: % set currentDir [pwd]
2: E:/Code
3: % set  msg "File created on [clock format [clock seconds]]"
4: File created on Thu Jul 08 10:36:52 British Summer Time 1999
5: % clock seconds
6: 931426626
7: % set msg
8: File created on Thu Jul 08 10:36:52 British Summer Time 1999
9: %
```

ANALYSIS   Line 1 defines a variable called currentDir whose value is the result of the Tcl command pwd. The pwd command returns the path of the working directory. Tcl commands can be nested, as shown in line 3. If you want to manufacture a string of text to be used as a time stamp, you can use the clock command. The clock command supports several subcommands. clock seconds returns the total elapsed time in seconds as an integer from an "epoch" (line 5). (See Tcl manual pages for further details regarding "epoch".) This integer can be formatted for human consumption using clock format as in lines 3–4. Note that the value stored is frozen, and it does not change. Lines 7–8 confirm this point.

Another useful command is incr which increments the value stored in a variable. The basic use of incr is demonstrated in Listing 2.6.

LISTING 2.6   Using incr Command to Change the Value Stored in a Variable

```
1: % set temperature 35
2: 35
3: % incr temperature
4: 36
5: % incr temperature -4
6: 32
7: % incr temperature 1.5
8: expected integer but got "1.5"
9: %
```

ANALYSIS   You store an integer value in the variable temperature in line 1. By default, incr increments by 1 as shown in lines 3–4. We can specify a negative increment as demonstrated in lines 5–6. Lines 7–8 emphasize that the command works only with integral increments. The same is true for the value stored. It would be wrong to increment the variable such as set x 1.5; incr x. General arithmetic is performed using the expr, which is introduced in Hour 3, "Working with Tcl Commands."

incr takes a variable name. You are asking Tcl to increment the value stored in a variable. Also, it works only on values that are integers.

incr returns an integer. For example, set x 012 defines an octal number because of the leading zero. The incr command returns 11, which is the decimal equivalent of the octal number 013.

An opening square bracket starts command evaluation. Thus, a close bracket can be used in variable names or values. For example, set sqR right] is acceptable, whereas set sqL left[is not. (If you happen to type this in the interpreter, and are wondering about the prompt, you can abandon the command by supplying a closing square bracket.)

Avoid combinations like the latter name for variable names. It is ugly.

Computing Variable Names

So far, you have been defining variables whose values are simple text or the result of evaluation of embedded variables and/or commands. In many practical situations, the names of the variables must be generated on-the-fly. As an example, consider the situation of storing the coordinates of top-left and bottom-right corners of a box. Normally, such information is stored in the variable names forming some sequence, say x0, y0, x1, and y1. This idea is illustrated in Listing 2.7.

LISTING 2.7   Computing Variable Names

```
 1: % set i 0
 2: 0
 3: % set x$i  20.0
 4: 20.0
 5: % set y$i 30.0
 6: 30.0
 7: % incr i
 8: 1
 9: % set x$i  40.0
10: 40.0
11: % set y$i 60.0
12: 60.0
13: % puts "TopLeft at: ($x0 , $y0)"
14: TopLeft at: (20.0 , 30.0)
15: % puts "BottomRight at: ($x1 , $y1)"
16: BottomRight at: (40.0 , 60.0)
```

ANALYSIS   You initialize a counter in variable i, to keep track of the numbering. The variable i has value zero. Line 3 defines the variable x0, and line 5 defines the variable y0. Notice the substitution of the variable i in line 3. The value 20 is stored in the variable x0. Similarly, the value 30 is stored in the variable y0. Now, you increment the variable i. As a result of the incr command in line 7, i has value 1 from now on. So, the value 40 in line 9 is stored in x1; and the value 60 is stored in y1. You can refer to these new variables names x0, x1, y0, and y1. This is shown with some annotation in lines 13–16.

When using the computed names for the variables, you need to be a bit careful and very precise. If you want to define a sequence of variables that contain filenames, starting from a base name, you compute appropriate names for the variables by prepending the basename as shown in Listing 2.8.

LISTING 2.8   Be Careful When Working with Computed Variable Names

```
1: % set baseName model
2: model
3: % set $baseNameData house.dat
4: can't read "baseNameData": no such variable
5: % set ${baseName}Data house.dat
6: house.dat
7: % set ${baseName}PS house.ps
8: house.ps
```

ANALYSIS   You store the generic name in the variable baseName in line 1. Using this base
name, you will create two additional variable names. First, you want to store the
name of the file that contains the (geometric) data in the variable modelData. To this end,
you try the command in line 3 using $baseNameData. Hmm! There is a problem. The Tcl
shell is looking for a variable named baseNameData (line 4). This is where your Tcl
grouping delimiters, curly braces, come to your rescue. You can clarify what is meant by
putting curly braces around the word baseName as in line 5, and the shell is happy. Line 7
is just another example to provide additional context.

Evaluation of Commands

Deferred evaluation occurs when you prepare a command to be evaluated later. This is
normally achieved with the help of eval command, which is introduced in Hour 3,
"Working with Tcl Commands," and further elaborated in Hour 5, "Working with Lists."
Commands in double quotes are evaluated immediately. The following simple example,
Listing 2.9, highlights these two types of commands.

LISTING 2.9   Immediate Versus Deferred

```
% set  t1 [clock format [clock seconds]]
Thu Jul 08 15:54:12 British Summer Time 1999
% set t2 {[clock format [clock seconds]]}
[clock format [clock seconds]]
% puts $t1
Thu Jul 08 15:54:12 British Summer Time 1999
% puts $t2
[clock format [clock seconds]]
% eval puts $t2
Thu Jul 08 15:55:07 British Summer Time 1999
%
```

The choice of an appropriate grouping mechanism depends on the application at hand. A thorough understanding of when evaluation takes place is important. To help you towards this goal, Table 2.2 summarizes different combinations of the possible evaluations.

TABLE 2.2   Variable and Command Substitutions Using the Variables `set h Hello;set w World`

Command	Value Stored in `st`	Remarks
`set st {$h $w}`	`$h $w`	Variables are not substituted.
`set st "$h $w"`	`Hello World`	Variables are substituted.
`set st "$h {$w}"`	`Hello {World}`	Inside double quotes, curly braces are treated as part of the text.
`set st [set h][set w]`	`HelloWorld`	No space between `Hello` and `World`.
`set st "[set h] [set w]"`	`Hello World`	You need the space between the two commands.
`set st {[set h] [set w]}`	`[set h] [set w]`	No command evaluation.
`set st [{set h}][{set w}]`		invalid command `"set h"` name.
`set st ${h}${w}`	`HelloWorld`	No problem with the variable substitution. It works even without curly braces.

Checking Up on Variables

When you are programming in an interpreted language, it is useful and desirable to reflect. The facility to inquire the status of the interpreter is provided by the `info` command. This command supports several subcommands. (See Appendix B for details.) Three of the useful `info` commands are shown in Listing 2.10.

LISTING 2.10   The `info` Command

```
 1: % info commands b*
 2: break binary bell bind button bindtags
 3: % info vars e*
 4: errorCode errorInfo env
 5: % info exists Money
 6: 0
 7: % set Money Penny
 8: Penny
 9: % info exists Money
10: 1
11: %
```

Analysis Line 1 inquires all the available Tcl commands that begin with b, and line 2 lists all the variables that begin with an e. The * is used as a wild card. You can check if a variable is already defined, as seen in line 5. A value of zero indicates that the variable does not exist in the interpreter (line 6). Next you set the variable Money (line 7) to the value Penny, and you confirm its existence in lines 9–10.

▼ Syntax

Do	Don't
Do use curly braces to protect embedded spaces.	**Don't** use special characters (See Table 2.1) in variable names unless you know what you are doing. Use alphanumerical characters for variable names.
Do use double quotes for variable and command substitution.	**Don't** use parentheses in variable names.
Do escape special characters with a back-slash.	

▲

Summary

In this hour, you have covered the basic ideas in Tcl. These include command, variable, and command substitution. A Tcl command is a group of words separated by spaces. The first word is the name of the command, and the remaining words are its arguments. Variables are defined with set and cleared with unset command. The value of the variable is obtained by preceding the name of the variable with a dollar sign. Note that variable substitution and command evaluation occurs using double quotes for grouping.

The most important slogan to take from this hour is: "Everything in Tcl is a string." As a consequence, all the numbers are treated as strings, and no arithmetic is performed automatically. You need to explicitly ask for it. Also, you need a tool to work with patterns in strings. In the next hour, you will learn to exploit these concepts to manufacture Tcl commands on demand and execute them.

Q&A

Q What is wrong with set velocity 15[m/s]?

A Square brackets are used for command evaluation in Tcl. When the interpreter encounters the opening square bracket, it is trying to evaluate the command named m/s, and there is no such command. If you intended to supply the units as part of the value of the variable velocity, you need to suppress the meaning of open square bracket. You might use set velocity {15 [m/s]}. Note that because command substitution occurs inside double quotes, you cannot use them for grouping here.

Q **What is wrong with set** `x 10` **and** `puts "Pocket money: \$x"`**?**

A Backslash suppresses the special meaning of the following character. As a result, the interpreter prints, `Pocket money: $x` to the screen. If you want to print the dollar symbol along with the value, you need an extra dollar before x. Thus the command `puts "Pocket money: \$$x"` prints `Pocket money: $10`.

Q **I have defined a variable as set** `point\[2\] 3.45`**. How do I use this variable?**

A First of all, avoid using such special characters for variable names. There is a much cleaner way to define arrays that is introduced in Hour 6, "Exploring Arrays." To continue with the question—when you are referring to such a variable, use `${point[2]}`. The curly braces suppress the meaning of square brackets.

Q **Can I use a period in a variable as in set** `pos.x 12.5`**?**

A Yes, you can. But be careful when referring to it subsequently, as shown below.

```
% set pos.x 12.5
12.5
% puts "The x coordinate: $pos.x"
can't read "pos": no such variable
% puts "The x coordinate: ${pos.x}"
The x coordinate: 12.5
```

Workshop

The quiz section, which follows, is designed to provide you with an opportunity to recall some of the important concepts introduced in this hour. These may be commands, command syntax, common mistakes, usage, and so on. The following exercises section helps you consolidate the material you learned via an example of practical value. Our aim is that these two sections should reinforce the knowledge you have gained in this hour. The answers to the quiz that follows can be found in Appendix A, "Answers to Quizzes."

Quiz

1. What is a Tcl command?
2. What is meant by variable substitution?
3. What is command substitution?
4. When do we use curly braces?
5. When do we use double quotes?
6. Are the commands inside curly braces evaluated?

7. Given the commands

```
1: set i 0
2: set y[set i] 1.3
```

what is the name of the variable in line 2?

8. What is wrong with the command `puts "Airfare: $250"`?

9. What is the command to list all the available Tcl commands that begin with `p`?

10. What is the value of the variable y in the following code?

```
1: % set x 5
2: 5
3: % incr x
4: 6
5: % set y $x
```

Exercises

Solutions to the exercises are on the CD-ROM that accompanies this book.

1. The command `set age 18` defines the variable age. Write a Tcl command to print the text "She will be 19 next year." including the double quotes.

2. Given the command `set w Root`, define two additional variables of the form `RootHeight` and `RootWidth` to store some relevant measurements.

HOUR 3

Working with Tcl Commands

In Hour 2, "Getting Started with Tcl," you learned how to define variables, and you studied the basics of variable substitution and command substitution. Also, you learned that everything in Tcl is a string. So how does one perform arithmetic? How does one process strings? In this hour, you address these questions, and then you move on to the basic concept of *regular expression*, a powerful tool for finding patterns in strings. This concept is essential for working with strings.

Tcl enables you to manufacture commands and evaluate them dynamically. This method of dynamic command invocation is illustrated with simple examples. We wrap up the hour with an introduction to procedures.

In this hour, you will learn

- To perform numerical computations using variables
- To use regular expressions for finding patterns in strings
- To create and evaluate commands
- To write simple procedures

Arithmetic Expressions

In the last hour, you learned that everything in Tcl is a string. So how do you perform numerical computations? Tcl provides an explicit command for carrying out numerical calculations. This command converts strings to numbers of appropriate type (for example, integer or floating point) for computation. Listing 3.1 shows an example.

LISTING 3.1   Sum of Integers Using expr

```
1:% set x 3
2: 3
3: % set y 5
4: 5
5: % puts "Sum of $x and $y is [expr $x + $y]"
6: Sum of 3 and 5 is 8
```

ANALYSIS   Lines 1–4 define two variables. In line 5, you invoke the expr command to carry out the required computation. Notice that the spaces surrounding the + are for clarity, and they are optional.

The complete list of available arithmetic operators is given in Table 3.1.

TABLE 3.1   Arithmetic Operators—the Operator Precedence Decreases as You Go Down the Table

Operator	Meaning
- ~ !	Unary minus, bitwise NOT, logical NOT
* / %	Multiply, divide, remainder
+ -	Add, subtract
<< >>	Bitwise shift left, bitwise shift right
< > <= >=	Boolean comparisons less than, greater than, less than or equal to, greater than or equal to
== !=	Boolean equals, Boolean not equals
&	Bitwise AND
^	Bitwise exclusive OR
¦	Bitwise inclusive OR
&&	Logical AND
¦¦	Logical OR
x?y:z	If x evaluates to nonzero, then y, otherwise z

The syntax for `expr` enables more complex expressions to be evaluated. You can mix and match Tcl commands and arithmetic expressions. This will be illustrated later in Hour 8, "Manipulating Strings." For now, look at an application of the *if-else* operator (the last item in Table 3.1). This operator is also referred to as *choice operator* or *ternary operator*. Listing 3.2 shows an example.

LISTING 3.2 If-else Operator

```
1: % set n 5
2: 5
3: % set iseven [expr ($n % 2 == 0 ) ? 1 : 0]
4: 0
5: % set n 8
6: 8
7: % set iseven [expr ($n % 2 == 0 ) ? 1 : 0]
8: 1
9: %
```

ANALYSIS You define a variable n with a value of 5 for illustration. The `if-else` operator is of the general form *expression* ? *true_branch* : *false_branch* and works as follows: If the *expression* evaluates to a nonzero value, *true_branch* is evaluated, otherwise *false_branch* is evaluated. In our example, the expression is ($n % 2 == 0) (line 3). For n = 5, $n % 2 returns 1, which is not equal to zero. Therefore, the expression in round brackets evaluates to zero, and the value in the false branch is assigned to the variable `iseven`. In lines 5–8, you check the `iseven` for n = 8. In this case $n % 2 is zero, and this time the value from the `true_branch` is assigned to `iseven`.

> The choice operator normally treats the terms in true and false branches as arithmetic expressions. If you want to assign string values, surround the values and the whole argument of expr with curly braces. For example, given an integer value in n, to store the text string positive or negative in the variable what, you should use the command:
>
> `set what [expr { ($n >0) ? {positive} : {negative} }]`

The `expr` command supports all the intrinsic mathematical functions. A few useful functions are given in Table 3.2.

TABLE 3.2 Some of the Built-In Mathematical Functions

Function	What it does
abs(x)	Absolute value of integer or floating-point number.
ceil(x)	Round x to integers toward infinity. For example: ceil(1.4) is 2.
hypot(xy)	Hypotenuse.$\sqrt{x^2 + y^2}$. For example, hypot(3,4) returns 5.
pow(x,y)	Returns x^y. For example, pow(2,0.5) is 1.414.
rand()	Returns a floating point number between 0 and just less than 1. No argument is required.
round(x)	Round towards nearest integer. For example, round(1.4) is 1, but round(1.6) is 2.
srand(x)	Sets the seed of random number generator. For example, srand([clock seconds]).
sqrt(x)	Square root. For example, sqrt(3).

Listing 3.3 shows a typical dialogue of using the built-in mathematical functions.

LISTING 3.3 Using Mathematical Functions

```
1: % set giga [expr pow(2,30)]
2: 1073741824.0
3: % set d [expr hypot(3,4)]
4: 5.0
5: % set x [expr round( 10*rand() ) % 10 ]
6: 5
7: %
```

ANALYSIS In line 1, we compute the number 2 raised to the power 30, which is stored in the variable giga. Line 2 computes the diagonal of a rectangle measuring 3 units by 4 units. A convenient way of generating random integers from zero to nine inclusive is shown in line 5. Clearly, the number you get when you type this command will be different.

Regular Expressions

What is a regular expression? These are patterns that describe the form of data you are interested in. Consider a simple example of finding calendar dates. Dates are normally written as *dayNumber-monthName-Year*. The separator need not be a -. You can be more flexible and possibly include a forward slash, /. Let us assume that you are interested in reading a file containing dates in this format, and you would like to identify these dates.

How do you describe the format? That is where regular expression comes in handy. You describe the pattern shown earlier by saying, two numbers followed by a minus or /, followed by three letters, followed by a minus or /, followed by four numbers. Using regular expression, you say the same thing as

```
set pat {([0-9]{1,2})[-/]([a-zA-Z])[-/]([0-9]){2,4}}
```

This is too complicated to tackle all at once. Look at a simpler example to understand the concept. For example, you want to identify a number consisting of several digits in a sentence. The pattern is simply one or more digits occurring together. Listing 3.4 illustrates a simple usage of the regexp command to identify a number occurring anywhere in a sentence.

LISTING 3.4   A Regular Expression to Match a Number

```
 1: % set p1 {[0-9]+}
 2: [0-9]+
 3: % set str "Total   tax paid: 750"
 4: Total   tax paid: 750
 5: % regexp $p1 $str
 6: 1
 7: % regexp $p1 $str match
 8: 1
 9: % set match
10: 750
11: % regexp $p1 {This line has no number.} match
12: 0
```

ANALYSIS   Line 1 defines the pattern for a number. The number you are interested in consists of digits zero through nine, and this range is specified by enclosing them in square brackets. Note that these square brackets have nothing to do with the Tcl command invocation; these are enclosed inside curly braces. The + after the character range indicates one or more instances of the preceding pattern. In this case, it means one or more digits. Line 3 is a sample string to try your regular expression. Line 5 invokes the regexp command in its simplest form. If regexp succeeds in finding a match, it will return 1; otherwise it returns 0. The matches found by the regexp command can be obtained by specifying a variable name while invoking regexp, as shown in line 7. You verify the result in lines 9–10. Line 11 shows an example where the regexp command fails, in which case it returns 0.

If you are encountering regular expressions for the first time, go through the preceding example once more. Try a different number of digits somewhere in the text.

What happens if you have two numbers in a line? Which number will the matcher pick? You can specify where the pattern to be matched should occur. You can match the pattern either at the beginning or at the end of the sentence.

NEW TERM *Anchoring patterns* is a way of constraining the pattern and specifying where a pattern match should occur. Listing 3.5 shows an example of an anchoring pattern at the end of the sentence.

LISTING 3.5 A Regular Expression to Pick Numbers at the End

```
 1: % set str2 "She lives in 36 Kaveri Rd., and her tax bill is: 745"
 2: She lives in 36 Kaveri Rd., and her tax bill is: 745
 3: % regexp $p1 $str2 match
 4: 1
 5: % set match
 6: 36
 7: % set p2 {[0-9]+$}
 8: [0-9]+$
 9: % regexp $p2 $str2 match
10: 1
11: % set match
12: 745
13: %
```

ANALYSIS Consider a string with two numbers (line 1) and apply your old pattern set p1 {[0-9]+}. Which number will it match? Will it match 36 or 745? Lines 3–6 show that you pick the first number, 36. If you intend to match the number at the end of the string, to match the amount of tax paid, you need to specifically construct a pattern. If the patterns occur at the beginning or at the end, you can specify this constraint by using the regular expression characters ^ (anchor at the beginning) and $ (anchor at the end). Line 7 defines one such pattern, {[0-9]+$}. This pattern says that you want one or more digits anchored at the end. Lines 9–12 demonstrate the result of this interaction.

NEW TERM *Subpattern* is a grouping of part of a pattern.

When you use a regular expression, the complete match can be saved in a variable. When you are interested in only part of that pattern for further processing, you can include this requirement when defining the pattern. These parts are called subpatterns. Enclosing the required pattern inside a pair of round brackets specifies subpatterns. To illustrate this feature, let's return to the pattern introduced at the beginning of this section. In Listing 3.6, you define a subpattern to identify the name of a month. This is further explained in Figure 3.1.

FIGURE 3.1

A regular expression to match the name of a month is enclosed between two dashes. The subpattern for the month *is enclosed in parentheses.*

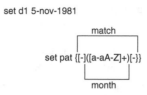

regexp $pat $d1 match month

LISTING 3.6   Simple Regular Expression to Pick the Name of the Month

```
 1: % set pat {[-]([a-zA-Z]+)[-]}
 2: [-]([a-zA-Z]+)[-]
 3: % set d1 5-nov-1981
 4: 5-nov-1981
 5: % regexp $pat $d1
 6: 1
 7: % regexp $pat $d1 match month
 8: 1
 9: % set match
10: -nov-
11: % set month
12: nov
13: %
```

ANALYSIS   Line 1 defines a pattern for identifying the characters between the two dashes (-). The pattern indicates single dash followed by one or more letters in a range. The range consists of the alphabet in either lowercase or uppercase. This range of letters is to be followed by a single -. Line 1 also includes a subpattern, ([a-zA-Z]+), for identifying the name of the month. Parentheses are used as delimiters when specifying a subpattern. Note that this does not verify the text you match is a genuine name of a calendar month. Note also that the pattern [a-zA-Z] represents one character, and it is the + character that is responsible for matching the pattern repeatedly.

Line 3 defines a typical date string. You can mix the case if you want to. You accounted for it in the pattern. Line 5 invokes the regexp command, together with the pattern and the date string stored in the variable d1. If the specified pattern is found in the string, regexp returns 1; otherwise, it returns 0. In this example, you have a successful match, and, therefore, the 1 in line 6. This is fine. Now, how do you get at the text you have matched. regexp enables you to specify additional names of the variables as its arguments. In line 7, you have specified two additional arguments, called match and month. When a successful match is found, the matched pattern and submatches are assigned to these variables. In this example, your pattern has a subpattern (to identify just the month name). Lines 9–12 show the values stored in these variables.

There are two points worth clarifying regarding the pattern that we used to match the - in the dates. This is a *special* character that has two meanings (beginning of an option, range separator in describing character ranges in regular expressions). It is possible to match a single character using the period, (.). If we insist on using -, you must remember that an unprotected dash will be misinterpreted as a command switch. The pattern [-] is a simple way to avoid some of the above pitfalls.

Mastery of regular expressions comes with practice. If you are not successful with the precise pattern you want, try something more general. The two examples in this section introduce the basic concept and use only simple constructs to explain the principle. A subset vocabulary of regular expressions is given in Table 3.3 for your convenience. For an extensive list of quantifiers and related information, see Tcl/Tk manual pages, under the command regexp.

TABLE 3.3 Regular Expressions

Pattern	Matches
re¦re	Either re
re*	Zero or more of re
re+	One or more of re
re?	Zero or one of re
.	Any single character except newline
^	The beginning of string
$	The end of string
\c	The special character c
[abc]	The set of characters included inside the square brackets
[^abc]	Characters not in the set
[a-z]	Range of characters a through z
[^a-z]	Characters not in the range
{m,n}	A sequence of m through n matches of the preceding re
( )	A subpattern

> The pattern (.*) matches the whole string. See the dialogue below for an
> example.
>
> ```
> % regexp {(.*)} {Regular expressions are beautiful.} match
> 1
> % set match
> Regular expressions are beautiful.
> ```
>
> To match any of the special characters *,+,?,.,^,$ literally, escape them with
> a back slash. For example, the command regsub -all {\^} {term =
> (x+y)^3.5} {**} new replaces ^ by **. Note that we don't escape the aster-
> isks in the substitution specification. The variable new has the value term =
> (x+y)**3.5

Manufacturing Tcl Commands on Demand

So far, you have seen that you can store values in variables, which can be the result of a
Tcl command. How about storing a Tcl command put together for a specific purpose,
and get it interpreted when you want it. A typical example is the capability to print a
custom-made time stamp when you press a button. You will extend this example in Hour
10, "Getting Started with Tk." In this hour, you will concentrate on the basic principle.
Your task now is to generate a command to print the time together with some annotation.
Listing 3.7 sets the scene.

LISTING 3.7 Why Use eval?

```
1: % set timeNow [clock format [clock seconds] -format %c]
2: Thu Jul 15 07:46:55 1999
3: % puts "Time now is: [set timeNow]"
4: Time now is: Thu Jul 15 07:46:55 1999
5: % puts "Time now is: [set timeNow]"
6: Time now is: Thu Jul 15 07:46:55 1999
7: %
```

ANALYSIS   In line 1, you define a variable to store the information. The -format option for
the clock format command returns the local date and time information as shown
in line 2. If you want to print the value held in the variable timeNow, you might try a
command such as that in line 3. This prints the value of the variable timeNow with some
annotation. Note that you could have used $timeNow instead of [set timeNow]. Both
result in the same output. Clearly, the value stored in the variable timeNow is manufac-
tured once and for all, as demonstrated in lines 4–6. You can enter them with a delay of a
few seconds to convince yourself.

Now you can assemble a Tcl command. For simplicity, use the words `clock seconds`. Can you store this as a Tcl command in a variable and get it interpreted later? Yes. A simple dialogue is shown in Listing 3.8 to motivate the concept.

LISTING 3.8   Storing a Command in a Variable for Evaluation

```
 1: % set timeCmd1 {clock seconds}
 2: clock seconds
 3: % eval $timeCmd1
 4: 932022994
 5: % set timeCmd2 {clock format [clock seconds] -format %c}
 6: clock format [clock seconds] -format %c
 7: % eval $timeCmd2
 8: Thu Jul 15 08:17:24 1999
 9: % puts "Time now is: [eval $timeCmd2]"
10: Time now is: Thu Jul 15 08:20:17 1999
11: % puts "Time now is: [eval $timeCmd2]"
12: Time now is: Thu Jul 15 08:20:43 1999
13: %
```

ANALYSIS   In line 1, you store just the text of the required command in a variable called timeCmd1, which contains the two words `clock seconds`. These words happen to be the commands that Tcl can interpret. So, you ask the interpreter as shown in line 3. Line 5 is very similar, but has more text. Note that line 5 contains [`clock seconds`]. Remember that no command evaluation takes place inside curly braces. (See Hour 2.) Line 6 is just the text you want, and it is ready to be sent to the interpreter. You send it in line 7. Now you can evaluate the command stored in timeCmd2 whenever you want and get the latest value of time as shown in lines 9–12.

In this example, you defined the variables precisely as required. You can assemble more powerful commands using list operations. You will be revisiting eval in Hour 5, "Working with Lists."

Understanding Eval

Tcl commands are evaluated in two steps. In the first step, the commands are parsed, and variable and command substitutions occur. In the second step, the parsed text is passed to an appropriate command procedure to do the required job. During this phase, the procedure can request a further round of parsing. A simple example of this process is illustrated in Figure 3.2.

FIGURE 3.2

At most, one round of substitutions occur for each character. The result of one substitution is not scanned for further substitutions. The eval command forces another round of evaluation as indicated by the dashed line in the second diagram.

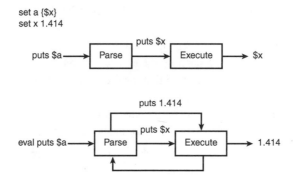

```
set a {$x}
set x 1.414
```

Consider a practical application of eval command. You will be using this command extensively, in subsequent hours, when working with Tk widgets interactively. Here, look at an example involving the topics covered so far. For example, you have created lots of variables in the interpreter, and you want to get rid of them in one fell swoop. Listing 3.9 shows what can go wrong and how to remedy the situation.

LISTING 3.9   Clearing Variables with eval

```
 1: % set xy1 1
 2: 1
 3: % set xy2 2
 4: 2
 5: % set xy3 3
 6: 3
 7: % info var xy*
 8: xy1 xy2 xy3
 9: % unset [info var xy*]
10: can't unset "xy1 xy2 xy3": no such variable
11: % eval unset [info var xy*]
12: %
```

ANALYSIS   You define some variables for demonstration in lines 1–6. You inquire the variables you just now defined with info command. The pattern xy* lists all the variables in the interpreter that begin with xy. If you want to unset all these variables in one action, you might be tempted to use a command such as in line 9. But there is a problem.

Why does the interpreter complain (line 10)? If you read the message carefully, you see that unset got a variable by the name xy1 xy2 xy3, as one word. Of course, there is no such variable. Here is what happened. When the interpreter got the command in line 9, it parsed the command. During parsing, the embedded command [info var xy*] was evaluated and given to the procedure that handles the unset command. The unset command received it as one word, which is a nonexistent variable name. Note that variable names can contain spaces. (See Hour 2.) The best way to cure this problem is to perform one more round of evaluation. The eval command takes its arguments and interprets them as a Tcl command. In your example, you pass unset and the result of [info vars xy*] as arguments to eval.

Special Variables

The interpreter defines some variables that are useful when developing programs interactively. A few of them are illustrated in the Table 3.5.

TABLE 3.5   Special Variables

Variable	Remarks
% set errorCode	Error code NONE
% set errorInfo	Displays most recent error message
% set tcl_library	Location of the library E:/TclTk81/Tcl/lib/tcl8.1
% set tcl_patchLevel	Current patch level of the interpreter 8.1.0
% set tcl_precision	Specifies the number of digits when converting floating-point values to strings 12
% set tcl_version	Current version in major.minor form 8.1

The special variable errorInfo is very useful when debugging errors in the interpreter. A simple example is shown in Listing 3.10, which also illustrates the problem of using in-line comments.

LISTING 3.10 Using `errorInfo`

```
1: % set x {Homer Simpson} # Doh...
2: wrong # args: should be "set varName ?newValue?"
3: % set errorInfo
4: wrong # args: should be "set varName ?newValue?"
5:     while compiling
6: "set x {Homer Simpson} # Doh... "
```

ANALYSIS In line 1, you force the interpreter to generate an error. In this example, you are trying to use an in-line comment in line 1. The interpreter immediately responds with an error message. You can look at what is stored in the variable `errorInfo`. The `set` command in line 3 sheds some more light on this.

The interpreter uncoils, and shows when the error was generated. This mechanism is quite powerful when debugging more complicated scripts. In this simple example, the error was generated, as the message says, while compiling the `set` command (line 6).

Now try to fix the problem. Read the error message again in line 2. The interpreter is expecting to find `set varName ?newValue?`. I know, you meant `# Doh...` to be an in-line comment. The `#` character should be the first character of the first word where Tcl expects to find a command. (See the online manual for further detail.) In this example, the `#` appeared where a value of the variable is expected. To satisfy the interpreter's requirement, you must separate the two lines with a semicolon (`;`). Replace line 1 by `set x {Homer Simpson} ;# Doh...`

Writing Simple Procedures

What is a procedure? A procedure is a group of Tcl commands that performs a specific task. Tcl procedures are analogous to subroutines or functions in other languages. If you find yourself virtually repeating lines of code, except for a few parameters, in all the programs you write, you will improve your productivity by using procedures. Procedures encourage reusable code. As you develop a large collection of these procedures, you will even be able to package them for other users. As an illustration of the syntax, consider a simple example for computing the cube of a given number. First, the procedure is shown in Listing 3.11.

The Syntax for proc

The following code shows the syntax for proc:

```
proc procName { ?arg1 arg2 ...? } {
body
?return?
}
```

where *procName* is the name of the procedure followed by a list of zero or more arguments enclosed within curly braces. The *body* includes an optional return command.

If a procedure has no arguments, you must still indicate this by a pair of braces—{}.

LISTING 3.11   Defining a Simple Procedure to Compute the Cube of a Number

```
1: # Simple procedure to compute the cube of a number
2:
3: proc cube { x } {
4:     set ans [expr $x*$x*$x]
5:     return $ans
6: }
```

ANALYSIS   One simple way of developing procedures is to store them in a file using an editor. Assume that the lines in Listing 3.11 are saved in a file called cube.tcl.

A procedure is a command, like any other Tcl command. It has three arguments. The first argument is the name of the procedure. The second argument is a list of arguments for the procedure. The third argument is the body of the procedure.

Line 1 is a comment. Line 3 starts the procedure command. In the present example, there is only one argument to the procedure. The curly braces are not really needed in this case, but they are included here to show you how they are generally used. The body of the procedure is contained in lines 4–5. Line 4 computes the cube of the number. You use an explicit return command in line 5. A typical interaction invoking the procedure is shown in Listing 3.12.

LISTING 3.12 Invoking a Procedure

```
1: % source cube.tcl
2: % cube 4
3: 64
4: % cube 2.5
5: 15.625
6: % cube -8
7: -512
8: %
```

ANALYSIS You have defined a command called cube in the procedure that is stored in the file cube.tcl. It is yours, and the Tcl interpreter has no knowledge of it. You bring the cube command into the interpreter by sourcing the file containing the procedure. If there is no error, the source command returns nothing.

Now, you are ready to invoke your command. Simply use it as any other Tcl command. Lines 2–6 show some typical examples of cubing an integer, a real and a negative number, respectively.

The return value of the source command depends on the way the procedure is defined. If there is no explicit return command in the procedure, the value of the last command is returned as the return value of the source command. If there is a return command, the source command returns an empty string.

Defining a Procedure to Solve a Linear Equation

To consolidate the material learned in this hour, look at a comprehensive, yet practical example. Let us consider the problem of solving a linear equation. The equation is specified in the form "Solve a*x + b = 0" as a string, where a and b are numbers. For example, "Solve 3*x + 6 = 0". You want to identify the numbers from the string and the variable, x, and return the solution as a string. In the above example, you compute the answer and return the string "x = -2".

The plan is as follows. You will use a procedure for generality. The procedure has one argument, which is the equation to be solved. Next, you define a regular expression to identify the numbers and the variable (such as x or r or p) and throw away the rest. After you have the numbers from the string, you invoke the expr command to do the actual computation, and the result is wrapped in a string. There is one subtle point to watch for in using expr, as explained in the following section. The procedure is shown in Listing 3.13.

3

LISTING 3.13   Identify Numbers and the Variable: Solution of Linear Equations

```
 1: # Procedure to solve linear equations
 2: # Input: string of the form 3*x + 5 = 0
 3:
 4: # Purpose: Use regexp to identify the variable and numbers
 5: #          and return the solution in a string
 6:
 7: proc solveLin { str } {
 8:     regexp {([1-9]+)\*?([a-z])[ ]+(.)[ ]+([1-9]+)} $str match a var op b
 9:     puts " a is : $a "
10:     puts " b is : $b "
11:     puts "op is : $op"
12:     return " $var = [expr (-$b.0/$a)] "
13: }
```

ANALYSIS   The procedure accepts one argument. All the hard work is done in line 8. You want to identify three things from the str variable—coefficient of variable (a), the variable itself (var), and constant term b. In general, identify the operator as well. You paraphrase the regular expression in line 8. It is saying, one or more digits followed by an optional *, followed by one or more spaces, followed by a single character, followed by one or more spaces, followed by one or more digits. Note that the literal *, (multiplication symbol) is specified by escaping it with a back slash. You have indicated the patterns for a, var, op, and b by placing them in round brackets.

After you have found the numbers, it is a straightforward matter to compute the answer using expr. Here comes the subtle point. expr uses decimal point (.) to recognize floating point numbers. If it encounters integers, only integer arithmetic is performed. For example, expr 3/4 returns 0, where as expr 3./4 returns 0.75. So, to account for this eventuality, you append .0 to one of the arguments in the expr command, as shown in line 12. Additional print statements are included for illustration. A typical dialogue using solveLin is shown in Listing 3.14.

LISTING 3.14   Using solveLin

```
 1: % source proc1.tcl
 2: % solveLin {3*x + 5 = 0}
 3:   a is : 3 4:  b is : 5
 5: op is : +
 6:   x = -1.66666666667
 7: % solveLin {2t + 8 = 0}
 8:   a is : 2
 9:   b is : 8
10: op is : +
11:   t = -4.0
```

```
12: % solveLin {4p+6 = 0}
13: can't read "a": no such variable
14: %
```

ANALYSIS The file defining the procedure is first sourced in line 1. Note that the argument to the procedure (line 2) `3*x + 5 = 0` contains blanks and, therefore, is enclosed inside a pair of braces. Line 7 is another example to check that the variable and the coefficient are matched correctly. The final example in line 12 checks the failure. It failed because you mandated at least one blank around the operator (see Listing 3.11, line 8).

This example can be improved in many ways and made robust. You should check the status of `regexp` command in Listing 3.11, line 8, and take corrective action. Also, the procedure is limited to positive integers. These additional checks can be included after you are introduced to conditional statements. (See Hour 4, "Controlling Your Program.")

3

Do	**Don't**
Do protect your patterns when using regular expressions.	
Do remember that the `expr` command returns an integer answer if you supply integer arguments for arithmetic operations.	
Do comment your procedures.	
Do remember that `eval` performs another round of substitution.	

Summary

This hour has been very busy. You have introduced essentially four main ideas—arithmetic, regular expressions, forcing another round of evaluation, and procedures. All these topics will be applied extensively in this book. This hour serves as an introduction to these ideas. The main message to take from this hour is the idea of procedures. Procedures enable you to write simple, elegant programs and test them independently. This helps you isolate any errors far more easily than you could in a monolithic program. You revisit procedures in Hour 7, "Building Your Own Procedures," where advanced material will be covered.

Note that all the commands return a value. In order to take an appropriate action depending on this value, you need a mechanism to control the flow of execution. This is your next topic of study.

Q&A

Q Do I need to protect spaces inside `expr` command?

A No.

Q When I perform some arithmetic with `expr`, I am getting peculiar results. What is wrong?

A You need to be careful when substituting variables and then performing arithmetic. The following code demonstrates one such problem. The user intends to compute the average of three numbers as

```
1: % set nums 1+2+3
2: 1+2+3
3: % set avg [expr $nums/3]
4: 4
5: % set avg2 [expr ($nums)/3]
6: 2
```

To explain the result in line 4, look at the command in line 3. After the variable substitution, you get `expr 1+2+3/3`. Now perform the arithmetic. You get 4. So, be warned when performing variable substitution and arithmetic.

Q When I am generating random numbers, I get the same sequence every time I run the program. Aren't they supposed to be different?

A Yes, you are right. They are supposed to be different. If you have merely invoked `rand()` in your procedure, that will generate the same sequence every time you invoke the procedure. You need to plant the seed for random number generator using `srand(arg)`, where arg is an integer which changes from run to run. Normally this number is chosen as `[clock seconds]`. Thus, you can try `srand([clock seconds])`. The command `srand([pid])` works equally well.

Q Can I return more than one result from a procedure?

A Yes. Use return `"$a $b $c"` where the variables a, b and c are the results you want to return.

Q I am trying to match the negative integers with the pattern `set p {-[0-9]+}` and `regexp $p "-226"`. Why does Tcl complain?

A Well spotted. When the variable is substituted, `regexp` command gets the arguments `-[0-9]+` and `-226`. The interpreter thinks that `-[0-9]+` is an option to `regexp` command. Remember that the options to arguments begin with a - (minus) sign. The best way to avoid such problems is to use `regexp -- $p "-226"`. The double minus signals the end of optional arguments and tells the interpreter that what follows are arguments to the command.

Workshop

The quiz section is designed to provide you with an opportunity to recall some of the important concepts introduced in this hour. These may be commands, command syntax, common mistakes, usage, and so on. In the following exercises section, we have introduced exercises that consolidate the material you learned by means of an example of practical value. The aim is that these two sections should reinforce the knowledge you have gained in this hour. The answers to the quiz that follows can be found in Appendix A, "Answers to Quizzes."

Quiz

1. What is the value of y in the following dialogue?

   ```
   % set x 5
   5
   % set y [expr ($x % 2 == 0 ) ? 1 : 0]
   ```

2. What are regular expressions used for?

3. What is the regular expression to find the three letter words in a string?

4. What is the command to generate random integers in the range of one through six?

5. What is returned by expr 1/4?

6. Given the following procedure, what does the command guessWhat 4 return?

   ```
   1: % proc guessWhat x {
   2: >     set y [expr $x * $x / 2]
   3: > }
   4: % guessWhat 4
   ```

7. What is the regular expression to pick Tcl comment lines?

8. What does set errorInfo do?

Exercises

Solutions to the exercises are on the CD-ROM that accompanies this book.

1. Write a procedure that returns the area and perimeter of a rectangle. Store the procedure in a file called rectangle.tcl.

2. Write a procedure, using the if-else operator that returns strings of the form "There are(is) 5 item(s) in the window" where the appropriate verb and noun are produced depending on the number.

3. Write a procedure to simulate a throw of a dice.

HOUR 4

Controlling Your Program

In the last hour, you learned the essential commands for doing arithmetic with `expr` and using `regexp` for identifying patterns in a string. You also learned how to define simple procedures for frequently used operations.

Controlling the flow of a program is an essential construct in any programming language. Tcl provides five constructs `if...elseif`, `for`, `foreach`, `while`, and `switch`, which extend the functionality of similarly named constructs in other languages.

In this hour, you will learn

- To use the logical conditional statements to control the flow of a Tcl program
- To use looping constructs `for`, `while`, and `foreach`
- To use the powerful `foreach` construct
- To use `switch` for multiway branching

Conditional Branching with `if-then-elseif`

The program flow can be controlled with an `if-then-elseif` command. The most important point in Tcl is that there are commands, not program statements. Command arguments are separated by spaces. When the arguments contain spaces or newlines, you protect them by using curly braces. Reminding yourself of this fact will help you understand the syntax of the `if-then-elseif` command better.

▼ SYNTAX

The Syntax for `if-elseif`

The following code shows the syntax for `if-elseif`

```
if expr1 ?then? body1 elseif expr2 ?then? body2 elseif ... ?else? ?bodyN?
```

where *expr1*, *expr2,* and so on are expressions that return boolean values. If *expr1* is true, *body1* is executed. Otherwise the condition in *expr2* is evaluated, and if true, *body2* is executed and so on. Note that the words `then` and `else` are optional. Note also that any condition or equation that produces a value other than zero is true, while a value of zero

▲ is false.

Look at a simple example to clarify some of the finer points. You can print sentences to say whether a given number is positive zero or negative.

LISTING 4.1   The `if-else` Command

```
 1: % set n 0
 2: 0
 3: % if {$n >0} {
 4: >     puts "$n is positive"
 5: > } elseif {$n == 0} {
 6: >     puts "$n is zero"
 7: > } else {
 8: >     puts "$n is negative"
 9: > }
10: 0 is zero
11: %
```

The `if` command in lines 3–9 has five arguments. It could have been written as one long line, but that wouldn't be easy to read! The first argument `{$n>0}` is a condition. If true, you execute the body in line 4. Otherwise, you check another condition, in line 5. You branch off to execute line 6 if the condition `$n == 0` is true; otherwise, you execute line 8.

Nested `ifs`

The `if` commands can be nested to an arbitrary depth. It is highly desirable for the sake of clarity to keep this nesting to a depth of two or three. Let us illustrate this feature with an example that assigns grades from numerical marks. The code is shown in Listing 4.2.

LISTING 4.2 Nested if

```
 1: % set mark 90
 2: 90
 3: % if {$mark > 80} {
 4: >     if {$mark < 85} {
 5: >         set grade  A-
 6: >     } else {
 7: >         set grade A
 8: >     }
 9: > }
10: A
11: %
```

ANALYSIS Lines 3–9 define an `if` command that contains another `if` command (lines 4–8). Using indentation and grouping with curly braces, there is no confusion as to which `if` the `else` command belongs. Note that the `else` part is optional. In the above example, the top-level `if` does not have an `else` part.

Conditional Branching—`Switch`

A `switch` command is more versatile in processing multiple choices. As an example, generate a string to say that a supermarket closes early on certain days. Let us say it closes early on Friday and Saturday; it completely shuts down on Sunday; it closes at 6:00 p.m. on the remaining days. The dialogue in Listing 4.3 shows a simple example.

The Syntax for `switch`

The following code shows the syntax for `switch`

```
switch ?options? string {
    pattern body
    pattern body
    default body
}
```

where the available options are `-exact` or `-glob` or `-regexp` or `--`. The `switch` command matches its *string* argument against each of the *pattern*s in order. If the *string* matches a *pattern*, the corresponding *body* is executed. If *string* does not match any of the patterns, and *default* pattern is not specified, the `switch` command returns a `null` string.

LISTING 4.3   Using the switch Command for a Multiway Decision

```
1: % set day Fri
2: Fri
3: % switch  $day {
4: >     Fri    { puts "Closes early on $day at 4 p.m." }
5: >     Sat    { puts "Closes early on $day at 4 p.m." }
6: >     Sun    { puts "Closed all day on $day" }
7: >     default { puts "Closes at 6 p.m.  on $day" }
8: % }
9: Closes early on Fri at 4 p.m.
```

ANALYSIS   For illustration, choose a day as you did in line 1. The switch command shown here has two arguments. The first argument is the value of the variable. You will make a choice based on this value. The second argument is the body of the switch command. The body consists of pattern action pairs. Our first pattern describes what to do if the $day matches with the literal text Fri. In this simple example, you just print appropriate text indicating the closing time. Similar pattern action pairs are defined for Sat and Sun (lines 5–6). The default pattern is a catchall situation and matches for any value of $day.

To test that this works for all other patterns, you can wrap a foreach loop around the switch block, which is introduced in the next section, "Looping—for, foreach, while."

You can be more flexible with the switch command and specify the type of matching you want to perform. The switch command supports three options, -exact for matching patterns exactly, -glob for glob style pattern matching and -regexp for matching patterns using regular expressions. Most popular is to use -regexp option for pattern matching because it offers more flexibility. Listing 4.4 demonstrates its use.

LISTING 4.4   Using Switch with Fall Through Actions

```
1: % set day Friday
2: Friday
3: % switch -regexp $day {
4: >      ^Fr.* -
5: >      ^Sa.* { puts "Closes early on $day at 4 p.m." }
6: >      ^Su.* {puts "Closed all day on $day" }
7: >      default { puts "Closes at 6 p.m. on $day" }
8: > }
9: Closes early on Friday at 4 p.m.
10: %
```

ANALYSIS In the body of the `switch` (lines 4–8), two ideas are introduced. The first shows the way you can specify patterns. The second idea is a fall through of an action. For greater flexibility in processing the value of $day, `-regexp` is used for matching patterns. It means that you can specify the variable day as short as Fr or as long as Friday. The pattern, in line 4, says match Fr followed by zero or more characters, and the corresponding action is just a dash. This dash signals the interpreter to use the following action. In the preceding example, the action used is that for `^Sa.*`, which prints the closing time as shown in line 5. (See Hour 3, "Working with Tcl Commands," to brush up on Regular Expressions.)

Note that the regular expression can be tightened a bit, but the preceding forms are used for simplicity.

We conclude this section with a cautionary example. Using simple values, such as those you have seen so far, for switch is fine. The problem arises when you want to use values such as `-font` or `-height`, and so on. This situation can arise if you are working with widget options, which are of this form. Listing 4.5 illustrates the problem and its remedy.

LISTING 4.5 Use `--` to Terminate Option Specification in `Switch`

```
 1: % set opt -font
 2: -font
 3: % switch -regexp $opt {
 4: >        -font { set f {Courier Bold 12}}
 5: >        -width { set w 15 }
 6: > }
 7: bad option "-font": must be -exact, -glob, -regexp, or --
 8: % switch -regexp — $opt {
 9: >        -font {set f {Courier 12 bold} }
10: >        -width { set w 15}
11: > }
12: Courier12 bold
13: %
```

ANALYSIS Line 1 defines a variable whose value begins with a dash. The first attempt (in lines 3–6) comes up with an error. If you read the message carefully, you find that the variable $opt, in line 3, was substituted and passed to the `switch` command, and the `switch` command thought that `-font` is one of the options for it. To avoid such confusion, you should specify a double dash, `--` to tell switch that what follows is an argument.

4

> Use -- to terminate option specification while using `switch`. For example,
> `switch -regexp -- $var { pat1 {body} ...}.`

Looping—for, foreach, while

Looping constructs enable you to repeatedly execute a group of Tcl commands. Properly constructed loops save time and make the code compact and eminently readable. Tcl provides three commands `for`, `foreach`, and `while`. These are discussed in turn below.

The for Loop

The `for` loop command is used for repeating a group of commands with uniform stride (or step size). A simple example is given in Listing 4.6.

The Syntax for `for`

The following code shows the syntax for the `for` command

`for start test next body`

where `start` contains the initialization of the loop variable (or parameter), `test` is the termination condition, `next` is a command to update the loop, variable and `body` means the lines of commands to be executed.

LISTING 4.6   Printing the Squares of Numbers Using the `for` Command

```
1: % for {set i 1} {$i <= 4 } {incr i} {
2: >    puts "Square of $i is [expr $i*$i]"
3: > }
4: Square of 1 is 1
5: Square of 2 is 4
6: Square of 3 is 9
7: Square of 4 is 16
8: %
```

ANALYSIS   Lines 1–3 define a simple `for` command. Remember that Tcl has commands and their arguments—not statements. The `for` command has four arguments—initializer, condition to terminate the loop, incrementer, and body of the loop. Here the loop variable is `i` and is initialized to `1` as `set i 1` (line 1). Next you want to check the bound on the loop variable. Here you want to execute the body as long as `i` is less than or equal to four. The next argument is the step size or stride of the loop variable. You want to increment the loop variable by 1. The final argument is the body of the loop that consists of a single command (line 2), which prints the number and its square.

The spaces between the arguments in the for loop must be used. This requirement catches many beginners who are accustomed to programming in other languages. Another point to remember is that incr command takes the name of the variable, not the value. (See Hour 2, "Getting Started with Tcl.")

foreach Loop

When you want to walk through a list of items in a variable, the foreach loop command provides a powerful mechanism. Using foreach, you can process a single item, a pair of items, or even a subset of contiguous items from the list in one go. The command comes in three flavors.

The Syntax for foreach

The following code shows the syntax for foreach

```
foreach varname list body
```

```
foreach varlist1 list1 ?varlist2 list2 ...? body
```

where *varname* and *list* is the list of items to be processed and *body* consists of a set of Tcl commands that process the items in the list in some way.

foreach with One Loop Parameter

The foreach command is used when the loop parameter does not have any uniform stride. Typically, you need to process all the items in a set. With a foreach loop, you can walk through an arbitrary list of items processing them as required. Consider a simple example. You want to compute the cubes of a given set of numbers. The numbers do not form any sequence. Listing 4.7 illustrates this. See also Figure 4.1 which clarifies how various loop parameters are assigned.

LISTING 4.7 The foreach Command—a Single Loop Variable

```
1: % foreach x {3 4 2 5 } {
2:     puts "Cube of $x is \t [expr pow($x,3)]"
3: }
4: Cube of 3 is     27.0
5: Cube of 4 is     64.0
6: Cube of 2 is     8.0
7: Cube of 5 is     125.0
8: %
```

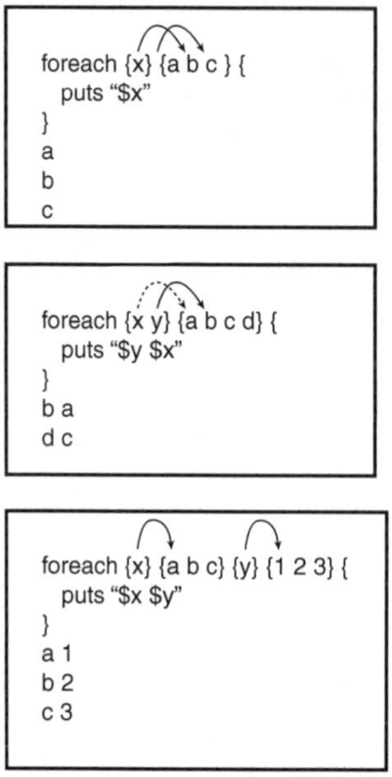

FIGURE 4.1

The three flavors of foreach *loop.*

```
foreach {x} {a b c } {
    puts "$x"
}
a
b
c
```

```
foreach {x y} {a b c d} {
    puts "$y $x"
}
b a
d c
```

```
foreach {x} {a b c} {y} {1 2 3} {
    puts "$x $y"
}
a 1
b 2
c 3
```

ANALYSIS Lines 1–3 define a simple foreach command. Here the loop variable is x. Each
entry in the list is processed in turn. First time round, x gets the value 3, and the
body of the loop is executed. It prints the value of the cube as in line 4. Remember, when
performing arithmetic, you need to invoke the expr command. Next time round, the loop
variable gets the value 4, and its cube is printed in line 5. The loop is continued until all
the elements in the list are processed.

foreach with Two Loop Parameters

Consider a simple example to illustrate the command. You want to process a list consisting of pairs of numbers x, y supplied as x0 y0 x1 y1 x2 y2 and so on. You want to
find the maximum x and y values respectively (refer to Figure 4.1).

LISTING 4.8   The foreach Loop with Two Loop Parameters

```
 1: % set xmax {}
 2: % set ymax {}
 3: % foreach {x y} {3 5 6 12 9 8} {
 4: >    if {$x > $xmax} {set xmax $x}
 5: >    if {$y > $ymax} {set ymax $y}
 6: > }
 7: % set xmax
 8: 9
 9: % set ymax
10: 12
11: %
```

ANALYSIS Lines 1–2 initialize two variables to null strings. In line 3, you use two loop parameters to process the items from the list in one go. The body of the loop updates the current `maxima`. When you finished scanning the list, you end up with the required `xmax` and `ymax`.

> `foreach` loop is an efficient way of scanning through a list of items. You will be able to solve many practical problems elegantly using the `foreach` command with multiple loop parameters. Master it now!

Walking Through Two Lists with Two Parameters

Our final form of `foreach` is a walk through using more than one list with separate loop parameters. Listing 4.9 shows a simple example, where you walk through a list of student names and each student's corresponding grade in a science class.

LISTING 4.9 Walking Through Two Lists Using `foreach`

```
1: % foreach n {Mike Phil Kathy} m {75 80 90} {
2: >        puts " $n has got $m in Sciences"
3: > }
4:   Mike has got 75 in Sciences
5:   Phil has got 80 in Sciences
6:   Kathy has got 90 in Sciences
7: %
```

4

ANALYSIS The `foreach` loop in lines 1–2 operates on two lists simultaneously. You also use two separate parameters n and m (refer to Figure 4.1). The first time around n gets `Mike`, and m gets 75. In this example, you merely print them. Other names and marks are assigned to the respective loop parameters as you go around the loop.

while Loop

The `while` command is used when you want to repeatedly execute a group of commands subject to a condition being satisfied.

SYNTAX

The Syntax for `while`

The following code shows the syntax for `while`

```
while test body
```

▲ where *body* is executed as long as the *test* evaluates to a nonzero value.

In the popular rhyme children use when learning to count, you see the basic operation of the `while` command. The code is shown in Listing 4.10.

LISTING 4.10 Looping Subject to a Condition Using the WHILE Command

```
 1: % set n 3
 2: 3
 3: % while {$n > 0} {
 4: >     puts "$n green bottles standing on the wall"
 5: >     puts "if one green bottle should accidentally fall ..."
 6: >     incr n -1
 7: > }
 8: 3 green bottles standing on the wall
 9: if one green bottle should accidentally fall ...
10: 2 green bottles standing on the wall
11: if one green bottle should accidentally fall ...
12: 1 green bottles standing on the wall
13: if one green bottle should accidentally fall ...
14: %
```

ANALYSIS Lines 3–7 define the while command that has two arguments. The first argument is a *test*. Here, you test whether the number of bottles is greater than 0. Because you have set n to be three, the test evaluates to 1, and the body of the while loop is entered. The second argument is the *body*, (lines 4–6). Here the body consists of printing some informative text to the screen.

The most important point to remember about the while loops is that you must update the variables defining the *test* so that the *test* fails eventually. If you don't, you end up in an indefinite loop. In line 6, you decrease the value of n, thus making sure that you exit the loop in a finite number of steps.

> Make sure that the while loop terminates properly. It is quite easy to get into indefinite loops. Check that the test fails at some point.
>
> 1 is always true. For example, while 1 { *body* } executes the *body* indefinitely.

break and continue

The break command provides an early exit from a loop. The break command exits the innermost loop. To illustrate the break command, consider searching for an item in a list. As soon as you find the item, there is no need to scan the rest of the items, and you make an early exit. The code is shown in Listing 4.11.

LISTING 4.11   Exiting Early with Break Command

```
1: % foreach n {Mark Phil Dave Shane} {
2: >        puts " Item  is $n"
3: >        if { $n == "Phil" } break
4: > }
5:  Item  is Mark
6:  Item  is Phil
7: %
```

ANALYSIS   You scan through a list of names as in line 1. To demonstrate an early break from the loop, you keep printing the item being processed (line 2). You make a simple check to match a specific name. If the check is satisfied, you break out of the loop. The remaining elements are not processed, as can be seen from lines 5–6.

In contrast to break command, the continue command enables you to proceed to the next iteration of the loop. It is typically used in the body of for, foreach, and while loops. Listing 4.12 illustrates a loop to process odd numbers only.

LISTING 4.12   The Continue Command

```
 1: % foreach n { 4  8 9 6 7 } {
 2: >        if { ($n%2) == 0 } {
 3: >            # ignore it
 4: >            continue
 5: >        } else {
 6: >            # do something with it
 7: >            puts $n
 8: >        }
 9: > }
10: 9
11: 7
```

ANALYSIS   The foreach loop (lines 1–9) iterates through a list of integers. Inside the body, you make a check for even numbers. If the number you are processing turns out to be even (line 2), you just ignore it and proceed to the next item in the loop, using the command continue. The else branch (lines 5–8), processes the case you are interested in.

Do	**DON'T**
Do include an `else` branch as often as you can. It helps you track the flow of logic better.	**Don't** forget that the `default` pattern in a `switch` command matches anything.
Do remember to include a blank space between all the arguments of the `if..elseif...else` command.	**Don't** include a comment line in a `switch` command where a pattern is expected.
Do use `break` command to exit early from a loop.	
Do remember to leave a blank space between all the arguments of any command.	
Do terminate the options for `switch` with `--`.	

Summary

In this hour, you have learned how to control the flow of a Tcl program. Tcl provides five constructs `if ... elseif`, `for`, `foreach`, `while`, and `switch` to control the flow. All these commands are analogous to similar constructs in other languages.

The main differences lie in the extended functionality offered by the Tcl flow control commands. The commands `foreach` and `switch` offer far greater flexibility to write compact code. Solutions to many practical problems can be expressed succinctly using these commands. A `foreach` loop can be used to operate on elements of multiple lists. The `switch` command consists of pattern-action blocks and is used to select a particular block depending on the value of a variable. The value of the variable can be matched to the pattern using any of the three options `-exact` or `-glob` or `-regexp`. Finally, the commands `break` and `continue` complete the set of flow control commands. A `break` command exits the innermost loop.

Thus far, you have worked with simple variables to store a value. To process a set of related items, you need a bit more flexibility than that offered by simple variables. Tcl offers two important data structures, lists and arrays, to manipulate data efficiently. These structures are introduced in the next two hours.

Q&A

Q **What is wrong with the commands set w Sunny and**

    if {$w == Sunny} { puts Sunny } else { puts "Not Sunny" } ?

A If you use the above command, the interpreter complains saying, "syntax error in expression "$w == Sunny " ". The problem lies in the way you have specified the logical equality. You need to compare them as strings. So rewrite the logical equality either as {$w == {Sunny}} or {$w == "Sunny"}. In fact using the string compare command will be more efficient. Strings are introduced in Hour 8, "Manipulating Strings."

Q **How do I use comments within the body of a switch script?**

A This is the trickiest process of them all. The rule is this. If the first nonblank character of a command is a #, all the characters from it to the next new line character are discarded by the interpreter. Consider the following lines:

```
1:     switch -regexp -- $a {
2:            # yes branch
3:         ^[Yy].* { puts $a }
4:            # no branch
5:         ^[Nn].* { puts $a }
6:            # default case
7:         default { puts $a }
8:         }
```

Placing the comments as in lines 2, 4, and 6 confuses the interpreter. For example, when the interpreter encounters line 2, it thinks that it is a pattern, and complains extra switch pattern with no body. The clue is in the error message. You cannot have comment lines where the interpreter is expecting to see a Tcl command. Place the comments inside the body of a pattern as shown below.

```
1: switch -regexp -- $a {
 2:      ^[Yy].* {
 3:          ;# yes branch
 4:          puts $a
 5:      }
 6:      ^[Nn].* {
 7:          ;# no branch
 8:          puts $a
 9:      }
10:      default {
11:          ;# default case (no semicolon here)
12:          puts $a
13:      }
14:      }
```

Note that we have used ;#. A semicolon separates Tcl commands.

Q **Why do I need to enclose the condition for `while` command inside curly braces? For example, the following code runs forever. What is going on?**

```
set cond 1
    while "$cond <5" {
    puts $cond
    incr $cond
}
```

A Do not type this code yet. The variable substitution for the test condition happened once and for all—that is,]1 < 5, which is always true. As a result the loop executes indefinitely. To convince yourself, you may insert the command `if {$cond == 10} break` after the `incr` command and run the script (or type it interactively). If the test for the `while` loop is specified as {$cond < 5}, the new value of the `cond` is taken into account, and the loop terminates as expected.

Q **Why can't I place the curly braces for `if` command on a separate line? For example, the code below appears to be unacceptable. Why?**

```
1:          set toggle 0
2:          if {!toggle}
3:          {
4:          set toggle 1
5:          }
```

A Remember the structure of a Tcl command. A newline terminates the command. So, the parser attempts to parse the command, in line 2, and finds that it has the wrong number of arguments. On the other hand, if you keep the opening brace on line 2 and hit return, that is fine, because everything in the curly braces is passed as the second argument to the `if` command.

Q **I am using a regular expression pattern in a switch block, and it appears to behave differently. For example, in the code below I was expecting the case for `Tue` to be handled by the `default` case. But it is not. Why?**

```
1: %set day Tue
2: %switch -regexp -- $day {
3: >     [Mo].* -
4: >     [We].* -
5: >     [Fr].* { puts "Closing Early" }
6: >     default { puts "Closes at 5:30 p.m." }
7: >}
8: %Closing Early
```

A Are you expecting the default pattern to be matched, and `"Close at 5:30 p.m"` to be printed? If so, read on. The pattern specified says, if my $day contains the letters Mo or We or Fr followed by zero or more characters print "Closing Early"; otherwise, print "Closes at 17:30". The pattern does NOT specify that M has to be followed by o, and so forth. The square brackets include a set of characters only. If you mean to say M followed by o, or W followed by e, or F followed by r, you must change the patterns to Mo.* (in line 3), We.* (in line 4) and Fr.* (in line 5). Now the reason for the output in line 8 should be clear. The given day Tue contains the letter e, and hence matches pattern in line 4, and because the action for that pattern is a fall through to line 5, you got the answer that is displayed.

Be patient with regular expressions, and understand clearly the patterns you are using.

Workshop

The quiz section that follows is designed to provide you with an opportunity to recall some of the important concepts introduced in this hour. These may be commands, command syntax, common mistakes, usage, and so on. The following exercises section helps you consolidate the material you learned via an example of practical value. Our aim is that these two sections should reinforce the knowledge you have gained in this hour. The answers to the quiz that follows can be found in Appendix A, "Answers to Quizzes."

Quiz

1. What is the syntax for an if...elseif...else command in Tcl?

2. What are the arguments for the switch command?

3. Why do you need to indicate termination of the options for switch?

4. What is wrong with this script:
   ```
   switch -- $answer {
           yes: { puts Ok }
           no:  { puts NotOK } }
   ```

5. What are the differences between the switch and if....elseif....else commands?

6. What are the admissible options for switch command?

7. What is the command to print a message if you are not using the latest version of Tcl?

8. Can I write an if..elseif...else command in a single line?

9. What happens when you use a - for specifying an action for a pattern in a switch command?

Exercises

Solutions to the exercises are on the CD-ROM that accompanies this book.

1. Use the `foreach` command to create four variables given by the surname of the person in the following list of personal information: name, age, some identification number, and job title; and rearrange the information to store the personal details using the surname as a variable name.

```
set personalList {Anderson 24 3249 Secretary Bingham 29 6234 \
> Salesman Carr 45 8627 Engineer McPherson 54 8729 Chairman}
```

2. Write a procedure, which returns the quadrant number of a point (in the two dimensions), to which it belongs. For example, the point (1,-1) belongs to the fourth quadrant. Use your procedure to print the quadrant numbers for the following points.

```
set pts {1 1 -1 1 -1 -1 1 -1 0 0}
```

3. Write a `for` loop to print the numbers 0 to 9 in the reverse order.

4. Lucky seven! Write a script to find how many times you will obtain a seven in 1,000 throws of a dice. (You may use the procedure in Exercise 3 of Hour 3, "Working with Tcl Commands," for throw of a dice.)

HOUR 5

Working with Lists

In Hour 4, "Controlling Your Program," you learned how to use conditional statements to control a program. In this hour, you will learn one of the most powerful yet simple constructs of Tcl—lists. Lists are used to create commands and evaluate them. Lists play an important role in developing powerful scripts.

What are Tcl lists? Simply stated, a list is a collection of words enclosed within curly braces and separated by whitespace characters—one or more blanks, tabs, or newline characters. (See Hour 2, "Getting Started with Tcl," for more information on whitespace.) The following is an example of a list:

```
{January February March April}
```

A list element can also be a list, and such elements are often referred to as sublists. A thorough understanding of the manipulation of lists pays rich dividends later on. In this hour, you will learn

- How to create lists and lists of lists
- How to extract an element from a list
- How to modify elements of a list

- How to search for an element in a list
- How to sort a list
- How to evaluate a list as a Tcl command

Manipulating Lists

List manipulation commands can be broadly categorized into two groups. The first group of commands queries properties of a list such as length of a list and the element at index position 3, and so on. The second group of commands alters the contents of the list in some way (for example, appending an element to a list). The complete set of list commands are shown in Table 4.1, which also includes two closely related commands.

TABLE 4.1   List Commands

Command	Result
lappend varName ? value value ...?	Appends one or more elements to a list. **The command takes the name, not the value of a list.**
lindex *list index*	Extracts the element at *index* position.
linsert *list index* element ?elt ...?	Inserts *element*s into a list at index position *index*.
list ?arg arg ...?	Returns a list formed by *arg*s.
llength *list*	Returns number of elements in a list. llength {a {b c} d} returns 3. A null list has zero elements.
lrange *list first last*	Returns a list of *first* through *last* elements inclusive.
lreplace list *first last ?value* ...?	Replaces with value *first* through *last* elements. Returns a new list, leaving original list intact.
lsearch ?[-exact|-glob¦ (default)-regexp]? *list pattern*	Index of the first occurrence of *pattern* in the *list* is returned.
lsort ?[-ascii¦-dictionary¦ -index ind¦-integer¦-real¦ -increasing¦-decreasing¦ -command cmdProc]? list	Sorts elements of a *list*.
join *list ?joinString?*	Joins elements of a list. E.g. join {a b c} {::} returns a::b::c.
split *string ?splitChars*	Splits *string* into a proper Tcl list. For example, split {Hello} {} returns the characters in a list.

Once a list is created, you can add additional elements to it. You can retrieve elements from a list. Two of the important list manipulation facilities are searching for elements and sorting elements in various ways. If you don't like the built-in comparator, you can define your own. Without further ado, let us get started.

In this section, we introduce the list manipulation commands with short examples, and we conclude the hour with a comprehensive example, where we define our own comparator.

Creating Lists

Lists are created by enclosing the elements included in the list within curly braces. Elements of a list are separated by whitespace characters. When a particular element happens to be another list, that list is enclosed within curly braces. Listing 5.1 is a short example.

LISTING 5.1   Creating Lists and Sublists

```
1: % set months {January February March April}
2: January February March April
3: % set  parts {i386  HPLaserJet6L  x5y x2y}
4: i386  HPLaserJet6L  x5y x2y
5: % set nums { {4 6 8 2} {7 9} }
6: {4 6 8 2} {7 9}
7: %
```

ANALYSIS   Line 1 defines a simple list consisting of four elements. Note that the output returned by the set command does not include the curly braces. Line 3 defines a list consisting of alphanumeric characters. You can also have a simple listing of numbers alone, as shown in line 5. Note that line 5 uses two sublists. In all the commands above, the lists are stored in some variables. This is not always strictly necessary.

Lists of Lists

Not all lists you encounter are simple. Often elements of lists are themselves lists. List syntax allows you to use sublists. Simply group the elements using the curly braces when defining them. Note that a sublist may be the result of a variable substitution. Variable substitution is covered in Hour 2, "Getting Started with Tcl." Both these situations are illustrated in Listing 5.2.

LISTING 5.2 Using the List Command

```
 1: % set cmdOpts {Edit {Cut Paste Undo Delete}}
 2: Edit {Cut Paste Undo Delete}
 3: % set address {Dear Mr.}
 4: Dear Mr.
 5: % set name Ash
 6: Ash
 7: % set addLine {$address $name}
 8: $address $name
 9: % set addLine [list $address $name]
10: {Dear Mr.} Ash
```

 Line 1 illustrates a typical use of lists to store some relevant information. In this example, certain options for Edit are stored in a sublist for convenience. Lines 3–10 demonstrate a common mistake.

Consider the scenario of constructing a line such as "Dear Mr. Ash". You can store the value "Dear Mr." in a variable (line 3) and the name of a person you are going to address in the variable name. If you want to generate the complete line, you might be tempted to try the command as in line 7. Oops! What has gone wrong? Of course, it is that variable substitution—it did not take place. So, to evaluate the variables, you might try to use double quotes. It will work, but there is an annoying side effect. They destroy the list structure. Listing 5.3 highlights this point. An elegant way of dealing with this situation is to use the list command as shown in line 9.

LISTING 5.3 Double Quotes Destroy List Structure

```
 1:  % set name {Ash Brown}
 2: Ash Brown
 3: % set addLine "$address $name"
 4: Dear Mr. Ash Brown
 5: % set addLine [list $address $name]
 6: {Dear Mr.} {Ash Brown}
```

ANALYSIS Ash is given as a last name in line 1 to highlight the effect. In line 3, you use double quotes to evaluate the embedded variables. As you can see, the variables are evaluated (line 5). Notice that the variable addLine loses the list structure. In line 6, you use an explicit list command that preserves the list structure of the embedded variables. This distinction is important when you learn about generating commands and evaluating them.(For more information, see the section "Generating and Evaluating Commands," later in this hour.)

Length of a List

The length of a list is the number of elements in a list. `llength` returns the length of a list. There are a couple of points to watch for. The first thing to notice is that the elements that happen to be sublists count as one. Second, watch for escaped whitespace characters. The simple usage of `llength` and the other points mentioned in this paragraph are illustrated in Listing 5.4.

LISTING 5.4 Watch for Escaped Whitespace Characters and Sublists When Calculating the Length of a List

```
1: % set fruits {Apples Peaches Kiwi}
2: Apples Peaches Kiwi
3: % llength $fruits
4: 3
5: % set fruits2 {Apples Straw\ Berries}
6: Apples Straw\ Berries
7: % llength $fruits2
8: 2
9: % set fruits3 {Apples {Straw berries}}
10: Apples {Straw berries}
11: % llength $fruits3
12: 2
```

ANALYSIS In line 1, you define a list of three elements. `llength` in line 3 returns the length of the list. In line 5, you use an escaped whitespace character, space. Because you suppressed its intended meaning, `llength` treats that character as part of the element, and hence the length of `fruits2` is 2 (lines 7–8). Sublists are counted as one element, as demonstrated in lines 9–12.

Be careful when using variable substitution or command evaluation while constructing lists and determining their lengths. This is illustrated in Listing 5.5.

LISTING 5.5 Watch for Substituted Variables When Calculating Length of a List

```
1: % set x {1 2}
2: 1 2
3: % set msg1 "Origin: $x"
4: Origin: 1 2
5: % llength $msg1
6: 3
7: % set msg2 [list Origin: $x]
8: Origin: {1 2}
9: % llength $msg2
10: 2
```

5

In this example, lists are constructed in two different ways. You define a variable to store a pair of numbers (line 1). Note the difference between the lengths of `msg1` and `msg2`. `msg1` is the result of variable substitution using double quotes, whereas `msg2` is the result of using the `list` command. The lesson here is that the list structure is preserved using the `list` command.

Retrieving Elements from Lists

A single element from a list is extracted using `lindex`. A contiguous set of elements are extracted using `lrange`.

Individual elements can be accessed from a list using a simple indexing scheme. The first element in a list has index `0`, and the last element has index `end`. Elements in-between are accessed by using the appropriate numerical index.

> The first element of a list has index `0`, and the last element has index `end`.

LISTING 5.6 Accessing Elements in a List

```
1: % set shopping {Milk Bread Fruits {Can Opener} Butter}
2: Milk Bread Fruits {Can Opener} Butter
3: % lindex $shopping 0
4: Milk
5: % lindex $shopping end
6: Butter
7: % lindex $shopping 3
8: Can Opener
9: %
```

First a simple list called `shopping` is defined. Note that the list contains a sublist in position 3. (Yes, it is 3. List indices start from 0.) `lindex` takes a list and an index. The index is either an integer or the logical name `end`. At index position 3, there is a sublist; and the whole sublist is extracted in one go.

> The logical index `end` is useful when accessing the last element from a list, particularly when the list is changing.

A contiguous set of elements is extracted using the `lrange` command. Listing 5.7 shows how to extract elements 1–3 from your shopping list.

LISTING 5.7   Extracting a Range of Elements from a List

```
1: % set shopping {Milk Bread Fruits {Can Opener} Butter}
2: Milk Bread Fruits {Can Opener} Butter
3: % lrange $shopping 1 3
Bread Fruits {Can Opener}
```

ANALYSIS The `lrange` command in line 3 takes the list contained in the variable `shopping` and two indices. In this example, you want to extract the elements at positions 1, 2, and 3. Note that if an element happens to be a sublist, the complete sublist is extracted.

Modifying Lists

Elements can be added to an existing list. `linsert` takes a list, an integer index, and a value that is to be added to the list. Listing 5.8 illustrates its usage.

LISTING 5.8   Inserting Elements into a List

```
1: % linsert  $shopping 3  Biscuits
2: Milk Bread Fruits Biscuits {Can Opener} Butter
3: % linsert $shopping  0 Veg
4: Veg Milk Bread Fruits {Can Opener} Butter
5: % linsert $shopping end  Ketchup
6: Milk Bread Fruits {Can Opener} Butter Ketchup
7: %
```

ANALYSIS Line 1 shows how to insert the element `Biscuits` into the list at position 3. You can insert elements at the end of the list as in line 5. Note the use of the end logical name for the index.

Continue the shopping list metaphor a little longer. If it turns out that you already have a `Can Opener` in the bottom drawer, you might want to drop that element from the list. You can replace elements using `lreplace`, which takes a list, two indices, and a value to replace with. If you do not specify a value, the specified elements are replaced by nothing. The twist in the tale is nothing happens to the original list. Listing 5.9 illustrates this point.

LISTING 5.9   When Replacing the Elements in a List, `lreplace` Does Not Change the Original List!

```
1: % set shopping {Milk Bread Fruits {Can Opener} Butter}
2: Milk Bread Fruits {Can Opener} Butter
3: % lreplace $shopping 3 3
4: Milk Bread Fruits Butter
5: % set shopping
6: Milk Bread Fruits {Can Opener} Butter
7: % set newShopping  [lreplace $shopping 3 3]
8: Milk Bread Fruits Butter
9: % set newShopping
10: Milk Bread Fruits Butter
```

ANALYSIS   Line 3 specifies that you want to replace elements in position 3 through 3 by nothing. The command did its job and returned its output. What happens to the original list? Nothing. It is not altered in any way (lines 5–6). If this behavior catches you unaware, try and remember that `lreplace` returns a list. Lines 7–9 confirm this point.

Searching Lists

A list can be searched for an element using `lsearch`. It supports three options for searches: `-exact`, `-glob`, and `-regexp`. With the `-exact` option, the list must contain an element identical to that specified in the pattern. Patterns specified as glob-patterns, or more generally as regular expressions, are more flexible. These are illustrated in Listing 5.10.

A glob-pattern is a way of specifying names using wild cards. The characters ? (matches any single character), * (matches zero or more characters), [`chars`] (matches any single character in the set `chars`), \x (matches the literal x), {a,b,...} (matches any one of the strings a, b, or c) are used for wild cards. For more discussion on glob-patterns and regular expressions, see Hour 3, "Working with Tcl Commands."

LISTING 5.10   Searching for Elements in a List

```
1: % set shopping {Milk Bread Fruits {Can Opener} Butter}
2: Milk Bread Fruits {Can Opener} Butter
3: % lsearch $shopping Fruits
4: 2
5: % lsearch  $shopping B*
6: 1
7: % lsearch -regexp $shopping {er$}
8: 3
9: % lsearch $shopping O*
10: -1
```

ANALYSIS Use the shopping list (line 1) to illustrate the syntax. You can use the default option to search for Fruits in the list. lsearch command requires a list and a pattern (line 3). The pattern can be a simple word, such as Fruits, a glob pattern (line 5), or a regular expression (line 7). If the search is successful, lsearch returns the position index at which the element has occurred first in the list. If the search fails, the command returns -1.

The glob pattern in line 5 says, "Look for element beginning with B followed by anything." In your list, there are two such elements. Remember, only the first occurrence counts. So the command returns 1 for the element Bread. In line 7, you use a regular expression pattern. The pattern says, "Look for elements that end in er." Note that the $ anchors the pattern to the end. Once again, there are two potential matches. Only the first occurrence is returned. In line 9, you use a glob pattern hoping to pick Opener. Because there is no such element, the command returns -1. Notice that the search does not look deep inside the sublists!

Appending to a List

A small application illustrates the lappend command. You have seen that lsearch returns the first occurrence of the element you are searching for. There are situations where it is useful to know all the positions where a particular element occurs. You can write a procedure to do this task, as shown in Listing 5.11.

LISTING 5.11 Procedure to Find All the Occurrences of an Element in a List

```
1: # lwhere list element
2: #    Returns a list of indices where the element occurs in the list.
3: #    Return a null list if the element doesn't occur in the list.
4:
5: proc lwhere { lis element } {
6:     set inds {}
7:     set size [llength $lis]
8:     set j 0
9:     for {set i 0} {$i < $size} {incr i} {
10:         set idx [lsearch -exact $lis $element]
11:         if {$idx >= 0} {
12:             lappend inds [expr $idx+$j]
13:             # drop the element from lis
14:             set lis [lreplace $lis $idx $idx]
15:             incr j
16:         } else {
17:             break
18:         }
19:     }
20:     return $inds
21: }
```

5

ANALYSIS You will now look at the procedure in some detail. The basic plan is to initially locate the first occurrence of an element. If the search returns a nonnegative index, you store that in a list and drop that element from the list. You then look for the next occurrence. You keep looking as many times as needed to work through the entire list. Note that the for loop index starts from zero. You make an early break out of the loop, at some stage, if you don't find an occurrence.

You define a list called inds to store the indices (line 6). In the for loop (lines 9–19), you keep looking for the given element. If the return value from lsearch is nonnegative, you take some corrective action. First, you append the index to your temporary list inds. Next, you drop that element from your list (line 14). Notice that you have stored the return value from lreplace into the same variable lis. Because you are dropping the found element from lis, you track this through the variable j to preserve the correct index position in the given list. Figure 5.1 explains the algorithm.

FIGURE 5.1

Finding all occurrences of a repeated element in a list.

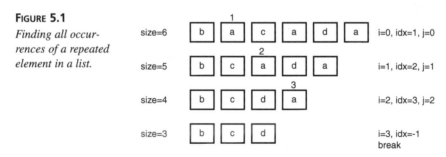

The procedure in action is shown in Listing 5.12.

LISTING 5.12   Procedure to Find All the Occurrences of an Element in a List

```
1: % source lwhere.tcl
2: % set liz {b a c a d a}
3: b a c a d a
4: % lwhere $liz a
5: 1 3 5
```

ANALYSIS The procedure you have defined is sourced in line 1. A simple list with multiple occurrences of an element is defined in line 2 of the illustration. The procedure is invoked in line 4. As expected, you have the indices where the element a has occurred in the list liz.

Sorting Lists

Elements in a list are sorted in a variety of ways. For example, a list can be sorted into an alphabetical order. A list of numbers can be sorted into an increasing or decreasing sequence. First, you will look at some simple usage of the command in Listing 5.13.

LISTING 5.13 A Simple Use of the `lsort` Command

```
1:  % set list1 {apples pears Avocados bananas oranges}
2:  apples pears Avocados bananas oranges
3:  % lsort $list1
4:  Avocados apples bananas oranges pears
5:  % lsort -dictionary $list1
6:  apples Avocados bananas oranges pears
```

A nice feature of `-dictionary` option is that embedded numbers in elements are sorted in numerical order. This is useful when you want to sort some data files that you named numerically, such as file1, file2,…file12, and so forth. Listing 5.14 illustrates this point.

LISTING 5.14 Smart Sorting with the `-dictionary` Option

```
1: %  set mixed {file1 file2 file12}
2: file1 file2 file12
3: % lsort $mixed
4: file1 file12 file2
5: % lsort -dictionary $mixed
6: file1 file2 file12
```

ANALYSIS A straightforward default sorting order produces file12 between file1 file2 (lines 1–2)! This could be disconcerting when presenting a list of files in a menu. The `-dictionary` option recognizes the embedded numbers in list elements and does the decent thing as shown in lines 5–6.

Given a list, `lsort` uses an ASCII comparison to sort the elements as shown in lines 1–2. With the `-dictionary` option (line 5), the case of the elements is ignored. When sorting integers or floating point numbers, you need to be vigilant as Listing 5.15 demonstrates.

5

LISTING 5.15   Beware Sorting Numbers!

```
1: % set nums {1 2 11 -5 4}
2: 1 2 11 -5 4
3: % lsort $nums
4: -5 1 11 2 4
5: % lsort -integer $nums
6: -5 1 2 4 11
7: % set floats {1.2 3.14 11.2 0.5 -4}
8: 1.2 3.14 11.2 0.5 -4
9: % lsort $floats
10: -4 0.5 1.2 11.2 3.14
11: % lsort -real $floats
12: -4 0.5 1.2 3.14 11.2
```

ANALYSIS   Remember that the default sorting order is `-ascii`. If you are not careful, you will get a surprise result, as in line 2. You need to specify the `-integer` option, if you mean to compare the list as integers (lines 5–6). Similar care is needed when comparing floating point numbers (lines 9–12). You need to use the `-real` option.

Generating and Evaluating Commands

The most frequent use of lists in Tcl scripts is for dynamic generation of commands. A clear understanding of what `list` does is essential to developing efficient scripts. You will be using this concept in many of the examples in the later chapters. The `eval` command is used to interpret the list as a Tcl command. Listing 5.16 introduces the concept.

LISTING 5.16   Evaluating a Simple List

```
1: % set pCmd {puts {Hello World}}
2: puts {Hello World}
3: % eval $pCmd
4: Hello World
```

ANALYSIS   Line 1 stores a simple list in a variable called pCmd. Note that the text "Hello World" is included as a sublist. Expressed as a list, `puts` does not have any special meaning and the value of the variable $pCmd is returned (line 2). A simple way to execute the command contained in the list is to invoke the `eval` command as shown in line 3. See Hour 3 for a discussion on `eval` command.

When the commands you are generating involve variable substitution, you need to be careful, as illustrated in the next example.

Command Lists with Variable Substitution

You want to define a custom-made puts command to print the line "Hello Mr. Pop Eye". You also want to keep the salutation and name in separate variables and pass them to puts. As a first attempt, you might try something along the lines of Listing 5.17.

LISTING 5.17   What Is Wrong with My eval?

```
 1: % set name {Pop Eye}
 2: Pop Eye
 3: % set  salutation {Hello Mr.}
 4: Hello Mr.
 5: % set pCmd "puts $salutation $name"
 6: puts Hello Mr. Pop Eye
 7: % eval $pCmd
 8: wrong # args: should be "puts ?-nonewline? ?channelId? string"
 9: % set pCmd [list puts $salutation $name]
10: puts {Hello Mr.} {Pop Eye}
11: % eval $pCmd
12: can not find channel named "Hello Mr."
13: % set pCmd [list puts "$salutation $name"]
14: puts {Hello Mr. Pop Eye}
15: % eval $pCmd
16: Hello Mr. Pop Eye
```

ANALYSIS   In lines 1–2, you define two variables to store the required information. As a first attempt, you define a variable pCmd (line 5) to store the puts command together with its arguments. The double quotes are needed to evaluate the variables. Next, you attempt to evaluate the command line stored in pCmd (line 7). What is wrong? puts wants a string. Instead, eval got the four words, Hello, Mr., Pop and Eye (line 6).

Illuminated by this, you might try preserving the list structure by using the list command as in line 9. From the output, you see that you are not out of the woods yet, because the value of pCmd is the three words, shown in line 10, and not a string. You should generate puts followed by a string. You then make up a list consisting of puts and another word returned by the evaluation of the embedded variables inside the double quotes. Yes, you do lose the list structure of the embedded variables, but you get a proper command (line 14). Now eval is happy.

Splitting Strings

There are two useful commands related to strings: split and join. A string of text is split into a list using a nominated character with split. The join command reconstructs the string using a nominated character. Listing 5.18 shows the use of the split command.

5

LISTING 5.18 Splitting Strings into a List

```
1: % set components [split [pwd] /]
2: E: TclTk81 Tcl bin
```

ANALYSIS You evaluate the path of the working directory and pass that string to split. You use the forward slash as the split character (line 1), and the result is stored in the list components.

By way of illustrating join, use the amusing code in Listing 5.19.

LISTING 5.19 Split, Join, and eval

```
1: % set n 123
2: 123
3: % set digs [split $n {}]
4: 1 2 3
5: % set e [join $digs +]
6: 1+2+3
7: % set cmd [list expr  $e]
8: expr  1+2+3
9: % eval $cmd
10: 6
```

ANALYSIS You use split with a null split character to extract digits from a number (line 1). Next, you join the list elements with a + character to form a string (line 5). Then, you construct a command using expr ready to be evaluated (lines 7–10). The above task is somewhat fictitious. Nevertheless, you can exploit the power of the language in avariety of ways.

Writing a Procedure for Sorting a List of Grades

Consider the situation where a list of grades must be arranged as a list of the form

```
{ {Name1 Mark1 Grade1} {Name2 Mark2 Grade2} ... }
```

The *Namei* is an ASCII string. *Marki* is a decimal integer. *Gradei* is represented by three letters A, B, C along with the modifiers + or -. A typical entry in that list is of the form {Dravid 85 A+}. Your task is to produce a sorted list using either the name field, numerical mark field, or the grade field.

The first two cases are fairly straightforward. A simple dialogue with your artificial list of students is shown in Listing 5.20.

LISTING 5.20   Sorting a List of Marks Using Name or an Integer Mark

```
 1: %set list {{Joe 95 A+} {Phil 88 A} {Simon 65 B-} {Amy 82 A-}}
 2: {Joe 95 A+} {Phil 88 A} {Simon 65 B-} {Amy 82 A-}
 3: %lsort $list
 4: {Amy 82 A-} {Joe 95 A+} {Phil 88 A} {Simon 65 B-}
 5: %lsort -decreasing $list
 6: {Simon 65 B-} {Phil 88 A} {Joe 95 A+} {Amy 82 A-}
 7: %lsort -index 1 $list
 8: {Simon 65 B-} {Amy 82 A-} {Phil 88 A} {Joe 95 A+}
 9: %lsort -index 1 -decreasing $list
10: {Joe 95 A+} {Phil 88 A} {Amy 82 A-} {Simon 65 B-}
```

ANALYSIS   First, you define a simple list of marks/grades to work with. You might restrict the names to first names for simplicity. This can be easily extended to store more complex names. A simple use of `lsort` (line 3) produces an alphabetical list. Note that the default sorting order is `-increasing`, hence the result in line 4. Note also that if the first elements are the same, the next element is used to decide the ordering.

You can reverse this with `-decreasing` option as in line 5. To sort using the integer marks, you have to specify the index where the data can be found. In this list, the numerical marks appear at index position 1, and the command in line 7 delivers the goods. Remember the default ordering is from low to high. If you require the top marks to appear first (that is the usual case), you must specify the option `-decreasing`.

Now to the interesting bit of sorting on the grades. Remember, you are restricting your list of grades to A+, A, A-, B+, B, B- to illustrate the point. You can easily extend to a full-blown scheme as used in an academic university. Had the grades been without modifiers, you could have used the ASCII sort on elements in index position 2. Note that the ASCII sorting order on the grades puts A+ after A. (You may try `lsort {A- A A+}`.) This is where the `-command` option comes into play.

You can define your own criteria to compare two elements. This is done by writing a procedure which takes two arguments, for example, a and b. The procedure should return `-1` if element a is to be placed before b, `0` if they are same, and `1` if element a is to be placed after b. This neatly fits with the grades you wish to list. Look at the required ordering. You want A+ to be placed before A, and A to be placed before A-, B+, B, and B-. Given two grades to the procedure, you first identify the letters and the corresponding modifiers.

5

If the letters are different, you do a simple string comparison that produces the desired effect. (A is placed before B, and so on.) If the letters are the same, you consider the modifiers. This is the case where you have to sort grades such as A and A+. Table 5.2 summarizes the values you need to return from the procedure, and the procedure is shown in Listing 5.21.

TABLE 5.2   Required Return Values to Sort Grades

Modifier 1 Value	Modifier2	Return	Remarks
+	+	0	No preference
+	-	-1	A+ before A-
+	{}	-1	A+ before A
-	+	1	A- after A+
•	0	No preference	
-	{}	1	A- after A
{}	+	1	A after A+
{}	-	-1	A before A-
{}	{}	0	No preference

LISTING 5.21   The Procedure to Compare Grades

```
 1: proc cmpG { a b } {
 2:     # extract the letter and modifier for each
 3:     regexp {([A-F])([+-]?)} $a match1 let1 m1
 4:     regexp {([A-F])([+-]?)} $b match2 let2 m2
 5:     if { [string compare $let1 $let2] == 0 } {
 6:     # letters are same, so compare their modifiers
 7:     switch -exact — $m1 {
 8:         "+" {
 9:         switch -exact — $m2 {
10:             "+" { return 0 }
11:             "-" { return -1 }
12:             ""  { return -1 }
13:         }
14:         }
15:         "-" {
16:         switch -exact — $m2 {
17:             "+" { return 1 }
18:             "-" { return 0 }
19:             ""  { return 1 }
20:         }
```

```
21:        }
22:        "" {
23:        switch -exact — $m2 {
24:            "+" { return 1 }
25:            "-" { return -1 }
26:            "" { return 0 }
27:        }
28:        }
29:    }
30:    } else {
31:    # compare the letters in ASCII
32:    return [string compare $let1 $let2]
33:    }
34: }
```

First let us see the procedure cmpG in action, as shown in Listing 5.22.

LISTING 5.22 Sorting the Marks/Grade List Using cmpG

```
1: % source cmpG.tcl
2: % set list {{Joe 95 A+} {Phil 88 A} {Simon 65 B-} {Amy 82 A-}}
3: {Joe 95 A+} {Phil 88 A} {Simon 65 B-} {Amy 82 A-}
4: % lsort -index 2 -command cmpG $list
5: {Joe 95 A+} {Phil 88 A} {Amy 82 A-} {Simon 65 B-}
6: % lsort -command  cmpG {B- B B+ A- A A+}
7: A+ A A- B+ B B-
```

ANALYSIS You source the file containing the procedure (line 1). A typical list is defined in line 2. The position of the elements on which you want to perform your sorting is specified with -index, as before. The comparison function is specified with the -command option (line 4). As expected, the high grades are listed first. line 6 is another test line (consisting of lowest grade to the highest) to make sure that the procedure cmpG is doing its job. Indeed it does.

There are a couple of things that can go wrong. In the switch command, be sure that you include a default case. Also be careful to put the comments in the right place in the switch block. (See Hour 4, "Controlling Your Program," regarding placements of comments in a switch block.)

Summary

In this hour, you looked at lists and their manipulation. A list is a collection of elements (or words) which are separated by whitespace characters. An element in a list can be a list in its own right. Such elements are referred to as sublists. The first element of a list is referred to using the index 0, and the last element is referred to using the logical name end. The length of the list is the total number of elements in the list. Sublists count as one. Here is a list (no pun!) of some salient points to take home:

- Use the list command, if you want to preserve list structure.
- lreplace does not alter the original list. Store the return value from lreplace in a variable, if you want the replaced list.
- lappend requires the name of a list, not what is contained in that list.
- Use eval to interpret the commands generated with list.

Lists are an example of a simple data structure. List commands provide the basic infrastructure for generating Tcl commands dynamically and interpreting them with a further round of evaluation. Although lists are adequate for most purposes, they are less expressive for storing semantically rich information. Arrays provide an elegant answer for manipulating such information and are the subject of your study for the next hour.

Q&A

Q In a long list, does it take more time to access the elements that are towards the end than the elements at the beginning?

A No. Lists are internally stored in such a way that they take constant time.

Q Is it a good idea to create complex data structures using lists and sublists?

A No. Lists are efficient for constructing dynamic commands and evaluating them. Arrays, which will be discussed in the next hour, are more efficient for creating complex data structures. Use lists for simple tasks such as storing simple elements, for example, options for a menu or list of file names. If you need to store and manipulate structured data, use arrays.

Q What is the advantage of using explicit list command?

A When the list you are creating has variable substitutions, the use of explicit list command preserves the list structure of the resulting list. Preserving this list structure is important when creating widget command callbacks, which are introduced in Hour 10, "Getting Started with Tk."

Q Is there a way to find the length of an individual element?

A Yes. For example, to find the length of the second element in the list set sample {It does work}, you can use the command llength [split [lindex $sample 1] {}]. Admittedly, this kind of approach is a bit convoluted. String commands, covered in Hour 8, "Manipulating Strings," provide a more direct approach. For example, to find the length of the second element in the list `set sample {It does work}`, you can use the command `string length [lindex $sample 1]`.

Workshop

The quiz section is designed to provide you with an opportunity to recall some of the important concepts introduced in this hour. These may be commands, command syntax, common mistakes, usage, and so on. The following exercises section helps you consolidate the material you learned via an example of practical value. Our aim is that these two sections should reinforce the knowledge you have gained in this hour. The answers to the quiz that follows can be found in Appendix A, "Answers to Quizzes."

Quiz

1. What is the length of the list `set la {Marks List {Phil 75}}`?
2. What is the length of the list `set la {a b\ c\ d end}`?
3. What is the command to extract the second element in the list `set la {Fruits: {pears mangoes apples}}`?
4. What is the command to extract the last element of the list `set makes {Ford Toyota Saab Audi}`?
5. What is the command to sort the numbers `set nums {-5 1 7 12 3}`?
6. What is the default sorting order for `lsort`?
7. What is the command to replace 12 by 36 in the list `set nums {-5 1 7 12 3}`?

Exercises

Solutions to the exercises are on the CD-ROM that accompanies this book.

1. Write a procedure to reverse the elements of a list.

```
# Reverses elements of a list
proc lreverse { list } {
    set len1 [expr [llength $list] - 1]
    set rList {}
    for {set i 0} { $i <= $len1 } { incr i } {
    # list indices start from 0
        lappend rList [lindex $list [expr $len1 - $i]]
    }
    return $rList
}
```

5

2. The following is a list of weather associated with cities. Sort the list so that sunny cities are listed first followed by fair, followed by cloudy, and then by rainy cities. Write an appropriate procedure for -command to sort the list containing the weather data of the form

```
set cityTemps { {Algeirs 26 Cloudy} {Athens 34 Fair}\
                {Bahrain 45 Sunny}  {Berlin 17 Rain} }
```

3. Write a procedure that returns unique elements of a list.

4. Find the one mistake in the following code:

```
1: set s {}
2: foreach e {1 2 3} {
3:     lappend $s $e
4: }
```

HOUR 6

Exploring Arrays

In the last hour, you learned about creating lists and manipulating them. During this hour, you look at arrays in some depth. The basic concept of an array is quite ubiquitous in programming languages. A closely related concept, the concept of associative arrays, has been very popular in scripting languages. A good understanding of these ideas is essential to designing powerful scripts. Accordingly, this hour is designed to provide you with a thorough knowledge of arrays and their manipulation.

In this hour, you will learn

- To create arrays
- To search through an array for an element
- To search array elements using patterns
- To use list commands on arrays
- To invert associative arrays
- To exploit the power of associative arrays for practical tasks

Using Arrays

The concept of an array is quite prevalent in programming languages. It is used to store a group of related values in a variable with a simple mechanism to refer to a specific value within that group. As for the access mechanism, there are two approaches. The first approach relies on an integral number to refer to an item. This is the most common approach in traditional languages. The second approach is to use character strings as indices. Arrays that support such a representation are referred to as *associative arrays*. Both these approaches are discussed in the following sections.

Indexed Arrays

The dialogue in Listing 6.1 shows a typical use of arrays using an integral index.

LISTING 6.1   Indexing Arrays with an Integer

```
1: % set CC(1) London
2: London
3: % set CC(2) Paris
4: Paris
5: % set CC(3) {New Delhi}
6: New Delhi
7: % puts "Capital of Uk is $CC(1)"
8: Capital of Uk is London
```

ANALYSIS   The array CC (for Capital Cities) stores the names of capital cities of several countries. For example, the value of CC(1) is set to London. You need to protect the whitespace characters with curly braces (line 5). You refer to a specific item by preceding the array name with a $. For example, line 7 displays the value contained in CC(1).

The major problem with this approach is that you need to know which index corresponds to which country. In this regard, this approach is similar to using a list and lindex to refer to its elements.

Associative Arrays

An associative array uses character strings as indices into the array to refer to a particular item. This approach is user-friendly, and lends itself easily to solving myriad programming tasks. Listing 6.2 illustrates an associative array to store the capital cities.

LISTING 6.2 Capital Cities in an Associative Array

```
1: % set CC(Uk)   London
2: London
3: % set CC(France) Paris
4: Paris
5: % set CC(India) {New Delhi}
6: New Delhi
7: % puts "Capital of India is $CC(India)"
8: Capital of India is New Delhi
```

In associative arrays, you can use any character string as an index into the array. Avoid special characters such as $ and # in array names, until you are a bit more familiar with Tcl. In lines 1–6, you use the names of the countries as the names of the elements. The case of the names is important, as it is with all Tcl variable names. You refer to the value of a particular item by preceding the element name (for example, India) with the array name (for example, CC), as in line 7.

In this approach, you don't need to remember any specific code to identify the country. You can simply use the string, that is, the name of the country with which you indexed the array.

There is only one type of array, and that is an *associative array*. They are internally stored as hash indices. Integers are used for array element names in Listing 6.1 to motivate the topic.

Both of the previous approaches are illustrated graphically in Figure 6.1.

FIGURE 6.1

Index arrays and associative arrays.

index	value		name	value
1	London		Uk	London
2	Paris		France	Paris
3	New Delhi		India	New Delhi
...			...	...

6

The array notation is explained in Figure 6.2.

FIGURE 6.2

Arrays are indexed using names and given values with the set command.

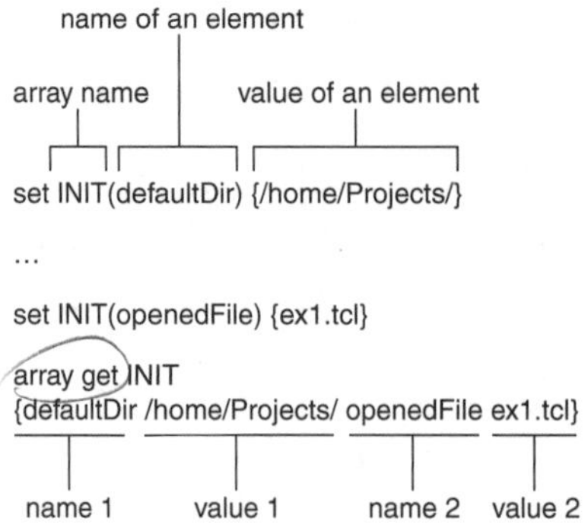

name of an element

array name | value of an element

set INIT(defaultDir) {/home/Projects/}

...

set INIT(openedFile) {ex1.tcl}

array get INIT
{defaultDir /home/Projects/ openedFile ex1.tcl}

name 1   value 1   name 2   value 2

Avoid using embedded whitespace characters for the names of array elements. If you must use embedded spaces, protect them with curly braces. For example, set FILES({Last Visited Files}) {a.dat b.dat}.

Retrieving from Arrays

You have already seen how to refer to a single item in an array. Now, you explore how to process the information contained in the array.

A simple method of scanning through the elements of an array is to use a foreach loop as shown in Listing 6.3.

LISTING 6.3   Working Through the Elements of an Array

```
 1: % puts [array names CC]
 2: Uk India France
 3: % foreach n [array names CC] {
 4: >     puts "Capital of $n   \t is \t $CC($n) " }
 5: Capital of Uk        is      London
 6: Capital of India        is      New Delhi
 7: Capital of France        is      Paris
 8: % foreach n [lsort [array names CC]] {
 9:     puts "Capital of $n   \t is \t $CC($n) " }
10: Capital of France        is      Paris
11: Capital of India        is      New Delhi
12: Capital of Uk        is      London
13: % parray CC
14: CC(France) = Paris
15: CC(India)  = New Delhi
16: CC(Uk)     = London
```

ANALYSIS You first obtain the element names with the `array names` command (lines 1–2). Now you iterate through that list. Notice the order in which element names have been listed. This ordering will almost certainly be different from the one you have originally defined. This behavior has to do with internal implementation of arrays as hash tables. A hash table is a collection of entries where each entry consists of a key and a value. As you are only interested in the values stored in a particular element, this order of internal storing is immaterial. However, if you want to process entries in a specific order, you need to pass the elements through an `lsort` command, as in line 8. The Tcl shell provides a useful command called `parray` to print the contents of an array; it is illustrated in line 13.

If you are continuing this example in the same interpreter from Listing 6.1, you will see those array element names as well. You can either unset `CC` or start a new session.

The output from `parray` cannot be stored in a variable, as it does not return what you are seeing on the screen as the return value of the procedure. It prints the array contents to the standard output. Note that the `parray` command returns an empty string. See the section "Writing Simple Procedures" in Hour 3, "Working with Tcl Commands."

`env`, `tcl_platform`, and `tkPriv` are three of the important arrays provided in the `wish` shell. The `env` array contains useful information such as pathnames to the home directory, processor details, and so on. The array `tcl_platform` contains details of your hardware platform. The `tkPriv` array contains information specific to widgets. Use the information stored in them to make your scripts more portable.

6

Array Inquiry Functions

Arrays can be set at any time. If the array by a given name doesn't exist, it will be created. You can obtain the name-value pairs of an array. These and related commands are illustrated in Listing 6.4.

LISTING 6.4 Using Array Inquiry Commands

```
 1: % array set RNUMS {one I two II three III four IV}
 2: % array get RNUMS
 3: four IV three III two II one I
 4: % array set RNUMS {five V}
 5: % array get RNUMS
 6: four IV three III five V two II one I
 7: % foreach {n v} [array get RNUMS] {
 8:     array set INV "$v $n" }
 9: % parray INV
10: INV(I)   = one
11: INV(II)  = two
12: INV(III) = three
13: INV(IV)  = four
14: INV(V)   = five
```

ANALYSIS You define an array, RNUMS, to hold the Roman numerals. For convenience, spelled-out Arabic numbers are used as array element names (line 1). Notice that array set returns an empty string. It just sets the array elements to a value. If you want to add additional entries to RNUMS, simply use RNUMS again (line 4). The beauty of it is that, if the array already exists, array set simply adds the new entries. It is not destructive. You can inquire what is stored in the array RNUMS with the array get command, as in line 2, which returns name-value pairs. This form of output is quite useful in many situations. For example, you can use this listing to invert the array (lines 7–8). The foreach loop works on each of the name-value pairs and reverses the order of $n and $v (line 8). Remember to protect the whitespace in "$v $n". Finally, check the result with parray in line 9. The same effect can be achieved by replacing line 8 with set INV($v) $n.

> The array get arrayName ?pattern? command returns name-value pairs as a list.

Modifying Arrays

An array name combined with the name of the element is a valid Tcl variable name. The value stored in an array can be modified in the normal way. This fact might come as a surprise to you initially, but after you have come to grips with it, it provides a powerful mechanism to solve some practical problems. Listing 6.5 gathers the number of times a particular value turns up in a given number of throws of a dice. It is convenient to store the scripts in a file and bring them into the interpreter, as shown in Listing 6.5.

LISTING 6.5   Frequency Counts of Values in 10,000 Throws of a Dice

```
 1: proc dice {} {
 2:     # simulate a throw of dice. Return sum of face values
 3:     set a [expr round( 5*rand() + 1 )]
 4:     set b [expr round( 5*rand() + 1 )]
 5:     return [expr ($a+$b)]
 6: }
 7:
 8: set valList {}
 9: # generate throws
10: for {set i 1} {$i<=10000} {incr i} {
11:     set val [dice]
12:     lappend valList $val
13: }
14: # initialize or increment COUNT(x) array
15: foreach x $valList {
16:     if {![info exists COUNT($x)] } {
17:     set COUNT($x) 1
18:     } else {
19:     incr COUNT($x)
20:     }
21: }
22: %source dice4.tcl
23: % parray COUNT
24: COUNT(10) = 818
25: COUNT(11) = 446
26: COUNT(12) = 91
27: COUNT(2)  = 100
28: COUNT(3)  = 374
29: COUNT(4)  = 801
30: COUNT(5)  = 1164
31: COUNT(6)  = 1625
32: COUNT(7)  = 1745
33: COUNT(8)  = 1618
34: COUNT(9)  = 1218
```

ANALYSIS   Lines 1–6 define a simple procedure that simulates the throw of a dice. (Refer to the section on simple procedures in Hour 3, "Working with Tcl Commands.") Lines 8–13 generate a list of face values that turn up in 10,000 throws.

6

Now you return to the essential task—the task of finding how many times a particular number appears. The list valList consists of numbers from 2 to 12 in some order (lines 10–13). Your job is to keep track of how many times a number, such as 7, appears in that list. Proceed as follows. As you scan the list, store the occurrences of that specific face value in an associative array. You use the face value itself as the element name. As you process the list, check whether a variable by that name exists. If it does not exist (as is the case initially), initialize the count to one (line 17). If the variable by that name already exists (which will be the case as you progress down the list), increment its count by one (line 19). At the end of the loop, the array COUNT contains the required numbers. Lines 24–34 show typical output. Note that number 7 occurs most frequently, and numbers 2 and 12 least frequently. Also note that the array names 10, 11, and 12 appear before 2 (lines 23–34). This has to do with the default ASCII sorting order used by parray.

Array variables are not initialized in Tcl. If you are performing arithmetic, initialize them appropriately.

An array should exist before you can use array commands, except for array set.

Searching in Arrays

It is convenient to have a facility that searches through the elements of an array to pick the corresponding values. We introduce the basic concept in Listing 6.6. For a more practical use of the search commands, see Listing 6.11.

Consider a simple array, COLORS, that stores RGB values of certain colors as hex values in an array. The dialogue in Listing 6.6 illustrates a simple way to search for a color name and pick its RGB value in hex format.

LISTING 6.6   Searching for an Element Name in an Array

```
 1: % array set COLORS {red #FF0000 green #00FF00
 2: >                   blue #0000FF lawn_green #7CFC00}
 3: % set id [array startsearch COLORS]
 4: s-1-COLORS
 5: % while {[array anymore COLORS $id]}  {
 6: >       set elt [array nextelement COLORS $id]
 7: >         if {$elt == "green"} {
 8: >             puts "Green color:  $COLORS($elt) "
 9: >             break
10: >         }
11: > }
12: Green color:  #00FF00
```

ANALYSIS   Line 1 defines some colors and their associated hex values. You initiate the search in line 3 with the array startsearch command. This command returns an identifier to refer to the search later on. In this example, you want to print the hex value corresponding to green. The array anymore command returns a boolean value for a search in a given array. Use this conditional to loop through the array, COLORS (lines 4–10). Every time the while condition is satisfied, you get the next element name from the array (line 6) and check if it is green. If it is not, you go around once more. If the next element is green, you print the corresponding hex value (lines 7–8) and break out of the while loop (line 9).

Using Patterns in Search

Array names and array get commands provide an optional argument that takes a glob pattern to filter out unwanted element names. The search patterns are limited to glob style patterns only. (Refer to Hour 3 for more on Regular Expressions and Hour 8, "Manipulating Strings.")

Listing 6.7 demonstrates the basic idea.

LISTING 6.7 glob-Style Patterns for Searching Through Array Element Names

```
1: % array set DATA {input1 a.dat input12 b.dat
2: >                 input1_old  y.dat output1 res.dat}
3: % array get DATA {input*}
4: input1 a.dat input1_old y.dat input12 b.dat
5: % array get DATA {input[0-9]}
6: input1 a.dat
7: % array get DATA {input[0-9][0-9]}
8: input12 b.dat
```

ANALYSIS Line 1 defines a sample associative array. You can filter those array names that begin with input followed by any group of characters, using the pattern input*. You can restrict the pattern to pick input followed by a digit (line 5) or input followed by two digits (line 7). When you use the pattern (lines 5 and 7), you must enclose the pattern within curly braces; otherwise the interpreter tries to evaluate 0-9 as a command!

Applications

Database of Countries

Consider a simple scenario of storing some relevant information about countries, such as their capital cities, currency, and population. Arrays provide a convenient mechanism to set up this data. This data can be defined in one file and easily can be made available to other procedures that require it. What is more, you can query for required data such as "What is the currency of Uk?" Listing 6.8 sets up a small database to illustrate these basic ideas.

6

LISTING 6.8　A Database of Countries Stored in `countries.tcl`

```
 1: # simple database of countries
 2: set CINFO(Uk,Capital) London
 3: set CINFO(Uk,currency) Pound
 4: set CINFO(Uk,population) 55
 5:
 6: set CINFO(France,Capital) Paris
 7: set CINFO(France,currency) Franc
 8: set CINFO(France,population) 45
 9:
10: set CINFO(India,Capital) {New Delhi}
11: set CINFO(India,currency) Rupee
12: set CINFO(India,population) 900
13:
14: set CINFO(Usa,Capital) Washington
15: set CINFO(Usa,currency) dollar
16: set CINFO(Usa,population) 100
```

ANALYSIS　You use an array `CINFO` to store the desired information. You want to store the capital of the country, its currency, and population size. You devise a suitable scheme for storing these attributes of a country. The array element name is split into two parts—country name and attribute name. Separate them by a comma for visual clarity. In fact, you can exploit this for your advantage later on. Lines 2–16 contain a typical data element/item. You can add more data and attributes if you wish.

Listing 6.9 demonstrates how to list all the countries in your database.

LISTING 6.9　Listing the Capital Cities in `CINFO`

```
1: % source countries.tcl
2: 100
3: % foreach c [array names CINFO *,Capital] {
4: >    puts "Capital is: $CINFO($c) "
5: > }
6: Capital is: Washington
7: Capital is: London
8: Capital is: New Delhi
9: Capital is: Paris
```

ANALYSIS　First, you source the file (line 1) `countries.tcl` that sets up the array `CINFO`. The return value from the source command is the return value from the last command in the file `countries.tcl`, which is displayed in line 2. The command `array names` takes an array name and a `glob` pattern (not a regular expression pattern). Use the `glob` pattern `*,Capital` (line 3) to list those element names that contain `,Capital` in them.

Listing all countries in our database requires some careful attention. Listing 6.10 illustrates the point.

LISTING 6.10 Countries' Names in `cinfo` with a `glob` Pattern on One of the Attributes to Avoid Repetitions

```
1: % foreach c [array names CINFO *,currency] {
2: >         regsub {,currency} $c {} cnew
3: >         puts "Name of the country: \t $cnew" }
4: Name of the country:     India
5: Name of the country:     France
6: Name of the country:     Uk
7: Name of the country:     Usa
```

ANALYSIS The naive approach of using `array name CINFO` (in line 1) will result in each country name appearing three times, together with the name of the attribute. This is where you can use a `glob` pattern to avoid repetition. You can use any of the attribute names. In line 1, the pattern `*,currency` generates the names. This list will contain the string `,currency`. Remove this using the `regsub` command. The resulting string is stored in the variable cnew. (String manipulations are discussed in Hour 8.)

To illustrate searching in an array, consider the following problem. You want to store the currency conversion factors and retrieve them. A simple array might consist of data as shown in Listing 6.11.

LISTING 6.11 An Array of Currency Conversion Factors

```
 1: # use an aray to store Currency conversion rates
 2:
 3: set CRATES(francTOpound) 0.0992
 4: set CRATES(francTOdollar) 0.158
 5: set CRATES(francTOrupee) 6.82
 6:
 7: set CRATES(poundTOdollar) 1.55
 8: set CRATES(poundTOfranc) 9.83
 9: set CRATES(poundTOrupee) 68.72
10:
11: set CRATES(dollarTOpound) 0.78
12: set CRATES(dollarTOfranc) 6.35
13: set CRATES(dollarTOrupee) 43.26
14:
15: set CRATES(rupeeTOpound)  0.0146
16: set CRATES(rupeeTOdollar) 0.0232
17: set CRATES(rupeeTOfranc)  0.147
```

6

ANALYSIS
The conversion factors are stored in the array CRATES. The element names are of the form currency1TOcurrency2. (The values can be obtained from newspapers or Web servers.)

You want to use the information stored in CRATES to fetch the required conversion factor. The procedure for this task is stored in the file cfactor.tcl and is shown in Listing 6.12.

LISTING 6.12 The Array CRATES Is Searched to Locate the Required Conversion Factor

```
 1: # get the conversion factor for a name
 2:
 3: proc getConvFactor { name } {
 4:     global CRATES
 5:     set sid [array startsearch CRATES]
 6:     while {[array anymore CRATES $sid]} {
 7:         set elt [array nextelement CRATES $sid]
 8:         if { $elt == $name } {
 9:             return $CRATES($elt)
10:             break
11:         } else {
12:             continue
13:         }
14:     }
15:     set msg  " \"$name\" is not a name of an element in CRATES."
16:     error $msg
17: }
```

ANALYSIS
The procedure accepts the desired factor as an argument that has to be one of the names of the elements used in CRATES. The array defining the conversion factors is brought into the procedure via the global command (line 4). The search in the array is initiated in line 5. The command array startsearch returns an identifier that can be used subsequently to refer to the search. The bulk of the work is done in the body of the while loop (lines 6–14). The basic idea is to get the name of an element (line 7), and compare it (lines 8–13) with what is passed to the procedure. If it is the same, you return the value associated with it and break out of the while loop (line 10). If not, continue looking (line 6). If the given name is same as that of an element name, return the corresponding value and break out of the while loop.

If you have exhausted the search and didn't find any match, print an error message. Listing 6.13 shows the procedure in action.

LISTING 6.13 Searching in Arrays

```
1: % source crates.tcl
2: 0.147
3: % source cfactor.tcl
```

```
4: % getConvFactor  dollarTOfranc
5: 6.35
6: % getConvFactor poundTOyen
7: "poundTOyen" is not a name of an element in CRATES.
```

ANALYSIS The array CRATES is defined in crates.tcl and is first sourced in line 1. Next, you source the file cfactor.tcl that contains the procedure getConvFactor. Line 4 invokes the procedure to obtain the multiplication factor for converting dollars into francs. Line 6 is a simple check to see what happens if you give a nonexistent name.

Note that this problem can also be solved by exploiting the command info exists CRATES(name). See Listing 6.14.

Inverting an Array

So far, you have considered examples of accessing values associated with array element names. That is, given the names, you can fetch the corresponding values. The opposite situation is equally important. That is, given a value stored in an array, find the corresponding name(s). Consider a simple situation. You have decided to store certain keywords occurring in a file as an associative array. A typical entry may be defined as set KWD(filename) {list for switch}. It is convenient to keep one entry per file. Next, you want to know the names of the files in which a particular keyword has occurred. This is inverting an array.

Listing 6.14 illustrates the process.

LISTING 6.14   Inverting an Array

```
 1: # Invert an array
 2:
 3: set KWD(file1) {switch if for}
 4: set KWD(file2) {set puts for}
 5: set KWD(file3) {foreach switch set}
 6:
 7: foreach { n v } [array get KWD] {
 8:     foreach e $v {
 9:         if {[info exists INV($e)] } {
10:           lappend INV($e) $n
11:         } else {
12:           set INV($e) $n
13:         }
14:     }
15: }
```

ANALYSIS Lines 3–5 define the associative array KWD containing three elements and their associated values. Given a value (such as switch), you want to find array element names with which it is associated. For example, the value of switch is associated with file1 and file3. So, your strategy is as follows. You create another associative array called INV to store the inverted array on-the-fly (line 12). Use a foreach loop collecting the name n and the value v in one swoop (line 7). The variable v is a list. You scan through the list (line 8) checking whether a particular element already exists. If the array element INV($e) does not exist, create it (line 12). If it exists, keep appending the name $n to it.

There are a couple of subtle points in the script. You use info exists INV($e) to check for the existence of a variable. Secondly, you use lappend in line 10. Here again, the name INV($e) is used as a variable name.

A typical dialogue is shown in Listing 6.15.

The array name together with the element name can be used as a variable name. For example, AR(nam) can be used where a variable name is required, for example, lappend AR(nam) {newItem}.

LISTING 6.15   Using the Script for Inverting an Array

```
 1: % source  invar1.tcl
 2: % parray KWD
 3: KWD(file1) = switch if for
 4: KWD(file2) = set puts for
 5: KWD(file3) = foreach switch set
 6: % parray INV
 7: INV(for)     = file1 file2
 8: INV(foreach) = file3
 9: INV(if)      = file1
10: INV(puts)    = file2
11: INV(set)     = file2 file3
12: INV(switch)  = file1 file3
```

 ANALYSIS   Assume that the lines in Listing 6.15 are stored in invar1.tcl. Because the script merely sets up the arrays KWD and INV, nothing appears immediately on the console. Invoke parray to check the values stored in KWD and INV. Yes, it has done the job!

The example of inverting an array is deliberately shown as a script. Passing arrays to a procedure requires additional concepts and is discussed in Hour 7, "Building Your Own Procedures."

Do	Don't
Do use arrays to pass information that is common to many procedures.	**Don't** forget to declare them as global in the calling procedure, if you require that data in other procedures.
Do use all capitals (or similar) for the array names to make them stand out, particularly if they happen to be global.	**Don't** use embedded whitespace characters for the array `element` names.

Summary

In this hour, you have learned what arrays are. An associative array uses character strings to index its elements, called element names, or simply names. Arrays are defined either with the `set` or the `array set` command. The `array set` command can be used subsequently to add additional elements. The `array get` command returns name-value pairs as a list. This list can be used in a double-subscripted `foreach` loop to process the array elements. Table 6.1 is a summary of the array commands.

TABLE 6.1 Summary of Array Commands

Command	Remarks
`array anymore arrayName srchId`	Returns 1 if there are more elements to be searched for in `arrayName` using `srchId`; 0 otherwise.
`array donesearch arrayName srchId`	Terminates search on `arrayName` using `srchId`.
`array exists arrayName`	Returns 1 if the variable name is an array variable; 0 otherwise.
`array get arrayName ?pattern?`	Returns a list of key-value pairs matching the `glob` pattern.
`array names arrayName ?pattern?`	Returns a list of all names in `arrayName` that match the `glob` pattern.
`array nextelement arrayName srchId`	Returns the name of the next element in `arrayName` using `srchId`.
`array set arrayName list`	Sets the value of `arrayName` to `list`. `List` is specified as key-value pairs.
`array size arrayName`	Returns the number of elements in `arrayName`.
`array startsearch arrayName`	Initializes an element-by-element search through `arrayName`.
`parray arrayName`	Prints the contents of `arrayName` to the standard output.

6

Q&A

Q **What is the difference between lists and arrays?**

A A list can be thought of as having a built-in indexing mechanism. A list element is accessed using a numerical index. Arrays have a more flexible indexing mechanism. You can use either a numerical index or a character string, as in associative arrays. Numerically indexed arrays are identical to lists in functionality. Note that you can define array-like structures using lists, but that is not necessary when you already have array commands. In the case of associative arrays, array elements are retrieved using the array element names, not numerical indices.

Both lists and arrays are internally stored efficiently so that accessing elements at the beginning or at the end of the list/array takes the same time.

Q **Why are the array elements listed in a different order from that when they were initially defined?**

A Arrays are stored internally using what is called a hash table. The order in which they are printed to the screen reflects this internal mechanism. For all practical purposes, you are interested in the element names and their values. If you need to process them in some specific order of element names, you must invoke appropriate list sorting commands. The following code clarifies this point:

```
1: % array set COLORS {red 1 yellow 2 purple 3 magenta 4 blue 5 green 6}
2: % array get COLORS
3: % blue 5 purple 3 yellow 2 green 6 magenta 4 red 1
4: % lsort [array names COLORS]
5: blue green magenta purple red yellow
6: % lsort -decreasing [array names COLORS]
7: yellow red purple magenta green blue
```

Q **Can I use array values as lists?**

A Yes. After you have retrieved the value of an element you want, you can use any of the list commands. The following code fragment illustrates:

```
1: % set FILMS(best) {Gone with the Wind}
2: Gone with the Wind
3: % lindex $FILMS(best) end
4: Wind
```

Q **Can I append new data to an existing array element?**

A Yes. Simply use lappend, supplying the array name together with the element name as shown in the following code:

```
1: % lappend FILMS(best) {Casablanca}
2: Gone with the Wind Casablanca
```

Workshop

The quiz section below is designed to provide you with an opportunity to recall some of the important concepts introduced in this Hour. These may be commands, command syntax, common mistakes, usage, and so on. The following exercises section helps you consolidate the material you learned via an example of practical value. Our aim is that these two sections should reinforce the knowledge you have gained in this hour. The answers to the quiz that follows can be found in Appendix A, "Answers to Quizzes."

Quiz

1. What is an associative array?

2. What is the size of the array FRUITS defined by the command
   ```
   array set FRUITS {Juicy Mango Fleshy Pear Crunchy Apple} ?
   ```

3. Given the array MODELS defined in the following code what is the command to list Ford models?
   ```
   % set MODELS(Ford90) {Fiesta Escort Modeo Ka}
   Fiesta Escort Modeo Ka
   % set MODELS(Citroen85) {Xantia Zx Bx}
   Xantia Zx Bx
   % set mfr Ford
   Ford
   ```

4. Write a `foreach` loop to extract all the bottom left coordinates from the array COORDS defined in the following code:
   ```
   1: % set COORDS(BottomLeft1) {1.0 2.0}
   2: 1.0 2.0
   3: % set COORDS(TopRight1) {10 20}
   4: 10 20
   5: % set COORDS(BottomLeft2) {3 4}
   6: 3 4
   7: % set COORDS(TopRight2) {30 40}
   8: 30 40
   ```

5. How do you set the array variable env(MYHOME) to point to a suitable directory path and print the contents of the array env?

6

Exercises

Solutions to the exercises are on the CD-ROM that accompanies this book.

1. The associative array COLOR contains the following color vales (as hexadecimal).

```
array set COLOR {
    green               #00FF00
    red                 #FF000
    medium_sea_green    #3CB371
    violet_red          #D2B48C
    lawn_green          #7CFC00
    tomato              #FF6347
    dark_olive_green    #556B2F
    pale_violet_red     #DB7093 }
```

Use a glob pattern to retrieve the green color values.

2. Add the filename new.tcl to the array element

```
set FILES(lastVisited) {abc.txt cmp.tcl clr.c}.
```

3. Write a script to generate frequency count of words in the sentence

```
set s {She sells sea shells on the sea shore}
```

4. Assume that the array CINFO contains some elements. What is wrong with the following code?

```
% foreach c {[array names CINFO]} {
    puts $c }
```

5. What is wrong with the following line?

```
set numbers [array set x {one 1 two 2 three 3}]
```

HOUR 7

Building Your Own Procedures

In the last hour, you have seen how arrays can be exploited to define power-ful data structures. Arrays combined with compact procedures will enhance your programming skills. The basic idea of a procedure is introduced in Hour 3, "Working with Tcl Commands." In this hour, you explore some of the finer detail and additional flexibility offered by this construct.

Two important concepts are associated with procedures. The first is the scope of a variable in a procedure and the context in which the body of the procedure is executed. The second is the method of passing arguments to a procedure. Both of these concepts are amply illustrated. The hour concludes with related topics of timing and tuning your procedures and making script libraries.

In this hour, you will learn

- To define procedures that can handle a variable number of arguments
- To set default values to arguments of a procedure

- To understand the scope of variables in a procedure

- To declare global scope for certain variables

- To execute the body of a procedure in a different scope

- To build personal script libraries

- To fine tune the procedures

Anatomy of a Procedure

A procedure is a command of the form proc *name args body*. When there is more than one argument for a procedure, each must be enclosed in braces. The *body* contains valid Tcl commands. When the procedure *name* is invoked, a local variable is created for each of the formal arguments to the procedure. In this section, two special features used in defining the input arguments are explained: the scope of variables in a procedure, and the general mechanism to execute a script in a different scope.

Input Arguments

A procedure need not have any input arguments. However, a pair of braces must indicate their absence. There are two powerful features that enable us to set default values for certain arguments and a mechanism to supply a variable number of arguments. These are discussed in the following sections.

Setting Default Values

So far, the examples explicitly supply all the arguments. Tcl procedure supports setting default values for input arguments. To illustrate this feature, consider an example in which you magnify a number by a given factor. By default, you want to double the number. If the magnification factor is supplied, you will use that number to magnify the given number. Listing 7.1 shows the required procedure. The commands shown in Listing 7.1 are stored in a file called magnify.tcl.

LISTING 7.1   Default Values for Input Arguments

```
1: proc magnify { x {fac 2} } {
2:     puts "x is $x ; fac is $fac"
3:     return [expr $x*$fac]
4: }
```

ANALYSIS The procedure has two arguments. The first argument is magnified by the factor supplied in the second argument. If the second argument is not supplied, the procedure uses a factor of two. Note that the default argument and its value are defined as a sublist. The arguments with default values must appear after the formal arguments. A dialogue with the procedure is shown in Listing 7.2.

LISTING 7.2 Using Default Values for Arguments

```
1: %source magnify.tcl
2: %magnify 4
3: x is 4 ; fac is 2
4: 8
5: %magnify 4 6
6: x is 4 ; fac is 6
7: 24
8: %
```

ANALYSIS The procedure is brought into the interpreter in line 1. First, you invoke the procedure with a single argument to magnify (line 2) the number by a default factor of 2. In this case, a default value of 2 is used for fac and the magnified number is returned (line 4). Next, you invoke magnify with two arguments (line 5). In this case, magnify uses a value of 6 for fac overriding the default value (line 7).

> The default arguments, if present, must be the last arguments. For example, defining magnify as proc magnify { {fac 2} x } { ... } will complain when invoked with a single argument.
>
> There must be enough actual arguments for all the formal arguments that don't have defaults, and there must not be any extra actual arguments.

Variable Number of Input Arguments

Another useful feature is the processing of a variable number of arguments. If the last argument in the argument list to a procedure contains the word args, the procedure may be invoked with a variable number of arguments. Consider computing the average of a set of numbers. You want to write a procedure that takes any number of arguments and returns their average. Listing 7.3 illustrates this. The procedure defined in Listing 7.3 is stored in the file avg1.tcl.

7

LISTING 7.3   The Average of a Set of Numbers—Using a Variable Number of Arguments

```
 1: # Return average of numbers
 2:
 3: proc average { args } {
 4:     set total 0.0
 5:     set n [llength $args]
 6:     foreach x $args {
 7:            set total [expr $total+$x]
 8:     }
 9:     return [expr ($total)/$n ]
10: }
```

ANALYSIS   The procedure has one argument that is the special name args (line 1). This mechanism enables you to pass a variable number of inputs to average. Inside the body of the procedure, you first initialize the variable total for storing the cumulative total. The number of elements passed to the procedure is stored in line 2. Next, you cycle through the elements in args adding to our total (lines 6–8). You compute the average in line 9 and exit the procedure. Listing 7.4 shows a typical dialogue with average.

LISTING 7.4   Sample Output Using the Procedure average

```
 1: %source avg1.tcl
 2: %average 1 2 3 4 5
 3: 3.0
 4: %average 25 30
 5: 27.5
 6: %
```

ANALYSIS   After sourcing the procedure in avg1.tcl (line 1), you invoke the procedure in line 2 with five input arguments. You also supply two input arguments in line 5. On both occasions, you get the right result.

Note a common pitfall here. If the numbers are stored in a variable as set nums {7 9}, and you invoked the procedure as average $nums, you get syntax error in expression "0.0+7 9". The reason is clear from the error message. The input argument args was passed as one word 7 9 , and the expr command doesn't know how to add that word to 0.0. A simple remedy is to put the command through another round of parsing using eval average $nums.

If the argument list to the procedure contains both defaults and the special word `args`, there will be no actual arguments available to be placed in `args`, and hence `args` is set to an empty string. See Q&A in this hour for an example.

Scope of Variables Within a Procedure

Pass-by-value refers to a method of passing arguments to a procedure. It can also be referred to as call-by-value. The variables in a procedure work on their own local copies of the values passed to them. This is demonstrated in Listing 7.5.

LISTING 7.5 Procedures Work on Their Own Copies of the Values Passed to Them

```
1: %set x 5
2: 5
3: %proc doubleIt x { return [expr 2*$x] }
4: %doubleIt $x
5: 10
6: %set x
7: 5
8: %
```

ANALYSIS A simple procedure to double an argument is defined in line 3. For dramatic effect, the input argument is named x. In the main scope, you define a variable x (line 1). The procedure `doubleIt $x` doubles the value and returns. What is the value of x after invoking `doubleIt`? Nothing happens to it, as verified in lines 6–7. The procedure was given a copy of the variable to work with.

Variables with Global Scope

Variables defined in the main scope (or toplevel scope) are not generally available inside the body of a procedure.

It is often convenient to pass data required in several procedures using a `global` command. You communicate any changes made in the procedure to the variable available in the main scope, instead of using long lists of input arguments to the procedures.

For example, you have a procedure to compute an employee bonus, given a salary figure. The rate at which the bonus is computed is determined by a complex formula and is required in other procedures for other calculations, such as tax calculations. You decide to pass the bonus rate figure as a global variable. The procedure that computes the bonus and a dialogue using it are shown in Listing 7.6 and Listing 7.7, respectively.

7

LISTING 7.6   The bonus Procedure

```
1: proc bonus { x } {
2:     global rate
3:     return [expr ($x*$rate/100.0)]
4: }
```

ANALYSIS   The procedure returns the bonus on the amount x based on the rate that is supplied to the procedure as a global variable.

LISTING 7.7   The Global Command

```
1: %source bonus.tcl
2: %bonus 1500
3: can't read "rate": no such variable
4: %set rate 5
5: 5
6: %bonus 1500
7: 75.0
8: %
```

ANALYSIS   A straightforward invocation of the procedure (lines 13–14) results in an error. To rectify this, you set the variable in line 4. You get the bonus (lines 6–7)! There is one subtle message in this dialogue. In the main scope (that is, in the interpreter), you didn't explicitly state that the variable rate is global. The very act of setting the variable in the global scope defines the variable in the global scope. This is convenient for interactive work, but can throw you off when initializing the rate in another procedure.

You need to declare the variable under consideration as global in the procedure initializing it, as shown in Listing 7.8.

LISTING 7.8   Global Variables Defined in a Procedure

```
1: proc initBonusRate {} {
2:     global rate
3:     set rate 5
4: }
```

Note that you have explicitly declared the variable to be global in line 2. Now you can use the variable rate using the dialogue in Listing 7.9. Note also that it is useful to restart the shell when experimenting with this type of example, until you have a better grasp of what is going on.

The global command should appear before the first use of the variable. By convention the command global is placed as the first command in a procedure body, except for comment lines.

LISTING 7.9   Accessing Global Variables

```
1: %source init2.tcl
2: %initBonusRate
3: 5
4: %bonus 1500
5: 75.0
6: %
```

ANALYSIS   The procedure in line 2 initializes the variable rate and, correctly, makes it available in global scope.

Global variables that are currently available in the interpreter may be inquired using info global *pattern*. For example, info global e* returns the names errorCode errorInfo env.

Executing Code In a Different Scope

By default, arguments to a procedure are passed by value. This poses a restriction on your capability to pass the arrays to a procedure. You can, of course, pass the array as a global and work on an array. What if you have more than one array? You end up repeating the same code several times. You need a generic solution to such problems. It is provided by the Tcl commands upvar and uplevel.

Motivating upvar

The following example illustrates the command upvar. Your task is to increase the value of a variable by 15%. The twist is that you want to pass the name of a variable, and expect to see the increased value after the invocation of the procedure. You can do this in two stages. The first stage (Listings 7.10 and 7.11) demonstrates why the call-by-value doesn't deliver what you want.

7

LISTING 7.10   Why upvar?

```
1: proc increase1 x {
2:     set x [expr $x*1.15]
3: }
```

LISTING 7.11   Increase the Value by 15%

```
1: %source increase1.tcl
2: %set pay 1800
3: 1800
4: %increase1 $pay
5: 2070.0
6: %set pay
7: 1800
8: %
```

ANALYSIS   You source your procedure increase1 in line 1. You then define a variable called pay in line 2. Now invoke the procedure increase1 $pay. Does the value stored in pay change? No, as can be seen from lines 6–7. According to the scoping rules of procedures, this is the right behavior. Recall that all the variables are passed by value. However, in some situations, you want to pass the name and modify the value of the variable. What you need is a mechanism similar to pass-by-name. In this style of argument passing, any changes made to the argument names are communicated to the caller's scope.

How can you pass the name of the variable, rather than the value, to a procedure so that you can work on the original variable itself? Consider the procedure in Listing 7.12.

LISTING 7.12   Simple Example of upvar—Procedure increase2.tcl

```
1: proc increase2 name {
2:     upvar #0 $name x   ;# x is an alias to name
3:     set x [expr $x*1.15]
4: }
```

ANALYSIS   You define the procedure increase2 with one argument. Inside the body, you create an alias to the argument passed to the procedure in line 2, using the command upvar. Listing 7.13 demonstrates the modified procedure.

LISTING 7.13   Dialogue with `increase2.tcl`

```
1: %source increase2.tcl
2: %set pay 1800
3: 1800
4: %increase2 pay   ;# passing name, not value
5: 2070.0
6: %set pay
7: 2070.0
8: %
```

ANALYSIS   You source your new procedure `increase2.tcl` (line 1), and define a variable for testing (line 2). Now how do you invoke your procedure? You invoke the procedure by passing the name of the variable whose value you want to increase. This is an important difference. As expected, the procedure returned the modified value. Has it really changed the value for pay? Now, the moment of truth. You confirm the value in lines 6–7. Your procedure indeed has done its job and increased your pay!

Passing Arrays to a Procedure

One problem with procedures is passing arrays to procedures as input arguments. You can simply pass an array name as you did with variable names. Remember that a copy of the variable is passed to the procedure. In the case of array input, Tcl has to make many copies. A more efficient way to handle this situation is to pass the name (or more technically call-by-name) and do the required manipulations inside the body of the procedure. This is done using a general mechanism provided by the `upvar` command, which creates an alias to a variable in the calling scope.

For example, you can write a procedure that increments the numerical values stored in an array by a given amount. Listing 7.14 shows the procedure.

LISTING 7.14   Passing Arrays to a Procedure

```
1: # increment elements of array by d
2:
3: proc incrA { a d } {
4:     upvar #0 $a x   ;# x is an alias to a
5:     foreach e [array names x] {
6:          set x($e) [expr $x($e) + $d ]
7:     }
8: }
```

ANALYSIS   The first argument to the procedure is an array name, whereas the second argument denotes the change required. The important step is in line 4. You make an alias to the array name a and call it x. The `upvar` command has an optional first argument to denote the level. A #0 indicates the toplevel scope. In line 4, you effectively make an alias to the array name supplied through the variable a. The alias is x. From now on, you can use x in place of a. All the operations on x are automatically reflected in the calling scope. The loop in lines 5–7 cycles through the elements of the array and increments them by $d. Note that if $d happens to be negative, the values are decremented. The procedure is shown in action in Listing 7.15.

LISTING 7.15   Using incrA Procedure

```
1: %source arr1.tcl
2: %array set A {First 80 Middle 75 Last 40}
3: %incrA A 10
4: %parray A
5: A(First)  = 90
6: A(Last)   = 50
7: A(Middle) = 85
8: %
```

ANALYSIS   You define an array A for testing your procedure in line 2. (Array commands are introduced in Hour 6, "Exploring Arrays.") You invoke the procedure incrA to increment the array values by 10 in line 3, and you make a quick check with parray command (lines 4–7).

> The command parray is a Tcl procedure which exploits this mechanism of argument passing-by-name. It is very instructive to look at the code for parray. You can use the command info body parray to display the code. Note that the parray command is auto-loaded into the Tcl shell, and hence you need to use the command before you can display the body of the procedure. You can use parray env to auto-load the procedure into the Tcl shell.

Defining Your Own Command

The uplevel command combines the benefits of upvar and eval. It evaluates its argument in the calling scope (or a specific scope nominated by you). The uplevel command takes an optional level and a command as an argument.

Consider an example. You define a procedure called change, which changes the value of a variable using incr in the main scope. The procedure is shown in Listing 7.16. The source file also contains another procedure for evaluating boolean expressions. The process is also illustrated in Figure 7.1.

FIGURE 7.1

Executing a command in a different scope (or level).

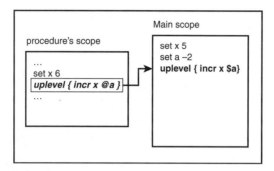

LISTING 7.16   A Simple Use of `uplevel`—Source File `uplevel1.tcl`

```
 1: #caller's scope is toplevel
 2: # a defined in caller's scope
 3: proc change x {
 4:      set x 6
 5:      uplevel { incr x $a }
 6: }
 7:
 8: 9: proc bool {} {
10:      uplevel {
11:            puts "Boolean expr: $e "
12:            puts [expr $e]
13:      }
14:}
```

ANALYSIS   The source file defines two procedures for illustration. In the first procedure (line 3), change has one argument that is to be modified. The body contains two lines (lines 4–5). You define a variable x to highlight the difference. Line 5 uses the uplevel command. By default, uplevel executes its argument { incr x $a } in the caller's scope. (See Figure 7.1.) You can think of the command being simply lifted and placed in main scope (or the interpreter). What is the result of the command { incr x $a }? Well, in the main scope, x has value 5, and a has value -2. Thus x has value 3. This dialogue is illustrated in Listing 7.17.

LISTING 7.17   Demonstration of `uplevel` Command

```
 1: % source uplevel1.tcl
 2: % set x 5
 3: 5
 4: % set a -2
 5: -2
```

continues

7

LISTING **7.17**   continued

```
 6: % change $x
 7: 3
 8: % set x
 9: 3
10: % set e {$x > 0}
11: $x > 0
12: % bool
13: Boolean expr: $x > 0
14: 1
15: %
```

ANALYSIS   You bring the two procedures into the interpreter in line 1. Two variables x and a
are defined in the interpreter, which is the mainscope. Now invoking change $x
(line 6), what do we expect to see for the value of x? As explained before, the procedure
changes the value of x in the caller's scope. Hence, you get the value of 3 for x.

Another example of evaluating a boolean expression is illustrated in lines 10–14. The
procedure bool is defined in Listing 7.16. The procedure simply evaluates the boolean
expression in the caller's scope, and hence the result in line 14.

You are now in a position to define your own command.

Defining Your Own do *body* while *test* Command

As explained earlier in this section, uplevel and upvar enable you to define additional
control structures. For illustration, define your own do *body* while *test* construct. A
production version will require stringent error checking. Listing 7.18 implements the
bare bones of such a construct.

LISTING **7.18**   The Procedure Defining the do *body* while *test*

```
 1: # define a do body while test loop
 2:
 3: proc do {body while  test } {
 4:     # execute the body at least once
 5:     uplevel $body   ;# remember it bumps up k
 6:     # test is first substituted and then sent upstairs
 7:     set t [uplevel "expr $test"]
 8:     # upstairs gets $k < 1, k is defined there
 9:     while { $t } {
10:         catch {uplevel $body} msg
11:         set t [uplevel "expr $test"]
12:     }
13: }
```

ANALYSIS The procedure has three arguments, body, while, and test. The second argument while is a noise word and is thrown away in the procedure. The important point about the do .. while block is that the body is entered first, and then the condition in test is evaluated. To this end, you evaluate the body in the main scope in line 5. Next, you evaluate the condition test again in the main scope (line 7), and store the result in t. Now, you use the Tcl while loop (lines 9–12) to execute the body as long as the condition (line 11) evaluates to true. The procedure is demonstrated in Listing 7.19.

LISTING 7.19   Using do...while Construct

```
 1: %set k 1
 2: 1
 3: %do {
 4:      puts " k squared is [expr $k*$k]"
 5:      incr k
 6:      } while {$k < 4}
 7:  k squared is 1
 8:  k squared is 4
 9:  k squared is 9
10: %set k 1
11: 1
12: %do {
13:      puts " k squared is [expr $k*$k]"
14:      incr k
15:      } while {$k < 1}
16:  k squared is 1
17: %
```

ANALYSIS To test your new construct, you define a variable k (line 1). Lines 3–6 define the do...while loop. In the body of the loop, you just print the square of the number and increment the value of k. Now check the condition $k<4 and keep going round the block while the value for k is less than four. The results of your labor are shown in lines 7–9. Is the loop entered at least once? We check this in lines 10–16, and lo and behold, it is.

Tuning Your Procedures for Performance

Tuning procedures for high-performance is an art and comes with practice. One of the first things to learn is to time the code.

The time command may be used to measure the performance of your scripts or procedures. The general form of the command is time *script* *?count?*. By default the *script* is executed once, and the command returns the elapsed time. A short example is shown in Listing 7.20.

7

LISTING 7.20   Timing a Script

```
1: %time {expr sqrt(2)} 10000
2: 3 microseconds per iteration
```

ANALYSIS   In this example, the script {expr sqrt(2)} is executed 10,000 times. The elapsed time is reported in line 2.

As an example, put x and y coordinates into separate lists from a single list containing the pairs. For example, a given list is of the form {x0 y0 x1 y1 x2 y2 ...}. You are required to keep all the x coordinates in one list, say Xs, {x0 x1 x2 ...} and Ys in the list {y0 y1 y2 ...}.

This can be done using either for loops or more versatile foreach loop. These are shown Listing 7.21 and Listing 7.22.

LISTING 7.21   The Script coords1.tcl

```
1: # pickout x,y from a list of points
2:
3: set pts {1 1 2 4 3 9 4 16 5 25 6 36 7 49 8 64 9 81 10 100 11 121}
4:
5: set x2 {}
6: set y2 {}
7:
8: for {set i 0} {$i < [llength $pts]} {incr i 2} {
9:     lappend x2 [lindex $pts $i]
10: }
11:
12: for {set i 1} {$i <= [llength $pts]} {incr i 2} {
13:     lappend y2 [lindex $pts $i]
14: }
```

ANALYSIS   You define two empty lists for storing respective coordinate information (lines 5–6). You walk through the list of points with a stride 2 to pick the next value. Note the different initializations for i in the for loops (line 8 and line 12).

LISTING 7.22   The Script coords2.tcl

```
1: # pickout x,y from a list of points
2:
3: set pts {1 1 2 4 3 9 4 16 5 25 6 36 7 49 8 64 9 81 10 100 11 121}
4:
5: set x {}
6: set y {}
```

```
 7: foreach {i j} $pts {
 8:      lappend x $i
 9:      lappend y $j
10: }
```

ANALYSIS Once again, you start with two empty lists (lines 5–6). The important difference is that you use two parameters as you walk the list.

It is instructive to compare the two scripts in Listings 7.21 and 7.22 with the procedure shown in Listing 7.23.

LISTING 7.23   The Procedure `coords3` Stored in `coords3.tcl`

```
 1: #  pickout x,y from a list of points
 2: #  set pts {1 1 2 4 3 9 4 16 5 25 6 36 7 49 8 64 9 81 10 100 11 121}
 3:
 4: proc coords3 { pts } {
 5:     set x {}
 6:     set y {}
 7:     foreach {i j} $pts {
 8:          lappend x $i
 9:          lappend y $j
10:     }
11:     return "$x $y"
12: }
```

The time commands comparing the three approaches are shown in Listing 7.24.

LISTING 7.24   Comparing `coords1.tcl` and `coords2.tcl` and the Procedure `coords3`

```
1: %time {source coords1.tcl} 1000
2: 3325 microseconds per iteration
3: %time {source coords2.tcl} 1000
4: 2564 microseconds per iteration
5: %source coords3.tcl
6: % set pts {1 1 2 4 3 9 4 16 5 25 6 36 7 49 8 64 9 81 10 100 11 121}
7: 2 4 3 9 4 16 5 25 6 36 7 49 8 64 9 81 10 100 11 121
8: time {coords3 $pts} 1000
9: 130 microseconds per iteration
```

ANALYSIS Each of the scripts are timed using a repeat count of 1000 for demonstration. The first script, which uses `for` loops, certainly took longer than the script using a `foreach` loop. You can experiment with different repeat counts, but the general message remains the same. The `foreach` command with multiple loop parameters is faster and more efficient. More important, the logic of the code is clearer and more elegant. Line 8

7

times the procedure `coords3` defined in `coords3.tcl` which shows a dramatic improve-
ment. Note that line 8 also shows the order of overhead incurred by sourcing the file.

An in-depth discussion of this topic is beyond the scope of this book. For general tips on
tuning your programs, see `http://mini.net/cgi-bin/wikit/`. (You may want to search
using the phrase Tcl Performance or Donal Fellows.)

Building Script Libraries

Tcl provides a simple and elegant mechanism to create libraries of frequently used code.
A thorough discussion of this topic is beyond the scope of this book. However, the concept is important; and we stick to obtaining a working knowledge of creating script
libraries. Let us say that you want the procedures defined in the files `lunique.tcl`,
`lwhere.tcl`, and `myhelp.tcl` to be kept in a library of your own. The process of creating
your personal script library is described in Figure 7.2, and the dialogue for creating this
library is shown in Listing 7.25.

FIGURE 7.2
*Creating personal
script libraries.*

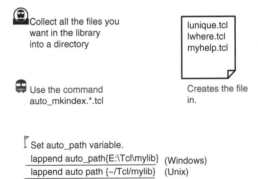

Collect all the files you
want in the library
into a directory

```
lunique.tcl
lwhere.tcl
myhelp.tcl
```

Use the command
auto_mkindex.*.tcl

Creates the file
in.

Set auto_path variable.
lappend auto_path{E:\Tcl\mylib} (Windows)
lappend auto path {~/Tcl/mylib} (Unix)

LISTING 7.25   Creating a Personal Library

```
 1: %cd E:/Tcl//mylib/
 2: %dir
 3: ./:
 4: lunique.tcl  lwhere.tcl    myhelp.tcl
 5: %auto_mkindex . *.tcl
 6: %lappend auto_path {E:/Tcl/mylib}
 7: E:/TCLTK8~1/Tcl/lib E:/TCLTK8~1/Tcl/bin E:/Tcl/mylib
 8: %pwd
 9: E:/
10: %lunique {a b a c b a c a}
11: % a b c
12: %
```

ANALYSIS You can put all the files to be included in the library into a directory called, let us say, E:\Tcl\mylib. You move into that directory as in line 1. Run the command (line 5) `auto_mkindex` that generates an index file. The command `auto_mkindex` takes two arguments. The first argument is the name of the directory where the library is located. The index file is named `tclIndex` and is written in the directory nominated in the first argument. This index is used by Tcl to locate the file and source it when needed. The file can be inspected and is written as an ASCII file. The final step is to append the newly created variable to the system variable `auto_path`. In line 6, you use `lappend` to add your newly created library. From now on, you can issue the command `lunique` from any subdirectory. It works just as does any other Tcl command.

Note that this is an alternative to explicitly sourcing the files yourself. It is instructive to inspect the `tclIndex` file.

After the library is working satisfactorily, you can customize your initialization files so that your library is picked up every time you open the shell (`tclsh` or `wish`).

> You need to regenerate the index whenever you modify the corresponding source files.

Do	**Don't**
Do remember that arguments with default values for arguments must appear at the end of the argument list.	**Don't** place the global command in the middle of a procedure body.

Summary

This hour concentrated on procedures in some detail. A procedure can have zero number of arguments. The arguments to a procedure can have default values defined. If they are present, they must occur at the end of the argument list. A variable number of arguments are passed to a procedure using the special name `args`. This must appear as the last argument. If you combine default values and the special name `args`, `args` will be set to `null` string.

There are two styles of argument passing called pass-by-value and pass-by-name. The arguments to a procedure are passed by value. That means each procedure works on its own local copy and doesn't interfere with a variable with the same name elsewhere.

7

Variables can be declared to have global scope. A convenient way of making common data available to several procedures is to store the data in an array and declare the array as a global.

Argument passing-by-name is implemented using the command upvar. A related command, uplevel, combines the flexibility of upvar and eval, which enables you to define custom-made control flow commands.

The hour concludes with related topics concerning creating Tcl script libraries and tuning your procedures. The time command provides a simple means to compare the performance of two scripts.

With procedures under your belt, you now can confidently move on to the topic of manipulation of strings.

Q&A

Q Can I have procedures within procedures?

A Yes. For example, you can define a procedure to deal with the square root of negative numbers as follows. If the number supplied is negative, you change the sign, and then take the square root. To emphasize that this is a complex number, append *i at the end of the number. Such a procedure is defined inside a procedure.

```
 1: proc within { x } {
 2:
 3:     puts "You gave me $x"
 4:     proc complexRoot { x } {
 5:  if { $x < 0 } {
 6:     set nx [expr -1*$x]
 7:     set ans "[expr sqrt($nx)]*i" ;# append *i
 8:  }
 9:     }
10:     puts "After: [complexRoot $x]"
11: }
```

A sample session with a within procedure is shown in the following code.

```
 1: %source procinproc.tcl
 2: %within -5
 3: You gave me -5
 4: After: 2.2360679775*i
 5: %complexRoot -4
 6: 2.0*i
 7: %complexRoot -1
 8: 1.0*i
 9: %
```

Although such little utility procedures can be conveniently defined inside a procedure, it is important to recognize those procedures are equally available in the main scope, as illustrated in lines 5–8.

Q Can the procedures be recursive?

A Yes. For example, we can compute the factorial of a number recursively, as shown here:

```
1: # recursive proc for factorial
2:
3: proc factorial { n } {
4:     if { $n <= 1 } {
5:   return 1
6:     } else {
7:   return [expr $n*[factorial [incr n -1]] ]
8:     }
9: }
```

A sample output using the procedure is shown below:

```
1: %source factorial.tcl
2: %factorial 5
3: 120
4: %factorial 4
5: 24
6: %factorial 0
7: 1
8: %
```

Q I am trying to write a procedure to compute powers of a list of numbers. Inputs to the procedure consist of a default parameter to indicate the powers to which the numbers are raised and a variable list of numbers through args. What is wrong with the following procedure?

```
1: proc powers { {p 2} args } {
2:     set ans {}
3:     puts "p is $p ; args is $args"
4:     foreach a $args {
5:   lappend ans [expr pow($a,$p)]
6:   puts " $a raised to $p is [expr pow($a,$p)]"
7:     }
8:     return $ans
9: }
10: %source powers.tcl
11: %powers 3 4 5  ;# compute squares of 3, 4, 5
12: p is 3 ; args is 4 5
13:   4 raised to 3 is 64.0
14:   5 raised to 3 is 125.0
15: 64.0 125.0
16: %powers
17: p is 2 ; args is
18: %
```

7

A When a procedure has default arguments and variable input arguments, there is a problem as illustrated in the preceding code. There is no way of NOT supplying the value for p. As demonstrated in lines 11–15, the first argument 3 is given to p, and the rest of inputs 4 5 are passed to args. The only time you can get at the default value for p is when you invoke powers without any arguments, and that doesn't solve our problem.

The problem can be solved elegantly using lists. A sample procedure is given in the following code:

```
1: # Raise to power p a list of numbers
2:
3: proc powers2 {  numList {p 2} } {
4:     set ans {}
5:     foreach a $numList {
6:   lappend ans [expr pow($a,$p)]
7:     }
8:     return $ans
9: }
```

A sample output follows.

```
1: %source powers2.tcl
2: %powers2 {2 3}
3: 4.0 9.0
4: %powers2 {4 5 6 8} 3
5: 64.0 125.0 216.0 512.0
6: %
```

Workshop

The quiz section that follows is designed to provide you with an opportunity to recall some of the important concepts introduced in this hour. These may be commands, command syntax, common mistakes, usage, and so on. The following exercises section helps you consolidate the material you have learned with an example of practical value. The aim is that these two sections should reinforce the knowledge you have gained in this hour. The answers to the quiz that follows can be found in Appendix A, "Answers to Quizzes."

Quiz

1. Can I have zero arguments for a proc?
2. What is the constraint on specifying default values for input arguments for a proc?
3. What is the purpose of the special argument args?
4. What is the scope of the variables defined inside a procedure?

5. What is the command to inspect the global variables?

6. How are arguments passed to a procedure?

7. What Tcl command enables you to implement a call-by-name method of argument processing?

8. What is the command to time a Tcl script?

9. What does the variable auto_path contain?

10. Can I declare an array as a global?

Exercises

Solutions to the exercises are on the CD-ROM that accompanies this book.

1. Write a procedure that initializes the top-left and bottom-right coordinates of a rectangle, and defines the height and width in a global scope. (Use the convention that the x-coordinates increase as you go farther right, and y-coordinates increase as you go farther down. This is consistent with drawing a rectangle in a canvas widget later in the book.) Write another procedure that uses the global variables height and width and computes the area of the rectangle.

2. Store a set of conversion factors (for example, from British units to Metric) in an array, which is declared global. Write a procedure of the form convert n units, that uses the conversion factors stored in the global array. If the units are not specified, default them to inches.

7

Hour 8

Manipulating Strings

In the last hour, you learned the details of Tcl procedures and how to build script libraries. You also learned how to tune the procedure for the best performance. In earlier hours, we have mentioned that everything in Tcl is a string. In this hour, you study strings in some detail.

Mastery of string manipulation is essential, if you want to get the last ounce of performance out of your code. String manipulation commands can be broadly categorized into two groups. The first group of commands is related to inquiry commands (for example, length of a string), and the second group of commands modifies the string in some way (for example, converting it to uppercase). String commands support two types of pattern matching that are discussed in detail. Two related commands for formatting strings are also introduced in this hour, as well as the reverse process of extracting formatted data from strings.

In this hour, you will learn

- To use string inquiry commands
- To use glob-style pattern matching for listing files

- To use regular expression patterns for string processing, extracting substrings, and locating substrings that match a pattern
- To replace the parts of a string that match a given pattern
- To generate string with specified format
- To extract required data from strings

String Commands

A string consists of characters in the ASCII character set. Note that only a subset of this character set is actually visible on the terminal screen. Special characters such as tabs can be included using a back slash or the corresponding Hex (or Unicode) code.

The Syntax for String Commands

SYNTAX

The following code shows the syntax for string commands:

```
string subCommand args
```

where the possible values for *subCommand* are given in Appendix B, and *args* are either strings or integers depending on the *subCommand*.

Some of the basic inquiry commands are shown in Listing 8.1. Figure 8.1 shows a simple example of a string.

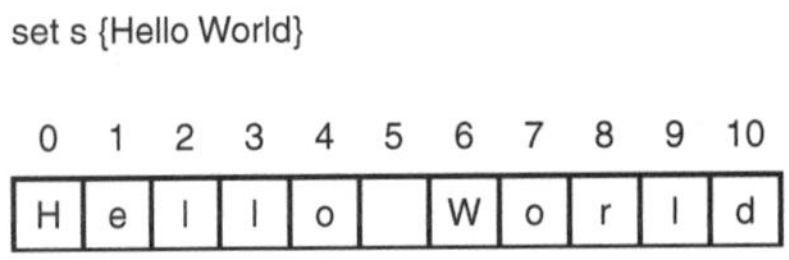

▲

FIGURE **8.1**

The length of the string is 11. The character at index position 0 is H, and the character at index position 10 is d. The last character can also be referred to using the logical name end.

set s {Hello World}

```
 0   1   2   3   4   5   6   7   8   9   10
┌───┬───┬───┬───┬───┬───┬───┬───┬───┬───┬───┐
│ H │ e │ l │ l │ o │   │ W │ o │ r │ l │ d │
└───┴───┴───┴───┴───┴───┴───┴───┴───┴───┴───┘
```

LISTING **8.1**   Simple String Inquiry Commands

```
1: %set s {Hello World}
2: Hello World
3: %string length $s
4: 11
5: %string index $s 4
6: o
7: %string range $s 4 end
8: o World
9: %
```

Line 1 defines a string you can experiment with. In line 3, you inquire the length of the string. Note that the number returned is the number of characters—including blanks and any special characters. Individual characters in a string are referred to using an integer index, starting from zero. For example, the first character in the string, H, is referred to using the index 0. In line 5, you query the character at index position 4 in the string s. A range of characters is extracted by specifying the starting index and the finishing index. The final index can be the logical name end as in line 7. Other string inquiry commands are illustrated in Table 8.1.

Strings Versus Lists

How do strings and lists differ? The basic unit of a string is a character, whereas the basic unit of list is a word. This distinction is demonstrated in Listing 8.2.

LISTING 8.2 String Length and List Length

```
1: %set s {Hello World}
2: Hello World
3: %string length $s
4: 11
5: %llength $s
6: 2
7: %
```

ANALYSIS Here the string Hello World stored in the variable s illustrates the distinction. In the context of a string (lines 3–4), the length is 11. The variable s used because the list has length 2.

The string inquiry commands are illustrated in Table 8.1, and some of the string manipulation commands are shown in Table 8.2.

TABLE 8.1 String Inquiry Commands

Command	Result
string compare $s $s	0
string compare $s {hello World}	-1
string compare {hello world} $s	1
string first o $s	4
string index $s 0	H
string last o $s	7

continues

TABLE 8.1 continued

Command	Result
string length $s	11
string match {*W*} $s	1
string range $s 6 10	World
string range 4 end	o World

TABLE 8.2 String Manipulation Commands—The String Defined in set s
{   Hello World   } Is Used for Illustration

Command	Result
puts "++[string tolower $s]++"	++ hello world ++
puts "++[string toupper $s]++"	++ HELLO WORLD ++
puts "++[string trim $s]++"	++Hello World++
puts "++[string trimleft $s]++"	++Hello World ++
puts "++[string trimright $s]++"	++ Hello World++

Comparing Strings

Strings are compared lexicographically (that is, in dictionary order), using the string compare command.

The Syntax for string compare

The following code shows the syntax for string compare:

```
string compare string1 string2
```

The command returns -1, if *string1* is lexicographically less than *string2* (that is, a before b, and so on). 0 is returned if they are the same, and 1 is returned if *string1* is greater than *string2*.

A simple example of a string comparison is shown in Listing 8.3.

LISTING 8.3 The String Comparison

```
1: % foreach item {rectangle oval Rectangle} {
2: >    set itemLc [string tolower $item]
3: >    if { [string compare $itemLc rectangle] == 0 } {
4: >        puts "Draw a rectangle in the canvas"
5: >    } else {
```

```
 6: >       puts "I don't know the item \"$item\" "
 7: >   }
 8: >}
 9: Draw a rectangle in the canvas
10: I don't know the item "oval"
11: Draw a rectangle in the canvas
12: %
```

ANALYSIS In this example, you cycle through a list of items that consists of strings describing the shapes of some objects. You want to take a particular action depending on the type of object, independent of the case. In line 2, you convert the item to lowercase. You make a string comparison to check whether the itemLc is a rectangle. Note that the string comparison command returns 0 if the items compared are the same, and hence the logical equality in line 3.

> A string comparison command returns zero if two strings are the same.

Pattern Matching in Strings

Two types of pattern matching are supported by string commands—glob-style and regular expression. Glob-style is useful for simple tasks, such as matching the first few characters in a filename. (See Hour 9, "Interacting with the Operating System," for additional examples.) Regular expressions offer more control when defining flexible patterns. These two pattern-matching techniques, which play an important role in processing strings efficiently, are described in the following sections.

Glob-Style Pattern Matching

A glob-style pattern is a simple way to describe a pattern, analogous to the use of wildcards in searching for text in editors or names of files in directories. A glob-style pattern is described using the characters in Table 8.3.

Table 8.3 Special Characters Used in Glob-Style Patterns

Special Character	Meaning
*	Matches any sequence of zero or more characters. For example, ca* matches car, card, career, cartoon.
?	Matches any single character. For example, ca?t matches cart and cast.

continues

Table 8.3   continued

Special Character	Meaning
[chars]	Matches any single character in the set. A range of characters is specified as [a–z]. The dash is not part of the set. For example, List_[0-9].dat matches List_1.dat, List_2.dat, and so on. It does not match List_12.dat. Remember to suppress the command evaluation by enclosing the pattern inside curly braces.
\x	Matches the literal character. Used to match the special characters *?[] in the pattern.
{str1, str2, ...}	Matches any of the strings. For example, glob {{Ch4,Ch8}/*.t[cx][lt]} matches files in the directories Ch4 and Ch8 with extension .tcl, .txl, .tct, and .txt.

Glob-style searching in strings is illustrated in Listing 8.4.

LISTING 8.4   Matching with Glob-Style Patterns

```
 1: %string match {A[mr]*} Armenia
 2: 1
 3: %string match {A[mr]*} America
 4: 1
 5: %foreach c {America Armenia India China} {
 6:        puts " Pattern *in* in $c: [string match *in* $c] "
 7:    }
 8:  Pattern *in* in America: 0
 9:  Pattern *in* in Armenia: 0
10:  Pattern *in* in India: 0
11:  Pattern *in* in China: 1
```

ANALYSIS   Line 1 illustrates a simple use of a glob-style pattern. You want to determine whether the string, Armenia contains the pattern {A[mr]*}. You use the letter A, followed by either m or r, followed by a sequence of zero or more characters. Clearly, the match in line 1 succeeds. The pattern must be enclosed within curly braces. Without them, the interpreter tries to evaluate a command by the name [mr], which isn't what you want. The same pattern is also found in America as shown in lines 3–4. Lines 5–7 cycle through four strings that contain the pattern *in*. Note that only the string China contains the pattern. The pattern will not match the string India because it contains the uppercase letter I. If you want to match the uppercase letters, you must include that requirement in your pattern.

This example illustrates some limitations of glob-style patterns. How do you match names that end in digits? Listing 8.5 discusses this problem.

LISTING 8.5 Limitations of the Glob-Style Pattern

```
 1: %set p {*[0-9][0-9]}
 2: *[0-9][0-9]
 3: %set data {file1 fileB file2 file23 fileA}
 4: file1 fileB file2 file23 file A
 5: %foreach n $data {
 6:     puts " Pattern $p: [string match $p $n]" }
 7: Pattern *[0-9][0-9]: 0
 8: Pattern *[0-9][0-9]: 0
 9: Pattern *[0-9][0-9]: 0
10: Pattern *[0-9][0-9]: 1
11: Pattern *[0-9][0-9]: 0
12: Pattern *[0-9][0-9]: 0
```

8

ANALYSIS The pattern in line 1 matches strings that end in digits. Ideally, you would like to specify one or more digits. But there is no way to specify this. Using this pattern, you can only match the string file23. If you attempt the pattern {*[0-9]*}, it will match all the strings in $data including fileB and fileA.

Regular expressions, which are far more flexible to solve problems of this type, are discussed in the next section.

Searching with Regular Expressions

The basic concept of regular expressions was introduced in Hour 2, "Getting Started with Tcl." Here you consider more complex patterns. You start with a simple example of identifying an integer by way of quick revision in Listing 8.6.

LISTING 8.6 A Regular Expression to Match an Integer

```
1: %set msg {The car was built in 1962 and costs nearly $35000.}
2: The car was built in 1962 and costs nearly $35000.
3: %regexp {[0-9]+} $msg year
4: 1
5: %set year
6: 1962
```

ANALYSIS The string in line 1 has two integers. A simple pattern to pick an integer is defined in line 3. The pattern uses a character range [0-9] to describe a single digit, and the + says one or more such digits. That completes the pattern for an integer. Note that the sign for the integer is not accommodated here. When the regexp command succeeds in finding the pattern in the given string, it returns 1 and also stores the match in a variable called year. This is verified in lines 5–6. Is there a way to match both the integers for the year and the price in line 1? Of course there is. Listing 8.7 explains how.

LISTING 8.7 Matching Two Integers

```
 1: %set p {([0-9]+)([^0-9]+)([0-9]+).*}
 2: ([0-9]+)([^0-9]+)([0-9]+).*
 3: %regexp $p $msg match year mid price
 4: 1
 5: %set match
 6: 1962 and costs nearly $35000.
 7: %set year
 8: 1962
 9: %set mid
10:  and costs nearly
11: %set price
12: 35000
```

ANALYSIS Because you want to identify two integers with some text in between, you use the pattern in line 1. Also the subpatterns are indicated by enclosing them within round brackets. The pattern simply reads: one or more digits (`[0-9]+`), followed by one or more non-digits (`[^0-9]+`), followed by one or more digits (`[0-9]+`), followed by zero or more characters. Lines 5–12 verify the matched patterns.

The regular expression can also be written more mnemonically, as in set p3 `{(\d+)(\D+)(\d+).*}` where `\d` stands for a digit class and `\D` stands for a non-digit class. (See the online manual for additional information.)

Substitutions Using Regular Expressions

Often it is convenient to replace substrings that match a pattern. Think of identifying calendar dates in a document and converting them from American style to European style. Listing 8.8 shows a simple example of replacing all the numbers in a string.

LISTING 8.8 Replacing Integers with `regsub`

```
 1: %set s {Distance: 25 km; Unit Cost: 35 p; Total Cost: 325.46}
 2: Distance: 25 km; Unit Cost: 35 p; Total Cost: 325.46
 3: %regsub -all {[0-9]+} $s XXX TopSecret
 4: 4
 5: %set TopSecret
 6: Distance: XXX km; Unit Cost: XXX p; Total Cost: XXX.XXX
 7: %
```

ANALYSIS In line 1, a string is defined with integers and a number containing a decimal point. The task is to replace these numbers by another string. In this example, they are replaced by XXX. Line 3 defines the required pattern and replacement string. The `-all` option is necessary here. Without that, the substitution will stop after the first replacement. The `regsub` command returns the number of replacements (line 4). Are you wondering why there are four substitutions? The pattern uses only specified integers and does not say anything about a decimal point. As far as `regsub` is concerned, string 325.46 has two matches. One final point about `regsub` is that the substituted string is stored in a variable name. In line 3, you specify the name `TopSecret` for the substituted string. Lines 5–6 verify that your substitution has worked very well indeed!

The Syntax for `regsub`

The following code shows the syntax for `regsub`:

```
regsub ?switches? exp string subSpec varName
```

substituting matched regular expression pattern *exp* in *string* by *subSpec*. The substituted string is stored in *varName* on a successful match. The possible values for *?switches?* are `-all`, `-nocase`, and `--`.

Back references provide a convenient mechanism to refer to the matched patterns. Let us consider an example to illustrate this concept. The task is to convert the date format used in America to that used in Europe. American dates are usually formatted as month/day/year, and in Europe they are formatted as day/month/year. Assume that the month is given as an integer. The problem requires a way to access matched patterns.

When a regular expression finds a match for a pattern, it stores the match in the temporary variables \1, \2, and so forth. These are referred to as *back references*. The plan is to match the month and date and swap them around using the back references. Generally, you allow either a dash or a forward slash as separators, and identify the separator used as part of the problem. A typical dialogue is shown in Listing 8.9.

LISTING 8.9 Converting Date Formats with `regsub`

```
 1: % set amd1 07/27/99
 2: 07/27/99
 3: % set pat {([0-9]+)([-/])([0-9]+).([0-9]+)}
 4: ([0-9]+)([-/])([0-9]+).([0-9]+)
 5: % regsub $pat $amd1 {\3\2\1\2\4} ed1
 6: 1
 7: % set ed1
 8: 27/07/99
 9: % set amd2 1-2-94
10: 1-2-94
11: % regsub $pat $amd2 {\3\2\1\2\4} ed2
12: 1
13: % set ed2
14: 2-1-94
15: %
```

ANALYSIS You start with a simple date in American format in line 1. Line 3 defines the regular expression to find the data. The pattern consists of four subpatterns that can be referred to using the back reference \n. The `regsub` command in line 5 uses the matched patterns. For example, the month number is stored in \1, separator in \2, day number in \3, and the year number in \4. (See Figure 8.2). The transformed string is stored in `ed1`. Lines 7–8 confirm that your substitution has worked. Lines 9–14 are another example using the dash as a separator without any leading zeros in the month or day number.

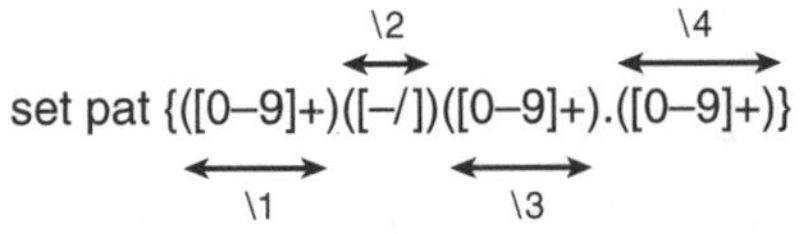

FIGURE 8.2

Using back references in the regsub command.

set pat {([0–9]+)([–/])([0–9]+).([0–9]+)}

Miscellaneous String Commands

Three commands that are closely related to strings are `format`, `scan`, and `subst`. The `subst` command enables another round of backslash, variable, and command substitutions; it is useful in constructing dynamic command strings.

Formatted Strings

You sometimes need to generate textual strings that are neatly formatted. These can be results you want inserted into a text widget, or simple messages that involve a computed result. By default, the computed results are printed to the screen in full precision (12 digits). The format command gives you flexibility to display data (numbers and strings) in a variety of ways. This command is analogous to `sprintf` in C with additional functionality.

The Syntax for `format`

SYNTAX

The following code shows the syntax for format:

```
format formatString ?arg arg ...?
```

where `formatString` describes the format using the `%` specifier for the data items `?arg arg?`.

The format string consists of a conversion specification. The specification consists of flags, a minimum field width, precision, and a conversion character. (See Figure 8.3.) A simple dialogue using a format command is shown Listing 8.10.

FIGURE 8.3

A simplified version of format string specification.

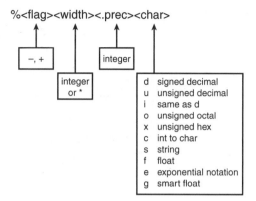

%<flag><width><.prec><char>

LISTING 8.10 Formatting Strings

```
1: % format "Square root of %d is %.4f." 2  [expr sqrt(2)]
2: Square root of 2 is 1.4142.
3: % foreach {n v} {UK London France Paris USA {Washington DC} } {
4:          puts [format "%+12s = %s" $n $v]
5:    }
6:          UK = London
7:      France = Paris
8:         USA = Washington DC
9: %
```

You cannot see the visual rendering just described if you are using the console window that comes with the Tcl/Tk distribution. The console window uses a variable width font and, as a result, the alignment is not perfect in lines 6–8!

ANALYSIS In line 1, you format two numbers. The first number is formatted as a decimal integer. The second number is specified to have four decimal places after the decimal point. Also, the number is represented as a floating-point number. Lines 3–5 show the versatility of the command. Here, you want to align the countries and their capital cities. You also want to right justify the text for the countries. In line 4, you format two strings using the specifier %s. The names of the cities are formatted using a %s specification. The names of the countries are formatted as strings, but you qualify this a bit more by asking for a minimum field width of 12. Within that width, you request that the text be right justified (+).

You can go one step further. You can even compute this minimum field width on-the-fly and pass it to the format string as an argument. The required amendments are shown in Listing 8.11.

LISTING 8.11   Pretty Printing with Format—Source file `fmt2.tcl`

```
 1: set maxLen 1
 2: # determine max length of country names
 3: foreach {n} {UK London France Paris USA {Washington DC} } {
 4:     set strLen [string length $n]
 5:     if { ($strLen > $maxLen) } { set maxLen $strLen}
 6: }
 7: set max2 [expr $maxLen + 3]
 8: foreach {n v} {UK London France Paris USA {Washington DC} } {
 9:     puts [format "%+*s = %s" $max2 $n $v]
10: }

 1: %source fmt2.tcl
 2:        UK = London
 3:    France = Paris
 4:       USA = Washington DC
```

ANALYSIS To determine the maximum length of the strings under consideration, you loop through the names of the countries (lines 3–6). You initialize a variable `maxLen` to 1. As you loop through the names, you find the length of the string and update the variable `maxLen` if it exceeds the current maximum. When you finish the loop in lines 3–6, you get the maximum length. You allow an additional three characters for grace (line 7). Now comes the important bit. How do you pass this value to format specification? Format strings allow a wild card specification, `*`, in place of the numbers you have been supplying so far (line 9). The actual number is read from the corresponding position in the argument list. In this example, it is supplied through $max2 (line 7). The remaining variables $n and $v are formatted as strings, just as they were earlier.

Some of the frequently used format specification strings are illustrated in Table 8.4.

TABLE 8.4 Examples of Formatting Strings, with a Pair of Vertical Bars Displayed to Show the Field Width

Command	Output	Remarks
format "¦%12d¦" 315	¦ 315¦	right justified in their field width by default
format "¦%12i¦" -315	¦ -315¦	same as %d
format "¦%12o¦" 12	¦ 14¦	integer to octal
format "¦%12x¦" 34	¦ 22¦	integer to hex
format "¦%-12x¦" 34	¦22 ¦	integer to hex left justified
format "¦%12c¦" 97	¦ a¦	integer to char
format "¦%12s¦" {The value of Pi}	¦The value of π¦	exceeds minimum width
format "¦%12.8f¦" [expr acos(-1)]	¦ 3.14159265¦	floating point
format "¦%12.8e¦" [expr acos(-1)]	¦3.14159265e+000¦	exponential notation
format "¦%12g¦" [expr acos(-1)]	¦ 3.14159¦	automatically switches to exponential format
format "%s = %g" "The value of \u03c0" 3.14159	The value of π = 3.14159	string contains Unicode character for π
format "¦%12G¦" [expr pow(10,-5)]	¦ 1E-005¦	
format "¦%s %.2f%%¦" {The tax rate is} 7.5%	¦The tax rate is 7.50%¦	use %% to print the literal %
format "¦%+*s¦ = %.2f%%" 15 {Rate} 7.5	¦ Rate¦ = 7.50%	the width spec is taken from the first arg

Scanning Strings

The scan command is the opposite of format in functionality and is used for parsing simple strings.

For example, consider a typical line that occurs in postscript files. The headers in these files contain a line such as %%Bounding Box: 0 0 596 842. The numbers indicate the coordinates of lower-left and top-right corners in units of printer's points. The task is to store this coordinate information in four variables. Listing 8.12 shows an example using scan for this task.

LISTING 8.12   Simple Use of the Scan Command

```
 1: %set str {%%Bounding Box: 0 0 596 842}
 2: %%Bounding Box: 0 0 596 842
 3: %scan $str {%[^0-9] %d %d %d %d} txt a b c d
 4: 5
 5: %puts "++$txt++"
 6: ++%%Bounding Box: ++
 7: %foreach x { a b c d } {
 8:       puts "$x   = [set $x] "}
 9: a   = 0
10: b   = 0
11: c   = 596
12: d   = 842
13: %
```

ANALYSIS   The scan command in line 3 uses the %d specifier to pick integers, and a regular expression to identify the string. Why can't you use %s for scanning strings here? Using %s, scanning stops as soon as it hits a whitespace character and after reading %%Bounding. Of course, you could scan the remaining text into another variable. Why use another variable when you can get away with one? Also, note the use of set in line 8 for printing the value stored in the variable.

Substitution

The subst command performs backslash, variable, and command substitutions in the string.

The Syntax for subst

The following code shows the syntax for subst

subst *?-nobackslashes? ?-nocommands? ?-novariables? string*

The command returns a fully substituted string after performing backslash, variable, and command substitutions.

For example, if you want to evaluate a formula to compute the area of a rectangle, you might put the formula in a string, together with dollar variables. You want this string to be replaced by the appropriate numbers. The dialogue in Listing 8.13 introduces this idea.

LISTING 8.13   A Simple Use of subst

```
 1: %set len 3
 2: 3
 3: %set width 4
 4: 4
 5: %set msg {The area of rectangle is [expr $len*$width]}
 6: The area of rectangle is [expr $len*$width]
 7: %subst $msg
 8: The area of rectangle is 12
 9: %set width 8
10: 8
11: %subst $msg
12: The area of rectangle is 24
13: %
```

ANALYSIS   You define two variables (lines 1–3)—len and width—and a formula to compute the area in a variable (line 5). Notice that the variable contains expr command and some variables, and nothing gets evaluated or substituted at this stage. In line 7, you invoke the subst command to substitute for variables and evaluate any embedded Tcl commands. This is quite handy when you want to re-evaluate your formula after some data items have changed (line 9). All you have to do is reissue the subst command, as in line 11, and the result is updated.

Note that eval $msg won't work here. Eval interprets the list as Tcl commands. In our example, eval $msg tries to interpret The as a Tcl command!

> To generate time stamps on application windows, define a string such as set title {File last modified: [clock format [clock seconds]]}, and issue subst $title to update the information.

Do	Don't
Do protect regular expression patterns either using curly braces or double quotes. **Do** remember that the string commands are highly optimized, and judicious use enhances performance.	**Don't** use bare [string compare *str str*] as a conditional in an if command. Form the logical expression such as [string compare *str str*]== 1 or another appropriate expression.

Summary

In this hour, you looked at string manipulation commands. These commands fall into two groups. The first group deals with inquiring some properties such as length, and the first occurrence of a substring. The second group of commands modifies the string in some way, for example, by removing trailing new lines.

You also revisited the regexp and its close friend regsub commands, which form the basis for an efficient string manipulation tool set. The main suite of string commands are complemented by format to generate neat text, scan to parse simple strings, and subst command for inplace evaluation of variables, commands, and backslash characters.

Many of these commands are used throughout the subsequent chapters, and additional examples will be provided in context. If there is one message to take from this hour, it is this—string compare str1 str2 returns zero when both str1 and str2 are the same. When you are in a position to manipulate strings, the natural question is how can you work with files and communicate with the underlying operating system? You will explore this topic in the next hour.

Q&A

Q What is wrong with the command string match A[mr]* America?

A The glob-style pattern must be enclosed inside curly braces. Without the curly braces, the interpreter tries to execute a command by the name [mr], which, of course, does not exist.

Q How do I match all the characters between two square brackets? The pattern {[(.*)]} isn't doing what I wanted.

A The above pattern is only specifying the set of characters enclosed within square brackets. In this case, you are asking the pattern to match the characters (or . or * or). The pattern is not specifying open square bracket followed by a subpattern consisting of zero or more characters, followed by closed square bracket. To get the desired behavior, a simple alternative is to escape the square brackets. The dialogue shows an example.

```
%set s {[expr $x*4]}
[expr $x*4]
%regexp {\[(.*)\]} $s ma x
1
%set x
expr $x*4
```

Q **Is there a neat way to extract a substring, ignoring the first word from a sentence? Note that my first word is of arbitrary length. For example, given the string set s {Name: Tom W Jones}, I want to extract the string Tom W Jones.**

A This is where the string action subcommands come in handy. A simple dialogue using two sample strings is shown below.

```
% set s1 {Name: Tom W Jones}
Name: Tom W Jones
% string range $s1 [expr [string wordend $s1 0]+1] end
 Tom W Jones
% set s2 {Address 2789 Springfield Av.}
Address 2789 Springfield Av.
% string range $s2 [expr [string wordend $s2 0]+1] end
2789 Springfield Av.
```

Note that the above solution doesn't depend on any characters in the data string.

Q **How do I align numbers nicely? For example, when I try the following code, I get the numbers in a zigzag.**

```
 1: % foreach n {-3 4 -7 8} { [
       puts [format "Cube of %d is %d" \[
                        $n [expr $n*$n*$n]]       }
 2: Cube of -3 is -27
 3: Cube of 4 is 64
 4: Cube of -7 is -343
 5: Cube of 8 is 512
 6: % foreach n {-3 4 -7 8} {
 7:          puts [format "Cube of % d is % d" $n [expr $n*$n*$n]]
 8:       }
 9: Cube of -3 is -27
10: Cube of  4 is  64
11: Cube of -7 is -343
12: Cube of  8 is  512
13: %
```

A By default, the numbers are right-justified in their field width. The format specifier can be further qualified either to include the sign or use a space character to get the correct alignment. In line 7, % d is used to achieve correct alignment. Note the space between % and d.

8

Workshop

The quiz section is designed to provide you with an opportunity to recall some of the important concepts introduced in this hour. These may be commands, command syntax, common mistakes, usage, and so forth. The following exercises section helps you consolidate the material you learned with examples of practical value. The aim is that these two sections should reinforce the knowledge you have gained in this hour. The answers to the quiz that follows can be found in Appendix A, "Answers to Quizzes."

Quiz

1. What is returned by

   ```
   set s {Hello World}
   string index $s [expr [string length $s -1]]
   ```

2. What is the result of the command `string compare C A`?

3. In the command `regexp {([0-9]+)-.*-([0-9]+)}` `{The card expires on: 30-Aug-2001} ma A B`, what is stored in the variable B?

4. Write a regular expression to match the two integers in the string `set msg {He is aged 12 and weighs 55 Kg.}`.

5. Why doesn't the command `if {[string compare OK OK]} {puts Fine}` work as intended?

6. What is returned by the command `string match {[Yy]*} yes`?

Exercises

Solutions to the exercises are on the CD-ROM that accompanies this book.

1. Write a procedure to extract the first contiguous set of comment lines in a Tcl source file. For example, if a file contains the following lines

   ```
   # First Line
   # Second Line

   # This line is not shown
   ...
   ```

   only the first two lines are displayed.

2. Write a script to produce the following table:

x	sin(x)	cos(x)
0.0000	0.0000	1.0000
0.4000	0.3894	0.9211
0.8000	0.7174	0.6967
1.2000	0.9320	0.3624
1.6000	0.9996	−0.0292
2.0000	0.9093	−0.4161
2.4000	0.6755	−0.7374
2.8000	0.3350	−0.9422

3. A window title is of the form `set title {The file name is: example.tcl}`. The file name is always shown after the colon `:`. Write a `regsub` command to replace the file name by `new.tcl`.

HOUR 9

Interacting with the Operating System

In the last hour, you have learned about string manipulation, which is an important aspect of application development. A significant part of the application development involves manipulating files on the system. Typical tasks are opening an existing file or creating a file for storing the strings you have been manipulating. The ability to work seamlessly with the underlying operating system is one of the essential features of an interpreted environment.

Communicating with the operating system is an important aspect of Tcl programming that you need to master. Tcl provides excellent support for communicating with the operating system and handling file operations such as reading and writing files to various devices. A file on the disk is a special case of a device, and we will be concentrating on disk files only. In this hour, you learn

- To use file inquiry commands
- To open a file for reading and/or writing
- To open a file for random access

- To execute external programs from Tcl shell (tclsh or wish)

- To trap exceptional returns from scripts or procedures

File Inquiry Commands

These are Tcl commands that allow the user to query any of the several properties of a file such as the size, its extension, time last accessed, and so on. What is more important is that these properties can be inquired in a portable fashion across all the platforms. Some of the frequently used commands are shown in Listing 9.1. For the complete set of file commands, see the online manual.

We will start our discussion with a simple example to check whether a file with a particular name exists in the current working directory.

LISTING 9.1   Checking Whether a File Exists

```
 1: %if {[file exists playsound.tcl]} {
 2:         puts " playsound.tcl exists"
 3: } else {
 4:         puts " playsound.tcl is not in [pwd]" }
 5: playsound.tcl exists
 6: %cd ..
 7: %if {[file exists playsound.tcl]} {
 8:      puts " playsound.tcl exists"
 9: } else {
10:      puts " playsound.tcl is not in [pwd]" }
11: playsound.tcl is not in E:/
12:
```

ANALYSIS   In lines 1–4, we check for the existence of a file named playsound.tcl. If it exists, we just print a message to that effect. Otherwise, we print an appropriate message, reminding ourselves the name of the path of the working directory (line 4) using the command pwd. We change the directory (line 6) to exercise the else branch (lines 7–10).

Next, we introduce a couple of other file inquiry commands through a practical application. The task is to generate a filename that forms a sequence subject to the following conditions: If the file with given name exists and has a number at the end of the root (for example, for the file name, tmp18.dat, the root is tmp18), we increase it by 1 and return the new name (for example, tmp19.dat). If the file exists and has NO number at the end of the root (for example, tmp.dat), we append 1 to the root and return (for example, tmp1.dat). If the filename doesn't exist, we simply return the filename with no alteration.

> Some refer to the file root as base. Tcl uses the terminology root, and we
> follow the same convention here.

Let us write it as a procedure, so you can customize it to suit your particular needs.
The procedure is shown in Listing 9.2.

LISTING 9.2   Source Code for `autoIncr.tcl`

```
 1: #-----------------------------------------------------------------
 2: # Purpose:  Generate a new file name using a numbering scheme
 3: #
 4: # Input(s): fn  - a file name with an extension
 5: # Output   : newName
 6: #-----------------------------------------------------------------
 7: #
 8:
 9: proc autoIncr { fn } {
10:     # check if fn exists
11:     if { [file exists $fn] } {
12:         # get the base name
13:         set base [file rootname $fn]
14:         set ext  [file extension $fn] ;# includes the dot
15:         # does the base have one or more digits at the end
16:         if { [regexp {([0-9]+$)} $base match digs] } {
17:             set nn [incr digs]
18:             regsub {([0-9]+$)} $base $nn newBase
19:             set newName ${newBase}${ext} ;# no need for the dot
20:         } else {
21:             # just append 1 to the base
22:             set newName ${base}1${ext}
23:         }
24:     } else {
25:         set newName $fn
26:     }
27:     return $newName
28: }
```

ANALYSIS   The procedure has one argument `fn` (line 8). Let us assume that the procedure
is supplied a name such as `tmp18.dat` for illustration and that it exists in the
current directory. The bulk of the procedure consists of two tiers of `if` commands
(lines 10–25). If the file exists, there is a lot of work to do. First we get the root name
with the command `file root` (line 12) and assign it to the variable `base`. Note that the
short form of the subcommand is acceptable, as there is no ambiguity. Similarly, we
extract the extension in line 13. Note that the extension includes the period.

Now, on to the interesting bit. Because the file exists when we come into this branch, we need to deal with two cases. In the first case, when the base has a number at the end, we replace it by its incremented value (lines 16–17) and reconstruct the full name in line 18. (The regsub command is introduced in Hour 8, "Manipulating Strings.") In the second case, when base does not have a number at the end, we just append 1 to the base name (line 21), and the extension. The case when the file doesn't exist is straightforward (line 24). Finally, we return the $newName (line 26).

Lines 16–17 might be replaced by regsub {([0-9]+$)} $base {[expr \1 + 1]} newBase and subst $newBase. The former command generates a value such as tmp[expr 18 + 1] for the variable newBase, and the subst command evaluates the embedded command. See Hour 8 for an explanation of back references and the subst command. The choice of which one is efficient depends on how many files are processed this way. The procedure in action is shown in Listing 9.3.

LISTING 9.3   Automatically Generated New Filenames

```
 1: %dir t*.dat
 2: ./:
 3: tmp.dat     tmp18.dat
 4: %source autoIncr.tcl
 5: %autoIncr tmp18.dat
 6: tmp19.dat
 7: %autoIncr tmp.dat
 8: tmp1.dat
 9: %autoIncr temp.dat
10: temp.dat
11: %
```

ANALYSIS   Current directory contains two files as shown in line 3, which are used for illustrating autoIncr in action. First, we supply an existing filename (line 5), and as expected, our procedure has generated the required name tmp19.dat. Line 8 confirms the case of a filename that does not end in digits. Finally, for a non-existent file, we get the input name back.

TABLE 9.1   Some File Inquiry Commands

Command	Remarks
file delete ?-force? ?--? fName1 fName2	Deletes given files.
file exists fName	Returns 1 if it exists, 0 otherwise.
file extension fName	Returns all the characters after the last dot and inclusive of the dot. File need not exist.

Command	Remarks
file isdirectory *fName*	Returns 1 if *fName* is the name of a directory, 0 otherwise.
file join *name ?name?* ...	Joins the arguments using the platform-specific separator. For example, `file join a x y z` returns `a/x/y/z` on Windows and UNIX, a:x:y:z for Macintosh.
file mkdir *dName ?dName?* ...	Creates directories of given *dName(s)*.
file rootname *fName*	Returns all the characters excluding the dot. For example, `file rootname autoIncr.tcl` returns `autoIncr`.
file tail *fName*	Returns all the characters after the last path separator. For example, `file tail E:/Ch9/rd2.tcl` returns `rd2.tcl`.

9

Opening and Closing Files

Files on the system (or hard disk) can be opened for reading, writing, or appending using the open command. The same command is also used for opening command pipelines and communicating with serial ports.

▼ SYNTAX

The Syntax for open

The following code shows the syntax for open:

```
open fileName
```

```
open fileName access
```

The command returns a handle (or identifier) to refer to the file for subsequent reading and writing. The acceptable values for *access* modes are shown in Table 9.2. The access mode refers to the purpose for which the file is opened.

▲

TABLE 9.2   File Access Modes

Mode	What it does
r	Opens an existing file for reading.
r+	Opens an existing file for reading and writing.
w	Opens a file for writing. Create it if it doesn't exist.
w+	Opens a file for reading and writing. Create it if it doesn't exist.
a	Opens an existing file for writing only. New data is appended to the file at the end of the file. Access position is at the end.
a+	Opens the file for reading and writing. Create it if it doesn't exist. Access position is at end.

Let us look at a simple use of open. We open an existing file in the current directory and display its contents in the console. Just to distinguish our lines, we add some additional annotation text such as line *n*, where *n* is computed as we write each line to the console. Listing 9.4 shows the example dialogue.

> The file playsound.tcl in Listing 9.4 is used only for illustration. You can replace it with any other ASCII file.

LISTING 9.4   Opening a File for Reading

```
1: %set fh [open playsound.tcl]
2: filed58c10
3: %set num 1
4: 1
5: %while {[gets $fh Line] >= 0} {
6:      puts "Line $num: $Line"
7:      incr num   }
8: Line 1: button .b -text {Play Tw} -command PB
9: Line 2: pack .b
10: Line 3: proc PB {} {
11: Line 4: exec "C:\\Program Files\\Real\\RealPlayer\\realplay.exe"
"C:\\Courses\\DefTech\\Expert\\tw3_8bit.wav"
12: Line 5: }
13: %
```

ANALYSIS   In line 1, we invoke the open command supplying a name of an existing file. It will be an error to try and open a nonexisting file for reading. The return value from the open command is an identifier to the file, also referred to as a *file-handle*. When you have got a handle on an opened file, you can use it to get lines of text from the file. Note that we don't need to use the actual value for the file-handle such as in line 2. Those values are not easy to remember, and they change from run to run.

That is why we store that information in a variable such as fh. We define a counter num for numbering our lines. Lines 5–7 define a simple while loop to read the contents of the file. Let us look at the conditional in the while loop, gets $fh Line. This command gets a line from the file referred to by the identifier, $fh and stores the string in the variable Line. The return value from the command is the number of characters successfully read from $fh, and the return value provides a simple conditional for the while loop. Notice also that the blank lines return 0, and hence the equality in line 5.

The body of the while loop (lines 6–7) contains simple commands to write the line to the console (or standard output) and to increment the counter num. Incidentally, the contents of the file is a genuine Tcl program, and it does work! The Tk commands are explained in Hour 10, "Getting Started with Tk."

> The gets command returns everything in the line excluding the end-of-line characters.

Reading from and Writing to Files

Let us illustrate reading from and writing to a file with an example. The task is to open a Tcl source file and copy its contents to another file except for blank lines and comment lines. We allow the comment lines to begin in column one, possibly with leading blanks or tab characters.

LISTING 9.5 Source File rd2.tcl—Copy a File, Stripping Off Blank Lines and Comment Lines in that Process

```
 1: # Copy file contents throwing away
 2: # Tcl comments lines and blanks lines
 3:
 4: set fhIn [open rd2.tcl]
 5: set fhOut [open rd2Out.tcl w]
 6:
 7: #Keep reading all the lines
 8: while { [gets $fhIn inLine] >= 0 } {
 9:     if { [string length $inLine] > 0 } {
10:     # is it a comment line
11:     if { [regexp {^[\t ]*#(.*)} $inLine] != 1 } {
12:         puts $fhOut $inLine
13:     }
14:     }
15: }
16:
17: close $fhIn
18: close $fhOut
```

ANALYSIS We open a file for reading in line 4 and another file for writing to in line 5. As an example, we use the file rd2.tcl itself for processing. Note that we open the output file rd2Out.tcl explicitly for writing only using the mode letter w. We also use two separate handles $fhIn (for reading the input file) and $fhOut (for writing our processed lines). Note that in this mode, if the file already exists, it is overwritten. We read the file exactly as in Listing 9.4 using a while loop (lines 8–15).

Inside the while loop, we check for blank lines (line 9) and make sure that the line currently read in is not a comment line (line 11), using two separate if commands for clarity. It might be tempting in this example to combine the two checks into one, using a single if command as if { ([string length $inLine] > 0) ¦¦ ([regexp {^[\t]*#(.*)} $inLine] != 1) } { ... }. This will not work because the comment lines satisfy the first condition! The correct connective to use is && in place of ¦¦. Having weeded out the blank lines and comment lines, we write the line into rd2Out.tcl using the file-handle fhOut (line 12).

It is good practice to explicitly close the files you opened in an application. It is true that when the application exits, it generally closes all the opened files. Explicitly closing files in an application makes a clean exit. This is what lines 17–18 do.

> The close command takes only one argument.

LISTING 9.6   Output from rd2.tcl

```
 1: %source rd2.tcl
 2: %type rd2Out.tcl
 3: set fhIn [open rd2.tcl]
 4: set fhOut [open rd2Out.tcl w]
 5: while { [gets $fhIn inLine] >= 0 } {
 6:     if { [string length $inLine] > 0 } {
 7:         if { [regexp {^[\t ]*#(.*)} $inLine] != 1 } {
 8:             puts $fhOut $inLine
 9:         }
10:     }
11: }
12: close $fhIn
13: close $fhOut
14: %
```

ANALYSIS In line 1, we source the script in rd2.tcl. No output is returned from the script. We check the contents of the output file rd2Out.tcl in line 2 with the type command. On UNIX platforms, you can use either cat or more to check the contents of a file.

Advanced File Operations

In the examples we looked at so far, we have been accessing files sequentially. After we get a line from the file, the next gets command retrieves the following text. You can

9

think of it as an imaginary pointer moving down the file. You can get to line 5 without reading line 4. Tcl has three commands, eof, seek, and tell to support nonsequential access to files.

When a file is opened, by default the contents are accessible from the beginning. Each file has an associated *access position* that can be set with the seek command; whereas the tell command gives us the current access position. The dialogue in Listing 9.7 illustrates the basic use of these commands. Table 9.3 gives a subset of File I/O commands (see the online manual for more details).

TABLE 9.3 Basic File I/O Commands

Command	Remarks
eof *fH*	Returns 1 if an end-of-file has occurred, 0 otherwise
read *fH nBytes*	Reads *nBytes* from *fH*
seek *fH* offset *?origin?*	Moves access position to *?origin?*+offset
tell *fH*	Returns current access position in *fH*

LISTING 9.7 Using read, seek, and tell

```
 1: %set fh [open sample.txt]
 2: filee621f0
 3: %read $fh 5
 4: avunc
 5: %seek $fh 0
 6: %read $fh 10
 7: avuncular
 8:
 9: %tell $fh
10: 10
11: %read $fh 10
12: backboard
13:
14: %tell $fh
15: 21
16: seek $fh 21
17: read $fh 10
18:
19: axiomatic
20: %
```

ANALYSIS In line 1, we open the file sample.txt to experiment with it. The contents of the file are shown in Figure 9.1. We set the access position at 2 bytes (shown as a hollow arrow in Figure 9.1), and after reading 3 bytes, the access position moves to the end of letter *c* (shown as a solid arrow in Figure 9.1). Line endings are platform dependent and are shown canonically as one empty square.

FIGURE 9.1

Nonsequential access of files.

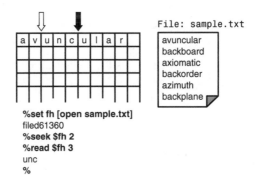

```
%set fh [open sample.txt]
filed61360
%seek $fh 2
%read $fh 3
unc
%
```

When we open a file, the access position is at the beginning. In line 3, we read 5 bytes from it. As expected, we got the first five characters. Note that each character is one byte. We change the access position to the beginning (line 5) and read the first word inclusive of carriage return/line feed characters. As expected, we got the return character along with our word (lines 9–10).

We check where we are with the command `tell` in line 11. Now the access position is at 10. Next we read another 10 bytes to read the next word together with carriage return (lines 14–15). To read the third word, we change the access position to 21 and read 10 bytes as in lines 16–19. Note that the word contains a newline character at the beginning, which can be removed either with a regular expression or using appropriate string commands.

On UNIX platforms, each line is terminated with a single newline character, \n. In view of that, access positions need to be computed accordingly.

Next we look at reading the whole file in one go and processing the contents using list operations.

LISTING 9.8   Read the File in One Go

```
1: %set fh [open sample.txt]
2: filed685c8
3: %set fSize [file size sample.txt]
4: 66
```

```
5: %set contents [split [read $fh $fSize] \n]
6: avuncular backboard axiomatic backorder azimuthal backplane {}
7: %
```

ANALYSIS Let us open the file `sample.txt` afresh (line 1) for this experiment. Otherwise, we might be reading the file from somewhere in the middle or from the end! You have learned that the `read` command accepts an optional size argument. So, why not determine the size with file inquiry command, and pass that value to it? This way, the whole file can be read in one go. Reading the file specifying a size value (that is, number of bytes to read) is much faster.

The next task would be to identify the individual lines. To extract lines of the file, we deploy the `split` command (see Hour 8) using `\n` as the split character. This results in a list, and we are home and dry. There is of course that little null string at the end, which can be removed in several ways. The simplest way is to extract items first through last but one from the list with the command `lrange $contents 0 [expr [llength $contents] -2]`.

> The command `read fileHandle` without any size specified reads the complete file, but will be slower, particularly when reading large files.

Executing System Commands

There might be occasions when you want to execute operating system commands from your application or in interactive use. For example, you might want to copy a file.

Operating system commands can be issued from the Tcl shell (tclsh or wish). For example, to list the contents of a file on a UNIX platform, you can invoke `cat fileName` and the contents are displayed in the shell. On Windows, you could invoke `type fileName` to achieve a similar effect. We give an example in Listing 9.9 to highlight some of the subtle differences between using system commands and Tcl commands. (You need to use the wish shell for the commands to work as stated here.)

> On UNIX platforms, `type operand` is a utility that returns a description of how *operand* would be interpreted if used as a command, and it does not produce a listing of the contents of a file.

LISTING 9.9   glob Versus dir Commands

```
1: %set files1 [dir *.txt]
2: ./:
3: ans.txt      junk1.txt  junk2.txt  qanda.txt  qq.txt      sample.txt
4: %set files2 [glob *.txt]
5: qq.txt ans.txt junk1.txt junk2.txt qanda.txt sample.txt
6: %list [llength $files1] [llength $files2]
7: 7 6
8: %
```

ANALYSIS   In line 1, we invoke the DOS command `dir` to list the names of the files in the current directory. Note that `dir` is NOT a tcl command. (There is no documentation for it!) When Tcl encounters a command that it doesn't know about, it passes the command and the arguments to `exec`, which in turn runs it as an application program. The beauty of it is the result from the command can be assigned to a Tcl variable and processed further.

Beware of some subtle points though. The return value might contain extra information as in lines 2–3. If you are using the length of the list `files1` to determine the number of files, you need to do some extra work. Let us compare this command with a similar Tcl command (and more general) to list the files in the current directory. The command `glob` takes a glob-style pattern (see Hour 8) as an input argument. In line 4, we use the wild card * to match one or more characters. Notice the difference in the lengths of lists `$files1` and `$files2`.

Protect the square brackets by enclosing them inside braces when specifying a range of characters in glob-style patterns. For example, to list the files that begin with a or s and end with any extension, the command `glob` `*.*` will raise an error.

On several machines, as happens to be the name of an executable file (typically assembler program). Remember that the square brackets perform a command evaluation. These commands are not necessarily Tcl commands, and they could be any system commands.

The correct way of listing the desired files is to use the command `glob` `{`*.*`}`. See also Hour 8 for some more examples of the `glob` command.

exec command

The exec command is used to execute programs that are external to Tcl.

9

The Syntax for exec

The following code shows the syntax for exec.

```
exec ?switches? arg ?arg ...?
```

The first arg, arg, is treated as a command and the remaining args are arguments to that command, and executed in a subprocess. The possible values for ?switches? are -keepnewline, to preserve the newline in from subprocess's output; and --, to mark the end of options.

For a simple illustration of the exec command, let us consider invoking RealPlayer (http://www.real.com), which can be used to play various types of sound files. The sound file tw3_8bit.wav is used as an example. You can replace it by any other .wav file you may have.

LISTING 9.10 Invoking External Application Programs

```
1: %exec {C:\Program Files\Real\RealPlayer\realplay.exe}  tw3_8bit.wav
2: %
```

ANALYSIS When invoking external programs, there are two important points you should remember. The first is that it is safe to specify the full path of the executable. If it is not either fully qualified or not defined in your environment variables, the exec command will fail. The second point is the path separator.

On PCs that use a back slash as a separator for directories, you need to suppress its special meaning. This can be done in three ways. Either enclose the whole path inside curly braces or double them up as in "C:\\Program Files\\Real\\RealPlayer\\realplay.exe". Alternatively, you can use the forward slash and let the Tcl shell convert them to the correct path separator. You can store the name of the program and files in Tcl variables and pass them to exec as

```
1: set soundFile {tw3_8bit.wav}
2: set prog {C:\Program Files\Real\RealPlayer\realplay.exe}
3: exec $pro $soundFile
```

On UNIX platforms, you have a command by the same name exec provided by the operating system shell. The Tcl command doesn't use the shell. It IS a pure Tcl command.

For additional examples of exec, see Hour 19, "Creating Tcl/Tk Interfaces to Legacy Applications."

> You can execute the programs in the background by including the ampersand (&) at the end of the argument list for exec. For example, exec winhlp32.exe {E:\TclTk81\Tcl\doc\tcl81.hlp} & will release the console for other operations.

Unknown Commands

The main mechanism for dealing with foreign commands is the use of the Tcl procedure unknown. In simple terms, this procedure runs the unknown command and its arguments through exec, passing all the arguments supplied.

> Issue the command info body unknown to learn more about how unknown commands are processed. This is also a good way of picking up new Tcl idioms.

Catching Errors

What happens when errors occur? In the interactive mode, the interpreter raises an error message and returns the control back to the user immediately. The user then can rectify the error condition and rerun the command. When the error occurs in a command in a procedure, both the command and the procedure in which it was used are aborted. Errors cause applications to be aborted because there is no sensible way to proceed further.

However, some errors are called *exceptions* that can be caught by the application and proceed with the application, in an appropriate manner. For example, inquiring the value of a nonexistent variable causes a script to be aborted. We might like to catch this error and to use a default action such as executing another script. This is achieved with the catch command.

The Syntax for catch

The following code shows the syntax for catch:

```
catch script ?varName?
```

Returns 1 if there is an error while evaluating the *script* and stores the message in *?varName?*. If there is no error, returns zero and stores the result of evaluating *script* in *?varName?*.

For this exercise, we will be using the built-in Tcl command `catch`. It is important that you understand how this works. To avoid any untoward errors, start this example in a fresh Tcl shell (tclsh or wish). That way you will avoid the variables used in the earlier examples. You can also `unset` the offending variable. In this case, `unset animSpeed`, if you believe you might have used it. Listing 9.11 shows an example.

LISTING 9.11 Catching Errors

```
 1: %if { [catch {set animSpeed} msg] } {
 2:        set animSpeed 10.5
 3:    } else {
 4:        puts "Animation speed is $msg"
 5:    }
 6: 10.5
 7: %set animSpeed 25.2
 8: 25.2
 9: %if { [catch {set animSpeed} msg] } {
10:        set animSpeed 10.5
11:    } else {
12:        puts "Animation speed is $msg"
13:    }
14: Animation speed is 25.2
15: %
```

ANALYSIS If you are trying this example, open a fresh console or make sure that the variable `animSpeed` is not defined before. Remember that you can `unset` `animSpeed`, if you happen to have one such variable.

Let us look at the `if` command block in lines 1-5. First time round, the `catch` command returns 1 because inquiring the value of a nonexistent variable is an error. The corresponding error message is saved in the variable `msg`. Our default action here is to give a default value to the variable as in line 2. Next, we would like to see what happens to our `if` block when the variable exists.

To convince ourselves, we change the value of `animSpeed` (line 7) and reinvoke the `if` block. This time, the `catch` command returns zero, and the `else` branch taken. Because the variable `animSpeed` exists, `catch` stores the result of the caught operation in the variable `msg`. In this example, `msg` contains the value 25.2, and hence the output in line 14.

To summarize, when the command successfully executes, `catch` fails, returns 0, and places the return value from the command in the variable `msg`. When the command fails—that is, raises an exception—`catch` succeeds and returns 1 and then assigns the error message to the variable `msg`.

Do	Don't
Do remember to protect square brackets when using glob-style patterns for searching files. **Do** close the files you have opened. **Do** catch the errors when using system commands.	**Don't** use exec date command on Windows. The Tcl shell tries to execute the Windows system command to reconfigure date and time information. Exec returns immediately and there is no opportunity for you to enter the information.

Summary

In this hour, we introduced two broad categories of commands. The first category deals with file operations. The second group of commands is related to executing application programs that are external to Tcl.

The next important topic in this group is handling exceptional conditions raised by procedures or scripts when they abort. Such errors are trapped by the catch command. This is very handy in that, when the command does catch an exception, it returns the error message in a variable; and when the command succeeds, the result of the caught command is stored in the same variable.

With this hour, we have covered all the basic concepts of Tcl. Now is the time to put all your Tcl knowledge into practice and develop interactive applications using widgets. What are they? Read on.

Q&A

Q How do I check the end-of-file?

A The end-of-file can be checked using the command eof *fileHandle*. For example, you can open a file for reading and keep getting a line until end-of-file is true. The following script shows an example:

```
1: %set fh [open qanda.txt]
2: %while { ![eof $fh] } {
3:       gets $fh Line
4:       puts "qanda.txt: $Line"
5:    }
6: qanda.txt: What does Tk stand for?
```

```
7: qanda.txt: </Question>
8: qanda.txt: <Answer>
9: ...
```

Q Why can't I invoke the DOS command cd with exec cd?

A The simple answer is cd happens to be a Tcl command. See the manual page for further information. The long answer is that the DOS commands on NT are invoked through the executable cmd.exe as exec cmd.exe cd.

Workshop

The following "Quiz" section is designed to provide you with an opportunity to recall some of the important concepts introduced in this hour. These might be commands, command syntax, common mistakes, usage, and so on. The "Exercises" section following the "Quiz" section helps you consolidate the material you learned via an example of practical value. Our aim is that these two sections should reinforce the knowledge you have gained in this hour. The answers to the quiz that follows can be found in Appendix A, "Answers to Quizzes."

Quiz

1. How do you open a file for writing?

2. Does gets $fh read blank lines in a file?

3. What does gets fileHandle Line return?

4. What is stored in the variable msg after executing the following sequence of commands?

   ```
   set x 2
   catch {incr x} msg
   ```

5. A file contains a single character followed by a return character. What is the size of the file?

Exercises

Solutions to the exercises are on the CD-ROM that accompanies this book.

1. Open a file of the form

   ```
   <Question>
   What does Tk stand for?
   </Question>
   <Answer>
   Toolkit
   </Answer>
   <Question>
   ```

```
Who is the creator of Tcl/Tk?
</Question>
<Answer>
John Ousterhout
</Answer>
...
```

and write the questions and answers to separate files appropriately numbered in the order read.

2. Write a procedure to create a subdirectory under the current directory if it doesn't exist, and then set the current directory to it. If it does exist, just move into that directory. Trap the condition of accidentally supplying the name of a file for the name of a subdirectory.

3. Write a script to list all files with zero size. (Create some zero size files with `foreach f {dum1 dum2 dum3} { open $f w }`, if you haven't got any.)

PART II
The Toolkit (Tk)

Hour

HOUR 10

Getting Started with Tk

The last eight hours provided you with a solid grounding in using the Tool Command Language—perhaps the most popular, versatile, and established scripting language in existence for gluing applications together to create a productive application environment.

The advent of the WIMP-based (Windows, Icons, Menus, and Pointer) desktop has established an expectation, even a *de facto* standard, for desktop applications. They must conform to WIMP-based graphical user interfaces (GUI) in providing an application-user front-end. Tcl caters to the programmer's need for developing graphical user interface front-ends for applications via the Tk toolkit. Beginning in this hour, you will progress toward becoming a confident Tk-based GUI builder, who can deploy your knowledge to develop any sort of interactive application.

The objectives of this hour are to teach you

- What Tk widgets are available
- How to create Tk widgets
- How to put Tk widgets together to create an application's user interface

- What a window manager is and its relationship to your application
- How to use Tk window manager commands to customize the appearance of your application

In Hour 11, "Adding Behavior to Your Widgets," you will learn how to customize the individual user-interface components, widgets, to look and behave the way you want them to.

Understanding the Toolkit (Tk)

The Tk extends Tcl and provides user interface controls for the development of Tcl-based GUI applications. It defines generic widget classes that determine appearance and behavior. For instance, `button`, `radiobutton`, and `checkbutton` might belong to the Tk button class. Each Tk widget, as mentioned already, is a window and is uniquely identified by its name. The name of a widget reflects the hierarchy within which the widget is placed. For instance, the widget name `.first.nextwidget` refers to a widget, `nextwidget`. This `nextwidget` is the child of a widget called `first`, which in turn is the child of the main widget, `.`. Each application has its own main `.` window. In other words, a Tk application is synonymous with the single-widget hierarchy of the main window and its children. This application widget hierarchy is analogous to a tree structure. (For a typical example of a widget hierarchy, see Figure 10.5.)

Tk Widgets

Tk provides classes of widgets such as buttons; scrollbars; lists; pull-down, pop-up, and option menus; the text widget; and the canvas widget. It also provides container widgets such as toplevel and frame widgets. Tk also provides commands to create and manipulate widgets.

The Tk widget commands are categorized into four groups:

- Commands for creating and deleting widgets
- Commands for communicating geometry management of individual groups of widgets
- Commands associated with each individual widget in a widget hierarchy of an application
- Commands for communication between widgets, between widgets and application data, and with other applications

In this hour, you will explore the first two of these four groups of commands. The last two groups will be discussed in Hour 11.

Even though the window manager commands are members of the communication class, in this hour, you will be provided with a complete picture of the geometry management of windows/widgets.

Widget Creation and Deletion Commands

The Tk widget creation command is of the form

```
widgetClass pathName ?option value?
```

In the previous line, `widgetClass` refers to the generic widget (button). The argument `pathName` is the name of this particular widget. Note that this `pathName` is actually its hierarchy, as we mentioned earlier. The option-value pairs are used to customize the widget's appearance and (where applicable) its behavior. Whenever a widget is created, Tk also creates a Tcl command for that widget. This command is known as the widget command, and its name is given by `pathName`.

For instance, the script line

```
button .but -text "I am a Tk button" -foreground green
```

creates a button named `.but`. It has the textual label `"I am a Tk button"` and the foreground color `green`.

At the same time, a command by the name `.but` is also created. You use this command to invoke any *action* on the widget. In this book, we refer to these widget manipulation commands as action subcommands. For example, if you want to change the foreground color to `red`, you use the most frequently used action subcommand `configure`. This is a typical Tcl command and takes the form `pathName configure ?option value?`. If an option is not specified, default values will be used. In Hour 11, you will learn to use this `configure` command, not just to set the options, but also to get the current value of each.

The concepts of hierarchy, inheritance, and class methods apply to Tk widgets. As a result, some options are common to all the widget classes, and some are specific to widgets belonging to a particular class.

Use the command `destroy pathName` to delete the named widget.

Bear in mind that the `destroy` command will destroy a widget and all its descendants.

Widget names cannot begin with an uppercase letter.

10

Creating a widget is a separate process from making it appear on the screen. Widgets appear on the screen when they are managed using a geometry manager. For this reason, it is useful to get into geometry management straightaway so that you can begin to create and visualize the Tk widgets.

Geometry Management

Tk provides three types of general-purpose GUI layout management. These are the Grid, the Placer, and the Packer. The creation and geometry management of Tk widgets are better explained with some interactive examples. Start a wish shell and try executing the various small sections of scripts shown in Listings 10.1–10.3.

The Grid Command

The Tk Grid geometry manager arranges slave widgets in rows and columns inside a master. The grid command grid slave ?option value? is used to communicate with the Grid geometry manager.

LISTING 10.1   Arranging Three Buttons Using the Grid Manager

```
1: % button .biscuit -text Biscuits
2: .biscuit
3: % button .coffee -text coffee
4: .coffee
5: % button .tea -text tea
6: .tea
7: % grid .biscuit -column 0 -row 0
8: % grid .coffee -column 0 -row 1
9: % grid .tea -column 0 -row 2
```

ANALYSIS   The left screenshot in Figure 10.1 shows the result of executing the previous lines of Tk script. Let us quickly analyze each line. Recall that widgetClass pathName ?option value? creates an instance of a widget named pathName of the type widgetClass and returns the widget's name. The interpreter parses each option specified, in turn, and assigns the value specified for this option. Lines 1, 3, and 5 create three button widgets. The first of these is called .biscuit. Its text is the string "Biscuits". It is the child of the application's main window, which is reflected in its name .biscuit. The interpreter returns the name of the widget it created, as shown in line 2. The second and third buttons, .coffee and .tea, are also children of the main window.

Lines 7–9 execute the grid command `grid slave -column n -row n` to arrange the buttons in a single column. Take note that the column and row numbering start from zero.

> In this example, we have not explicitly specified the master in which the slave should be packed. Tk automatically treats the parent of the slave as the master in such cases. Note that the master has to exist in this case before the slave is created and arranged.

Note that you can just as easily vary the column as you have varied the value of the row in the previous example. This is achieved by using the grid configure command `grid configure slave ?option value?`, as shown in Listing 10.2.

10

LISTING 10.2   Using the Grid Configure Command

```
1:% grid configure .coffee -column 1 -row 0
2: % grid configure .tea -column 2 -row 0
```

The result of the previous commands is shown in the middle screenshot of Figure 10.1. The right image in Figure 10.1 shows yet another grid setting reconfiguration given in Listing 10.3.

LISTING 10.3   Using Grid Configure to Rearrange a Row Column (Version 2)

```
1: % grid configure .coffee -column 1 -row 1
2: %grid configure .tea -column 2 -row 2
```

> If you fail to specify the row column options, the default grid placement is to place the slaves right-to-left, column-wise.

FIGURE **10.1**

*The Grid geometry
manager.*

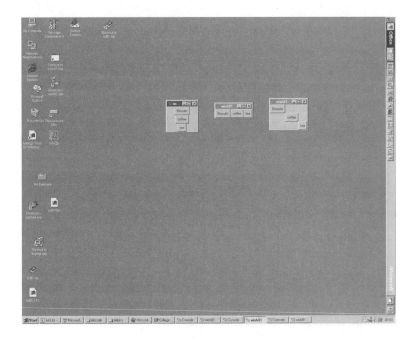

You can use other combinations to specify the positioning of the slaves using the option value pairs. For instance, by default, the command `grid slave slave -column m -row n` places the second slave in the parent of the first. The command `grid slave slave -in anotherMaster -column n -row n` changes this default and places the second slave in `anotherMaster`.

The master has to be either the parent of the slave or the descendant of the parent of the slave.

The grid algorithm works by requesting the master to change its size to the combined size of all its slaves. One of the admissible options is Propagate. If this option is set to the value 0, it disables the capability of the master to change its size. Consider this option if you want to ensure that the master window does not change its size.

In Tk, the most recently created widget has the highest stacking order. Use this fact when you want to place a slave in a master that is not its parent. Create the master before the slave to ensure that the master doesn't obscure the slave.

If you fail to specify the row column options, the default grid placement places the slaves right-to-left, column-wise.

The Placer

The *Placer geometry manager* is a simple Tk geometry manager that provides fixed or rubber-sheet type placement of a slave window within its master. With the Placer, you can specify the size and location of the slave, either in exact terms within the master or in terms of the dimensions of the master. In the latter case, when there are changes in the size of the master, the slave changes size and location in response. You can, of course, mix these styles of placement, for instance specifying that the slave always has a fixed width and height, but is always centered inside the master.

LISTING 10.4   Using the Place Command

```
1: %button .b1 -text button1
2: .b1
3: %radiobutton .b2 -text button2 -variable radvar
4: .b2
5: %checkbutton .b3 -text button3 -variable chkvar
6: .b3
7: % place .b1 -x 0 -y 0
8: % place .b2 -x 50 -y 0
9: % place .b3 -relx 0.25 -rely 0.1
10: %label .l -text "Type in your name: "
11: .l
12: % entry .e -relief sunken -bd 2 -width 20 -textvariable  entvar
13: .e
14: % place .l -relx 0.1 -x 10 -rely 0.7 -y 6
15: % place .e -relx 0.4 -x 60 -rely 0.7 -y 6
```

ANALYSIS   Listing 10.4 introduces you to the radiobutton, checkbutton, label, and entry widgets. Note how the command widgetClass pathName ?option value? is used to create a widget instance of the type widgetClass. The radiobutton is used to enable the user to make a one-of-many choice. The checkbuttons enable many-of-many choices. The label widget has no behavior. In this case, you are using the label as annotation to the entry widget. The entry widget is used to get single or multiline text/string input from the user.

In lines 3, 5, and 12, while creating the radiobuttons and checkbuttons and the entry widgets, we use the option -variable with a variableName as its value. When the user selects these buttons, the choice associated with a button is assigned to that variable. Now your script can use the current value of this variable elsewhere. In the case of the entry widget, the input from the user (his name in this instance) is stored in the variable entvar.

We now will explore the placement of these widgets using the Placer. Figure 10.2 shows the placement scheme used by the Placer geometry manager.

FIGURE **10.2**

*A schematic diagram
of various location
options used by geom-
etry managers.*

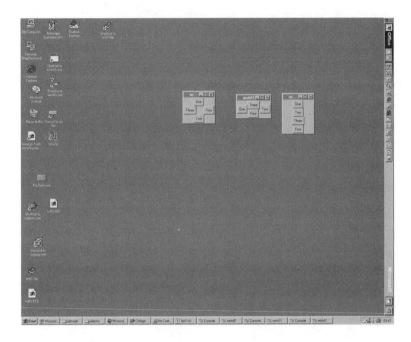

In your script, button .b1 is placed at the top-left corner of its master. Line 8 specifies
the x and y coordinates of the placement anchor point for the top-left corner of the button
b2. These values are specified in screen units (for example, pixel coordinates) and are relative to the master's. In line 9, the placement positions are specified as a proportion of
the master widget's dimensions. Script lines 14 and 15 instruct the Placer to locate the
label and entry widgets side by side. The combination of -rely 0.7 -y 6 is interpreted
as 6 pixel units from the left of the position marked by 0.7 times the vertical dimension
of the master. The positioning along the X direction is also interpreted similarly. Figure
10.3 shows the various widgets introduced by the script in Listing 10.4.

The Packer

The *Packer geometry manager* is the most commonly used geometry manager. It provides powerful, dynamic geometry management. The Packer is analogous to packing a
suitcase. When you have packed one or more slaves in the master (items in your suitcase
analogy), there will be a rectangular spare area called a *cavity* left in the master. When
another request for packing is received, the Packer allocates a subspace of the cavity
called a *parcel* for the slave. The Packer decides one of the dimensions of this parcel
from the available space within the master and the other from the requested size of the
slave. As the third and final step, the slave is slotted into its parcel. The syntax for the
pack command is: pack slave slave ?option value?.

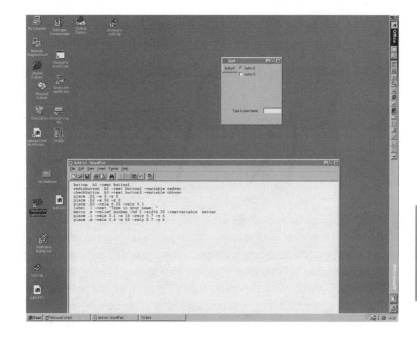

The options are -after, -before, -side, -anchor, -expand, -in, and -fill. The options -before and -after take the name of another window and insert all the slaves either before or after it. Pack uses the master of this other window as the master for packing all the slaves. The -anchor option specifies the gravity or anchor, such as north, south, or center of the parcel, to position the slave in its allocated slot. For instance, the value center will place the slave at the center of its parcel. The default gravity is the center. The -side option specifies that a parcel for a slave should be allocated in the specified side of the available space within the master. The admissible values are top, bottom, left, and right. The value for the -expand option is a boolean—0, 1, no, or yes. This will instruct the slave whether it expands to occupy extra space in the master when the master's size changes. The -fill option specifies how the slave is stretched (if it is) to include its contents. The admissible values are none, x, y, or both.

Here again, these concepts associated with the pack command are better demonstrated by executing the sample scripts given in Listing 10.5. For an excellent tour of packing widgets, visit the URL referred to in the "Exercises" section.

LISTING 10.5 The Pack Command

```
 1: button .c -text "One"
 2: .c
 3: button .m -text "Two"
 4: .m
 5: button .o -text "Three"
 6: .o
 7: button .r -text "Four"
 8: .r
 9: foreach win {.c .m .o .r} s {top bottom left right} {
10:        pack $win -side $s
11: }
```

ANALYSIS Lines 1, 3, 5, and 7 are rapidly becoming familiar for creating four button windows whose names are .c, .m, .o, and .r. Each of these widgets has its -text option set to the names of different numbers. In line 9, we use a single foreach loop iterating through two lists, the first of which is a list of the names of the widgets. The second contains the values for the -side option. The body of the foreach loop consists of a single script line to pack each widget with its packing side option given by the elements of the second list. The result is shown on the left of Figure 10.3.

Listing 10.6 is a continuation of Listing 10.5. You can execute the code interactively at the wish shell command prompt. Note how the bottom widget, .r, is placed at the center of its parcel. The primary reason for trying this interactively is to see how the Packer allocates the parcel. Try changing the widget text labels to smaller or larger strings.

If you are not executing this script interactively, please ensure you create the widgets by copying lines 1, 3, 5, and 7 of Listing 10.5. Skip the first line of Listing 10.6.

LISTING 10.6 The Pack Command

```
1: %pack forget .c .m .o .r
2: %foreach win {.c .m .o .r} s {left right top bottom} {
3:    pack $win -side $s
4:    }
```

ANALYSIS Line 1 uses the pack command with an action to forget the previous packing order assigned. You need to execute this command to refresh the packing order and make the Packer reallocate the parcels again. Lines 2–4 are similar to lines 9–11 in Listing 10.4, except that we have reordered the values of the -side option. The Packer essentially rearranges the widgets to produce the middle screenshot shown in Figure 10.3.

Let us try just one more arrangement. The reason you are being asked to try several of these arrangements is to emphasize how important it is to understand how the Packer works. You are more likely to use the Packer than any of the other geometry managers, because of its power and flexibility in laying out and managing groups of widgets.

LISTING 10.7 The Pack Command

```
1: %pack forget .c .m .o .r
2: %pack .c
3: %pack .r -side bottom
4: %pack .m -after .c
5: %pack .o -before .r
```

ANALYSIS Again, we assume that you are executing the script as a continuation of Listing 10.5. If not, remember to create the widgets (lines 1, 3, 5, and 7 of Listing 10.5). Line 1 in Listing 10.7 executes the pack subcommand `forget` once again to unpack the widgets. Remember to do this whenever you want to explore other options for achieving an ordered packing.

> Note that using `pack forget slave` does not destroy the slave, just unpacks it. So you don't have to recreate the slave to repack it.

In line 2, we pack `.c` with all default options. So it gets packed centred at the top. By default, the cavity management, GUI and>is the area below `.c`.

> In general, the Packer shrink-wraps the master around the slave widgets as they get packed. In this example, the master is the main `wish` shell, which has a defined minimum dimension based on its window's top border icons. The blank spaces on either side of `.c` are its parcel rather than the cavity in the master. For more information, see the "Exercises" section.

In line 3, we packed the widget `.r` with `-side` set to `bottom`. The last two lines, 4 and 5, instruct the Packer to pack `.m` after `.c` and `.o` after `.r`. The result is the right-most image in the screenshot shown in Figure 10.4.

FIGURE **10.4**

Results from various packing orders of four buttons.

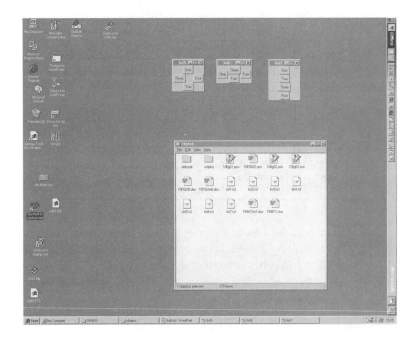

An Application

You will often group widgets into organizational units that require different types of geometry management. For instance, you might want certain groups of widgets to remain the same size, whereas others to expand in a particular fashion. You might also want to add a few options that make the appearance of the application more attractive. In this section, you will develop a simple application that introduces the Tk frame, a container widget, and additional options of the Packer.

Copy Listing 10.8 in a Tcl script file and execute it from a `wish` command prompt by sourcing the file.

Recall from Hour 1, "What Is Tcl/Tk?" that for Tk applications, you can use either file name extension `.tcl` or `.tk`. It is a matter of personal preference.

When you execute a Tk application from a source file, the interpreter usually returns only the return value of the last command. So you might not get to see the widget or path names of each widget or window returned as they are created. That happens only when you are executing each widget creation interactively at the command prompt.

In this simple application, you will create three groups of widgets. Each of the first two groups contains a label and an entry. The third group has three buttons. Each group is created as a child of a `frame` widget. Each `frame` is a child of the main window. The schematic diagram, Figure 10.5, shows the window hierarchy.

FIGURE 10.5

The widget hierarchy of the group of widgets in Listings 10.8 and 10.9.

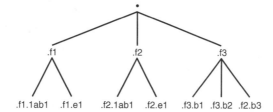

The simplest script to create the hierarchy of Tk widgets is given in Listing 10.8.

LISTING 10.8 Packing a Group of Widgets (Version 1)

```
1: frame .f1
2: pack .f1
3: frame .f2
4: pack .f2
5: frame .f3 -bd 2 -relief groove
6: pack .f3 -after .f2  -side bottom
7:
8: label .f1.lab1 -text "Userid: "
9: entry .f1.e1 -width 12
10: pack .f1.lab1 -side left
11: pack .f1.e1 -side left
12:
13: label .f2.lab1 -text "Password: "
14: entry .f2.e1 -width 12
15: pack .f2.lab1 -side left
16: pack .f2.e1 -side left
17:
18: button .f3.b1 -text Submit
19: button .f3.b2 -text Cancel
20: button .f3.b3 -text Help
21: pack .f3.b1 .f3.b2 .f3.b3 -side left
```

ANALYSIS Lines 1, 3, and 5 use the Tk `widget creation` command to create the three widgets `.f1`, `.f2`, and `.f3` of the widget class `frame`. You have used the default top packing of these frames into their parent master, the main window in lines 2, 4, and 6. Note that the `-after` option is somewhat redundant. You have specified that frame `.f3` is packed with `-side` option set to `bottom`. This will ensure that, if the user resizes the

10

main window of your application, the last group of widgets will always be placed along the bottom, retaining visual consistency.

Lines 8–11 and 13–16 perform similar tasks. Each set of these lines creates a label widget (.f1.lab1 and .f2.lab1) and an entry widget (.f1.e1 and .f2.e1) and packs them into their parent master with the -side option set to left and the packing master set to their parents, .f1 and .f2, respectively. The text of the labels .f1.lab1 and .f2.lab1 are "Userid" and "Password", respectively. The entry widgets are assigned a width of 12 characters each.

You then create three buttons, .f3.b1, .f2.b2, and .f3.b3 (in lines 18–20). These, too, are packed into their parent master .f3 starting from the left.

> Note that when you specify a number of slaves to be packed using a single pack command, the Packer traverses left to right for the packing order.

The result of executing this script is shown in the left-hand image of Figure 10.6. Your immediate reaction on seeing that screenshot, we guess, will be to wonder how to align the entry widgets to improve the visual appeal. The script in Listing 10.9, which follows, will achieve that goal. Please note that the script in Listing 10.9 is identical to that in Listing 10.8, except for the highlighted changes. You can copy or directly amend your previous script.

LISTING 10.9   Packing Group of Widgets (Version 2)

```
 1: frame .f1
 2: pack .f1
 3: frame .f2
 4: pack .f2 -after .f1
 5: frame .f3 -bd 2 -relief groove
 6: pack .f3 -after .f2  -side bottom
 7:
 8: label .f1.lab1 -text "Userid: "
 9: entry .f1.e1 -width 12
10: pack .f1.lab1 -side left -in .f1
11: pack .f1.e1 -side left -in .f1
12:
13: label .f2.lab1 -text "Password: "
14: entry .f2.e1 -width 12
15: pack .f2.lab1 -side left -in .f2
16: pack .f2.e1 -side left -in .f2
17:
18: button .f3.b1 -text Submit
19: button .f3.b2 -text Cancel
```

```
20: button .f3.b3 -text Help
21:
22: pack .f3.b1 .f3.b2 -ipadx 2 -pady 1 -ipady 1 -side left -in .f3
23: pack .f3.b3 -side right -in .f3
24: pack configure .f3.b3 -ipadx 2 -pady 1 -ipady 1
25: pack configure .f1 .f2 -pady 10
26: pack configure .f1 .f2 -anchor e
```

ANALYSIS By default, the button widgets were packed shrink-wrapped in the initial configuration. Tk provides Packer options to request extra padding of space in and around the slaves. The external padding options, *-padx* and *-pady,* force the Packer to allocate a larger than required parcel for the slave, so that there will be extra spacing around the slave and its neighbors. The *internal* padding options, -ipadx and -ipady, enlarge the slave by the requested spacing, as well as allocate additional parcels for it.

The values for these padding options are given in terms of all acceptable forms of screen units. You use combinations of external and internal padding to space out the buttons .f3.b1 and .f3.b2 while packing them in line 22 and while packing button .f3.b3 in line 24. In line 25, you request external spacing of 10 pixels along the y direction for the frames .f1 and .f2 using -ipady, thereby creating some vertical spacing between the three groups of widgets. Note that you use the pack configure command to achieve much of this padding. This illustrates this command's use in rearranging the packed slaves.

You must still solve the nonalignment of the two groups of label and entry widgets. The last command in script line 26 achieves this alignment. Recall the -anchor option, mentioned in the section on the Packer geometry manager. Here that anchor is set to e for the parent masters .f1 and .f2 of the label and entry widgets. This ensures that these widgets move right as you drag the main window to the right using the mouse pointer. The image second from the left in Figure 10.6 shows this improved interface.

As you move and resize the main window, you might notice that, unfortunately, the button widgets can get completely squashed to a slit, as shown in the third image from the left in Figure 10.6. If you want to ensure that these widgets always remain visible in a legible form, you should pack these before you pack all the other widgets. An exercise that follows the hour provides a drill to do this.

When you create a customized, dialog-box type application, as you did earlier, you might want to ensure that the applications window remains a fixed size so that no distortion of the widget placements takes place (as it did in the rightmost image in Figure 10.6). One way of achieving this is to disable the -propagate option, selectively.

However, if you want to apply resize restrictions globally to the toplevel application window or even add decorations, you will need to use the Tk window manager commands. The next section introduces these window manager commands and shows you how to get useful information about your application from its main window.

FIGURE **10.6**

Screenshots for the evolving scripts in Listings 10.8 and 10.9.

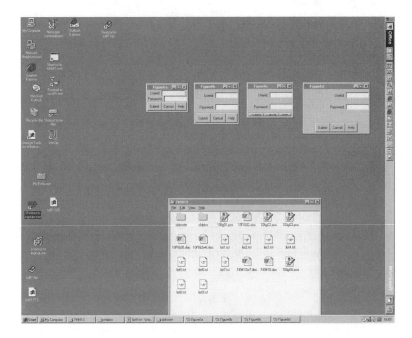

Relative Merits

The Grid geometry manager is most useful when you want to create tabular arrangements of widgets. The Placer is easy to understand and use. However, remember you are using absolute/relative coordinate-based positioning. As a result, whenever you have lots of widgets, changing one forces you to correct several others. It is also difficult to manage complex arrangements with the Placer. Do become familiar with Packer. Try to mix and match the geometry managers, for instance, by creating and packing a set of buttons in a frame and then placing that frame in a toplevel window using `grid`.

Window Manager Commands

Window systems provide a specialized application with priority that manages the display, allocating screen space requests made by all applications. The window manager monitors application windows, as well as user interactions with input devices (such as the keyboard and mouse) over these windows. The window manager for instance, processes all user-initiated window-resize commands and lets the application know the current state. It also conveys to the application other user interactions such as key presses.

In practice, you might never make many lower-level window manager calls, because the Tk applications are built to manage these communications automatically. However, you might want to use the Tk built-in commands to get and set the application's appearance and state.

There are two groups of window-related built-in Tk commands: the wm commands communicate with the manager, and the *winfo* commands return window-related information. Listing 10.10 shows a sample use of wm and *winfo* commands.

LISTING 10.10 Tk Window Manager Commands

```
1: %wm title . "My Wish..."
2: %winfo children .
3: .ok .cancel
```

Do	**DON'T**
Do remember that creating a widget does not realize it on the screen. Pack it to make it appear.	**Don't** leave any blank space between the "-" sign and the optionName when you execute a command such as button .b -text Button.
Do remember that if you want master windows to retain their sizes, you should set -propagate to 0 when packing the slave.	**Don't** forget that, if all you want to do is unpack a slave, you don't need to destroy it.
Do remember that the packer allocates a parcel for a slave in the side requested or on the current default side.	**Don't** use elaborate window decorations and so forth for transient windows such as pop-up dialogs.
	Don't use too many options for pack until you gain a good understanding of the pack mechanism. Use pack configure to progressively add the options.

Summary

In this hour, you learned the basic structure and methodology of developing graphical user interfaces. You have begun to learn what widgets (in particular, Tk widgets) are, how to create and destroy them, how to manage them, and what built-in support exists for dynamic placement and management of the hierarchy of widgets and window manager communication and query.

Tk provides four groups of commands that are used for

- Creating and deleting widgets
- Geometry management of individual groups of widgets
- Adding logical behaviors to individual widgets so they respond to user and application manipulation
- Communicating between widgets and between widgets and applications

The twin pillars of widgets are their look and feel—how they appear and how they behave. It is pretty difficult to describe widgets without describing the functionality they offer. In the next hour, "Adding Behavior to Your Widgets," you will be introduced to more Tk widgets and their look and feel.

Q&A

Q **Why won't the command `destroy [winfo children .]` work?**

A The command `winfo children .` returns a list of all the children of the root window. The destroy command expects individual widget names separated by space as arguments. The command will try to treat the list as a single unit and complain. Use `eval destroy [winfo children .]` to force another layer of parsing.

Q **You want to create and pack a list widget with a scrollbar, as shown in Figure 10.7. Will the following script deliver the result?**

```
wm title . QA1
listbox .lst
scrollbar .scr
pack .lst .scr -side left
```

A No. The scrollbar took its default size, because the `-height` option was not specified. The available cavity for the scrollbar was largely determined by the default size of the `listbox` widget, and hence the parcel allocated was larger than the default scrollbar size. It was, therefore, packed at the center of this parcel, with the result shown in Figure 10.8. In order to stretch the scrollbar to fill its allocated parcel, you must use the `-fill` option. In this case, the value for the option is `-y`. Use the command `pack configure .scr -fill y` to achieve the desired result.

The `pack configure slave slave ?option value?` command rearranges the packing with the option(s) specified. The correct script is

```
wm title . QA2
listbox .lst
scrollbar .scr
pack .lst .scr -side left
pack configure .scr -fill y
```

FIGURE **10.7**

A list widget and a
scrollbar packed
together.

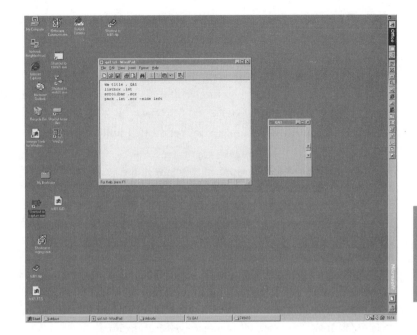

FIGURE **10.8**

A list widget and a
scrollbar packed
together with -fill y.

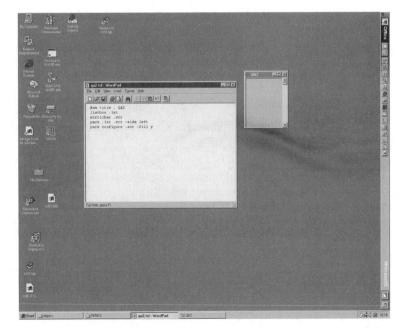

Q **What is the difference between `pack` and `pack configure`?**

A The `pack` command has several subcommands such as `forget` `info` `propagate` and `slaves`. If these subcommands are not present and the first argument for `pack` is the name of a window, the commands `pack` and `pack configure` behave identically. So, you can be forgiven for considering `pack configure` to be the command `pack` with the subcommand `configure`. In fact, that is what it is.

Q **What is the difference between `-fill` and `-expand`?**

A The `-fill` option takes the values `x`, `y`, or `none` and stretches the slave to fill the allocated parcel space, as you saw in the first Q&A. The `-expand` option, if set to `1`, stretches the slave when its master's size changes. Note that you use these action subcommands with `pack`.

Workshop

The "Quiz" section that follows is designed to provide you with an opportunity to recall some of the important concepts introduced in this hour. These may be commands, command syntax, common mistakes, usage, and so forth. The "Exercises" section helps you consolidate the material you learned via an example of practical value. Our aim is that these two sections should reinforce the knowledge you have gained in this hour. The answers to the quiz that follows can be found in Appendix A, "Answers to Quizzes."

Quiz

1. What does widget hierarchy mean?
2. What is the name of the toplevel widget when you start a `wish` shell?
3. How do you inquire the children of the toplevel widget?
4. How do you add a title to your application?
5. How do you delete a widget?
6. What are `frame` widgets used for?
7. How many geometry managers are there in Tk?
8. What are the main differences between the Grid, the Placer, and the Packer?
9. Where is the widget `.f.b` packed by default?

10. What is the default side for the pack command?

11. How do you unpack slaves?

12. How will you find the default minimum size of your application's main window?

Exercises

Solutions to the exercises are on the CD-ROM that accompanies this book.

1. Create three buttons as shown in Figure 10.9. Write a command to remove (not destroy) the middle button with the text "More ...", and reinstate it exactly where it was.

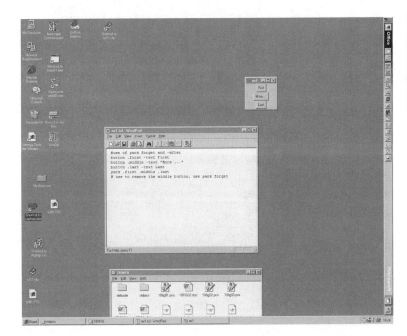

2. Create the arrangement shown in Figure 10.10. Add a title such as "Data base entry ..." to the window. Make the window resizable in the horizontal direction only.

FIGURE **10.10**
*Constrain the window
to resize in horizontal
direction only.*

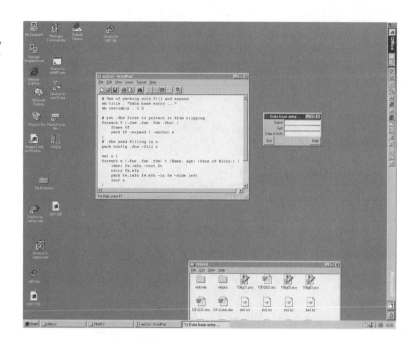

3. Create a list box and two scrollbars as shown in Figure 10.11.

FIGURE **10.11**
*A list box and two
scrollbars.*

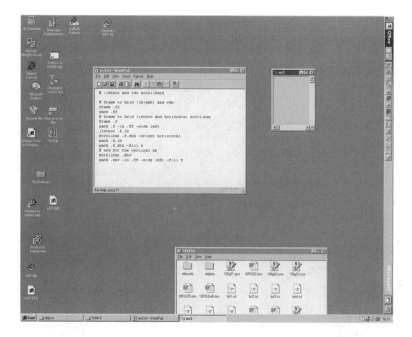

4. Explore the "Widget tour" under `<WHERE_TCL_IS_INSTALLED>/lib/tk8.*/demos`.

5. Familiarize yourself with the way the Tk packer works using the excellent tkPack application at `http://www.scriptics.com/plugin/contrib/packLet.html`.

10

Hour **11**

Adding Behavior to Your Widgets

In Hour 10, "Getting Started with Tk," you learned that the primary concept behind GUI toolkits, such as Tk, is to provide application builders with off-the-shelf, reusable user interface components with a predefined look and feel.

To recap, *look* refers to the external appearance of the various user interface elements of a toolkit, as well as the appearance of the application that is built using that toolkit. The term *feel* refers to how these interface components behave when the user interacts with them using the mouse and keyboard. You will find the term *direct manipulation* being used in literature to refer to this type of interaction.

In response to user interaction, the widgets invoke an appropriate behavior—either in themselves (for example, change color) or from the application behind them. (For instance, a file might be saved or a piece of text might be deleted.)

The user interface components must reflect their state (for instance, that they are active and can respond to user interaction). They must also respond to the application functionality behind them in semantically and conceptually meaningful ways. Your goal, as an application user interface designer and developer, is to create effective user interfaces and to enable the user to interact with the application.

In the last hour, you learned how to create and manage Tk widgets and create user interface layouts using the Tk geometry managers. You also learned how to use the Tk window manager commands. The objectives of this hour include learning how to customize the appearance and behavior of individual Tk widgets. In particular, you will learn

- The Tk widget commands and how to use them to configure widget options
- The Tk commands for communication between the user and the application
- More about the Tk widgets

Configuration Options, Widget Commands, and Bindings

In order to support a consistent look and feel, each widget class is defined in terms of attributes that determine its appearance and a set of methods. These methods invoke responses to user actions (such as a mouse button being pressed on the widget). Recall that the user actions are referred to as events that invoke the methods or callbacks. In the terminology of Tk, the widget attributes are known as configuration options or options, for short. You have already encountered some of the options in the last hour, where you specified the options at the time you created a widget.

Invoking Actions in Individual Widgets

Most often, you will need to specify the options for a widget after its creation or modify the options you set when you created the widget. You might also want to invoke other actions in the widgets. In Tk, this is achieved via the widget command. Recall that when TK creates a widget, it automatically creates an associated widget command for it. The name of the widget command is the same as that of the widget. For example, if you create a button widget named `.b`, Tk creates a widget command called `.b`. Widget command can be used subsequent to widget creation to configure any option for that widget. The widget configuration action subcommand is of the form `pathName configure ?option value?`. The current value of any option can be queried using the widget subcommand `cget` that has the form `pathName cget option`.

> The term *action subcommand* is used to refer to the action that the widget
> is being asked to invoke. You can use the terms *subcommand* and *action*
> interchangeably. You can say either that you are issuing the subcommand
> `configure` to the widget, or that the widget is being instructed to carry out
> a `configure` action.

All widget classes support the common options and the `configure` action. Complex widgets such as list boxes and menus have complex internal states that require subcommands other than just `configure` to change them. Hence, some widget classes define additional class-specific actions. For instance, you will learn in Hour 14, "Doing More with the Text Widget," that menus support actions to add items or modify existing ones, and dialog boxes to `grab` focus onto themselves.

Invoking Widget Response for User Interaction

A binding is the Tk mechanism to bind a user event (such as a keystroke or a mouse movement) on a widget to an action (such as execution of a Tcl script by that widget). The `bind` command takes any one of the forms given in Table 11.1, which follows. Each Tk widget class supports many default bindings. For instance, as you will learn in Hour 13, "Using the Tk Text Widget," one of the default text widget class bindings is the text selection action. This action is bound to an event sequence that consists of the user dragging the mouse along the text to be selected, keeping the left mouse button pressed from the start to the end of the selection.

A binding need not always invoke default actions. In fact, the major part of developing interactive applications is to implement your own actions via what are often interchangeably referred to as scripts, event-handlers, or callback functions. You attach these action scripts to the widgets in your application's graphical user interface, to be executed when the user initiates an appropriate sequence of events using the mouse and keyboard.

In Tk bind syntax, the term *tag* is used to refer to a window, widget, or string. If this argument starts with a ., then the interpreter knows that the argument is pointing to a window, main or internal. If it is a text string that does not resolve into a window/widget path name, it will be considered to apply to a tagged item. Hour 13 and Hour 16, "Using Canvas Widgets," introduce the concept of tagging items of text and drawing.

Action scripts, event handlers, and callback routines refer to the same mechanism. The particular term is part of the convention of the toolkit you are using. For instance, the terms *action script* and *event handler* are used in Tk. Other X Window System–based toolkits use *callback* and *event handler*.

Some Tk widget classes, such as the button, support a -command option that invokes an action script whenever a left mouse button click event happens over a button widget. You can consider the -command option to be analogous to a default binding for a particular event, in this case the Button1 event. The Tk bind command, on the other hand, is more general and enables you to explicitly associate a widget, an event, and an action script of your choice.

TABLE 11.1   Summary of Bind Command Syntax

Command	Action
bind *tag* <*event*sequence> script	Specifies that whenever *event*sequence takes place over a widget, a top-level window or a class of widgets specified by *tag*, the associated script is invoked by that widget.
bind *tag* <*event*sequence> +script	Same as above, except that if binding already exists, the new script is added to the existing script.
bind *tag* <*event*sequence>	If a binding for *tag* and <*event*sequence> *event*sequence exists, this command returns the associated script.
bind *tag*	Returns a list of all *event*sequences for which the widget has bindings (default and user-defined).

Note that if a default binding already exists, the command bind tag <event> script will replace it.

If you want to append to a default binding, put the prefix + before the script—that is, use the command bind tag <eventsequence> +script. Be sure you do not leave a blank space between the + and the script.

> If the script in the command `bind tag <event> script` is an empty string,
> the specified binding for that widget is removed.

Events

Events are part of the fundamental building blocks of GUI applications. Events are most commonly generated by a user with a physical device—such as keyboard or mouse—to issue commands to an application for carrying out specific tasks. The WIMP-based application typically defines a hierarchy of windows or widgets that the user can interact with using the mouse or keyboard. It initializes the application and its data structures and enters into an event loop waiting to process the events from the user.

> Note that, in this sense, there is a generic and fundamental event handler at
> the heart of the window system and all the applications that are running on
> a display. It is perhaps conceptually easy to consider layers of event handlers
> doing specific tasks.

Events can be classed into physical events (such as mouse or keyboard events) and virtual ones (such as cut and paste). Physical events may consist of single actions (such as a button press) or a sequence (such as pressing the Del button while simultaneously holding down the Control and Alt keys).

You need to know the Tk event syntax for defining your Tk widget bindings. Table 11.2, which follows, gives a summary of the most commonly used events. Typically, the syntax for an event in a `bind` command is in the form `<modifier-type-detail>`. The *modifier* is an event that acts as a prefix to the event specified by the *type*; the *detail* qualifies the *type*. In this example, the holding down of the Control and Alt keys is the modifier, whereas the `Del KeyPress` event is the type. The `Del` key qualifies the KeyPress. The <> acts as a delimiter to convey the idea that the sequence is to be treated as a single unit.

TABLE 11.2 Summary of Commonly Used Events

Event Name	Modifier/Detail	Description
Activate/Deactivate		For Macintosh systems—these events correspond to an application being activated or deactivated.
Button, ButtonPress	1,2, or 3	Specifies a mouse button press event. The type Button can be omitted and only the detail be given. For example, <1> can be used rather than <Button-1> or <ButtonPress-1>.
ButtonRelease	1,2, or 3	Event generated when a mouse button is released.
Circulate		Generated when the window stacking order has changed.
Colormap		Generated when the color map is modified.
Configure		Generated when a change to the size, position, border, or stacking order takes place. Circulate is included in this event.
Enter, Leave		Events generated when the mouse pointer either enters or leaves the window.
Motion/Drag	B1-,B2-,B3-	Events generated when the mouse pointer moves within the window. Holding down one of the mouse buttons acts as a modifier and generates a drag event out of the motion event.
Key, KeyPress	keysym	Generates keypress event.
KeyRelease	keysym	Event generated when a keyboard key is released.
Property		This indicates there has been a change to a property of the window, including possibly its deletion. Circulate, Destroy, Expose, FocusIn, FocusOut, Gravity, Map, Reparent, Unmap, and Visibility are encompassed in this event. It can also be used to indicate independent events on its own.

Key/KeyPress (as well as the angle brackets) can be left out if the key detail is given. Try this simple example to understand the keysym definition. Start up a wish. Execute the two commands

```
set w .
bind $w <KeyPress> {puts {Keysym for %%K=%K is 8bit ISO \
character value %%A=%A}}
```

Keep the mouse pointer in the wish shell, press any keyboard key a few times, and read the returned value.

When you are using the mouse events, you probably want to pass the current position, that is, the X,Y coordinates of the pointer. Tk provides a formatter, similar to that in C, for this purpose. Giving %x and %y as input arguments to the binding script delivers the widget relative X and Y coordinates of the mouse position. %X and %Y, however, pass the coordinate values relative to the screen. In both cases, the top-left corner is taken to be the origin.

A Simple Application for Widget Configure and Cget Commands

The simple application that follows shows how to use the configure and cget subcommands. Try this interactively by starting a wish shell and executing these script lines.

LISTING 11.1 Widget Configure and Cget Commands

```
 1: %button .b  -text "Time please..." -background green \
 2: >       -textvariable tn
 3:  .b
 4: %pack .b
 5: %.b cget -command
 6:  %
 7: %.b configure -command {set tn [clock format [clock seconds]]; \
 8: >    .b configure -background red}
 9: %.b cget -command
10:  set tn [clock format [clock seconds]];\
11: >    .b configure -background red
```

11

ANALYSIS In lines 1–2, you create a simple push button named .b, the child of the main window. Recall from Hour 10 that the command widgetClass pathName ?option value? creates a widget. You specify the options -text, -background, and -textvar at the time you create this button. These two options are set to the values "Time please .. ", green, and tn, respectively. The interpreter returns the widget/path name of your button widget in line 3, after creating it.

In line 4, you execute the pack command to manage and, therefore, see the widget on the screen. The -textvariable is a common Tk widget configuration option. It assigns the value of an associated global variable to the widget. Whenever the value of that variable changes, the associated option in the widget gets updated.

Line 5 uses the widget command .b with the subcommand/action cget to query the current setting of the -command option. The interpreter quite correctly returns the empty string. The result is shown in the left-hand image of Figure 11.1.

In script lines 7 and 8, you execute the widget command .b with the subcommand con-figure to set .b's -command option to a Tcl script. The first line of this script sets the variable tn to the formatted clock time. This is followed by a .b configure -option value command which configures the -background.

The script [clock format [clock seconds]] is a nested execution of the Tcl built-in command clock. clock seconds returns an integer value that denotes the elapsed time in seconds from a predefined epoch. The variable tn is assigned this value. The command clock format converts this integer value to the more user-friendly form of date and time in seconds. The option -textvariable associates a global variable to some textual value of the widget for which this option is specified. The value is dependent on the widget's class. The utility of this option is that whenever the value changes, the new value can be retrieved from the global variable associated with it. In this case our button's -textvariable is set to tn. The value changes every time you click mouse button 1 on .b and this value is assigned to tn. The second configure action results in the background color of the button being set to red. The result is shown in the right-hand image of Figure 11.1.

If you re-execute the .b cget -command, as in line 9, you now see that the interpreter returns a nonempty string, showing the script that will be executed in response to the button1 event.

Wherever abbreviating does not cause ambiguity, you can use abbreviations for the options. For instance, you can use -textvar, -com, and so forth.

You may be tempted to enclose the script for the -command option within quotes. Note that if you do that, the interpreter returns the script with the nested clock command evaluated. As a result, the time shown will not be updated.

You may also be tempted to enclose the clock commands within curly brackets for deferred evaluation, but it will not produce the desired effect of updating the time at every button press. The time will never get updated. The reason is that the clock command gets evaluated immediately, and the value of tn remains fixed to the value at the time of evaluation as seen by the following code:

```
pack [button .b -text time -textvar tn]
% .b config -com "set tn {[clock format [clock seconds]] }"
% .b cget -com\
set tn {Sat Sep 11 19:46:48  1999 }
```

You can also use .b configure -command {.b configure -text [clock format [clock seconds]]; .b configure -background red} to produce a similar effect, without setting the -textvar option.

FIGURE 11.1

A simple application to demonstrate widget, configure, *and* cget *commands.*

An Application to Explore the bind Command

You can consolidate the concept of Tk binding via another simple example. Take, for example, the small GUI that contains only a couple of entry widgets and buttons to enable the user to input a userid and password. Listing 11.2, which follows shows the use of the Tk bind command in action with the GUI that appeared in Listing 10.5.

LISTING 11.2 Bind and More Widget Commands

```
 1: wm title . "Bind and Entry widget commands"
 2: wm geometry . 300x128+40+40
 3:
 4: frame .f1
 5: pack .f1
 6: frame .f2
 7: pack .f2 -after .f1
 8: frame .f3 -bd 2 -relief groove
 9: pack .f3 -after .f2  -side bottom
10:
11: label .f1.lab1 -text "Userid: "
12: entry .f1.e1 -width 12
13: pack .f1.lab1 -side left -in .f1
14: pack .f1.e1 -side left -in .f1
15:
16: label .f2.lab1 -text "Password: "
17: entry .f2.e1 -width 12
18: pack .f2.lab1 -side left -in .f2
19: pack .f2.e1 -side left -in .f2
20:
21: button .f3.b1 -text Submit
22: button .f3.b2 -text Cancel
23: button .f3.b3 -text Help
```

continues

11

LISTING 11.2 continued

```
24: pack .f3.b1 .f3.b2 -ipadx 2 -pady 1 -ipady 1 -side left -in .f3
25: pack .f3.b3 -side right -in .f3
26: pack configure .f3.b3 -ipadx 2 -pady 1 -ipady 1
27: pack configure .f1 .f2 -pady 10
28: pack configure .f1 .f2 -anchor e
29:
30: .f2.e1 configure -show *
31:
32: .f3.b1 configure -command  "puts {You are logged on}"
33: .f3.b2 configure -command "puts {Press control+alt+del key if you changed
your mind}"
34:
35: bind .f1.e1 <Return>  "checkEntry .f1.e1 .f2.e1"
36: bind .f2.e1 <Return>  "checkEntry  .f2.e1 .f1.e1"
37:
38: proc checkEntry  {en1 en2}  {
39: if {[string length [$en2 get]]  <=0 } {
40:    puts "You need to enter both userid and a password for the system to log
you on\n"
41:    $en1 delete 0 [string length [$en1 get]]
42:    } else {
43:        puts "Ok, You are logged on\n"
44:    }
45: }
```

ANALYSIS The lion's share of the previous code, lines 4–29, must be familiar to you as Listing 10.5, which you developed in the last hour. The user interface you developed there is used to add behavior in this hour. Lines 1 and 2 use the Tk window manager commands wm title and wm geometry to add a title to your login window and set a size for it.

In this example, the primary purpose is to further explore the -command option and widget binding. In lines 30–33, you use the configure widget subcommand on the password entry widget and the two buttons with labels submit and cancel.

Recall that the complex widget classes support additional options, as well as actions beyond those that are shared by all widget classes. The button widget class, for instance, supports the -command option, which is equivalent to a widget binding for the mouse button-1 press event on instances of this class of widgets.

In contrast, the entry widget does not have a -command option as such, because you do not invoke an entry widget. The -show option of an entry widget takes a character for an input argument and uses that character to mask the real characters that are input by the user. Such a utility is very useful for inputting passwords. Here, in line 30, you have specified the masking character to be *. Figure 11.2 shows the graphical user interface with the masking character replacing the password.

11

FIGURE 11.2

A simple login window application.

The `-command` option for the two button widgets is configured to print a message. You could, of course, add any complex script.

You now must access the contents of the entry widgets for processing that content. There is more than one way to do this. The first method is to make use of the entry widget's `-textvariable` option. You can specify the name of the variable that Tk makes available globally (see the "Quiz" section). Here you want to make use of widget binding. In lines 35 and 36, you use the `bind` command to bind the `Return KeyPress` event to the two entry widgets with an associated script defined in the procedure `checkEntry`.

Lines 38–45 define the procedure `checkEntry`. Recall that complex widgets support additional actions and commands. In the case of an entry widget, the command `pathName get` retrieves its contents. The procedure `checkEntry` takes two input arguments. The first is the name of the entry widget that received the `Return KeyPress` event, and the second is the name of the other entry in the GUI. The procedure makes use of the `get` command to check whether the other entry has nonempty content. If not, the entry widget get action command `delete` is used to clear the calling entry, and the user is alerted to provide input to both entries. If both entries have nonempty strings, the message is printed to the console stating that the user is logged on.

You might find occasions where you do not wish to provide an entry widget binding for the `Return KeyPress` event. Even in this example, you can just as easily execute the `checkEntry` script by making it the same value as the `-command` option of the button widget `.f3.b1` and not provide the binding. Users might not be accustomed to pressing the Return key. A good interface design guideline is to be prepared for all such situations, gather the input as necessary, and ensure that the user gets feedback for all actions.

Difference Between the Action Subcommands and bind

One question you might have about the preceding example is why you bother with binding at all. You know that the combination of options and actions (such as -textvariable and pathName get) of certain widget classes (such as entry) can be effectively combined to provide the same outcome. The answer is that the bind command provides greater flexibility, enabling you to associate any possible and reasonable event sequence to any individual instance of any widget class. Thus, binding extends the basic functionality of a particular widget. In contrast, options and action commands are predefined for each class of widget and are customizable. It is necessary to appreciate that the combination of binding, options, and built-in action subcommands provides you with a rich and versatile development environment.

An Application

Tk provides widgets such as radio and checkbuttons, option menus, and list boxes to provide choices for the user. Let us build a simple example to explore these widgets. You will revisit this example in Hour 12, "Understanding Intercommunication Commands," to see how the various parts of this application can be brought together to provide a simple functional Tk application.

This application might look lengthy, but it is fairly representative of any application you might develop and, therefore, provides you with an opportunity to pick up skills. The Tk script of this application is given in Listing 11.3, which follows. We suggest that you develop this code in a script file.

Tk is more precise than other toolkits, but even with Tk, you can see that the code becomes longer. You should try to test out this code in chunks that suit you, even trying out a couple of commands interactively. It is worth your while to go through this code without breaking continuity. The code length is one of the primary motivations for using extensions such as [incr widgets] and BLT, which are covered in Hour 20, "Understanding Object-Oriented Programming with Tcl/Tk," and in Hour 23, "Using Tcl/Tk Extensions."

LISTING 11.3   Tk Widgets for Choice Input

```
1: set w .main
2: wm title . "STY Tcl/Tk in 24 Hours - Pizza Order Form"
3: wm geometry . 600x400+40+40
4: frame $w
5: pack $w
```

```
 6: label $w.lab1 -text "Make your choice and press the button Order now" \
 7:         -font {Courier 14 bold }
 8: foreach x { 1 4 5} {
 9:     set w$x $w.f$x
10: }
11: frame $w1
12: frame $w4   -bd 2 -relief groove
13: frame $w5   -bd 2 -relief groove
14: pack $w.lab1 $w1 $w4 $w5 -in $w -padx 1 -pady 4
15: set w2 $w1.f2
16: set w3 $w1.f3
17: frame $w2   -bd 2 -relief groove
18: frame $w3   -bd 2 -relief groove
19: pack $w2 -side left -in $w1 -anchor w
20: pack $w3 -side right -in $w1 -anchor e -padx 10
21:
22: label $w2.lab1 -text "Type" -font {Courier 14 bold }
23: radiobutton $w2.rb1 -text "Deep pan" -variable ptype \
24:             -value deeppan
25: radiobutton $w2.rb2 -text  "Thin Crust" -variable ptype \
26: -value thincrust
27: grid $w2.lab1 -column 0 -row 0  -sticky w
28: grid $w2.rb1 -column 1 -row 0 -sticky w
29: grid $w2.rb2 -column 1 -row 1 -sticky w
30:
31: label $w2.lab2 -text "Size" -font {Courier 14 bold }
32: radiobutton $w2.rb3 -text  "Medium" -variable psize -value medium
33: radiobutton $w2.rb4 -text  "Large" -variable psize -value large
34: grid $w2.lab2 -column 2 -row 0  -sticky n
35: grid $w2.rb3 -column 3 -row 0 -sticky w
36: grid $w2.rb4 -column 3 -row 1 -sticky w
37:
38:  label $w4.lab1 -text "Drinks" -font {Courier 14 bold }
39:  checkbutton $w4.chkb1 -text Coke -variable coke
40:  checkbutton $w4.chkb2 -text "Diet Coke" -variable dietcoke
41:  checkbutton $w4.chkb3 -text "7up" -variable 7up
42:  grid $w4.lab1 -column 0 -row 0  -sticky w
43:  grid $w4.chkb1 -column 1 -row 0 -sticky w
44:  grid $w4.chkb2 -column 1 -row 1 -sticky w
45:  grid $w4.chkb3 -column 1 -row 2 -sticky w
46:
47:  label $w4.lab2 -text "Extras" -font {Courier 14 bold }
48:  checkbutton $w4.chkb4 -text Coleslaw -variable coleslaw
49:  checkbutton $w4.chkb5 -text "Garlic bread" -variable bread
50:  checkbutton $w4.chkb6 -text "Green salad" -variable salad
51:  set opt [ tk_optionMenu $w4.optm icecream Almond Banana \
52:      Blueberry Chocolate "Chocolate chip" Coconut Coffee Fudge \
53:      Mango "Maple Syrup" Mint Pistachio Raspberry "Raspberry Ripple" \
54:      Strawberry  Tuti-fruti Vanilla Walnut ]
55:  grid $w4.lab2 -column 2 -row 0  -sticky w
```

11

continues

LISTING 11.3 continued

```
56:  grid $w4.chkb4 -column 3 -row 0 -sticky w
57:  grid $w4.chkb5 -column 3 -row 1 -sticky w
58:  grid $w4.chkb6 -column 3 -row 2 -sticky w
59:  grid  $w4.optm -column 4 -row 1 -sticky w
60:
61:  scale $w5.nums -orient horizontal -digit 0 -from 1 -to 10 -label Number \
62:      -showvalue 1 -length 10c -variable nums
63:  button $w5.order -text "Take order" -command {takeOrder $w3.lst $tops}
64:  pack $w5.nums -side left -padx 12
65:  pack $w5.order -side bottom -anchor e
```

ANALYSIS This is long Tk script considering that you are only into the second hour of learning to use the Tk toolkit! However, much of it is rather familiar from the last hour, and it is straightforward. Nevertheless, it might be easier if you refer to the graphical user interface, shown in Figure 11.3, which is generated by this script.

FIGURE 11.3

An application to demonstrate Tk choice widgets.

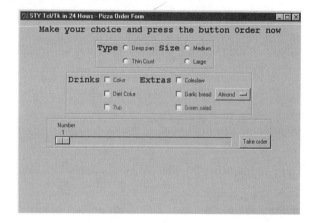

The tasks this application will accomplish are the following:

- Specify whether the pizza is deep pan or thin crust.
- Specify whether the size is medium or large.
- Select one or all from a list of side dishes, consisting of coleslaw, green salad, and garlic bread.
- Select a flavor of ice-cream.
- Select any or all from a list of the three drinks Coke, Diet Coke, and Seven Up.

Note that the previous script uses the options -padx, -pady, -ipadx, and -ipady quite generously. We recommend that you alter the values for these options and experiment.

Note also that this example uses the Grid and Pack geometry managers together. Please go through the geometry management lines carefully. Listing 11.3 is analyzed in detail in the following sections.

Layout Partitioning

In lines 2 and 3, you use the Tk window manager commands `title` and `geometry` to decorate the border and fix the window size. The application main window contains a frame `$w` that is partitioned into three by the three frame widgets `$w.f1`, `$w.f4`, and `$w.f5`. Note that you have used the `-border` (`-bd`) and `-relief` options to partition the real estate.

> The options `bd` and `relief` go together. `Relief` will not have any effect unless you have specified a positive border.

The first frame `$w.f1` contains two further frames, `$w.f1.f2` and `$w.f1.f3`. These internal frames are packed with the `-side` option set to `left` and `right` in lines 19 and 20. You also have used the `-anchor` option set to `w` and `e`, to ensure that these two containers retain their respective sides and aspects when the window is resized.

Radiobuttons for One-of-Many Choice

The choice between thin crust and deep pan and the choice between medium and large size are made using two sets of two radiobuttons. Each pair of radiobuttons shares a common global variable. This variable holds the value of the current choice, which is made by selecting one of the radiobuttons. Tk creates this global variable automatically for you if you specify the option `-variable` for each radiobutton.

If a group of radiobuttons works together, as they do here, you specify the same variable for them, but the value of that variable is distinct for each button in that group. In this case, the global variable for the type of pizza is `ptype`, as shown in lines 23 and 25; but the value is `deeppan` or `thincrust`, depending on which radiobutton the user selects (as specified in lines 24 and 26). Similarly, the global variable for the size of the pizza is `psize`, as shown in lines 32 and 33. The values are `medium` and `large` as shown in those lines.

Two labels are created in lines 22 and 31, one for each pair of radiobuttons. The two groups of one label and two radiobuttons are packed in their master parent `$w2` using the Grid manager as shown in lines 27–29 and 34–36.

> The Grid manager is by far the easiest and conceptually clearest geometry manager to use for the configuration you have here.

Checkbuttons for Many-of-Many Choice

You have a very limited selection of soft drinks and side dishes, but you want to allow more than one beverage and side dish choice. Checkbuttons are ideal for presenting these many-of-many choices, if the list of choices is not long. Tk creates a global variable for each checkbutton whose value is set to 1 or 0 automatically when that button is selected or deselected. Giving meaningful names to these checkbutton variables makes them easier to remember and also makes your code readable.

> Each checkbutton holds its own variable independent of its group members. It is inappropriate to use checkbuttons if you want to toggle and allow only a one-of-many choice. Use radiobuttons with a common global variable instead.

You have used a set of one label and three checkbuttons for drinks and a similar set for side dishes. These widgets are created in lines 38–41 and 47–50. The Grid geometry manager is used to position these widgets in the desired layout in lines 42–45 and 55–58, respectively.

Option Menus for One-of-Many Choice

An option menu can be used for saving screen real estate when you are presenting a one-of-many choice, where the choice is a long list. The label of the option menu displays the current choice. Tk associates a global variable with option menu, as well. The current choice is stored in this variable.

The option menu is an appropriate widget to present the flavors of ice cream, as shown in lines 51–54. The tk_optionMenu command is of the form tk_optionMenu w varName value ?value?. It creates an option menu button and returns the name of the menu associated with that button. The menu is a top-level window, and it cannot be packed. Instead, you pack the menu button $w4.optm as shown in line 59.

Getting Numerical Value Input

Having made all these choices, you can specify the quantity that you want. (This makes a simplistic assumption that everyone likes the same options!) You can then place the order and confirm the choice. The penultimate widget in this GUI is the Tk scale widget, created in lines 61–62. It's a highly customizable widget with a puck, labels for current value, and scale divisions. It updates its variable (in this case nums) to the currently active value selected by the user.

The resulting graphical user interface is shown in Figure 11.3. Selecting the button with the text Take order will invoke the evaluation of the procedure takeOrder, which will be defined in the next hour.

Do	Don't
Do check available options for a widget class by using the command pathName configure.	**Don't** overwhelm the user with too many radiobuttons and checkbuttons. Use option menus and lists.
Do use the global variables associated with widget classes to store and retrieve values associated with widgets of that class.	**Don't** make windows too large for their purpose.
Do provide bindings to support users' style on interaction. For example, if users press the Return button in an entry widget, implement a binding to respond to it.	**Don't** use unusual and complicated key sequences for modifiers of event sequences.
	Don't use more than two modifier keys. You will increase the cognitive overload for the user.
Do check for existing bindings before replacing them.	**Don't** forget to declare global variables within the scope of event handlers.
Do provide an explicit geometry management policy so that the window layout does not get skewed due to changes in window sizes.	
Do use lists when you are presenting a long list of one-of many or more-of-many choices.	

11

Summary

In this hour, you learned the Tk widget commands that enable you to add a rich set of interactive behaviors to your application. With Tk, every time you create a widget, an associated command for that widget is also created. You can use this command to customize that widget, add behavior, and bind events and event-handlers.

In Hour 12, "Understanding Intercommunication Commands," you will learn how to communicate between widgets in a GUI and how to use menu bars, menus, and dialog widgets to create a whole application that has rich interactive functionality.

Q&A

Q **Why won't the following script work the way it is expected to (that is, update the text properly)?**

```
button .b  -text "Time please..."
pack .b
.b configure -command ".b configure \
   -text {[clock format [clock seconds]]};  \
   .b configure -background red "
```

A You will find that the first time you click the left mouse button the appropriate time will be shown, but the same time will be repeated for all subsequent button clicks. Execute this code and execute .b cget -command interactively at the wish prompt. You will find that the clock commands have been evaluated once and for all when the interpreter parsed the script. Using -textvariable or the -text options, as shown in Listing 11.1, updates the label correctly.

Q **What is wrong with the script** foreach w {ok cancel help} { button .$w -text $w -command {puts "Button is $w"}; pack .$w }?

A The script for the -command option for each button has differed evaluation; that is, the script is not immediately evaluated when the interpreter is parsing the option. Instead, the script is evaluated every time the command is invoked. As a result, when evaluation takes place, the current value of $w is substituted. Using {} causes the evaluation to be differed and using " " forces immediate evaluation. One correct way of specifying the desired result is: foreach w {ok cancel help} { button .$w -text $w -command "puts \"Button is $w\""; pack .$w }. Note the escape sequence for the inside double quotes in this nested use.

Q **How do I prevent the user from selecting choices he shouldn't?**

A If selecting a widget or an option will cause the application to carry out an inappropriate action and produce an error, prevent this by making the choice unavailable. If you set the -state option to disabled, user action on the widget will be ignored. Make the inactive states of widgets obvious by setting the

-disabledForeground option to a duller shade of gray or a stippled pattern. This will prevent the user from being frustrated by not knowing whether a widget is active and available.

Workshop

The following "Quiz" section is designed to provide you with an opportunity to recall some of the important concepts introduced in this hour. These may be commands, command syntax, common mistakes, usage, and so on. In some ways, the material in this hour is at the heart of developing interactive Tk applications. It is important to gain confidence in using the concepts and programming methodology introduced here. Our aim is that the "Quiz" and "Exercises" sections should consolidate and reinforce the knowledge you have gained in this hour. The answers to the quiz that follows can be found in Appendix A, "Answers to Quizzes."

Quiz

1. What is a widget command?
2. What are the widget actions or subcommands that are common across all Tk widget classes?
3. What does the action subcommand `pathName cget option` do?
4. What is the syntax of the `bind` command?
5. What is the syntax of the event sequence for a `bind` command?
6. How will you find out if a binding is defined for a widget?
7. What is the command to examine the action script associated with a particular binding of a widget?
8. What is the difference between the `-command` option and a widget binding?

Exercises

Solutions to the exercises are on the CD-ROM that accompanies this book.

1. Create three button widgets: `first`, `middle`, and `last`. Attach a command to the middle button that will insert additional buttons when it is selected.
2. When an alphanumeric input is sought from the user, the input value is generally not validated until the user has completed the input. It may be more efficient to process `KeyPress` events as they are being typed. Write a small application with a label and an entry widget. Use `KeyPress` event binding to accept only numeric, `BackSpace`, and `-` characters. Note that the `BackSpace` is necessary if the user wants to correct a value already inputted. The `-` is a useful character to separate the numbers. Note that the entry widget should accept no other keyboard input, including `<Return>`.

Hour **12**

Understanding Intercommunication Commands

In Hour 11, "Adding Behavior to Your Widgets," you saw how to add behavior to widgets so that they individually respond to a user's interaction with them. In any real application situation, you require widgets within the application to communicate with each other and the application data structures in order to support user tasks. For instance, in a text editor application, you will expect a menu item called File Open to pop up a file selection box that returns a filename to the application. The application then can open that file and read it into a text widget for editing. Tk widgets support intercommunication between themselves and the application-using options, event handlers, and bindings.

Sometimes your application must attract the user's attention and explicitly require a response from him or her before it can continue. In such circumstances, it might be necessary to temporarily suspend the user's interaction with any other widget or window. Tk provides built-in commands such as grab, focus, and tk_wait to enable you to achieve this. Typically, you will use these commands in conjunction with modal pop-up dialog boxes. In this hour, you will learn to create and use Tk menus and dialog widgets, together with intercommunication commands that make them work together cohesively.

In particular, you will learn how

- To use intercommunication commands
- To build menubars and attach menu items to your application windows
- To construct pop-up menus
- To use message boxes to provide information to and seek information from the user

Extending the Application with Intercommunication Commands

Let us extend the pizza ordering application of the previous hour to achieve the objective—learning useful intercommunication commands. Listing 12.1 gives this extension.

 Note that this is a continuation of listing 11.3 and will not work without that earlier listing. Copy that listing into a script file and append the following code to complete your pizza order.

LISTING 12.1 Communicating with Other Widgets, Windows, and Applications

```
 1: set tops {Anchovies Cheese Ham Jalapeno Mushroom Olives Onions
 2:       Pepper Pepperoni Pineapple Sweetcorn Tomatoes Tuna }
 3: label $w3.lab3 -text "Extra toppings" -font {Courier 14 bold }
 4: scrollbar $w3.scr -command "$w3.lst yview"
 5: listbox $w3.lst -yscrollcommand  "$w3.scr set" \
 6:   -selectmode multiple
 7: pack $w3.scr -side right -anchor n -in $w3 -fill y
 8: pack $w3.lab3 -ipadx 1 -ipady 1 \
 9:        -padx 12 -side left -anchor n -in $w3
10: pack $w3.lst -ipadx 1 -ipady 1 -padx 6 -side left \
11:        -anchor n -in $w3
12: for {set i 0} {$i <= [llength $tops]} {incr i} {
13:        $w3.lst insert $i [lindex $tops $i]
14:        }
```

```
15:
16: proc takeOrder {win t} {
17: global psize ptype nums salad bread coleslaw coke 7up dietcoke icecream
18:  set toppings  [$win curselection ]
19:  set selected {}
20:  foreach i $toppings {
21:      lappend selected [lindex $t $i]
22: }
23: set extras {}
24:  if {$bread == 1} {
25:      lappend  extras "Bread\n"
26: }
27:  if {$coleslaw == 1} {
28:      lappend extras "Coleslaw\n"
29: }
30:  if {$salad == 1} {
31:      lappend extras "Salad\n"
32: }
33:  set drk {}
34:  if {$coke == 1} {
35:       lappend drk "Coke\n"
36: }
37:  if {$dietcoke == 1} {
38:       lappend drk "Diet Coke\n"
39: }
40:  if {$7up == 1} {
41:       lappend drk "7UP\n"
42: }
43: set s "You have ordered $nums $psize sized $ptype pizza with: \n"
44: foreach i $selected {
45:      append s " $i "
46: }
47: append s " for extra topping,"
48: foreach i $extras {
49:      append s " $i "
50: }
51: foreach i $drk {
52:      append s " $i and "
53: }
54: append s " $icecream icecream"
55:  append s ".\n"
56: toplevel .top
57: wm title  .top "Your order"
58: frame .top.fr -bd 1 -relief raised -width 5i -height 5i
59: message .top.fr.m -width 4i -text $s
60: button .top.dismiss -text Dismiss -command {destroy .top}
61: pack .top.fr .top.dismiss
62: pack .top.fr.m
63: grab set .top
64: raise .top
65: tkwait window .top
66: }
```

12

In the listing, you are essentially

- Adding a long list of toppings to choose from
- Gathering all the input to present it to the user for confirmation when he or she selects the Take Order button

In order to choose your pizza toppings from a large selection, you will want to make a multiple-choice list. You can use the scrollable listbox widget to present many-of-many choices, as shown in Figure 12.1 (which is the modified version of Figure 11.3). Listing 12.1 is analyzed in detail in the following sections.

FIGURE 12.1

An application to demonstrate Tk inter-communication commands.

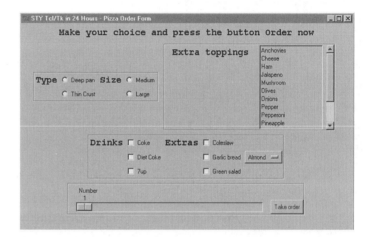

A Scrollable Listbox for Many-of-Many Choices

In line 4, you create a scrollbar, $w3.scr. The scrollbar is made of two arrows and a slider. The position and size of the slider indicate which portion of the document is visible in the widget/window associated with the scrollbar. In this case, lines 5–6 create a listbox widget, $w3.lst, to be associated with this scrollbar.

The option -selectmode, in line 6, enables you to specify whether you want the selection to be single, multiple, browsed, or extended. (Extended involves pressing mouse button 1 and dragging along the list of items to select all the items under the mouse motion.) Thus, the listbox provides a complex selection mechanism.

Scrolling

The scrollbar and listbox demonstrate intercommunication between widgets. When the user interacts with the scrollbar (for example, by dragging the slider with the left mouse button pressed down on it), the scrollbar notifies the listbox that the listbox must change the view it is presenting. The scrollbar makes this notification by evaluating the Tcl script generated from the scrollbar's -command option.

The usual script for the -command option is a single Tcl command, which requests a change of either *yview* or *xview* of the associated widget. The choice *xview* or *yview* is based on whether the scrollbar's -orientation option is set to *horizontal* or *vertical* (default).

The Scroll Command

The -yscrollcommand option specified in line 5, passes a list of two real fractions to the scrollbar. The values of these two fractions are specified as a proportion of the contents of the associated widget. Hence, each value ranges between 0 and 1. If the widget associated with the scrollbar is a listbox, as in this case, the first element gives the position of the first or top item in the listbox, relative to the size of the listbox as a whole.

The second element gives the position of the listbox element just after the last one in it, again relative to the listbox as a whole. If the associated widget is a text widget, the scrolling fractions are computed as a proportion of the text to be displayed in the text widget. If the associated widget is a canvas, an additional option, -scrollregion, is also specified to indicate the rectangular boundary of information that is scrollable. The scrolling fractions are computed as a proportion of this information.

In lines 7–11, you pack the listbox, its scrollbar, and an associated label into their container frame $w3 with -side and -anchor options set to left and n to align their tops.

Note that we have used a -fill y specification with the scrollbar packing. If you do not specify the -fill option while packing the scrollbar, it is displayed with a default size that can fall well short of the length of the listbox it serves.

12

Inserting Items in a Listbox

Next you need to display the toppings as listbox items. The variable tops is a list of toppings, which is set in lines 1–2. The for loop in lines 12–14 inserts the items from tops one below the other in the listbox using the listbox action subcommand pathName insert index value.

Gathering All Input

Selecting the button Take order invokes the Tcl procedure takeOrder, defined in lines 16–66. This procedure takes two input arguments—the listbox and the list of pizza toppings. Note that all the global variables associated with all the widgets need to be declared in the body of the takeOrder procedure to make these available within the scope of this procedure. Please refer to Hour 7, "Building Your Own Procedures," for a detailed discussion on variable scope within procedures.

In line 18, you execute the listbox widget command `pathName curselection` to get the list of indices that represent the current choice and assign it to `toppings`. In line 19, you create an empty list called `selected`. In line 20, the list of indices stored in `toppings` is used to extract the actual names of the chosen toppings and appended to `selected`.

Next, you retrieve the side dishes and drinks ordered. If a selection is made here, the variable associated with it will be equal to 1. If no selection is made, it is equal to 0. In line 23, you create an empty list `extras` to hold the side dishes selection. The simple numerical comparison in lines 23–32 gives you all the selections that the user has made. Similarly, you collect the list of drinks selected by the user in the list `drk` in lines 33–42.

Presenting the Input

The only thing that remains to be done is to present all the choices the user has made so that he or she can confirm them. This task illustrates how

- To create more than one toplevel window for your application
- To create a window that will ensure that the user sees it and responds to the information or query it presents
- To redirect the keyboard focus automatically, so that subsequent user input is sent to a specified window

Message Widget

In lines 43–55, you gather all the user choices and create a single string s using the Tcl `append` command. Please refer to Hour 8, "Manipulating Strings," for detailed discussion on string creation and manipulation. You assign this string to the `-text` option of the built-in Tk widget `message`. The Tk widget `message` has the simple function of presenting a formatted string.

The Toplevel Widget

The Tk `toplevel` window is a child of the application's root or main window. Frequently, these windows are used as transient dialog or menu windows, but they also can be used as supplementary `toplevel` windows for an application. A `toplevel` window is automatically displayed, and you do not need to pack and manage its geometry. If these windows are transient in nature, you can use the Tk window manager commands to instruct the window manager not to decorate its borders or allow window resize, and so forth. You use a top level and some children in lines 56–60 to present the data.

In line 56, `.top` is created as the child of the main window `.` and, in lines 58–60, you create a frame `.top.fr` to contain your message window `.top.fr.m`, and a button `.top.dismiss`. This button's `-command` option is set to destroy `.top` when the user selects `.top.fr.dismiss`. In lines 61–62, you pack the frame, the message, and the button.

Note that you need to pack the frame .top.fr before you pack .top.fr.m.

Grab, Raise, and tkwait Commands

When the procedure takeOrder is invoked, all the input is gathered, and the toplevel window and all its children are created and managed. You want to make sure that the user sees this window and the message it contains. You want to ensure that he or she acknowledges that he or she has seen it by clicking on the .top.fr.dismiss so that you can take down .top and all its children. Tk provides built-in commands to support these application tasks.

In line 63, you set the grab to .top. The Tk grab set action command processes keyboard and mouse events only if these happen within the window or widget subtree given as an argument to this command. You can set grab to be global or local. If it is a global grab, all keyboard and mouse events in windows other than the grab window will be ignored. With local grab, the restriction is confined only to the application of which the grab window is a subtree.

In line 64, you set .top to raise to the top of the window stack on the display, so that it is not hidden behind other windows. This is essential. Otherwise, the application will fail to process any of the user's input, and the user (because he or she doesn't know the reason for this failure) can become frustrated with your application.

In line 65, you use the tkwait command to temporarily suspend processing until .top is destroyed. The tkwait variable/visibility/window name command releases the grab command when the value of the variable represented by the name changes, when the visibility of the window with the name changes, or when the named window is destroyed. One of these events will take place when user interaction with the dialog box is complete. Note that you are most likely to use these commands when presenting dialogs to elicit user response that is vital for continuation of the application. In important cases, you will also use the Tk focus command in conjunction with them. These intercommunication commands should be used with care.

Menubars and Menus

In Tk, a menubar is basically a manager widget, a toplevel window that hosts menu items displayed in a pull-down style. When selected, the items in a menubar spawn pull-down menus that display application commands and functions. The menubar is designed for the economical use of screen real estate. It tidily hides the whole set of commands or

12

menu items in an organized manner, and yet the menubar banner makes visible the fact that these functions are available.

The Tk menu widget can accept a set of entries that it arranges in a column to provide different styles of menus such as pull-down menus, cascading menus, and, of course, pop-up menus. The menu entries are cascade, command, checkbutton, and radiobutton. These entries behave like widgets, even though they are not distinct widgets. Another useful menu entry is the separator, which enables you to provide visual clues about the grouping of items within a menu.

> When constructing menus, use the same font for every menubutton and menu, left-align menu labels for a tidy appearance, and extend separators right across the menu groups to keep visual separation looking neat. Don't position menubuttons too close to each other in a menubar. It will make it difficult to distinguish one topic from another. Don't use multiple rows of menubars unless it is absolutely necessary. It will take up the vertical space in your application window. Don't give endless lists of choices in a slab of menu. Try using option and list widgets instead.

It will be to your benefit to grasp this menu entry concept right at the outset. Start a wish application and execute the Tk commands in Listing 12.2 interactively by typing them in directly at the wish command prompt. When you try this piece of code interactively, you will note that the command menu pathName ?option value? returns an identifier, but the other commands do not. It will also help you to observe the evolving menu structure.

Figure 12.2 shows the result. Run your mouse cursor over the posted menu. Use the left mouse button to select one or more of the display styles, and then select any one of the fonts. Note the appearance of the last item, the cascade entry.

LISTING 12.2   The Menu, Menu Add, and Menu Post Commands

```
1: % menu .m
2: .m
3: % .m add checkbutton -label Bold
4: % .m add checkbutton -label Italic
5: % .m add checkbutton -label Underline
6: % .m add separator
7: % .m add radiobutton -label Times
8: % .m add radiobutton -label Courier
9: % .m add radiobutton -label Helvetica
10: % .m add separator
11: % .m add cascade -label Size
12: % tk_popup .m 456 256
```

FIGURE 12.2

A basic Tk menu.

ANALYSIS In line 1, the widget command menu creates a menu and returns its name .m. Three checkbutton items are added to this menu in lines 3–5. Each checkbutton has its label option set to Bold, Italic, or Underline, respectively. Notice that when a .m add menu_item ?option value? command is executed, the interpreter does not return a widget name. The entries, as we noted earlier, are not widgets even though they behave in a similar fashion.

The bindings and key traversal for entries are built-in with the menu mechanism. Lines 6 and 10 add two separators to the menu. Note that the separators add a visual effect that automatically conveys the grouping of the entries.

In lines 7–9, you add three more entries of type radiobutton to the menu. These, too, have their labels set to different font names.

In line 11, you add a cascade entry to the menu. Cascade entries are the means to add walk-through submenus to the original menu. You attach the submenu to the cascade entry using its menu option. When the mouse passes over a cascade entry, it automatically posts the submenu, generally to its right, as indicated by the cascade entry's arrow. However, if there is no space to the right, the cascade will automatically post its menu to its left.

You can see this menu with its entries by posting it on the screen. Use the built-in Tk command tk_popup menuName x y. The variables x and y refer to screen pixel coordinates. The menu will be positioned in such a way that, if an entry is specified, the menu item indicated by the entry will be over the given point. If the entry is null, the menu's upper-left corner is positioned at the given point. After a menu is posted, keyboard traversal and shortcuts also work for pop-up, if these are defined. Move the cursor over the items, selecting the items. Notice the changes in their visual appearance.

The Pull-down Menu

Pull-down menus are the most common style of menus used in application windows, with a menubar occupying a top strip of the window. In Tk, a frame widget is generally used as a menubar for this purpose. A set of menubutton widgets is attached to this frame. Each menubutton is associated with a menu, which is created with the menu command as before. Menu items are attached to each menu using the menu widget command pathName add menu-item ?option value?. You can construct a menubar and a set of pull-down menus as shown in Listing 12.3. Figure 12.3 shows the result.

12

From now on, you will be modifying, adding, and reusing the code in Listing 12.3. You can start creating these lines of code in a Tcl/Tk script file in your current working directory. Call this script file `menu.tcl`.

LISTING 12.3   A Menubar with Pull-down Menus

```
 1: set w .main
 2: frame $w
 3: set m $w.mbar
 4: frame $m -relief raised -bd 2
 5: set tf $w.txtframe
 6: frame $tf
 7:
 8: pack $w
 9: pack $m -in $w -side top -fill x
10:  pack $tf -after $m -side bottom -fill x
11:
12:  scrollbar $tf.ys -command "$tf.t yview"
13:  text $tf.t -width 40 -height 20 -wrap none \
14:      -yscrollcommand "$tf.ys set" -relief sunken -bd 2
15:
16:  pack $tf.t $tf.ys -in $tf -side left -fill y
17:
18:  menubutton $m.file -text File -underline 0 -menu $m.file.m1
19:  menubutton $m.edit -text Edit -underline 0 -menu $m.edit.m1
20:  menubutton $m.find -text Find -underline 0 -menu $m.find.m1
21:  menubutton $m.help -text Help -underline 0
22:  pack $m.file $m.edit $m.find -in $m -side left
23:  pack $m.help -in $m -side right
24:
25:  menu $m.file.m1
26:  $m.file.m1 add command -label Open
27:  $m.file.m1 add command -label Save
28:  $m.file.m1 add command -label "Save As"
29:  $m.file.m1 add command -label Quit
30:
31:  menu $m.edit.m1
32:  $m.edit.m1 add command -label Cut
33:  $m.edit.m1 add command -label Paste
34:  $m.edit.m1 add command -label Copy
35:  $m.edit.m1 add command -label Clear -com "$tf.t delete 1.0 end"
36:  #find menu
37:  menu $m.find.m1
38:  $m.find.m1 add cascade -label "Find" -menu $m.find.m1.fmenu
39:  $m.find.m1 add command -label "Replace"
40:  $m.find.m1 add command -label "Tag"
41:  menu $m.find.m1.fmenu
42:  $m.find.m1.fmenu add radiobutton -label Forward
43:  $m.find.m1.fmenu add radiobutton -label Backward
```

ANALYSIS Note that, in this script, you are making use of the Tk frame widgets. Frames are good containers for organizing the layout of your application windows. The example above illustrates this point.

> Because you must specify widgets by their full pathnames, make it a habit to assign short variable names to full pathnames, particularly when you know that you will be using the pathnames repeatedly. You can see the convenience afforded by this in the following analysis of the preceding script.

In lines 1, 3, and 5, you assign three widget pathnames to the variables w, m, and tf, respectively. In lines 2, 4, and 6, you create three frames with names specified by w, m, and tf. The first frame is a child of the root and acts as the base for the other two frames, which are packed one below the other. You want the frame at the top to act as a menubar and the frame below to hold the scrollbar and text widget. The three frames are packed accordingly in lines 8–10.

Next, you create the scrollbar .main.txtframe.ys ($tf.ys) and the text widget .main.txtframe.t ($tf.t) as children of the text frame window .main.txtframe ($tf) in lines 12–14, associating each with the other. In line 16, the text window and scrollbar are packed into the frame $tf, as you will see in Hour 13, "Using the Tk Text Widget."

Script lines 18–21 create a set of four menubuttons named $m.file, $m.edit, $m.find, and $m.help. The underline option specifies a letter from the text label of the menubutton that will be assigned for keyboard traversal. This will enable the user to invoke the pull-down menu associated with that menubutton by using the keyboard rather than the mouse pointer.

The menu option specifies the name of the pull-down menu associated with the menubutton. The File, Edit, and Find menubuttons are packed into the menubar in that order, from the left to the right as specified in line 22. The Help menubutton is packed into the menubar right-justified by the script in line 23. You have now created a menubar in keeping with the current style of desktop applications!

You now define three pull-down menus—$m.file.m1, $m.edit.m1, and $m.find.m1. You leave the Help button without any added behavior.

In line 25, the widget command menu pathName is used to create the menu $m.file.m1. The script in lines 26–29 adds four command entries. The labels of these entries are Open, Save, Save As, and Quit. You are familiar with the command menu add entryType ?option value? from Listing 12.1. Notice that the entries here represent a basic set of file commands that you will want to use with a text widget. Now you can guess where we are heading!

12

You can add callbacks to entries using the -command option, but don't add callback event bindings until later. First, complete the construction of the remaining pull-down menu definitions instead. The edit menu $m.edit.m1 is pretty similar to the File menu, except that its labels represent common editing tasks such as Cut, Copy, Paste, and Clear.

The Find menu, defined in script lines 37–42, contains a cascade and two command entries. The cascade entry Find Selection has an additional walk-through submenu to specify whether the intended search will go forward or backward from the current insertion position in the text widget. Script lines 41–43 define this submenu with two radiobutton entries.

> Note that the entries permitted for a menu are cascade, command, checkbutton, and radiobutton. Even though the menubutton posts a menu when selected, it is a widget and is not an admissible menu entry. The cascade entry is provided for the spawning of a menu from it. Use it for constructing walk-through level submenus.

FIGURE 12.3

An application window with one menubar and several pull-down menus.

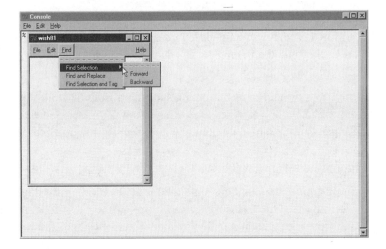

The Pop-up Menu

Another frequently used type of menu is the pop-up menu. This style of menu can be used in your applications to present application commands and other window-system–related commands. This menu is also useful to invoke other applications from the current cursor position. Users might find it annoying if they are required to leave their current working positions and return to the application window frame simply to access some frequently used command. Keyboard shortcuts can be attached to menus to obviate this problem. However, it is good user-interface–development practice to provide mouse-pointer–based interactions for novice users who might want to browse the available commands before invoking them. These options are also helpful for users who are not comfortable with keyboard shortcuts. Pop-up menus are designed to cater to these users' needs.

Pop-up menus are generally bound to the right mouse button.

One important consideration a with pop-up menu is that it must always be posted within the boundary of its application window. In Tk, you can use the indexes %x and %y to guarantee that a pop-up pops up within its application window. Pop-up menus are posted using the built-in Tk command tk_popup, which you already encountered in Listing 12.2.

Note that %X and %Y represent the position with respect to the whole screen, whereas %x and %y represent the pixel coordinates of the current position of the cursor within the currently active window.

The example in Listing 12.4 demonstrates the use of a pop-up menu. Figure 12.4 shows the result of executing this script.

LISTING 12.4 Pop-up and Option Menus

```
 1:  menu .mu -tearoff 1
 2: .mu add checkbutton -label Bold
 3: .mu add checkbutton -label Italic
 4: .mu add checkbutton -label Underline
 5: .mu add separator
 6: .mu add radiobutton -label Times
 7: .mu add radiobutton -label Courier
 8: .mu add radiobutton -label Helvetica
 9:
10: proc postMenu {x y} {
11:     tk_popup .mu $x $y
12: }
13:
14: set w .main
15: pack [frame $w]
16: pack [text $w.t -width 80 -height 20 ]
17: bind $w.t  <Button-3> {postMenu %x %y}
```

12

ANALYSIS Line 1 defines a menu .mu using the menu widget command. The tearoff option is set to 0 so that the menu may not be cloned. Lines 2–8 use the command menuName add entryType ?option value? to add three checkbuttons, three radiobuttons, and a separator to .mu. Recall that this bit of the script has already been encountered in Listing 12.2.

The procedure postMenu is defined in lines 10–12. It takes two inputs, the x and y coordinates of the mouse cursor position with respect to the display, and it executes the command tk_popup menuName x y to pop up the menu .mu.

You create a single frame widget $w, the child of the root window in line 15. A text widget, $w.t, is created and managed in line 16. In line 17, you add an event binding to this text widget for the right mouse button. Whenever the right mouse button is pressed, the script associated with this binding reads the mouse cursor position and calls the tk_popup procedure with these values to post the menu .mu as a popup. The top-left corner of the menu is positioned over x,y.

The result of executing this script is shown in Figure 12.4.

FIGURE 12.4

The pop-up menu.

Message and Dialog Boxes

Message and dialog boxes serve an essential role in graphical user interfaces of applications. They display information to and query information from the user with a heightened visual effect that ensures the user's attention and response to the information. Some functions in an application do not occur frequently, even though they are important and detailed enough to warrant explicit user response. It would be confusing, cumbersome, and even annoying if these were allowed to clutter the application's window. As a good interface designer, you should allocate these to pop-up message boxes within your application and, thereby, present the information or query only when required.

A dialog box is a compound widget with a top level that contains an optional icon, a message, perhaps an entry widget for alphanumeric input, and one or more pushbuttons. There are adequate numbers of built-in Tk message boxes for use in all the situations that require them. In Tk, you create a message using the command tk_messageBox ?option value?. Important options for this command are -title, -message, -icon, -type, and -parent. Tk provides built-in information, question, warning, and error icons. The –type option is either abortretrycancel, ok, okcancel, retrycancel, yesno, or yesnocancel.

It is easier to explain and understand the use of message boxes using an example. The following example asks the user whether he wants to select a Tcl file from a current directory. If the user agrees, the Tk built-in fileselection dialog is presented. If the user selects a file, the application checks whether it is a Tcl script file. This is done in a simple way by checking the filename extension. If it is, indeed, a .tcl file, the application tells the user the chosen filename and asks the user whether he wants a repeat performance. If the chosen file is not a Tcl script file, the application inquires whether the user wants to retry. This introduces the various built-in message facilities. The script is given in Listing 12.5.

LISTING 12.5 Message and Dialog Boxes

```
 1: proc checkFile { fname } {
 2: set ext [file extension $fname]
 3: if {$ext == ".tcl"} {
 4:    set answer [tk_messageBox -icon info -type yesno -title "Tk Dialog boxes" \
 5:              -message "You have selected [file tail $fname].\n
 6:                Click Yes to browse directory again. \
 7:                No to exit."  -parent .]
 8:         switch — $answer {
 9:                no exit
10:                yes { selectFile }
11:                      }
12:         } else {
13:                set answer [tk_messageBox -icon error -type retrycancel \
14:                         -title "Tk Dialog boxes" \
15:                -message "Select a TCL file. \nRetry to browse again \n \
16:                Cancel to exit."  -parent .]
17:                switch — $answer {
18:                         cancel exit
19:                         retry { selectFile }
20:                      }
21:               }
22: }
23: proc selectFile {} {
24: set fltyp {
25:         {"Tcl scripts" {.tcl}  }
26:         {"Text files"   { .txt .doc }   }
27:         {"Text files"    {}       }
28:         {"C source files"       {.c .h} }
29:         {"All source files"     {.tcl .c .h}     }
30:         {"Image files"          {.gif .jpeg .jpg}       }
31:         {"All files" *}
32:         }
33:         set fname [tk_getOpenFile  -filetypes $fltyp -parent .]
34:           if {$fname == ""} {
35:                retryEmptyInput{}
```

12

continues

LISTING 12.5 continued

```
36:                     } else {
37:                             checkFile $fname
38:                     }
39: }
40: set answer [tk_messageBox -icon question \
41:       -type ok -title "Tk Dialog boxes" \
42:       -message "Click OK to browse current directory." \
43:       -parent .]
44: switch — $answer {
45:    ok { selectFile }
46: }
```

The analysis of this script is best explained with the schematic diagram in Figure 12.5.
ANALYSIS The explanation starts bottom up when you view it in terms of the line numbers.

Line 40 creates and pops up a question dialog/message box to query whether the user
wants to browse the current working directory to select a Tcl file. When the user clicks

FIGURE 12.5

*Schematic diagram
of a message box
example.*

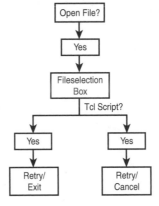

on OK, he or she assigns that string to the variable answer. The switch statement in line
44 invokes the procedure selectFile defined in script lines 23–39. The Tcl switch
command is similar to the C control flow procedure and is described in Hour 4,
"Controlling Your Program."

Script lines 24–32 set up a list of lists fltyp. This variable describes the various file
types, the first item in each list, and a list of their associated extensions (which comprise
the second item). To refresh your knowledge of these structures, see Hour 5, "Working
with Lists."

The built-in Tk command tk_getOpenFile ?option value? automatically pops up the built-in Tk `fileselection` box and returns the filename specified by the user. As always, the appropriate options enable you to specify the directory, default file, parent for this widget, file types to be filtered in, and so on. In this example, you are restricted to -`filetype` and -`parent`, for which we specify `$fltyp` and the root window, respectively. The `fileselectionbox` can appear anywhere on the screen, but it usually appears at the center. The returned filename is assigned to the variable `fname` in script line 33. The procedure `checkFile` will be invoked with `fname` as input.

Script lines 1–22 define the `checkFile` procedure. This simple procedure uses the Tcl built-in command file extension `fileName` to extract the extension of the selected file. If it is `.tcl`, then a YESNO message box pops up to show the selected file and invites the user to select another file. If the user does not want another file, the application exits. If he or she does, the `selectFile` procedure is invoked again.

If the selected file is not a Tcl script, a RETRYCANCEL message box pops up to invite the user to retry selecting the file or exit from the application.

> The -`type` option indicates the type of message box. Note also that the returned value is a string representing the button pressed. This string is used as the enumeration argument for the switch statement.

The message boxes invoked are shown in Figure 12.6.

FIGURE 12.6

Various Tk message and dialog boxes.

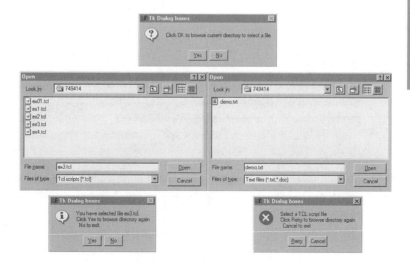

12

NEW TERM A modal dialog occurs when a message window grabs the focus of the keyboard and mouse, relinquishing these only when the user has responded to the dialog. The file selection box and the initial login window of your computer are examples of modal dialog widgets. Modal dialogs are useful when you want to ensure that the user responds to the query in a message box.

Tk makes creating modal dialogs easy. The Tk dialog boxes are just like message boxes, but they are modal. You can create dialog boxes similar to the message boxes using the built-in Tk command `tk_dialog window ?option value?`. The set of options and values enable you to customize the dialog widget with the message and the number of buttons, and so forth.

Do	Don't
Do ensure that message and dialog boxes are automatically closed/destroyed when the user makes a choice or when he hits the return key after inputting data.	**Don't** parent inappropriate windows as parents for menus. Use toplevel or frame windows.
Do ensure that messages in dialog and message boxes are concise and clear. Avoid verbose statements. Use short, sharp commands.	**Don't** design message and dialog boxes to be larger than your application window.
Do use single word verbs or nouns in menu labels.	

Summary

In this hour, you learned how to use intercommunication commands and how to create menus, message boxes, and dialog windows. This hour also introduced the concept of modal and modeless interaction. Together these commands, these widgets, and their behavior enhance the interactivity and appeal of your application and the productivity of its users.

In addition to all the widgets you studied here, Tk also provides versatile and sophisticated text and canvas widgets. These are introduced progressively in the next hours, starting with Hour 13.

Q&A

Q What is `sel` tag?

A When a text widget is created, Tk automatically creates a special tag known as `sel`. This sel tag is automatically associated with the current selection in the text widget. Note that you can select text in a text widget even when its status is disabled. Please go through Exercise 2, which makes use of `sel` tag.

Q How do I create pinnable menus?

A Setting the value of the `-tearoff` option to `1` while creating a menu with the widget command `menu menuName ?option value?` creates a clone of the menu created with that command. Clicking on the dotted-line (visible in Figure 12.3 or 12.4), pops up the clone as a toplevel window.

Workshop

The quiz section below is designed to provide you with an opportunity to recall some of the important concepts introduced in this hour. In the following exercises section, we have introduced exercises that consolidate and slightly extend the material you learned by using examples of practical value. Our aim is that these two sections should reinforce the knowledge you have gained in this hour. The answers to the quiz that follows can be found in Appendix A, "Answers to Quizzes."

Quiz

1. What are intercommunication commands used for?
2. What does the `grab` command do?
3. Why doesn't the Tcl/Tk interpreter return a widget or path name when you execute a command of the type `menu add entryType ?option value?`?
4. What are the types of entries can you use for a menu?
5. Can you use a menubutton to spawn a submenu?
6. What are the differences between an option menu and a list?
7. What are the built-in Tk message icons and types?
8. What is a modal dialog?

12

Exercises

Solutions to the exercises are on the CD-ROM that accompanies this book.

1. Write a Tk application to represent a function of a service station. The user should be able to select the type of gas. He should be able to start and stop the filling of his tank. As filling takes place, update the amount of gas filled and the price due. Use the built-in Tcl command `after ms ?script?`, which executes `script` after a time delay given by `ms`.

2. You are given a moderately large ASCII file containing about 2,000 words, each containing nine letters. Write a simple game application in which a word is randomly selected, jumbled up, and presented. The user has to unscramble the word. Provide a Hint button that will give a letter in the correct order each time.

Hour 13

Using the Tk Text Widget

In the last three hours, you were introduced to the Tk widgets, their basics uses, and the commands you can use to manipulate these widgets. In this hour and the next, you will learn about the Tk text widget in detail. This widget has many powerful and versatile features that you will want to exploit for your own applications. For instance, the Tk text widget enables you

- To display text in different styles by attaching text tags
- To add marks that refer to logical positions within the displayed text
- To create hypertext type links that activate other Tcl commands, using the tag mechanism
- To embed other widgets and images within the text and activate them

Marks, tags, embedded windows, and embedded images collectively provide four different types of annotation techniques within the Tk text widget. Understanding the extent of the Tk text widget's features and learning how to use them will enhance your repertoire of Tk knowledge.

Frequently, you need to search in text widgets for certain phrases. You will learn how to search for phrases using a simple, useful text editor application.

In this hour you will learn

- To create a simple text widget
- To insert text into the widget
- To use some of the built-in text widget bindings
- To use more useful text widget options
- To customize display styles with tags
- To search for phrases in text displayed in a text widget

Creating a Text Widget

The Tk built-in command `text pathName ?option value?` creates a text widget. Start a wish shell and experiment with the code in Listing 13.1. Try executing it at the Tcl command prompt in the wish application's console.

LISTING 13.1 The Text Widget

```
1: %text .t -width 80 -height 20 -bg gray
2: .t
3: %pack .t
```

ANALYSIS Line 1 creates a simple text widget, `.t`. Recall that the Tk command of the type `widgetClass pathname ?option value?` creates a widget of the specified type with a unique identifier. It will have all the appropriate attributes with default values, except for those values that will be taken from the user-specified list of options and values. The command returns the widget path name as shown in line 2. You have set the width, height, and background color when you created this widget. The values for these options render a text widget that is *80* characters wide and *20* lines long with a *gray* background. Line 3 packs the widget.

So far, it is not very exciting. But wait until you have some real text in this widget. The next section shows you how to do this.

Inserting Text Using Indices

Recall that when Tk creates a widget, it also creates a widget command associated with that widget. The name of a widget command is the same as the name of the widget with which it is associated. You will make extensive use of the widget command mechanism for configuring, customizing, and manipulating widgets in Tk applications.

The widget command is used in conjunction with the command `insert` when you want to insert text into a Tk text widget. In this sense, `insert` can be thought of as a widget action subcommand. The Tk text `insert` command takes an `index` for the first argument and the text to be inserted as the second argument. The syntax for an index is of the form `base ?modifier modifier?`, where `base` specifies a starting point, and any number of optional modifiers adjust the index from this starting point. An example is the indexing syntax `"fourth line from the end of text"`. Here, the end is the base for the index, the `fourth line from the end` modifies that base, and the index is calculated. In the following section of code, Listing 13.2, you can experiment with inserting text in the text widget using some of the available indices and modifiers.

LISTING 13.2   Inserting Text in a Text Widget

```
1: % .t insert 1.0 "My first line"
2: % .t insert end " My second line"
3: % for {set i 0} {$i < 10} {incr i} {
4: >    .t insert end "This is line number $i\n"
5: >}
6: % .t insert "end - 3 lines" "Third line from bottom"
7: % .t insert "end - 7  lines lineend" "HELLO"
```

ANALYSIS In line 1, the phrase `"My first line"` is inserted at a position defined by an index whose base is of the form `line.char`. In this instance, it is the first character of the very first line.

>   Note that the line numbers start from 1, whereas the character positions within each line start from zero, as they do in many system editors.

Line 2 inserts `"My second line"` at the end of `"My first line"`. Why? The special base end indicates the end of text, usually the character just after the last newline character. In this case, there was no newline, and as a result, `"My second line"` appears in the first line of the text window. In lines 3–5, you have created nine new lines of text using a `for` loop.

So far, you have used the index bases of the type `line.char` and end without any modifiers. In line 6, the base end is modified with `"- 3 lines"`, so that the text `"Third line from the bottom"` is inserted exactly in that line. Note that the insertion has taken place at the start of that line by default. In line 7, you further modify the specification by insisting that you want the new phrase to be inserted at the end of the seventh line from the end of the last newline.

13

You can use character count instead of line count in a similar way. There are two other special modifiers based on words—wordend and wordstart. These work similarly. Figure 13.1 shows the result of the experiment so far. Please refer to the Tcl/Tk manual pages for the list of available index bases and their modifiers.

FIGURE 13.1

Inserting text in a text widget using indices.

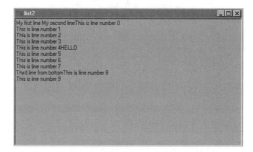

 The index base @x,y indicates the coordinates of the pixel containing a character in a text widget. This type of indexing is very useful. It is used by widget bindings when you are interacting with the text widget using the mouse and keyboard. From these, you can dynamically inquire the position coordinates of the insertion cursor when the text widget has the current input focus. After you have these position coordinates, you can alter the displayed text at that position.

The base end will always refer to the last character in the text widget. The modifiers can be applied before but not after. That means "end -2 chars" is OK, but "end + 2 chars" is not. When there is more than one modifier, remember to protect the embedded spaces by enclosing the whole thing in either " " or {}. However, remember that if you do use {}, then variable substitution will not happen.

Built-in Bindings of the Tk Text Widget

Recall from Hour 11, "Adding Behavior to Your Widgets," that widget binding is the mechanism that causes a Tcl script to be evaluated when a specified event, such as button press, occurs in a window for which the binding is defined. The Tk text widget has an extensive set of built-in binding functionality that your applications can exploit. For instance, you can carry out many ordinary editing tasks in interactive mode, without having to develop any script for such tasks. You can set the insertion cursor by pressing the mouse button1 at any point in the displayed text of a text widget. This enables you to directly type text at that point. You also can press and hold the left-mouse button and select the text by dragging the mouse across it. You then can use the delete or backspace keys on your keyboard to delete the selected text. Inserting/typing new text also deletes the selected text and replaces it with what you are currently typing.

You can use the copy/cut keys on your keyboard to copy text from either another part of the text window itself or from another application on your desktop. You then use the paste key to paste that text in to the text widget. After copying, you press mouse button2 at the desired location in the text window to paste the selection.

You can press and hold mouse button2 and drag the mouse up and down for fast scanning of the text. Double-click on a word to select it or triple-click to select the complete line.

If you are an Emacs user, the Tk text widget supports many of the <Meta> and <control> key combinations for editing characters and similar tasks.

Take a few minutes to try the built-in bindings of the text widget to familiarize yourself with the built-in capability.

Using More Tk Text Widget Options

You can display all the default options available to configure a widget by using the widget command and the subcommand `configure` without any further input arguments. Now type `.t configure` at the Tcl console window to see the complete listing of options available for configuring the text widget. Notice that most of the options are common to other widgets that you saw in the widget tour in Hour 10, "Getting Started with Tk." However, some of the options are new, and some of these are specific to complex widgets such as the text widget.

Some of the text-widget–specific options you might want to use are

- The selection of the background and foreground colors
- The insertion cursor shape
- How the lines of text that exceed the width of the text window are to be wrapped
- The default spacing above and below each line of text

The Tk text window can also be configured with the `-setgrid` option to resize to an integer number of characters in both length and width. This option will also automatically wrap the text if the window is resized.

The text widget is one of the Tk widgets that has the `-yscrollcommand` and the `-xscrollcommand` options. Recall that these options enable you to create a text widget that can be scrolled vertically and horizontally using scrollbars. You will explore the text-scrolling concept with an example given in Listing 13.3. To do this, you can import any

13

piece of text you have available. You can copy the vr.txt file or create your own example.txt file for experimenting with this part of the exercise. In the Listing 13.3, which follows, you will also try the selection of foreground, background, and text wrapping.

LISTING 13.3   The Scrollable Text Widget

```
 1: scrollbar .ys -command {.t yview}
 2: .ys
 3: text .t -width 60 -height 20 -bg grey -yscrollcommand {.ys set}
 4: .t
 5: pack .t .ys -side left -fill y
 6: .t configure -selectforeground red \
 7: -selectbackground yellow -wrap word
 8: if {[file exists "vr.txt"] == 1} {
 9:     set f [open "vr.txt" r]
10:     while {[gets $f line] >=0 } {
11:         .t insert end "$line\n"
12:         }
13:     } else {
14:     .t insert end "Can't open file\n"
15: }
```

ANALYSIS   You should now have a vertically scrollable text widget with the contents of "vr.txt" displayed, as shown in Figure 13.2. Now you can analyze what this code does. Recall that Tk built-in commands of the type widgetClass pathName ?option value? create a widget of the specified type and return the widget name. Following the logic of this syntax, line 1 creates a scrollbar ".ys". Recall from Hour 12, "Understanding Intercommunication Commands," that the option -command lets the scrollbar notify the widget .t associated with this command that it must change its view.

Line 3 creates the text widget with width and height specified in the units of the characters of the default font. In this case, it is 60 characters wide and 20 lines long. The widget background is set to gray. The -yscrollcommand sets .ys to be the vertical scrollbar associated with the text widget. It passes a list of two real fractions to the scrollbar. Recall from Hour 12 that these fractions indicate the start and end of the proportion of text that is displayed in the visible part of the text widget. This will enable the scrollbar slider to size and position itself along the scrollbar.

Line 4 returns the text widget name. Line 5 specifies the packing order from the left and adjusts the scrollbar height. Line 6 uses the widget action subcommand .t configure to wrap the text at a complete word and to set the selection foreground to red and background to yellow.

The value for the wrap option is character, word, or none.

Line 8 checks for the existence of a text file named "vr.txt". If the file exists, it is opened with read permission and the variable f is assigned the file handle returned by the open command. The while loop in lines 10–12 reads each line in the text file and appends it at the end of the current text in the text widget. The while loop continues until the end of the file is reached. If the file does not exist or if it cannot be opened for any reason, an error message is displayed in the text widget.

If you get any error when executing this piece of code, please check that you have read access to the directory and the file. You can use the Tcl catch command to trap this error rather than using the if file exists else route.

Note how the scrollbar uses the default values from the text widget's -yscrollcommand to adjust itself when the text is loaded.

FIGURE 13.2
The vertically scrollable text widget.

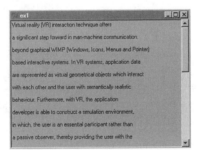

13

Using Symbolic Marking in Text Widgets

In the last section, you handled positions within the displayed text, as well as within the text window, in terms of numbers calculated in several forms. You passed this to the Tk text widget position specifier index. Tk also enables you to use symbolic names, called marks, for specifying positions within the text widget. You can also use these with widget commands. The syntax for mark takes much the same form as that for index; unlike index, however, mark refers to the same logical position within the text, persisting even when you add or delete any of the text.

For instance, .t mark set sty 1.4 sets a mark named sty to refer to the gap between character 4 in the first line and the character preceding it. If you remove a character from the first line, sty will automatically refer to the gap between character 3 in the first line and the character preceding it. Even if you add a whole line, sty will mark the new position of that gap! An example of this is shown in Listing 13.4.

LISTING 13.4   Using Mark in a Text Widget

```
1: % .t mark set sty 3.0
2: % .t index sty
3: 3.0
4: % .t get sty
5: a
6: % .t insert 3.0 "STY Tcl/Tk in 24 hours. \n"
7: % .t index sty
8: 4.0
```

ANALYSIS Line 1 in Listing 13.4 sets a mark sty at the gap preceding the first character of line 3. You inquire this setting by using the index widget command, passing the mark sty as the argument in line 2. Line 3 returns this value to be 3.0 as you expect. You can also use the get widget command, as in line 4. Tk returns the character to the right of the mark by default, as shown in line 5. You insert a new string "STY Tcl/Tk in 24 hours. \n" in line 6. If you inquire what the index is referred to by sty, you will see it is 4.0!

You can decide how a mark behaves by setting the gravity using the command .t mark gravity sty <value>. If a mark has left gravity, it is attached to the character on its left, remaining to the left of any text inserted at the marked position. With the default right gravity, new text inserted at the marked position will appear to the right of the mark. Listing 13.5 illustrates this point. Figure 13.3 shows the result of executing the Tcl commands in Listings 13.4 and 13.5.

LISTING 13.5   Using the Gravity Setting for a Mark in a Text Widget

```
 1: % .t mark set sty1 6.0
 2: % .t mark gravity sty1 left
 3: % .t index sty1
 4: 6.0
 5: % .t get sty1
 6: b
 7: % .t insert 6.0 "STY Tcl/Tk in 24 hours. \n"
 8: % .t get sty1
 9: S
10: % .t index sty1
11: 6.0
```

ANALYSIS

You can pass mark as the base and/or base modifier to index for inserting or deleting text. All the index base modifiers work with mark.

The Tk text widget mark persists, even if the characters on either of its sides are removed. You have to use the unset command to remove a set mark.

insert and *current* are two special marks that cannot be removed with pathName mark unset command. These two are created automatically when the text widget is created. insert identifies the location of the insertion cursor that you can modify (as you do with index). current identifies the character underneath the mouse pointer in the text widget.

FIGURE 13.3
Using mark *and configuring its gravity.*

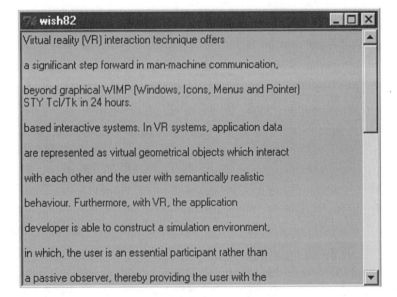

Controlling Display Styles with Text Widget Tags

A tag, like a mark, is another annotation technique used with Tk text widgets. Tags are used to control the display style of the associated text, to bind events to the associated text, and for use with the primary selection of text in the text widget. We will discuss the display styles in this hour and defer the discussion on the second and third purposes until Hour 13, "Using the Tk Text Widget."

A tag is a text string that is associated with one or more characters in displayed text. You can use many tags with the same set of characters or the same tag with many sets of characters. A priority order is defined among tags when they are created. This order is then used to implement some of the tag-related functions. When a tag is defined, it is given a priority higher than any existing tag. This priority order can be changed using the widget commands pathName tag raise and pathName tag lower.

The default display style of characters in a text widget is determined by the widget's background, foreground, and font options. You can change this default display style for any character(s) by associating the character with a tag that has a different display option. That means you create a tag, configuring a display option in that creation process. When you attach this tag to one or more characters, the tagged characters will take on the display style of the tag. The tag's display options thus override the default display style of characters it is attached to. You will explore this concept, as well as gain an insight into the built-in text display styles supported by the Tk text widget, using the code in Listing 13.6.

LISTING 13.6   Defining Tags for Display Styles

```
 1: % .t tag configure Bold -font {Times 18 bold}
 2: % .t tag configure bgstipple -background black \
 3: -borderwidth 0 -bgstipple gray12
 4: % .t tag configure fgstipple -fgstipple gray50
 5: % .t tag configure uline -underline on
 6: % .t tag configure centre -justify center
 7: % .t tag configure subS -offset -2p -font {Courier 10}
 8: % .t tag configure superS -offset 2p -font {Couier 10}
 9: % if {[winfo depth .t] > 1 } {
10:     .t tag configure cl1 -foreground green
11:     .t tag configure cl1 -background red
12: } else {
13: .t tag configure cl1 -foreground white
14: .t tag configure cl1 -background black
15: }
16: .t tag configure raiseTxt -relief raised -borderwidth 1
17: .t tag configure lowerTxt -relief sunken -borderwidth 1
18: % .t delete 1.0 end
19: % .t insert end  "STY Tcl/Tk in 24 hours \n" Bold
20: % .t insert end  "We are experimenting with " cl1
21: % .t insert end "text display styles." bgstipple
```

ANALYSIS In lines 1–17, you define a series of tags using the widget command `pathName` `tag configure tagName ?option value?`. When the tags are defined, you want to try them. In line 18, you cleared the text widget of previous trials using the widget command `.t delete`. In lines 19–21, you insert three text strings with different display styles using the familiar `insert` command. Note that you append the tag name just after the end of the string to be inserted into the text widget using the `insert` command. Figure 13.4 shows the result.

> You need to ensure that your hardware can support some of the tags defined in the previous listing. This is done in the `if ... else` section starting at line 9.

FIGURE 13.4

Associating tags with a range of characters in text.

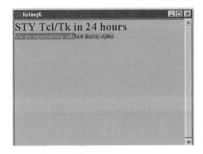

Searching for Phrases

One of the natural tasks users want to perform is looking for specific words and phrases in a text. It is also natural for most programmers to want to write a simple text editor as a way of coming to grips with the programming language they want to master. You combine these two needs to create a simple application. You can construct it in such a way that you consolidate your skill in creating and manipulating menus and dialogs.

The script in Listing 13.7 adds behavior to the Open and Find menu items. It enables you to open an ASCII text file into your text widget. You can then select the find `forward` or `backward` menu item. This provides a pop-up dialog for you to enter a word and conduct a search for that word in the displayed text. The first time the word is found, it is highlighted, and the insertion cursor is placed at that position.

13

LISTING 13.7 An Application

```
1: proc findDialog { w } {
2: global searchDir
3: toplevel .top
4: # window title to distinguish from other apps
5: wm title .top "Searching in text widget $w"
6: frame .top.f1
7: pack .top.f1
8: label .top.f1.find -text {Find: }
9: entry .top.f1.e
10: bind .top.f1.e <Return> "findWord $w .top"
11: pack .top.f1.find .top.f1.e -side left -expand 1
12:
13: # dismiss button
14: button .top.b -text Dismiss -command "findWord $w .top"
15: pack .top.b -fill x
16:
17:  }
18:
19: proc findWord { w w1 } {
20: global searchDir
21: set str [$w1.f1.e get]
22: destroy $w1
23: if {$str != ""} {
24:         $w tag config search -background yellow
25:         if { $searchDir == "fwd"} {
26:             set idx [$w search -forwards -exact $str 1.0 end]
27:             $w insert $idx ""
28:           } else {
29:             set idx [$w search -backwards -exact $str end 1.0]
30:             $w insert $idx ""
31: }
32:         $w tag add search  $idx "$idx wordend"
33:         } else {
34:          set answer [tk_messageBox -icon error -type retrycancel -title
            ➥"Tk Message boxes" \
35:           -message "Empty word to search. \nClick Retry to input search
            ➥word. \n \
36:            Cancel to exit."  -parent .]
37:           switch -- $answer {
38:                          cancel exit
39:                          retry {findDialog $w  }
40:                  }
41:          }
42:
43:   }
44:
45:  proc openFile {w} {
46: set fltyp {
```

```
47:            {"Tcl scripts"  {.tcl}  }
48:            {"Text files"   {}        }
49:            {"Text files"   { .txt .doc }   }
50:            {"C source files"      {.c .h} }
51:            {"All source files"    {.tcl .c .h}    }
52:            {"Image files"         {.gif .jpeg .jpg}      }
53:            {"All files" *}
54:            }
55:            set fname [tk_getOpenFile -filetypes $fltyp -parent .]
56:            if {[file exists $fname] == 1} {
57:                    set f [open $fname r]
58:                    while {[gets $f line] >= 0} {
59:                            $w insert end "$line\n"
60:                    }
61:            } else {
62:                    $w insert end "Can't open file: \"$fname\".\n" {Bold}
63:            }
64:
65: }
66:
67: set w .main
68: frame $w
69: set m $w.mbar
70: frame $m -relief raised -bd 2
71: set tf $w.txtframe
72: frame $tf
73: pack $w
74: pack $m -in $w -side top -fill x
75:  pack $tf -after $m -side bottom -fill x
76:
77:  scrollbar $tf.ys -command "$tf.t yview"
78:  text $tf.t -width 40 -height 20 -wrap none \
79:      -yscrollcommand "$tf.ys set" -relief sunken -bd 2
80:
81:  pack $tf.t $tf.ys -in $tf -side left -fill y
82:
83:  menubutton $m.file -text File -underline 0 -menu $m.file.m1
84:  menubutton $m.edit -text Edit -underline 0 -menu $m.edit.m1
85:  menubutton $m.find -text Find -underline 0 -menu $m.find.m1
86:  menubutton $m.help -text Help -underline 0
87:  pack $m.file $m.edit $m.find -in $m -side left
88:  pack $m.help -in $m -side right
89:
90:  menu $m.file.m1
91:  $m.file.m1 add command -label Open -command {openFile $tf.t}
92:  $m.file.m1 add command -label Save
93:  $m.file.m1 add command -label "Save As"
94:  $m.file.m1 add command -label Quit -command {exit}
95:
96:  menu $m.edit.m1
```

13

continues

LISTING 13.7 continued

```
 97:  $m.edit.m1 add command -label Cut
 98:  $m.edit.m1 add command -label Paste
 99:  $m.edit.m1 add command -label Copy
100:  $m.edit.m1 add command -label Clear -com "$tf.t delete 1.0 end"
101:  #find menu
102:  menu $m.find.m1
103:  $m.find.m1 add cascade -label "Find Selection" -menu $m.find.m1.fmenu
104:  $m.find.m1 add command -label "Find and Replace"
105:  $m.find.m1 add command -label "Find Selection and Tag"
106:  menu $m.find.m1.fmenu
107:  $m.find.m1.fmenu add radiobutton -label Forward \
108:          -variable searchDir -value fwd -command "findDialog $tf.t"
109:  $m.find.m1.fmenu add radiobutton -label Backward \
110:          -variable searchDir -value bwd -command "findDialog $tf.t"
```

ANALYSIS The primary purpose of this script is to show you how to attach callback scripts to menu items, create and delete custom message or dialog boxes, and pass user-provided data from the dialog to the application. Script lines 1–17 define the procedure findDialog. This procedure takes the text window's name as its input argument. Its purpose is to create and display a toplevel dialog with a label, an entry, and a button widget. The base for the popup is a toplevel window .top. You add a window title using the command wm title windowName "Title String". Window manager functions are discussed in Hour 10. The entry, label, and button widgets are packed into the frame .top.f1, which is the child of the top level of the dialog. The entry is to be used for inputting the search word or phrase.

The findDialog procedure is the callback script attached to the radiobutton entries you attached to your Find cascade menu. When these radiobutton entries are created, a global variable is also created to store the value selected. In this case, you allocate searchDir to be this global variable. Declaring this global variable in both findDialog and findWord makes it available within both procedures. Recall variable scope from Hour 4, "Controlling Your Program."

Note that the entry widget does not have a command option. Instead, you use the built-in command bind tag <eventType> {script}. This command is discussed in detail in Hour 11. When you hit Return after you have input the search word in the entry widget, or when you click on the Dismiss button, you invoke the callback procedure, findWord, defined in lines 19–43.

It is good practice to provide the user the choice to hit Return after his input string or to click on the Dismiss button.

The procedure findWord takes the text widget and the toplevel window of the dialog widget as input arguments. It retrieves the contents of the entry widget using the widget command widgetName get and assigns it to the variable str. The widget command pathName search -direction -exact $str indexstart indexend retrieves the position at the beginning of the first occurrence of the search word from the current position. This search is carried out in the specified -direction. The insertion cursor is moved to this position. The search word is highlighted in yellow by attaching a display tag. If the user has input an empty string as the search word, the application pops up a warning dialog. This dialog is of type RETRYCANCEL. It explicitly asks the user whether he wants to try again.

The procedure openFile is identical to selectFile, described in Listing 12.4.

In script lines 90, 93, and 99, you have added the -command option to the command entries to open a selected file, exit, and clear the text widget, respectively.

Note that in lines 107 and 109, the two radiobutton entries from Listing 12.3 have additional options specified. As explained earlier, you assign the name searchDir for the global variable associated with these radio entries. Selecting one of these entries will set the value of this global variable.

FIGURE 13.5

A simple text editor, with tear-off pull-down menus.

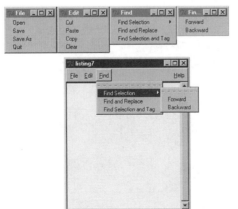

13

Searching and Tagging Repeated Phrases

Let us wrap up this hour with a very simple application to search and tag a repeated phrase in the text displayed in a text widget. It shows you how to use regexp and the Tk command scan to achieve this objective.

For this exercise, create a Tcl script file (for example, ex.tcl) and enter the following code in the file. Ensure that the file is executable. You can then invoke the wish application or source this file in a wish application that is already running. Please ensure that you destroy any widgets named .t and .ys if you are going to reuse a wish application that tested code previously. You can do that by executing the widget command destroy .t .ys.

If you want, you can include a whole range of style tags that are listed in Listing 13.6. The result of executing this script is shown in Figure 13.6.

LISTING 13.8   Associate a Tag to a Phrase in a Text Widget

```
 1:  proc attachTag {w pattern tagtype} {
 2:    scan [$w index end] %d nlines
 3:    for {set i 1} {$i < $nlines} {incr i} {
 4:        $w mark set last $i.0
 5:        while { [regexp -indices "$pattern" \
 6:                [$w get last "last lineend"] indy] } {
 7:                $w mark set first "last + [lindex $indy 0] chars"
 8:                $w mark set last "last +[lindex $indy 1] chars \
 9:                    + 1 char "
10:                $w tag add $tagtype first last
11:                }
12:            }
13:    }
14: scrollbar .ys -command ".t yview"
15: text .t -width 80 -height 20 -yscrollcommand ".ys set"
16: pack .t .ys -side left -fill y
17: .t configure -selectforeground red \
18:     -selectbackground yellow -wrap word
19: .t tag configure Bold -font {Times 18 bold}
20: if {[file exists "vr1.txt"] == 1} {
21:    set f [open "vr1.txt" r]
22:    while {[gets $f line] >= 0} {
23:      .t insert end "$line\n"
24:        }
25:    } else {
26:      .t insert end "Can't open file\n" Bold
27:        }
28: attachTag .t VR Bold
```

ANALYSIS Lines 1–12 above describe a procedure called attachTag. It takes the name of a window, search pattern, and tag as input arguments. The scan command, which has the form scan string formatString ?varName varName?, takes a string. This command assigns values to the list of variables subject to the format specified. It uses the ANSI C sscanf command. In this case, the evaluation of the command $w index end returns the number of lines in the text widget. The scan command assigns the integer part to nlines. Within the for loop, the mark last is assigned to each line of text that is searched for the pattern. If the regular expression pattern is found, the indices of the phrase within that line are assigned to the list indy in line 6.

In line 7, the mark first is assigned to the gap preceding the first character of the phrase, and in line 8 the mark last is assigned to the gap succeeding the last character. Line 10 associates the choice of tags to the range of characters between first and last. Note that this procedure makes use of your knowledge of regular expressions, list manipulation, and marking. Lines 14–27 have already been discussed in this hour in Listings 13.3 and 13.6. Line 28 calls the procedure attachTag with the text widget .t and the word VR with the tag Bold. Try executing this procedure repeatedly with other words in the displayed text and other tags.

FIGURE 13.6

Exercise 2—A procedure to associate a tag with a repeated set of characters.

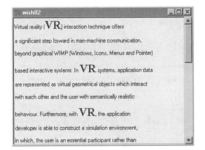

Summary

In this hour, you have learned how to create a text widget, make it scrollable, and then insert text in the style and at the position you want. The text annotation techniques mark and tag were also introduced to you. In this hour, you learned how to use tags to alter the default display style. Tag is a novel and powerful mechanism in Tk, and you will revisit it in Hour 14, and again when we are learning about the canvas widget. You also learned to search for phrases in the text widget.

In the next hour, you will learn how to use tags as event bindings and how to execute Tcl commands. In Hour 14, you will also learn two more annotation techniques, namely embedded windows and embedded images in text widgets.

13

Do	Don't
Do remember that a mark persists even when the character it is assigned to disappears.	**Don't** forget that end+ doesn't work.
Do remember to unset marks to remove them.	**Don't** forget that there should be no space between the - sign and the option name that follows it.
Do remember that pathName get/index markName gives the range of characters around and the position of a mark.	**Don't** forget to protect your modifiers with {} or "".

Q&A

Q What do the -xscrollcommand and -yscollcommand do?

A They pass the parameters for the scrollbar widget command set, so that the slider in the scrollbar can reset itself. The scrollbar then invokes the text widget action subcommand yview or xview of the widget associated with the scrollbar (which is the widget that had the scrollcommand in the first place).

Q What will be the result of executing the following text widget command: .t insert end Sample Line?

A "Sample" will be appended to the end of the text that is already in the text widget. Line will be taken as the name of a tag attached to this phrase "Sample". The point to remember is to protect your text with "Sample Line" or {Sample Line}, if that is what you mean to do.

Q Can you assign more than one tag for the same set of characters?

A Yes, you can assign more than one tag to the same range of characters. The command syntax is .t insert end "tagged text string" {tag1 tag2}. If a set of characters has several tags associated with it, and the tags have conflicting display options, the option of the highest tag is used. If the display options are different, they are all used.

Q Can you assign the same tag to several sets of characters?

A Yes, you can. You repeat the basic syntax of associating a tag with a set of characters for each.

Q What happens to a tag when you remove the range of characters associated with it?

A A tag disappears when you remove the characters associated with it—unlike mark, which persists even when you remove the character associated with it.

Workshop

The "Quiz" section, which follows, is designed to provide you with an opportunity to recall some of the important concepts introduced in this hour. These may be commands, command syntax, common mistakes, usage, and so forth. In the "Exercises" section, we have introduced exercises that consolidate the material you learned by using an example of practical value. Our aim is that these two sections should reinforce the knowledge you have gained in this hour. The answers to the quiz that follows can be found in Appendix A, "Answers to Quizzes."

Quiz

1. Where will the following command insert text in the text widget: `.t insert "end - 5 chars"`?
2. What is the syntax of index?
3. What is the command to determine the number of lines displayed in a text widget?
4. What is the command to insert some text at the point where the mouse is clicked?
5. How do you create a mark called `"lastbutone"` to mark the start of the second last line of text?
6. How do you find the current position of a mark?
7. How do you list a range of characters using a mark?
8. How would you configure a tag for overstrike display style?
9. What is the command to attach a tag to a text string?

Exercises

Solutions to the exercises are on the CD-ROM that accompanies this book.

1. Add an `-xscrollcommand` to the text widget and display some long lines of text.
2. Create a keyboard shortcut to save a file. (Hint: Use any of the listings in this chapter, except 13.5. Insert some text, any text, and use it for saving to a file called demo.txt in the current working directory.)
3. Use the relevant parts of Listing 13.3 or 13.6 to create a text widget and a file menu in a menubar. Open an ASCII text file of your choice into the text widget. Configure three display tag styles—Bold, Underline, and Overstrike. Create a pop-up menu using these three display styles. Write a callback to each menu item that will apply the display style to selected text. (Hint: Use the `sel` tag to retrieve the selected text. Bind the menu popping up to the right mouse button.)

13

HOUR 14

Doing More with the Text Widget

Hour 13, "Using the Tk Text Widget," introduced the Tk text widget. You were taught how to create one, make it scrollable, insert text, create text marks, and attach different text display styles using the tag mechanism. The text widget also supports more advanced forms of annotations. For example, a Tcl script can be executed in response to certain events in the text widget using the tag mechanism that you are already familiar with.

The tag mechanism supports the creation of a hypertext type information display that can be selectively expanded or hidden in response to user actions, such as a mouse click on a specific item.

This hour will help you to explore these advanced annotation features further. In particular, this hour will show you how to

- Use the tag mechanism to create hypertext, such as characters and words in the display
- Embed other Tk widgets in a text widget
- Embed images in a text widget

All these elements in the text widget respond to user actions, such as mouse-button clicks, to invoke interactive behavior in the display.

Tag Bindings

Recall from Hour 13, that a tag is just a text string that you can associate with one or more characters in a text widget. You can associate more than one tag with each such set of characters. You can also associate the same tag with any number of sets of characters. Looked at this way, the tag is recognizable as a grouping mechanism that enables you to refer to the associated group members as if they are a single entity. Tags are user-friendly and an easy way of manipulating the grouped item(s).

> You can also use tags to compose behaviors for the associated items. *Tag binding* responds to mouse events on tagged items with the execution of Tcl commands. That is, the tag binding operates much the same way as the event-callback mechanism that is typical of interactive graphical user interface-based toolkits such as Motif.

To add behavior to the tagged text in a widget, the widget command `pathName tag bind tagName <eventType> {script}` is used. It binds the event specified as `eventType` to the tag `tagName`. The command attaches the script as the callback to be executed when the event happens over the set of characters that are associated with the tag. You will explore the use of this command with an example in Listing 14.1.

An Application Using Tag Bindings

The example in Listing 14.1 is a small, but useful application. In this application, you add a tag to a single phrase `"ShowMe"`. You bind four events to this tag. The first event, `Any-Enter`, tracks the mouse-pointer as it moves on top of the tagged text. When this event happens, you want to send a visual cue to the user so that he can select this word, if desired. You indicate this by changing the cursor to a hand icon. The second event you are interested in is `Any-Leave`, which represents the mouse-pointer leaving the tagged word. Whenever this event happens, you restore the cursor. The third event occurs when the cursor is on the tagged word, and the user clicks the left mouse button, sending a `Button-1` (or just `1`) event. When this happens, you want to execute a Tcl script that will append the callback script at the end of the current text in the text widget. The fourth binding is for the `Shift-Button-1` event. The binding executes the script that deletes the newly inserted lines from the text widget. Figures 14.1 and 14.2 show the results of executing this code successfully.

This code is rather long. We advise you to create a Tcl script file named tagb.tcl in your current working directory and enter the code in it. You can then source this file to execute the script.

Remember that if you use a text editor such as Notepad, it may automatically add a .txt filename extension.

PC users: Remember that if you are using a NT/PC, and if you have set the PATHEXT environment variable correctly, double clicking on the *.tcl script file will automatically invoke the wish application and execute your script. If you have not set up the PATHEXT variable to include the Tcl extensions, invoke the wish application and source this script at the tclsh console window.

LISTING 14.1 The Tag Bind Widget Command

```
1: scrollbar .ys -command ".t yview"
2: text .t -width 60 -height 20 -font {Courier 14} \
3:        -yscrollcommand ".ys set"
4: pack .t .ys -side left -fill y
5: .t insert end "This is short demonstration of tag bindings. \n"
6: .t insert end "The word ShowMe is given a tag. \n"
7: .t insert end "Pressing <Button-1> will display the code, \n"
8: .t insert end "and pressing <Shift-Button-1> will erase the added text. \n"
9: .t tag config tgShowMe -background LightSteelBlue
10: .t tag add tgShowMe "2.10 wordstart" "2.10 wordend"
11: global inserted
12: set inserted 0
13:
14: proc showMeCB {} {
15: global inserted
16: set cb [.t tag bind tgShowMe <Button-1>]
17: if { $inserted == 0 } {
18: .t insert  end "\n The body of the proc ShowMeCB that \
19:          inserted this text: \n [info body $cb] \n" {newTxt}
20:     .t tag config newTxt -foreground CornflowerBlue -font {Times 12}
21:      set inserted 1
22:  } else {
23:         return
24:   }
25: }
26:
27: proc eraseTxtCB {} {
```

continues

LISTING 14.1   continued

```
28: global inserted
29: if {$inserted == 1} {
30:     set rng [.t tag range newTxt]
31:     .t delete [lindex $rng 0] [lindex $rng 1]
32:     set inserted 0
33: } else {
34:     return
35: }
36: }
37:
38: .t tag bind tgShowMe <Any-Enter> {.t config -cursor hand2}
39: .t tag bind tgShowMe <Any-Leave> {.t config -cursor xterm}
40: .t tag bind tgShowMe <Button-1> showMeCB
41: .t tag bind tgShowMe <Shift-Button-1> eraseTxtCB
```

ANALYSIS   Lines 1–4, in the previous listing, create a scrollable text widget `.t`, which is 60 characters wide and 20 lines long. Its default font is set to `Courier` 14pt. Please refer to Hour 12, "Understanding Intercommunication Commands," to refresh your knowledge of the scrollbar set up, the command, and the `-yscrollcommand` options.

Lines 5–8 insert some explanatory text in the text widget, telling the user how to interact with the displayed text.

In line 9, you configure a tag called `tgShowMe` with a `LightSteelBlue` background.

You can, of course, change it to a color of your choice. You can choose the color by executing the command `tk_chooseColor`. This will put up an interactive application to help you choose a color. The application returns the color in hexadecimal code. Use this portable form rather than a logical color name. Note that the named colors are also fewer, and the system defaults to the closest match if given a named color.

Normally, you can get the names of the available colors from /usr/lib/X11/rgb.txt or its equivalent. Alternatively, you can run the widget demonstration under your Tk lib/demos directory to browse a selection of possible colors.

Line 10 uses the widget command `pathName tag add tagName range`. The range is specified by two indices, each of which has the now familiar syntax `base ?modifier ?modifier`. In this example, the bases for both indices are the same—the tenth character of the second line of text. The modifiers are, of course, the `wordstart` and `wordend` keywords. As a result, you have added the tag `tgShowMe` to the word `ShowMe` in the text! The result of executing these lines is shown in Figure 14.1. Note the changed cursor in the figure.

FIGURE 14.1

The scrollable text widget with the tagged text ShowMe *highlighted.*

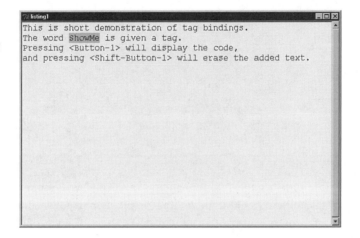

```
listing1
This is short demonstration of tag bindings.
The word ShowMe is given a tag.
Pressing <Button-1> will display the code,
and pressing <Shift-Button-1> will erase the added text.
```

In line 11, you declare a global variable called `inserted` and, in line 12, you initialize it to `0`. The purpose of this variable is to act as a flag to check whether the callback Tcl script is currently displayed in our text widget. If it is, any further inadvertent `Button-1` events are ignored. This avoids displaying the script many times over and cluttering the text widget.

Before executing the tag bindings, specify the callback scripts that these bindings must execute. Lines 14—37 do just that; they define the two callback procedures `showMeCB` and `eraseTxtCB`.

Procedures must be defined before they can be used. We highlight this just to remind you that if you are developing and testing your GUI interactively, the behaviors defined in procedures will come into play and can be tested only after you have defined the procedures.

Line 15 identifies `inserted` as the globally scoped variable for the procedure `showMeCB`. Refer to Hour 7, "Building Your Own Procedures," for variable scope within procedures. The Tcl command `[.t tag bind <Button-1>]` returns the procedure `showMeCB` that is assigned to the variable `cb` in line 16. If the value of `inserted` is zero, that is, if the left

14

mouse button has never been clicked on the tagged text before, the body of the `showMeCB` procedure is appended to the end of the current text in text widget. Otherwise, the procedure just returns. The result is shown in Figure 14.2.

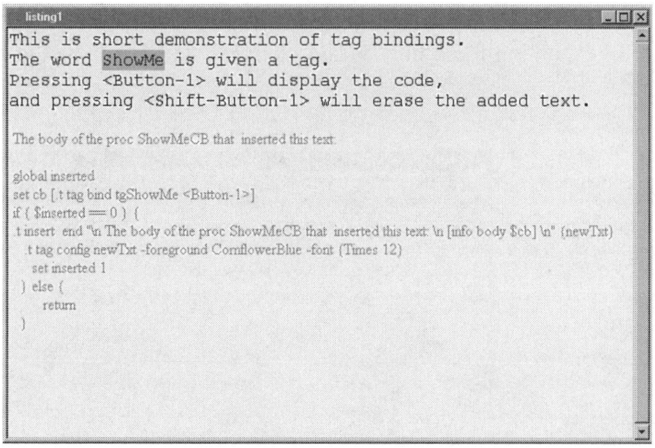

FIGURE **14.2**

The result of Button-1 *tag binding—*showMeCB *script appended in the text widget.*

Note that in line 17, the Tcl command, [info body $cb], returns the body of the `showMeCB` script from lines 15–25 as a string. You have assigned the tag `newTxt` to the new string, which is a concatenation of several lines of Tcl script. These lines are appended to the text widget. The display style is altered by the tag display style of `newTxt` configured in line 20. This procedure gives a good insight into the elegant power that tags offer. The grouping of several lines with a single tag enables you to manipulate them as if they are a single entity, as you will see shortly.

Lines 27–36 define the procedure `eraseTxtCB`, the callback for a `<Shift-Button-1>` event. Here again, the globally scoped variable `inserted` is identified as such. If the value of that variable is identically equal to 1, that is, if the `showMeCB` script has indeed been inserted in the text widget, you set out to delete those lines of text. In line 30, you retrieve the range of the tagged text by executing the command [.t tag range newTxt]. This returns a list containing the start and end indices of the tag `newTxt`. You then delete the tagged lines using the text widget command .t delete *index ?index??*. The Tcl list action command [lindex $rng 0] and [lindex $rng 1] extracts the two indices from the list returned by the widget command tag range in line 30.

In lines 38–41, the widget command pathName tag bind tagName <eventid> {script} is used to declare the four tag bindings for tgShowMe.

Embedded Windows

Text tag bindings make your text-widget–based Tk applications interesting and interactive by making the text elements respond to mouse-pointer–based user actions on them. For the execution of some scripts, however, you might be required to elicit from the user input other than mouse-pointer clicks, for instance, an alphanumeric value. You might want to present a list of options to the user in a compact and dynamic form. You might also want to compose and present interactive pictorial elements along with your tagged text elements as annotation. It is more intuitive and visually compact to present this information using appropriate user interface components. Such a user interface will immediately convey the "look and feel" affordance of that individually identifiable atom. The Tk text widget supports this type of user interface development in the text widget via embedded windows. That is, you can embed any Tk widget in the Tk text widget at any given position. The embedded widget occupies a character of index space and provides all the functionality that it provides as a widget.

An Application Using Embedded Windows

The simple yet powerfully elegant programming interface of Tcl/Tk extends to embedded windows, too. Without further ado, you will develop a simple application, as shown in Listing 14.2, using a text widget with embedded windows. In this application, you embed an entry widget to ask the user to enter a string, actually a Tcl command, to find the number of Tcl commands. You then check whether the input is correct and use that command to display the actual number of Tcl commands, but only if the user wants to know that information. Figure 14.3 and Figure 14.4 show the results of your endeavor.

You have the choice to experiment with the code that follows interactively at the `tclsh` command prompt or to execute it by sourcing the script file.

LISTING 14.2   Embedded Windows

```
 1: scrollbar .ys -command ".t yview"
 2: text .t -font {Courier 12} -wrap word -width 40 \
 3:    -height 20 -yscrollcommand ".ys set"
 4: pack .t .ys -side left -fill y
 5:
 6: .t tag config cl1 -foreground indianred -font {Courier 12 bold}
 7: .t tag config cl2 -foreground green -font {Courier 12 bold}
 8: .t tag config cl3 -foreground purple4 -font {Courier 12 bold} \
 9:      -justify center
10:
11: proc showAnswer {} {
12:    .t mark set bgnAns current
```

14

continues

LISTING 14.2 continued

```
13:    .t insert end "As many as \
14: [llength [info commands]] built-in Tcl commands exist" {cl3}
15: }
16:  proc chkAns {} {
17:     set ans [.entri get]
18:     set rtans {llength [info commands]}
19:     if {[string compare "$ans" "$rtans"] == 0} {
20:        .t insert end "\n Yes you are right. \n" cl2
21:        } else {
22:         .t insert end "\n Sorry, the right answer is:\n\t$rtans\n" {cl1}
23:        }
24: .t insert end "\n"
25: .t window create end -window .b
26: .t insert end "to find out the total \n"
27: }
28:  .t insert end "\n \nEnter the command to enquire\n \
29:     the total number of Tcl built-in commands "
30:  button .b -text "Click here" -command showAnswer
31:  entry .entri -width 25 -relief sunken -bd 2
32: bind .entri <Return> chkAns
33: .t window create end -window .entri –padx 20 –align center
```

ANALYSIS Lines 1–4 generate the standard scrollable text widget! In lines 6–9, you define three tags cl1, cl2, and cl3. In line 28, you insert a guidance text in the text widget asking the user to insert the Tcl command that returns the total number of Tcl built-in commands.

Recall, from Hour 10, "Getting Started with Tk," that the Tk command widgetClass pathName ?option ?value? creates an instance of the widget of the type widgetType, with configuration specified by the option value pairs. It also returns the widget name pathName. Following this syntax, you create a button widget .b with a text label "Click here" and an associated command option to execute the procedure showAnswer when this button is selected. Similarly, in line 31, you create an entry widget named .entri, as the child of the root window. This entry widget is a single line, 25 characters long, that has a sunken relief with a distinguishable border of 2 pixels width. Line 31 binds the <Return> event in this entry widget to the callback routine chkAns, which is defined in lines 16–23.

The widget command of the form pathName window create *index* window windowName embeds the window windowName in the widget pathName at the location specified by index. The option -padx positions the entry widget to the right of the current text by a given value and the option -align. It also adjusts the center of the embedded window with the line of text. Figure 14.3 shows the result of executing the preceding lines of script.

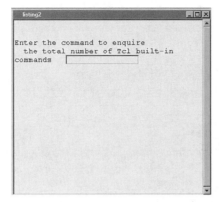

```
listing2                                    _ □ ×
Enter the command to enquire
   the total number of Tcl built-in
commands         [          ]
```

In line 17, you retrieve the content of the entry widget by executing the widget command .entri get and assign it to the variable ans. The right answer is, of course, llength [info commands], which is assigned to the variable rtans in line 18. Please refer to Hour 2 for the Tcl command information and Hour 5, "Working with Lists," for the Tcl command llength. A straightforward string comparison of ans and the right answer rtans is made in line 19. Lines 20–22 display appropriate messages in the text window based on the result of the comparison. It is at this point that you embed the button widget .b in the text widget and invite the user to click on it to execute the llength [info commands] command and get the answer. The result of this is shown in Figure 14.4.

FIGURE **14.4**

The button window is embedded in the text widget when required.

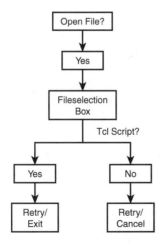

14

For geometry management purposes, the embedded window has to have the text widget either as its parent or the descendant of its parent. When text in the text widget is adjusted or the window is scrolled, the embedded windows are automatically updated.

Embedded Images

Ivan Sutherland said that a picture conveys a thousand words. Images do let you convey the information more succinctly. For this reason, images are used extensively and effectively in information displays all around us. It should come as no surprise, then, that the fourth and last form of annotation afforded by the Tk text widget is embedded images. That is, you can create and embed an image element in a text window and refer to it directly. The embedded image can be any image supported by Tk. For instance, it can be a GIF. You can embed the same image many times within the Tk text window and refer to the image by its name.

Embedded images, like embedded windows, occupy one character's worth of index space in the text widget. You can attach tags to the character of the embedded image and invoke Tcl scripts.

Creating an Embedded Image

The Tcl command `image create imageType` creates an image with specified options. These options primarily include the image format and the filename of the image data. The `imageTypes` supported by Tk are `bitmap` and `photo`. The formats currently supported are XBM, PPM, PGM, GIF, and JPEG. Listing 14.3 is a simple demonstration of how to use embedded images. The tag binding invokes the `exec` command to start the World Wide Web (WWW) http–protocol-based browser. The first or front page of the uniform resource locator (URL) is also passed via this command, and it is used by the browser to display that page. This method of invoking the WWW browser is quite crude and perhaps inadvisable. It is fraught with issues relating to the opened communication link between the caller and the called. In Hour 24, "Building Web-Based Applications with Tcl/Tk," you will revisit this aspect and learn how to use the http package to implement a better way of invoking Web pages.

This application and the Tcl command are discussed here because we feel that exploiting the widespread popularity of the WWW interface in your Tk text-widget–based application increases its appeal. Figure 14.5 shows the result of executing this code.

Tk provides support for creating, including, and manipulating images in your applications at all levels. For instance, in this hour and in Hour 17, "Working with Images in the Canvas," you will learn how to embed and manipulate image data in Tk text and canvas widgets. Once you have mastered Hour 18, "Using C with Tcl/Tk," you will know how to make use of the built-in Tk library routines that allow you to create your own image formats and use them in your Tcl/Tk applications. For more information, consult the online manual pages too.

Be sure you have copied the image file to your current working directory. Alternatively, insert the correct pathname to it.

Ensure that your application can connect to the Web host you will refer to in the example.

INPUT   **LISTING 14.3**   Embedded Images

```
1: scrollbar .ys -command ".t yview"
2: text .t -font {Courier 12} -wrap word -width 40 \
3:    -height 20 -yscrollcommand ".ys set"
4: pack .t .ys -side left -fill y
5: .t mark set m1 end
6: set m [.t index m1]
7: set p1 [image create photo -format GIF -file logo.gif]
8: .t insert end "\n \n"
9: .t image create 2.0 -image $p1 –name cookbook –padx 16
10: .t insert end "\n The Tcl/Tk Cookbook\n"
11: .t tag add tn $m "4.0 wordend"
12: .t tag bind tn <1> "showWebpage"
13:
14: proc showWebpage {} {
15: exec \
16: "C:\\Program Files\\Netscape 4.05\\Communicator\\Program\\netscape.exe" \
17: "http://www.itd.clrc.ac.uk/Publications/Cookbook/index.html" &
19: }
```

You can also set environment variables for the browser, the URL, and the directory of your image file(s). You retrieve these from the built-in array env.

14

ANALYSIS By now you know lines 1–4, which create a scrollable text widget, by heart. In line 5, you set a mark m1 to identify the end of text in the widget and retrieve and assign its index to the variable m in line 6. The `image create imageType ?option value?` command is used in line 7 to create the image to be embedded in the text widget. The image name is returned by the command and is assigned to the variable p1. In line 9, you embed the image in the text widget `.t` using the command `pathName image create index -image imageName -name instanceName ?option value?`. The padx option positions the image with spacing on either side. In line 10, you insert a title. In line 11, you add the tag tn to the set of characters whose index ranges from the mark m1 to the end of word in the fourth line of text. The tag bind is for `button 1` event and the call-back script is `showWebpage`. These are specified in line 12. The procedure `showWebpage` calls the exec command to invoke the Netscape Communicator and display the page specified by the URL: `http://www.itd.clrc.ac.uk/Publications/Cookbook/index.html.\`

The `pathName image create index -image imageName -name instanceName` command returns the image name specified with the option name. If the option name is not specified, the command instead returns the `imageName`. If more than one instance of the same image is embedded in the text widget, each instance is named with an `imageName#nn` convention by default. Remember that all subsequent references to the instance of an embedded image are made using its name.

When the character associated with the indexed position of a embedded window or image is deleted, so is the embedded element. The commands of the type `pathName image ?cget¦delete?` are available for you to manipulate the image.

Do	**DON'T**
Do check existing binds for text widgets before defining new ones.	**Don't** remove built-in functionality in text widget by allocating existing event sequences to new behavior.
Do remember that when you delete a tagged text, the tag gets deleted too.	**Don't** forget that you can't use index modifiers for character positions beyond that specified by the end of the text in the text widget.
Do remember, when inserting text around embedded annotations, that embedded windows and images occupy just one character's worth of index space.	**Don't** forget that when you delete a character associated with an embedded annotation, the embedded annotation will get deleted too.

Summary

In this hour, you learned more about the built-in capabilities of the Tk text widget and how to use them. The advanced annotation capabilities of the Tk text widget are the tag bindings for events such as mouse-pointer clicks, embedded windows, and images. Any interesting Tk text–widget-based application must have an extensive set of these annotations. All these text widget commands and annotations have rich sets of options and values, which help you to customize your application, making it visually pleasing, behaviorally intuitive, rich, and engaging.

Q&A

Q In Listing 14.1, the command `.t delete [lindex $rng 0] [lindex $rng 1]` deletes all the text associated with the tag `newTxt`. Will this always work?

A Not always. Consider the case where several sets of disconnected lines of text or words have all been tagged with the same tag `newTxt`. In such a case, the command `.t tag range newTxt` will still return a list of more than one pair of values. Each pair of values in this list represents the start and end of each range of tagged text associated with that tag. The above command will only delete the very first set of characters associated with the tag—not the rest.

Q What is the command to achieve the goal in the situation stated in the question above?

A Use `eval pathName delete [pathName tag range tagName]`. The `eval` command, described in Hour 3, "Working with Tcl Commands," will force the widget command `delete` to evaluate the list properly and apply itself to each pair of values.

Q What is the command for writing the full contents of a text widget to a file?

A The command `pathName dump switches index1 index2` returns the contents of the text widget from `index1` up to, but excluding, `index2`. It will include the text and information about any marks, tags, and embedded windows. The return format is `key1 value1 index1 key2 value2 index2 ...` for which the key values are `text`, `mark`, `tagon`, `tagoff`, and `window`. The corresponding value is the `text`, `markName`, `tagName`, or `pathName`. The index value is the index of the start of the text, the mark, the tag transition, or the window. The possible values for the switches are one or more of the following: `all`, `command`, `mark`, `text`, and `window`.

Workshop

The "Quiz" section is designed to provide you with an opportunity to recall some of the important concepts introduced in this hour. These might be commands, command syntax, common mistakes, usage, and so on. In the "Exercises" section, we use exercises that consolidate and slightly extend the material you learned with examples of practical value. Our aim is that these two sections should reinforce the knowledge you have gained in this hour. The answers to the quiz that follows can be found in Appendix A, "Answers to Quizzes."

Quiz

1. What is the use of text tags?

2. What happens to a tag when the characters or words associated with the tag disappear?

3. Is this code correct?

```
eval .t delete [.t tag range newTxt]; .t tag remove newTxt 1.0 end
```

4. Explain the need for line 20 in Listing 14.1.

5. How many characters does an embedded window or image take in the text widget's index space?

6. Embedded images in a text widget are there primarily as visual annotations. How can you make them appear more interactive?

7. Can two embedded windows have the same name?

8. What is the naming convention for embedded images?

9. What geometry management rules apply for embedded windows?

10. What is the scope of variables in tag bindings and binding callbacks?

Exercises

Solutions to the exercises are on the CD-ROM that accompanies this book.

1. Write a script to assign any three display style tags, such as bold, overstrike, and underline. Create a text widget with three lines of text, each of which is highlighted when the mouse-pointer moves over it and is changed to one of the display styles when button-1 is clicked on it. Script a tag binding that the displayed style can revert to the original style.

2. Embed an image of your choice in a text widget. (You can also use logo64.gif, which comes with Tcl and is under lib/images.) Associate a tag to it. Add a tag binding to display some text about the image in another embedded text window. Make this embedded window uneditable. Delete the embedded text window at alternate button-1 clicks on the image.

Hour 15

Getting Started with the Canvas

You are now on the last leg of learning to use the Tk widgets. From Hour 10, "Getting Started with Tk," to Hour 14, "Doing More with the Text Widget," you learned the rich variety of Tk widgets and the even richer behavioral functionality they provide for the development of interactive applications. Did you get the feeling that there is something missing in all this richness? If you did, you are right. A major component of interactive applications is the visualization of images and drawings with support for manipulating and annotating them.

Once more, recall Ivan Sutherland's famous quote, "A picture speaks a thousand words." It emphasizes how important it is to incorporate accurate visualization and pictorial description of information, wherever and whenever it is appropriate and economical to do so. We did touch upon embedding images in the Tk text widget, but most applications will require more extensive and sophisticated visualization functionality. Tk supports this via the canvas widget.

The *canvas widget* is a widget that supports the creation of structured graphics, called *canvas items*. These include lines, rectangles, ovals, and arcs. The widget structures them into groups and manipulates them as entities or objects with behavior using its internal geometry manager. Recall from Hour 10 that the fourth type of geometry manager that Tk provides is the internal geometry manager of the canvas widget. This geometry manager enables you to position, scale, and translate items and groups of items in a canvas. You can also embed images and windows in a canvas.

All canvas items have common attributes such as fill, outline, width, stipple pattern, color, and so forth. They also have item–type-specific attributes. For instance, a line may have arrowhead ends. Starting in this hour and continuing in the next two, you will progressively learn to exploit these functionalities.

In this hour you will learn

- To create a canvas widget
- To create items in the canvas window
- To manipulate these items using canvas widget commands
- To create a scrollable canvas window
- To create a simple interactive application based on canvas window

You have a lot of flexibility to experiment using the scripts in Listing 15.1 to Listing 15.4 interactively, that is at the wish shell prompt level.

Creating Canvas Window and Canvas Items

By now, you are familiar with the concept that when Tk creates a widget of any sort, it also creates an associated widget command. In Hour 11, "Adding Behavior to Your Widgets," you learned that complex widgets support additional widget subcommands, beyond `configure` and `cget`, that enable the widget to invoke complex actions. The action subcommands for a canvas widget are just as rich as they are for the text widget. Quite predictably, most of the action subcommands of the canvas are used for creating graphic primitives, structuring them, and manipulating them. The commands are generally either of the form

```
pathName action-subcommand option ?value?
```

or of the form

```
pathName action-subcommand tagOrId option ?value?
```

where `tagOrId` refers to the identifier/handle for a canvas item.

New Term The *item identifier* is the unique integer identifier created by Tk when a Tk canvas item is created.

You can also define one or more character strings called *tags* for each item. Tags are covered, in detail, in the next hour, "Using Canvas Commands." A list of all such identifiers and tags is maintained by the canvas widget's display list.

You will make extensive use of item handles to manipulate items in the canvas. Start an interactive wish shell and try the script given in Listing 15.1. This listing shows how to create a Tk canvas widget and create most of the basic built-in graphics primitives.

LISTING 15.1   The Canvas Create Command

```
 1: % set c .canvas
 2: .canvas
 3: % canvas $c
 4: .canvas
 5: % pack $c
 6: % set id1 [$c create rectangle 20 20 200 120]
 7: 1
 8: % puts $id1
 9: 1
10: % set id2 [$c create line 250 100 280 100 300 100 \
11: >            -width 8 -arrow both ]
12: 2
13: % set id3 [$c create oval 250 150 300 180 -width 2 -outline red \
14: >          -fill yellow]
15: 3
16: %  set id4 [$c create arc 250 20 300 80 -outline red -width 1 \
17: >            -extent 45 -start 0 -fill black -style pieslice]
18: 4
19: % set id5 [$c create polygon 80 150  50 180 110 180 80 150 \
20: >       -fill indianred -outline black -width 2]
21: 5
22: % set id6 [$c create text 180 200 -font {Courier 18 bold italic} \
23: >     -text "This is a text item "]
24: 6
25: % set id [$c create text 180 250 -font {Courier 18 bold italic} \
26: >       -text "in Tk canvas widget" ]
27: 7
28: % $c find all
29: 1 2 3 4 5 6 7
```

Analysis In line 1, you set the variable c to .canvas. In line 3, you use the widget creation command widgetClass pathName ?option value? to create the canvas $c. Note that this is the child of the root/application main window. You have set all the options to default values. Packing this canvas will manage it and make it appear on the screen.

In line 6, the canvas widget action subcommand create is used to create a rectangle. The item creation command is of the form pathName create type x y ?x ?y? ?option value?, where type refers to the type of the graphic primitive. The trailing x, y pairs define the coordinates of points that define the item—in this case, the coordinates of the top-left and bottom-right corners of our rectangle in pixel units.

> The coordinate system for the canvas is based on the X Window System convention. The top-left corner of the canvas is the origin. The x-axis values increase along the left-to-right direction, and y increases down the screen. Tk canvas coordinates and distances are specified in terms of screen units. These are floating-point numbers followed by an optional unit-specifier. If no unit-specifying letter is supplied, the distance is in pixels. The letter m denotes that the distance is in millimeters on the screen; if it is c, the distance is in centimeters; i stands for inches; p gives the distance in terms of printer points (== 1/72 inch).

The option-value pairs also depend on the type. You have not specified any of the options for your rectangle, so Tk uses default values. The item creat action returns a unique integer identifier for the item it creates. In this case, this identifier is assigned to the Tcl variable id1 so that it can be accessed using that variable name. Check what this id is by printing it, as shown on line 8, and you will see that it is the value 1, as the output in line 7 shows.

The line is the next type of item you have created in lines 10–11. The canvas supports the definition of the line in terms of a series of connected segments, whose start and end points are the consecutive x,y coordinates given with the create command. Using the options, you can specify whether you want the line to have arrowheads at either or both ends, whether the end points of each segment are to be round or miter, and so forth. In this case, you have opted to define the line to consist of two segments, to have arrowheads at both ends, and to be eight pixels wide. The identifier is stored as id2.

Oval is one of the graphic items supported by the canvas. Oval is the generic primitive used to draw circles and ellipses in Tk. Oval is specified by giving the coordinates of the two diagonally opposite corners of the rectangular region that will enclose the oval shape. In lines 13–14, you create an oval shape, this time specifying some of the options. For instance, you want the oval to be drawn as a filled shape with a prominent border. The return value from the execution of the create command is set to id3.

15

Arc, an arc-shaped region, is yet another graphic item that you can create in the canvas. An arc is a section of an oval delimited by two angles that are specified by the -start and -extent options. Tk supports several styles of arc, namely pieslice (the default), chord, or arc. The arc's region is defined as a section of an oval's perimeter plus two line segments connecting the center of the oval with each end of the perimeter section. If the arc type is chord, the arc's region is defined by a section of the oval's perimeter plus a single line segment connecting the two end points of the perimeter section. If type is arc, the arc's region consists of a section of the perimeter alone. Items of type arc appear on the display as arc-shaped regions.

> The -fill option is ignored if the arc's type is arc!

The arc is defined in terms of the oval, and hence the coordinate specification of an arc is of the form x1, y1, x2, y2. These four values give the coordinates of two diagonally opposite corners of a rectangular region enclosing the oval that defines the arc. The option -extent (whose value is specified in degrees) gives the size of the angular range occupied by the arc. This range extends counter-clockwise from the starting angle.

> The degrees for the -extent option of an arc can be negative. If it is greater than 360 or less than −360, degrees modulo 360 is used as the extent.

id4 gives you the handle for the arc you created in lines 16–17. In lines 19–20 you create one more basic Tk canvas item, the polygon. A polygon is made of three or more points. The create command takes the coordinates of each vertex as input arguments in order. You can specify whether the polygon should have straight edges or be made of Bezier curves. This one, id5, is a filled triangle.

You have created two text items, id6 and id, in lines 22–23 and 25–26. The -text option is to be used for specifying the text string to be drawn. Two of the many attributes that Tk canvas supports for the text item are font and justify. Your canvas widget should now look like Figure 15.1.

You learned that Tk assigns a unique integer identifier for each canvas item it creates. A list of these identifiers is maintained by the canvas widget's display list. The canvas widget subcommand pathName find ?searchspec? lists the item identifiers that fit the searchspec. In line 25, you have set the searchspec to all, which returns a list all the currently defined items as shown in line 29. Table 15.1 provides the list of all seearchspec and their description.

FIGURE **15.1**

The Tk canvas widget items.

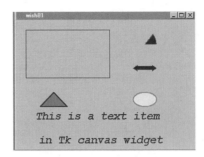

TABLE 15.1   Tk Canvas Search Specification Parameters

Search Specification	Description
above *tagOrId*	Get the item just after the one given by *tagOrId*. Note that the identifiers are allocated in ascending order.
all	Select all the items in the display list.
below *tagOrId*	Get the item just before the one given by *tagOrId*.
closest x y *marker start*	Select the topmost item that is closest to the point whose coordinates are given by x,y. If there is any item, other than marker, closer to the given position, that item is considered to overlap it and only the topmost of the overlapping items is returned.
enclosed x1, y1, x2, y2	Get all the item completely enclosed within the region bounded by the diagonally opposite points whose coordinates are x1, y1 and x2, y2.
overlapping x1, y1, x2, y2	Select all the items that overlap within the region bounded by the diagonally opposite points whose coordinates are x1, y1 and x2, y2. Note that this will also return all the items that are enclosed within the region specified.
withtag *tagOrId*	Searches for all items given by *tagOrId*.

Canvas Widget Commands for Manipulating Items

All Tk canvas widget commands can be passed the integer identifier as input when you want to query, configure, or manipulate the items. For example, five out of the seven search specifications for the `find` action subcommand discussed in the previous section are stated in terms of item identifiers. Listing 15.2 gives a sample set of Tk canvas widget commands and canvas widget action subcommands to manipulate canvas items.

One of the important manipulations you perform on graphic items is to modify their attributes. The second most important might be to animate them. In Listing 15.2, you will query and configure items. Simple animation is postponed to another section.

Having created a rectangle, you will access it using its identifier and change some of its attributes.

> Individual items may be moved or scaled using widget commands, but they cannot be rotated.

LISTING 15.2 Canvas Widget Action Commands

```
 1: # Append Listing 15.01 before this or continue in that same wish shell
 2: %$c itemconfigure $id1 -fill blue
 3: %$c coords $id1
 4: 20.0 20.0 200.0 120.0
 5: %$c coords $id1 40 30 80 120
 6: %$c bbox $id1
 7: 39 29 81 121
 8: %$c itemcget $id1 -outline
 9: black
10: %$c itemconfigure $id1 -outline red -width 2
11: %$c scale  $id1 0 0 1.5 2
12: %$c find enclosed 0 0 300 300
13: 1
14: %$c itemconfigure $id2 -joinstyle miter
```

ANALYSIS The script in the previous listing is a continuation of the script in Listing 15.1 because it involves the `rectangle` item `id1` that you created in that listing. You can either continue with the previous script in the same wish shell or append this listing to that in Listing 15.1 in a script file. If you use a script file, take care to exclude all the output lines in Listing 15.1. We recommend that you execute these lines interactively. They are quite dynamic. If you take a moment to observe the results after you issue each command, you will gain a lot of insight into the canvas widget's item management.

> If you plan to execute these lines from a Tcl/Tk script file, skip the output lines 4, 7, 9, and 13.

The canvas widget action subcommand `pathName itemconfigure tagOrId option value` can be used to reconfigure any attribute of any canvas item after it has been created. In script lines 2, 10, and 14, this action is invoked on the rectangle and line items `id1` and `id2`. In line 2, you specify that the rectangle should be drawn filled in with the color blue. In line 10, you define the width of the rectangle's outline to be two pixels wide and that the outline is drawn in red.

The widget action subcommand `pathName coords tagOrId ?value?` queries or sets the coordinates of the top-left and bottom-right corners of the rectangular region occupied by the item given by `tagOrId`, depending on whether or not the `?value?` part is present. In response to executing this command in script line 3, the interpreter has returned the coordinates of the diagonally opposite corners of the rectangle `id1` in line 4. In line 5, you specify the modified coordinates for these two points using the same command. The execution of this script results in a modification to the items in the canvas widget `.canvas` (as shown in the left-hand image of Figure 15.2).

Did you expect the rectangle to move on top of the triangle and text and obscure them? It didn't! Why? Remember the statement that the Tk canvas supports structured graphics. It allocates a unique integer identifier for each item as it is created. These identifiers are consecutive and are ordered. The internal geometry manager and the canvas widget commands use this ordering intrinsically. If items overlap, the items are drawn with a traversal of the display list starting from the bottom. On the other hand, the `find` action with the closest search specification returns the top-most item closest to a given position!

Execute the script in Listing 15.3 at the wish command prompt, and you will see the result shown in the right-hand image of Figure 15.2. The rectangle is now laid over the triangle and parts of the text!

LISTING 15.3 How to Raise or Lower a Canvas Item

```
1: $c find all
2: 1 2 3 4 5 6 7
3: $c raise $id1 $id6
4: % $c find all
5: 2 3 4 5 6 1 7
```

ANALYSIS You have already encountered the `$c find all` action in Listing 15.1. It returns a list of all item identifiers in the canvas's display list as shown in line 2. The Tk built-in canvas command `pathName raise tagOrId anothertagOrId` raises the identifier associated with the `tagOrId` above `anothertagOrId` in the display list. Check the display list again by executing `$c find all`. Notice how the integer identifier 1 (`==$id1`) has shuffled its place, as shown in line 5.

You can similarly lower an item in the display list for the purposes of drawing and search traversals. Note that raising or lowering only changes the position of the item in display list. It does not alter the identifier associated with the item.

FIGURE 15.2

Tk canvas item manipulation commands.

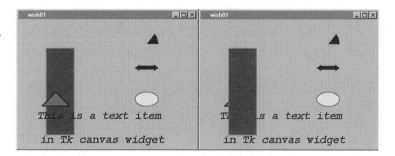

Binding Events to Canvas Items

The item creation and configuration functions that you have seen so far are quite useful in themselves. However, you often want to create more versatile behavior, such as animation of the graphical items. You can, for instance, provide the user with the ability to interact with a presented item. For example, you might want to move or stretch an item using the mouse pointer. You want to be able to track the mouse position in the canvas and, by processing that information, to manipulate displayed canvas items. The example that follows and the exercises in this hour (and the next two hours) are designed to teach you this expertise.

Listing 15.4 creates a simple polyline in a canvas. It binds to the polyline the three events: enter, leave, and Button-1-Motion. When the mouse pointer is close enough to an item, the color of the item changes from blue to red. When the mouse pointer moves away from the item by more than the minimum specified distance, the color is restored to blue. The Button-1-Motion binding lets the item follow the mouse pointer as you drag the mouse while pressing and holding the left mouse button *on* the item (*on* refers to when the pointer is within the area of sensitivity of the item).

LISTING 15.4   Event Bindings to Canvas Items

```
 1: canvas .c
 2: # to hold buttons
 3: frame .fb -background lightblue
 4: button .fb.qb -text Quit -command {destroy .}
 5: pack .c
 6: pack .fb.qb -side right
 7: pack .fb -fill x
 8:
 9: set item [.c create line 10 10 20 5 40 30 80 5 \
10:               -fill blue]
11:
12: puts "You have to be [.c cget -closeenough] pixel close to item\n"
13: .c configure -closeenough 10.0
14:
15: .c bind $item <Enter> "setUp .c $item %x %y"
16: .c bind $item <Leave> "restore .c $item "
17: .c bind $item <B1-Motion> "itemDrag .c $item %x %y"
18:
19: proc restore { c item  } {
20:         # store current $item color
21:         global originalCol
22:         $c itemconfig $item -fill $originalCol
23: }
24:
25: proc setUp { c item x y} {
```

15

```
26:          global prevX prevY originalCol
27:          # store current $item color
28:          set originalCol [$c itemcget $item -fill]
29:          $c itemconfig $item -fill red
30:          set prevX [$c canvasx $x]
31:          set prevY [$c canvasy $y]
32: }
33:
34: proc itemDrag {c item x y} {
35:          global prevX prevY
36:          set x [$c canvasx $x]
37:          set y [$c canvasy $y]
38:          $c move $item [expr $x-$prevX] [expr $y-$prevY]
39:          set prevX $x
40:          set prevY $y
41: }
```

ANALYSIS In line 1, you create a canvas .c with all default options, and it is packed in line 5. In line 3, you create a frame widget .fb with lightblue background to hold a Quit button, .fb.qb, to exit the application when you tire of it. The .fb.gb button itself is created in line 4. The -command option of the button is set to execute the simple built-in Tk command destroy with the application main window as an argument. The button is packed, right justified in its parent master (the frame in line 6). In line 7, the frame window is packed with -fill option set to x. When the main window is stretched, the frame will stretch to cover the X direction expansion. You then create, in lines 9–10, a simple line item with four connected segments and the fill color blue.

When you want to select an item in a canvas, an important factor is the proximity of the mouse pointer to the item. When the mouse pointer is within this proximity, it is considered as being "inside" the item and hence the item is selected. The canvas widget option -closeenough is set to a desired value for this purpose. The default value of this option is set to 1.0. You can check this by executing the script in line 12. The command .c cget -closeenough returns the default value for this option and the puts command prints it to the console. You want to increase this default value to a less stringent 10 pixels, and you do so in line 13 using the command .c configure -closeenough 10.0.

Another related issue is the tracking and returning the current position of the mouse pointer in the canvas. Tk supports this requirement by providing the special codes %x, %y and %X and %Y, which return the x and y coordinates of the current mouse position with respect to the widget and the root window respectively. This information can be passed as an input argument to any script that might require it.

Next, you define three event bindings for the polyline item in lines 15–17. The syntax for an item event binding for the canvas widget is

```
pathName bind tagOrId <eventsequence> {script}.
```

You can see that the event binding command and its syntax take much the same forms as those for the text tag bindings that you learned in Hour 14, "Doing More with Text Widget." For the polyline, you want to define three event bindings. One is for the event sequence enter, which is generated when the mouse pointer is within the region of sensitivity of the item. Another is for the leave event sequence which is generated whenever the pointer moves outside this region of proximity. The third binding is for the event sequence generated when the mouse pointer is dragged along the canvas while the left mouse button is pressed and held down.

The item event binding scripts associated with the leave, enter and Button-1-Motion event sequences are defined in the procedures restore, setUp and itemDrag in lines 19–23, 25–32, and 34–41, respectively. The procedure restore takes the canvas widget and the identity of the canvas item as an input argument and restores the item's original color, stored in the global variable originalCol. The command pathName itemconfig -fill is used to achieve this end.

The procedure setUp is executed whenever an enter-event is generated. It takes the canvas, the item, and the current x and y coordinates of the mouse pointer as input arguments. First the command pathName itemcget tagOrId -option is executed to retrieve the original color of the item, and this value is stored in the global variable originalCol. Next, the item's -fill option is reconfigured to change its color to red. In script lines 30–31, the commands $c canvasx $x and $c canvasy $y are executed to retrieve the x and y coordinates of the mouse cursor position in terms of canvas coordinates. These values are stored in the global variables prevX and prevY, respectively.

The procedure itemDrag similarly takes the identities of the canvas, canvas item, and the X and Y coordinates of the current position as input arguments. The item is then moved by an amount given by subtracting the value of each coordinate of the current position from the respective value stored in prevX or prevY. The values of the global variables prevX and prevY are updated with the current values.

A Scrollable Canvas

Your next task is to make your canvas scrollable. More information can be displayed on a scrollable canvas, without the need to create large application and canvas windows that obscure your computer screen and other applications running on it. As with text and listbox widgets, the solution lies in creating and associating horizontal and vertical scrollbars with the canvas widget. Please refer to Hour 14 for related information on scrollbars and the text widget. You must specify a scroll region, which defines the bounds of information to be displayed in the canvas.

Finally in this hour, revisit the canvas coordinate system. You have already learned that it is based on the X Window System with the top-left corner designated as the origin. The script shown below (in Listing 15.5) illustrates both these aspects. Figure 15.3 shows the result of executing this script (left-hand image) and the scrolled window displaying the rest of the canvas contents (right-hand image).

15

LISTING 15.5   The Scrollable Canvas Widget

```
 1: wm title . "DrawTool V0.0"
 2: wm minsize . 50 50
 3:
 4: frame .f -bg grey -bd 5;# to hold canvas and scrollbars
 5: pack .f
 6: frame .f.sub  -bg indianred -bd 2 ;# to hold canvas and vertical scroll bar
 7: pack .f.sub -in .f
 8: canvas .f.sub.c -relief sunken \
 9:                 -scrollregion { 0 0 1000 1000 } \
10:         -xscrollcommand ".f.sch set" \
11:         -yscrollcommand ".f.sub.scv set"
12:
13: scrollbar .f.sub.scv -command ".f.sub.c yview"
14: pack .f.sub.c .f.sub.scv -in .f.sub -side left -fill y
15:
16: scrollbar .f.sch -orient horizontal -command ".f.sub.c xview"
17: pack .f.sch -in .f -side top -fill x
18:
19: frame .b -bg grey
20: pack .b -fill x
21:
22:
23: button .b.quit -text Quit -command quitApp
24: pack .b.quit -side right -padx 4 -pady 4
25:
26: proc quitApp { } {
27:         foreach w [winfo chil .] { destroy $w }
28: }
29:
30: proc showGrid { w } {
31:  set ytop [.f.sub.c cget -height]
32:  set xtop [.f.sub.c cget -width]
33:  set x 0
34:  set dx [expr "$xtop/6"]
35:
36: # draw x = constant lines
37: for {set i 0} {$i <= 6} { incr i} {
38:         $w create text [expr $x+5] 10 -text "$x,0" -justify center
```

continues

LISTING 15.5 continued

```
39:        $w create line $x $ytop $x 0
40:  set x [expr $x+$dx]
41:        }
42: # draw y = constant lines
43:  set y 0
44:  set dy [expr $ytop/6]
45:
46:  for {set i 0} {$i <= 6} {incr i} {
47:     $w create text 5 [expr $y+5] -text "0,$y" -justify center
48:     $w create line 0 $y $xtop $y
49:     set y [expr $y+$dy]
50:
51:  }
52:
53: } ;# end of showGrid
54:
55:
56: showGrid .f.sub.c
```

ANALYSIS   In lines 1–2, you use the Tk built-in window manager commands to declare a title and minimum size for your application main window. In line 4, you create a frame window .f to hold the horizontal scrollbar and two further frames, .f.sub (line 6) and .b (line 19). Script lines 8–11 create a canvas widget with the options -xscrollcommand, -yscrollcommand, and -scrollregion specified. The -scrollregion specifies a list of four coordinates that are the left, top, right, and bottom coordinates of the rectangular region to be used for scrolling purposes. This region is taken to be the boundary of the information in the canvas window.

The -yscrollcommand invokes the scrollbar command .f.sub.scv set. It tells the vertical scrollbar associated with the canvas widget what the current vertical view of the canvas is. It passes this view position as a list of two real fractions. The values of these two fractions are specified as a proportion of the content within the canvas window, and hence each value ranges between 0 and 1. If the first fraction is 0.0, the first element gives the position of the topmost part of the content of the canvas, relative to its full content. If the second fraction is 0.4, the second element gives the position toward the 40% of the canvas contents, again relative to the full window. The -xscrollcommand has a similar interpretation for the horizontal scrollbar—.f.sch. You can, of course, let Tk allocate the default values for these.

In script line 13, you create the vertical scrollbar. The scrollbar option -command "pathName yview" specifies the widget action subcommand pathName <yview/xview>, depending on whether the scrolling requested is vertical or horizontal. It is invoked to change the view in the widget given by pathName associated with the scrollbar. When a user requests a view change by manipulating the scrollbar, the Tcl command is invoked by the widget pathName. In this case, this -command option is set to .f.sub.c yview. The canvas is asked to act on the changed vertical view whenever the user interacts with the vertical scrollbar.

> All scrollable widgets (such as canvas, text, and listbox) have xview and yview commands that take additional arguments exactly as appended by the scrollbar. Conversely, these scrollable widgets also have -xscrollcommand and -yscrollcommand that provide the arguments for the associated scrollbars to initialize their positions.

In line 14, you pack the canvas and the vertical scrollbar in their parent master .f.sub with -side option set to left and -fill option set to y. This ensures the scrollbar will cover the entire height of the window.

In line 16, you create the horizontal scrollbar in much the same way as the vertical one; and in line 17, it is packed in its parent master .f with -side set to top.

In line 19, you create a frame to hold a Quit button created in line 23. The button is created to provide a mechanism to quit the application without exiting your wish application shell. The quitApp script associated with the Quit button's -command option retrieves each child of the application main/root window and destroys it. Note that a simple exit will destroy the root window, too.

The procedure showGrid defined in lines 30–51 creates a grid pattern and textual labels to mark the axes of the grid in the canvas. The primary purpose is to show that the canvas coordinate system extends left-to-right and top-to-bottom. The values of xtop and ytop are retrieved using [.f.sub.c cget -width] and [.f.sub.c cget -height]. The variables x and y are initialized to 0, and the variables dx and dy set a region of the canvas into six equal parts horizontally and vertically using the execution of the commands [expr $xtop/6] and [expr $ytop/6]. Recall the Tcl expr notation from Hour 3, "Working with Tcl Commands." The two for loops increment the x and y variables in their respective directions to position text and create the lines. Note how the specification increases x and decreases y! Line 56 executes the showGrid procedure to produce Figure 15.3 that follows.

FIGURE 15.3

The scrollable canvas window.

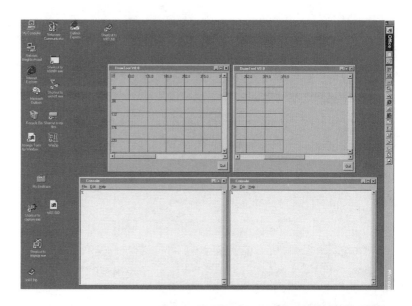

Do	Don't
Do remember to set the -scrollregion option to make your canvas scrollable. **Do** remember that the view within the canvas is not set outside the canvas scroll area by default.	**Don't** forget the ordering of canvas item identifiers in the display list and the resulting order in which they are drawn.

Summary

In this hour, you have learned the basics of using the Tk canvas widget that supports the creation and manipulation of structured graphic items. You also learned how to configure their attributes and add behaviors. You learned how to make the canvas scrollable. You have also been introduced to basics such as the canvas coordinate system, the display list associated with the canvas, and the method for raising and lowering items in the display list.

Any canvas items you have not used yet will be covered in Hour 17, "Working with Images in the Canvas." In the next hour, "Using Canvas Commands," you will learn how to add tags and tag bindings to canvas items.

Q&A

Q **Can I delete an item from the canvas?**

A You can use the command `pathName delete tagOrId` to delete items. Note that the canvas display list does not reallocate the unique integer identifier of an item. Every time an item is created, a unique integer identifier is created for that item, and it is placed on the top in the display list stack. You can, of course, reallocate your variable assigned to the item.

Q. **Can I use other structured graphics packages with the Tk canvas?**

A. Tk canvas supports structured graphics in the sense that a display list is maintained with an inherent ordering. You can, in fact, add more meaningful structures and grouping using the tag mechanism that you will learn about in the next hour. However, if you want to use traditional structured graphics, such as PHIGS or OpenGL or any other visualization packages, you can do so by extending the interpreter or by adding packages. These will be discussed in Hour 22, "Adding Tcl/Tk Extensions," and Hour 23, "Using Tcl/Tk Extensions."

Workshop

The quiz section below is designed to provide you with an opportunity to recall some of the important concepts introduced in this Hour. These may be commands, command syntax, common mistakes, usage, and so on. The following exercises section helps you consolidate the material you learned via an example of practical value. Our aim is that these two sections should reinforce the knowledge you have gained in this hour. The answers to the quiz that follows can be found in Appendix A, "Answers to Quizzes."

Quiz

1. What are the canvas items you can use?
2. What do the input arguments x1, y1, x2, and y2 refer to in the creation of the canvas item rectangle in the command `pathName create rectangle x1 y1 x2 y2 option ?value?`
3. What styles of arcs can you have with Tk?
4. What do the options `-extent`, `-start` mean for the canvas item arc?
5. What does setting `-scrollregion` do?
6. What does `-xscrollcommand` do?
7. What is the syntax for binding an event sequence to a canvas item?
8. What does the command `pathName find enclosed x1, y1, x2, y2` do?

9. What does the command `pathName find overlapping x1, y1, x2, y2` do?

10. What is the difference between the commands `pathName bbox tagOrId` and `pathName coords tagOrId`?

Exercises

Solutions to the exercises are on the CD-ROM that accompanies this book.

1. Create a canvas window and a button widget with text label `Fill`. Create two nested rectangle items in the canvas, the inner one filled, the outer with just the outline. Add a command script to the button, so that every time the button is pressed, the height of the inner rectangle increases, until it reaches the limit. The limit is the top of the outer rectangle. That means you are asked to create a very simple visual effect of a fluid level reader. The effect should appear as shown in Figure 15.4. (Hint. Reduce the ratio of increment as the fill reaches the top. Any simplistic algorithm will do.)

FIGURE **15.4**
Canvas item scaling.

2. Optional exercise—See if you can fit the above solution into the empty slot on the left-hand side of the gas station exercise in Hour 11.

HOUR 16

Using Canvas Commands

In the last hour, "Getting Started with Canvas," you learned the basics of Tk canvas widget, namely how to create it as well as how to use some of the basic canvas widget commands. In particular, you learned how to create graphic items in the canvas, customize their attributes, and add event bindings to produce simple behaviors. These were done using the unique integer identifiers that are automatically generated and associated with canvas items by the Tcl/Tk interpreter when each item is created. This identifier acts as a useful and unique identifier-handle for each item in the canvas.

In addition to these tools, you will now learn about a more powerful mechanism that can group several items into higher order structures so that they can be treated as a single entity semantically. This is done when you want to change an item's attributes or define some group behavior. Tk supports this requirement with the canvas item tag mechanism. Tags are character strings that provide a mechanism to attach meaningful symbolic names to items in a canvas. Their functionality is similar to the text widget tags that you learned in Hour 13, "Using the Tk Text Widget."

In this hour, you will learn

- How to attach canvas item tags
- More on canvas commands that use item tags
- How to bind event sequences to canvas items, via tags, to execute behavior
- How to bind events to the canvas
- How to do animation in canvas

Because the canvas widget, animation, and visualization are fundamentally useful tools, this hour provides quite a few examples as does the Exercise Section which follows.

Canvas Item Tags

Canvas item tags are not just symbolic names that are easy to recall. Their role is to provide an effective mechanism to group items. Although items and their integer identifiers have a one-to-one relationship, tags have a many-to-many relationship with items. That is, you can attach more than one item to a tag and associate more than one tag to an item. This flexibility enables you to create higher order structures for the grouping of items. The resulting group can be manipulated as a single entity. At the same time, you have the fine control needed to manipulate individual items.

The other advantage that tags have over item identifiers is their global scope. This means that you have the same access to tags from procedures as you do to with identifiers, without having to declare them as global variables. You will explore the concept of the canvas item tag via the example in Listing 16.1. Executing this script creates a simple model of a car! You can use a script file for this application because you will be using this example extensively.

Put the listing below in a source file listing1.tcl, for instance. Start a wish shell and source this file at the Tcl prompt. Note that the Tcl/Tk interpreter prompt % is missing in the listing below because this is the Tcl script sourced from a script file. Refer to Hour 1, "What is Tcl/Tk," to refresh yourself on the modes of execution.

LISTING 16.1 Creating Canvas Items with Tags

```
1: wm title . "A simple car"
2:
3: canvas .c
4:
5: frame .f -bg yellow
```

```
 6: pack .f .c -side left -fill y
 7:
 8: set id0 [.c create polygon \
 9:   0.7 1.7 .5 1.7 0.5 1.5 0.8 1.1 1.0 1.0 2.0 1.0 2.5 1.4 \
10:   3.0 1.5 3.0 1.7 -fill red -tags body]
11:
12: puts "[.c itemcget $id0 -tag]"
13:
14: .c addtag car withtag body
15: puts "[.c itemcget body -tag]"
16:
17: .c create oval  0.8 1.5 1.2 1.9 \
18:   -fill black -tags {bwheel car}
19: .c create oval  2.5 1.5 2.9 1.9 \
20:   -fill black -tags {fwheel car}
21:
22: .c create polygon  1.6 1.1 1.9 1.1 2.2 1.4 1.6 1.4  \
23:   -fill gray -tags {fwindow car}
24:
25: .c create polygon  1.5 1.1 1.5 1.4  0.9 1.4 1.15 1.1 \
26:   -fill gray -tags {bwindow car}
27:
28: .c scale car 0 0 38 38
```

ANALYSIS In line 1, you give a title to your first application of the hour. In line 3, the command `widgetClass pathName ?option ?value` is used to create the canvas widget `.c`, and in line 5, it is used to create a frame window `.f` with a yellow background.

> You can always use the short form of an option whenever it exists unambiguously.

You pack the canvas and the frame with `-side` and `-fill` options set to `left` and `y` respectively.

> The frame widget does not have a significant default size. It always expands to accommodate its children and slaves like a shrink-wrap. You will notice how the yellow frame in the figure is barely visible because it doesn't contain any widgets. You can of course use the `-height` and `-width` options to specify a start up size. You can also use the `-relief` option to specify visual delimiters.

In lines 8–10, you create the body of the car. It is made of a simple filled polygon. Please refer to Hour 15, "Getting Started with the Canvas," to refresh your memory of the polygon creation.

> The list of coordinate pairs specifies the vertices of the polygon. The first and last of these pairs can be the same. Whether or not you specify a last pair of coordinates that are the same as the first pair, Tk automatically closes the region.

The fill color is red, but the important option to note here is -tags. This applies the specified symbolic name to the item created. In this case, the tag associated with your polygon is body. You also assign the item identifier to the variable id0 in line 8.

You know that you are drawing a car as a sum of its parts. You might, in some cases, want to refer to the whole car, rather than a part. You, therefore, want to add another symbolic name to this body part. Before doing so, check the current list of tags attached to id0 by executing the pathName itemcget tagOrId -option and printing that output through the puts command. The puts command in line 12 should produce the result body in your console.

In line 14, you use the canvas widget action subcommand addtags to add the tag car to the item, which already has the tag body. Check the list of tags for your item once again. You will see that the item now has two tags, car and body printed in the wish console.

> You can add more than one new tag to an item using the addtags action subcommand. Remember to protect the tags using curly braces or double quotes.

> The command pathName itemcget tagOrId -tag can accept either the item's identifier or its tag. This command returns a list of all the currently valid tags for the item. If the value you give for tagOrId is a tag that is attached to more than one item, this command returns the tag list for the first item with the specified tag.
>
> Remember, however, that an item's identifier and a tag that is unique to that item can be used interchangeably for all the canvas action subcommands. If the tag is not unique to the item, the action is applied to all the items with that tag.

The action subcommand `addtags` is used to attach new tags to an item after its creation. You can, in fact, assign all the tags you want to apply to an item in a single specification when the item is created (if you have decided on the tags in advance). You have followed this second option while creating the other parts of the car in the rest of the script. Lines 17–20 create the back and front wheels, attaching the tags `bwheel` and `fwheel`, as well as `car`, to both these parts. Recall from Hour 15 that the coordinates x1, y1, x2, and y2 in the command `pathName create oval x1 y1 x2 y2 ?option value?` refer to the top-left and bottom-right points of the rectangular region that will enclose the oval.

In lines 22–26, you create two polygons to represent the front and back windows for the car, again with tags `fwindow` and `bwindow`, as well as the common tag, `car`. The result of executing this script is shown in Figure 16.1.

16

FIGURE 16.1

A simple car made up of polygons for body and windows and ovals for tires.

A Moving Experience

You learned that the power of item tags lies in how they group items. You can explore this in action using the car defined in Listing 16.1. The script in Listing 16.2 (which follows) is a continuation of the first listing. You are basically extending your application by including a couple of buttons and attaching action scripts to manipulate your car.

LISTING 16.2 Manipulating Tagged Items in Canvas

```
 1: wm title . "Still a simple car"
 2:
 3: canvas .c
 4:
 5: frame .f -bg yellow
 6: pack .f .c -side left -fill y
 7:
 8: # put some buttons in .f
 9: button .f.move -text Move -command [list moveCar 10 0]
11: button .f.reset -text Reset -command [list resetCar 10 0]
12: button .f.quit -text Quit -command exit
```

continues

LISTING 16.2 continued

```
13:
14: pack .f.move .f.reset -side top -fill x
15: pack .f.quit -side bottom -fill x
16:
17: .c create polygon 0.7 1.7 .5 1.7 0.5 1.5 0.8 1.1 1.0 1.0 2.0 \
18:     1.0 2.5 1.4 3.0 1.5 3.0 1.7  -fill red -tags {body car}
19: .c create oval 0.8 1.5 1.2 1.9  -fill black -tags {bwheel car}
20:
21: .c create oval 2.5 1.5 2.9 1.9 -fill black -tags {fwheel car}
22:
23: .c create polygon 1.6 1.1 1.9 1.1 2.2 1.4 1.6 1.4  \
24:    -fill gray -tags {fwindow car}
25:
26: .c create polygon 1.5 1.1 1.5 1.4  0.9 1.4 1.15 1.1 \
27:    -fill gray -tags {bwindow car}
28:
29: .c scale car 0 0 38 38
```

ANALYSIS The highlighted code creates three buttons labeled Move, Reset, and Quit within the frame widget you created earlier. The code is self-explanatory, and we will not go through it in minute detail. The gist of it is that you attach two procedures, moveCar and resetCar, and the built-in action exit as event-handlers to these buttons. Please refer to Hour 11, "Adding Behavior to Your Widgets," to recall the concept of event-handlers and callbacks. These buttons are packed in their parent master, the frame .f, with the Quit button appearing close to the bottom. The resulting widget GUI layout is shown in Figure 16.2.

FIGURE 16.2

GUI layout for the moving car.

You now define the event-handlers you have declared in Listing 16.2.

Canvas Widget Action Subcommands Using Tags

We have already encountered the three canvas action subcommands that use tag as an argument:

```
.c itemcget tagOrId ?option
```

```
.c addtags newTag withtags tagOrId
```

```
.c scale tagOrId x1 y1 x2 y2
```

Literally, all the canvas widget commands that you can execute using the item identifier can also be used with tags. However, the global scope of tags provides much greater flexibility. In addition, all items with a particular tag are treated as a single entity. The event-handlers exploit both these aspects, as you can see from Listing 16.3. Listing 16.3 is a continuation of Listing 16.2, and hence also of Listing 16.1. Please copy, insert, or type in only the highlighted script if you are adding to your evolving program in a Tk script file.

LISTING 16.3   Event-Handler Scripts for the Car

```
 1: wm title . "A moving car"
 2:
 3: canvas .c
 4:
 5: frame .f -bg yellow
 6: pack .f .c -side left -fill y
 7:
 8: # put some buttons in .f
 9: button .f.move -text Move -command [list moveCar 10 0]
10: button .f.reset -text Reset -command [list resetCar 10 0]
11: button .f.quit -text Quit -command exit
12:
13: pack .f.move .f.reset -side top -fill x
14: pack .f.quit -side bottom -fill x
15:
16: .c create polygon \
17:    0.7 1.7 .5 1.7 0.5 1.5 0.8 1.1 1 1 2 1 2.5 1.4 3 1.5 3 1.7 \
18:    -fill red -tags {body car}
19:
20: .c create oval \
21:    0.8 1.5 1.2 1.9 \
22:    -fill black -tags {bwheel car}
23: .c create oval \
24:    2.5 1.5 2.9 1.9 \
25:    -fill black -tags {fwheel car}
```

continues

LISTING 16.3 continued

```
26:
27: .c create polygon \
28:    1.6 1.1 1.9 1.1 2.2 1.4 1.6 1.4  \
29:    -fill gray -tags {fwindow car}
30:
31: .c create polygon \
32:    1.5 1.1 1.5 1.4  0.9 1.4 1.15 1.1 \
33:    -fill gray -tags {bwindow car}
34:
35: .c scale car 0 0 38 38
36:
37: proc moveCar { dx dy } {
38:
39: # stop moving the car if the bounding box hits the right edge
40: # canvas
41: set redge [.c cget -width]
42: set curX  [lindex [.c bbox car] 2] ;# use bottom right coord
43: if { [expr $curX <= [expr $redge -4] ] } {
44:     .c move car $dx $dy
45:     return
46:     } else {
47:         puts "Hitting the right edge. Can't move"
48:     }
49: }
50:
51: proc resetCar { xpos ypos } {
52:
53: set curX [lindex [.c bbox car ] 0]
54: if { [expr $curX > $xpos] } {
55:     .c  move car [expr -$curX + $xpos] $ypos
56:   } else {
57:     puts "Cannot go any further back\n"
58:   }
59: }
```

ANALYSIS The procedure moveCar, defined in lines 37–49, takes two increments in x and y directions as input arguments. The x coordinate of the right edge of the canvas is extracted in line 41 using the widget action subcommand cget. It is assigned to the variable redge. You then query the bounding box of the car entity. This returns a list of four values that give the approximate coordinates of the two diagonally opposite points of the rectangular region enclosing the car. From this list, you retrieve the right-most x coordinate using the lindex command. Recall from Hour 5, "Working with Lists," that list indices start from 0.

> Notice how tagging all the parts as car has resulted in the bbox action to return the coordinates of the collective boundary when the argument to this action subcommand is the common tag.

Now, make a very simple check to see if the x coordinate of the right-most point of the car is less than or equal to 4 pixels short of the right-most edge of the canvas. If it is, the car is moved by the incremental values. If it is not, a message to that effect is printed to the console. You can, of course, reverse the car or reorient it as an exercise.

The procedure resetCar is defined in lines 51–59 and is very similar in structure to moveCar. In this case, check whether the car's left-most edge (along the x axis) has moved beyond the minimum start position. If it has (as it will when you press the move button every time), the car is pushed back by an amount equivalent to the initial x position. That position is passed to this procedure as input argument.

In themselves, these procedures are quite simplistic, but they demonstrate the simple elegance and power that tagging affords. It enables you to group canvas items into semantically related entities in order to manipulate them. The procedures also introduce the canvas widget action subcommands that are available to access and manipulate tagged items.

Tag Binding

Item tagging enables you to bind event sequences to tagged items so that when an event happens over the tagged item or items, the associated script is invoked. You already used this mechanism in action with the item identifier in Hour 15. With tags, you can invoke the behavior in a group of items or on individual items as required. Tag binding provides a powerful mechanism for animating canvas items.

LISTING 16.4 Canvas Bindings

```
 1: wm title . "Wheel Repairs"
 2:
 3: canvas .c
 4:
 5: frame .f -bg yellow
 6: pack .f .c -side left -fill y
 7:
 8: # put some buttons in .f
 9: button .f.move -text Move -command [list moveCar 10 0]
10: button .f.reset -text Reset -command [list resetCar 10 0]
```

continues

LISTING 16.4   continued

```
11: button .f.quit -text Quit -command exit
12:
13: pack .f.move .f.reset -side top -fill x
14: pack .f.quit -side bottom -fill x
15:
16: .c create polygon \
17:    0.7 1.7 .5 1.7 0.5 1.5 0.8 1.1 1 1 2 1 2.5 1.4 3 1.5 3 1.7 \
18:    -fill red -tags {body car}
19:
20: .c create oval \
21:    0.8 1.5 1.2 1.9 \
22:    -fill black -tags {bwheel wheels car}
23: .c create oval \
24:    2.5 1.5 2.9 1.9 \
25:    -fill black -tags {fwheel wheels car}
26:
27: .c create polygon \
28:    1.6 1.1 1.9 1.1 2.2 1.4 1.6 1.4  \
29:    -fill gray -tags {fwindow car}
30:
31: .c create polygon \
32:    1.5 1.1 1.5 1.4  0.9 1.4 1.15 1.1 \
33:    -fill gray -tags {bwindow car}
34:
35: .c scale car 0 0 38 38
36:
37: proc moveCar { dx dy } {
38:
39: # stop moving the car if the bounding box hits the right edge
40: # canvas
41: set redge [.c cget -width]
42: set curX  [lindex [.c bbox all] 2] ;# use bottom right coord
43: if { [expr $curX <= [expr $redge - 4] ] } {
44:     .c move car $dx $dy
45:     return
46:     } else {
47:     puts "Hitting the right edge . Can't move"
48:     }
49: }
50:
51: proc resetCar { xpos ypos } {
52:
53: set curX [lindex [.c bbox car ] 0]
54: if { [expr $curX > $xpos] } {
55:     .c  move car [expr -$curX + $xpos] $ypos
56:   } else {
57:     puts "Cannot go any further back\n"
58:     }
59: }
```

```
60: .c bind wheels <Enter> {.c itemconfigure current -fill orange}
61: .c bind wheels <Leave> {.c itemconfigure current -fill black }
62: .c bind wheels <Button-1> { changeTire .c }
63: proc changeTire { w } {
64:
65: set idtags [ $w gettags current ]
66: set ctag [ lindex $idtags 0 ]
67:
68: if { $ctag == "bwheel" } {
69:     if { [.c type current ] == "oval" } {
70:         $w delete bwheel;
71:         $w create arc 0.8 1.5 1.2 1.9  -tags {bwheel wheels car}\
72:                 -style chord -extent 240 -start -30 -fill black
73:
74:     } else {
75:         $w delete bwheel;
76:         .c create oval 0.8 1.5 1.2 1.9 \
77:                 -fill black -tags {bwheel wheels car}
78:         }
79:         $w scale bwheel 0 0 38 38
80:
81:     } elseif { $ctag == "fwheel" } {
82:         if { [.c type current ] == "oval" } {
83:             $w delete fwheel;
84:             .c create arc  2.5 1.5 2.9 1.9 -style chord -extent 240 -start -
30\
85:                     -style chord -fill black -tags {fwheel wheels car}
86:         } else {
87:             $w delete fwheel
88:             .c create oval 2.5 1.5 2.9 1.9 \
89:                     -fill black -tags {fwheel wheels car}
90:             }
91:
92:         $w scale fwheel 0 0 38 38
93:     }
94:
95: }
```

16

ANALYSIS   Much of the preceding code is continued from Listings 16.1–16.3. The newly inserted script lines are highlighted. For this example, you have assigned a new common tag, wheels, to both the front and back wheels. The purpose is to assign event bindings of the event sequences Enter, Leave, and Button-1 to the tag wheels. The events Enter and Leave refer to the mouse cursor entering the region occupied by the items. The aim is that both the wheels display similar behaviors when any mouse event happens over them.

Lines 60–62 define the three bindings. All the three bindings make use of the built-in default tag called current. This tag is automatically assigned to any item currently under the mouse cursor. Note the elegant power of tags. You can use the common tag wheels to guarantee that both wheels display identical behavior when mouse events happen over them. You can also use the current tag to ensure that the action happens only on the wheel that is currently under focus and not on both at the same time. The situation is not intuitive in this case. If you want such behavior, you can, of course, use the tag wheels. The flexibility is provided for you.

The Enter and Leave bindings are quite straightforward. Whenever the mouse cursor enters the region of either of the wheels, that wheel changes its color to orange. When the cursor leaves the wheel, it is restored to black.

Whenever the left mouse button is pressed over either of the wheels, the procedure changeTire will be invoked. If the tire is found to be flat, it will be changed. In the body of the procedure changeTire, use the Tk canvas widget action subcommand gettags to retrieve the list of all the tags that the item with the current tag has. You check the first element of this list to see if the selected item is either the back or front wheel. If it is either of those, you use the action subcommand cget to check the type of the item. If the type is oval, the wheel is not flat. Proceed to flatten it.

Because this example is not about creating perfect visualization, you get away with changing the type of the item from a oval to an arc whose style is set to chord with the -extent and -start options set to 240 and -60, respectively. If, on the other hand, the wheel is already flat, you repair it.

> If you have used item identifiers, you must assign the binding for each wheel separately. In such a case, the current tag is still available to you. Also, remember to assign a variable to represent each wheel. That variable will then hold the current value of the item identifier of the wheel, no matter how many times Tk exchanged the oval and arc to recreate each wheel.

Binding Event Sequences to the Canvas

The tag bindings are effective mechanisms to manipulate individual items or groups of items in the canvas. You might also want to bind events to the canvas itself. For instance, you might want to recognize click button and drag mouse events to draw rubber bands around items, stretch items, or sketch items. Unlike text widget, the canvas does not have any default event bindings. You can define your own. Listing 16.5 provides a script that enables you to create a canvas in which you draw a line by pressing, holding the mouse button 1, and dragging it along. The line ends when you let go of the button.

LISTING 16.5   Canvas Binding

```
 1: wm title . "Canvas bindings"
 2: canvas .c
 3: pack .c
 4: frame .fb -background lightblue
 5: button .fb.qb -text Quit -command {destroy .}
 6: button .fb.clear -text Clear -command clearItems
 7: set info {Click B1 in canvas and move the mouse}
 8: set infoWidth [string length $info]
 9: label .fb.info -text $info -width $infoWidth -background lightblue
10: pack .c
11: pack .fb.qb .fb.clear  -side right
12: pack .fb.info -side left
13: pack .fb -fill x
14:
15: # bind B1 B1-Motion and B1Release to draw a line
16:
17: # store the initial position
18: bind .c <Button-1> {
19:    set lastX %x
20:    set lastY %y
21: }
22:
23: bind .c <B1-Motion> {
24:    .c delete tempLine
25:    .c create line $lastX $lastY %x %y -tags tempLine
26: }
27:
28: bind .c <ButtonRelease-1> {
29:    .c delete tempLine
30:    .c create line $lastX $lastY %x %y -tags theLINE
31: }
32:
33: bind .fb.clear <Enter> {.fb.info config -text "Clear items on canvas" }
34: bind .fb.clear <Leave> {.fb.info config -text $info}
35:
36: proc clearItems { } {
37:    .c delete theLINE
38: }
```

ANALYSIS   This script creates a canvas widget and a frame window. Within the frame, a label and two buttons are created and packed. The label is used to display the instruction asking the user to click, hold, and move mouse button 1. Selecting the Quit button will exit the application. Selecting the Clear button invokes the procedure `clearItems`. The procedure `clearItems` executes the widget action command `delete` on all items that are tagged with the name `theLINE`.

There are three bindings for the canvas window itself: one for `Button-1` event, one for `Button-1-Motion`, and the last for `ButtonRelease-1`. When the left mouse button is pressed in the canvas, the coordinates of the point under the mouse cursor are stored in the variables `lastX` and `lastY`. As the mouse is dragged along with the left mouse button down, a line item is created with the tag `tempLine`. This line is drawn from the point whose coordinates are `lastX` and `lastY` to the current position given by `%x` and `%y`. The execution of this command is preceded by deleting the same line drawn between the point (`lastX`, `lastY`) and the position just before the current position. Figure 16.3 shows a snapshot of using these event bindings to draw some lines.

> The execution of the command `.c delete tempLine` will do nothing the very first time it is used because there will be no line item with the tag `tempLINE`.

When the mouse button is released, the line is redrawn for the last time, and a new tag `theLINE` is added.

You do not have to declare `lastX` and `lastY` as global. Go through Listing 16.5 with care. It shows you how to bind event sequences and associated event handlers to the canvas widget. However, the binding syntax `bind pathName <event sequence> {script}` is something you are already familiar with from Hour 11. The other purpose of this script is to remind you that bindings are executed in global scope. This is demonstrated in the use of the variables `lastX` and `lastY`.

There is a take-home message here concerning the scope of variables. If by some chance you have used `lastX` with a set value `1` and also used a local variable `lastX` (within a binding script) with a value set to `3`, the binding script, while being parsed, will alter the main variable to `3`! In order to avoid such confusion, it is always safer to define bind scripts in procedures when you are going to set and use local variables in that script.

Finally, you can define bindings for any widget by associating the `Enter` and `Leave` events with the buttons. When the mouse pointer is on the button, a short message giving its command is displayed. When the pointer leaves, the original text is restored.

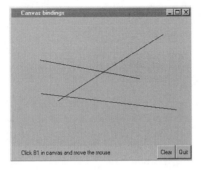

FIGURE 16.3

*An application for
canvas event bindings.*

16

Constrained Motion in a Canvas

There might be occasions you want a canvas item to move along a given locus, regardless of the mouse movement. An example is a situation when the user needs to provide a
direction or angle as input. For such input, you want to provide a dial and needle whose
range varies from 0–360 degrees. It is not necessary or easy to make the user place the
mouse cursor precisely on the edge of the needle to drag it along. He can also drag in the
canvas at a distance. To support such an easy interaction, you interpret the mouse movement in the canvas in terms of distances along the locus.

A simple example, Listing 16.6, shows a bead that is constrained to move along the circumference with the <Button-1-Motion>. This example also emphasises the importance
of the canvas coordinate system and the need to make the necessary transformations in
all the appropriate expressions.

LISTING 16.6   Constrained Movement

```
 1: wm title . "Constrained Motion"
 2: global x0 y0
 3: pack [canvas .c]
 4: .c create oval  160 120 260 220 -fill {} \
 5:     -width 2 -tags { rim }
 6: # put a bead at pi/4 rads
 7: # Center at:  (210,170)
 8: # Radius:      50
 9: #
10: set pi [expr acos(-1)]
11: set x0 210; set y0 170
12: set x1 [expr $x0 + 50*cos($pi/4)]
13: set y1 [expr $y0 - 50*sin($pi/4)]
14:
15: .c create oval [expr $x1-5] [expr $y1-5] \
16:     [expr $x1+5] [expr $y1+5] \
```

continues

LISTING 16.6   continued

```
17:      -fill #a46fce -tags { tgBead }
18: # light yellow
19: frame .f -bg #f9fc8f
20: pack .f -fill x
21: label .f.label -bg #f9fc8f \
22:      -text {B1-Motion moves the bead along the rim.}
23: pack .f.label -side left
24: button .f.b -text {Quit} -command {exit}
25: pack .f.b -side right
26:
27: proc moveBead { x y } {
28:      global x0 y0
30:      set xr [expr $x-$x0]
31:      set yr [expr -($y-$y0)] ;# flip the sign as canvas y increases down
32:      ;# if you don't the bead moves opposite to the mouse pointer
33:      set theta [expr atan2($yr,$xr)]
36:      set x1 [expr $x0 + 50*cos($theta)]
37:      set y1 [expr $y0 - 50*sin($theta)]
38:      .c delete tgBead
39:      .c create oval [expr $x1-5] [expr $y1-5] \
40:      [expr $x1+5] [expr $y1+5] \
41:      -fill #a46fce -tags { tgBead }
42:      update
43: }
44: # bind
45: bind .c <B1-Motion> {moveBead %x %y}
```

ANALYSIS   In line 1, you use the window manager command to set a title for your application window. You then declare two global variables x0 and y0 that are the coordinates of the center of a circular rim along which you want to move a small bead. In line 3, a canvas widget .c is created and packed. In lines 4–5, you create the circular rim and attach the tag rim to it with the -tags option. The next task is to select a point on the circle. Given the center (x0,y0), one point on the circumference of a circle will be given by x1=X0+r*cosp/4 and y=y0=r*sinp/4, where r is the radius of the circle. These formulae apply in a system where the origin is situated at the bottom left. Specifying the value of p as [expr acos(-1)], as you have done in line 10, ensures that the value used is the highest accuracy afforded by the machine. The center of the circular rim is set to 210 and 170 in line 11, and the radius is taken to be 50 screen units. Lines 12 and 13 give the computational expression for x1 and y1. Note anything? Yes, you have corrected for the top-left origin by reversing the sign of the second term for computing y1.

Lines 17–19 create a small bead, whose enclosing rectangular region is defined in terms of the initial x1, y1. You have taken these diagonal points to be (x1-5,y1-5) and (x1+5,y1+5). You have attached the tag tgBead to your bead.

Next, you have defined a frame with a yellow background to provide demarcation cues. In this frame, you can provide a label with a crisp instruction telling users about the mouse cursor usage and a button to be used for exiting the application.

In line 45, you define the binding of the event sequence B1-Motion to the canvas and attach the event handler script in procedure moveBead to this binding. The procedure itself is defined in lines 27–43. The procedure takes two input arguments, the x and y coordinates of the current position of the mouse cursor. As a first step, the procedure transforms the coordinates x and y in terms of the center of the circular rim. Note that you have corrected for the canvas coordinate system by changing the sign of yr. If you don't perform this correction, the bead moves in an opposite direction to the mouse cursor motion.

Now, you need to compute the coordinates for the rectangular region that encloses the current position of the bead following the mouse motion. To compute this, you need to determine the direction of the line given by (x,y) and (x0,y0). This is given by atan2(yr,xr). You can use atan2 to ensure that the returned value lies between 0 and 2p. If you use atan, you get the value between 0 and p/2. Note that the value returned by atan2 is in radians.

Finally, at every move of the mouse, the bead is accessed using its tag name tgBead, and the command .c delete tgBead deletes it from the canvas. The bead is redrawn (recreated) using the new coordinates. Figure 16.4 shows the application layout.

FIGURE 16.4
GUI layout for constrained motion of a bead along a circular rim.

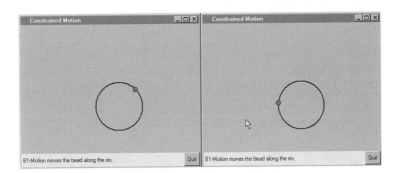

Animation in Canvas

The last topic in this hour covers how to create animation with canvas items, and in particular, how to implement a confined motion that stipulates how a given body moves within the confines of a given boundary. You can demonstrate this via the script in Listing 16.7 that follows. The script enables you to select a speed with which a given ball moves within a region bounded by four lines.

The user can control the update time delay by selecting the value using the scale. This value is passed as the input argument to the Tk `after` command. The `after` command suspends the process by an amount equivalent in milliseconds to its input. So a smaller value of this parameter makes the ball move faster because the delay between each move is smaller. The application layout is shown in Figure 16.5.

LISTING 16.7 Confined Movement

```
 1: wm title . "Confined motion"
 2: global stopped
 3:
 4: pack [canvas .c -width 3.5c -height 4.5c]
 5: # use 4 separate lines for the box to check for collision
 6: .c create rectangle 10 10 105 160 -tags { topWall box } -width 4 \
 7:                -outline blue
 8:
 9: # get a random number between the limits
10: proc randBetween { a b } {
11:     # x is between a and b
12:     set x [expr round( ($b-$a)*rand()+ $a ) ]
13: }
14:
15: # put a billiard ball somehere
16: set xti [randBetween 10 100]
17: set yti [randBetween 10 155]
18: set xbi [expr $xti+10]
19: set ybi [expr $yti+10]
20: .c create oval $xti $yti $xbi $ybi -fill indianred -tags { ball }
21:
22: set stopped 1
23: set speed 50
24: # moveBall
25: proc moveBall {} {
26:     global stopped speed
27:     set xNew [randBetween 15 100]
28:     set yNew [randBetween 15 155]
29:     if { $stopped } {
30:         return
31:     } else {
32:         after $speed  moveBall
33:
34:         .c delete ball
35:         .c create oval $xNew $yNew \
36:                [expr $xNew+10] [expr $yNew+10] \
37:                -fill indianred -tags { ball }
38:     }
39: }
40: scale .sc -orient horizontal -show 1 -from 5 -to 290 \
```

```
41:         -length 5c -label {Delay update by ...} -variable speed \
42:         -tick 70
43: pack .sc -side top
44: .sc set 20
45: frame .f
46: pack .f -fill x
47: button .f.b -text MoveBall -command {
48:     if $stopped {
49:         set stopped 0
50:         moveBall
51:     }
52: }
53: button .f.stop -text Stop -command {set stopped 1}
54: pack .f.stop .f.b -side right
```

ANALYSIS   In this script, you create a canvas and a frame that are packed from top to bottom. The frame contains a scale widget and two buttons. The scale enables the user to set the parameter for the built-in Tk command `after`. This command introduces a time delay in the execution process. The `MoveBall` button sets the global variable `stopped` to `0` (False) and executes the procedure `moveBall`. The `Stop` button is used to invoke a command that sets a global parameter to `1`.

Script lines 6–7 create a rectangle that acts as a bounding region for the ball, which is created in line 20. The random initial position of the ball is generated in lines 16–19. The procedure `randomBetween` takes two input arguments. It calls the built-in function `rand` and normalizes the generated value to be one lying between the two input arguments. You, of course, round it to generate an integer value, as you need position values.

Next, the script uses the procedure `randBetween` to generate two random numbers between 10 and 100 and between 10 and 155. It then creates the four coordinates required to specify the two diagonally opposite points of the bounding box of the ball. Recall that these points are required for the canvas widget action subcommand `create` to create the oval shape that represents the ball.

Script lines 25–39 define the procedure `moveBall`. This procedure checks whether `stopped` is set to `true` or `false`. If stopped is `false`, then a new random position for the ball is generated. The old instance of the ball is deleted from the canvas and the new instance is drawn. This process is repeated at the rate specified by the variable `speed`, which is passed to the `after` command. So, if the speed variable is set to 5 milliseconds, the old instance of the ball is deleted and a new instance of the ball is created every 5 milliseconds. Figure 16.5 shows the application layout for this script.

16

Figure 16.5

Application layout for confined motion.

Do	Don't
Do use patterns and semantically intuitive names in tags where possible. They can be exploited for your advantage later.	**Don't** forget that all items associated with a given tag are affected when you execute a reconfiguration using the common tag.
Do clear up any left over `after` events with `after cancel [after info]`	**Don't** forget that tags also are ordered similar to item identifiers. Traversal ordering applies to all items whether a call to reconfigure an item is made using an item identifier or tag; that is, items lower in the stack will be drawn first.
Do remember that you can use tag and item identifiers interchangeably, and all action subcommands that apply to items using their integer item identifiers can also be issued using their tag.	

Summary

In this hour, you learned about the creation and use of canvas item tags, one of the most powerful, flexible, and yet simple mechanisms supported by Tk. Item tags are used to group individual canvas items so that they can be subsequently manipulated as a single entity. Concepts, such as tag bindings and canvas bindings, were also introduced using examples.

In this hour, you also learned more about the canvas coordinate system and how to handle it for animation of items, alongside constrained and confined motion of items in a canvas. The canvas widget and action subcommands act using both integer item identifiers and item tags.

You continue to learn about Tk canvas widgets in the next hour, "Working with Images in the Canvas." That final phase will show you how to exploit the Tk built-in image manipulation commands and include them in your application. It will also show you how to embed other widgets in a canvas. Equally important, you will learn how to get hard copies of your canvas contents.

Q&A

Q How can I rotate an item in the canvas?

A There is no generic support for rotating items in the canvas. This is partly because there is no viewing model. However, you can emulate a rotation about a point or an axis by writing the computational code yourself. Remember that the canvas origin is at the top-left corner. As a result, computing rotated vertices using the textbook rotation matrix does not yield the desired result. To help you understand the mechanics of rotating an item, we provide an illustration. We use an L-plate and rotate it by 60 degrees clockwise. Figure 16.6 gives a schematic diagram of this example. The script is given in Listing 16.8 that follows. Figure 16.7 is the result of executing Listing 16.8, which implements this rotation.

FIGURE 16.6

Sketch of polygonal item 'L'. Vertices of an item with respect to different origins.

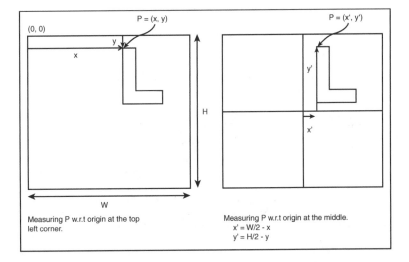

Measuring P w.r.t origin at the top left corner.

Measuring P w.r.t origin at the middle.
$x' = W/2 - x$
$y' = H/2 - y$

LISTING 16.8 Rotating Canvas Items

```
# Simple rotation by theta
#    use the origin at the middle
#
# use the default width and height
pack [canvas .c]
# vertices of 'L' are defined so that the shape appears
# in the first quadrant.
# Start from top left and go anti-clock wise, A, B, C, ...
# Bottom right vertex is 'C'.

global axisMode
# showAxis
```

continues

LISTING 16.8   continued

```
#
proc showAxis {} {
    global axisMode
    # draw axis
    if { $axisMode } {
    .c create line 189 0 189 265   -tags axis
    .c create line 0 132.5 378 132.5 -tags axis
    set axisMode 0
    } else {
    .c delete axis
    set axisMode 1
    }
}

set A {200 20}
set B {200 120}
set C {250 120}
set D {250 100}
set E {220 100}
set F {220 20}
set pts "$A $B $C $D $E $F" ;# double quotes will flatten the list
eval .c create polygon  $pts -fill red -tags { tgPlate }

set th [expr acos(-1)/4]
set trPts {}

# convertPoints
# Input: pts  List of points x0 y0 x1 y1 ...
# Outputs: newPts List of points expressed with ref to the mid point of
#                  canvas dimension as the origin
# Algorithm: x coords remains the same
#            y coords computed as H -yi, where H is the canvas Height
#
# Note: Converts from one style to another
#
proc convertPoints { pts } {
    set newPts {}
    set H 265       ;# [.c config -height]
    set W 378
    foreach { x y } $pts {
    lappend newPts [expr $W/2-$x]
    lappend newPts [expr $H/2-$y]
```

```
        }
        set newPts
    }

    # coordinates w.r.t origin at the middle
    #
    set pts2 [convertPoints $pts]

    # rotatePoints
    # Inputs: pts    List of points of the form x0 y0 x1 y1 ...
    #         theta  Angle of rotation in radians
    # Outputs: newPts List of rotated points
    #                 rotated clock-wise
    #
    proc rotatePoints { pts th } {
        set newPts {}
        foreach {x y} $pts {
        set p [expr $x*cos($th)-$y*sin($th)] ;#  clock-wise
        set q [expr $x*sin($th)+$y*cos($th)]
        lappend newPts $p
        lappend newPts $q
        }
        return $newPts
    }

    # put some rotated L-plates

    for {set i 1} {$i < 6} {incr i} {
        set pts2 [convertPoints $pts]
        set th [expr $i*acos(-1)/3]
        set trPts [rotatePoints $pts2 $th]
        set newPts [convertPoints $trPts]
        set clr [format #%02x%02x00 [expr 255-$i*20] [expr 255-$i*20] ]
        eval .c create polygon $newPts -fill $clr -tags plate$i
    }

    # frame, buttons
    frame .f -bg lightblue
    pack .f -fill x
    button .f.b -text Quit -command {exit}
    set axisMode 1
    button .f.axis -text {Show Axis}  -command  showAxis
    pack .f.b -side right
    pack .f.axis -side left
```

16

FIGURE **16.7**

Rotating a polygonal item.

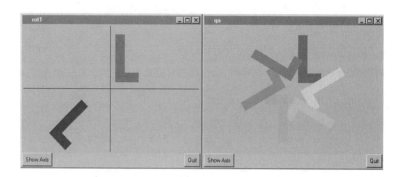

Workshop

The quiz section below is designed to provide you with an opportunity to recall some of the important concepts introduced in this hour. These may be commands, command syntax, common mistakes, usage, and so on. The following exercises section helps you consolidate the material you learned via an example of practical value. Our aim is that these two sections should reinforce the knowledge you have gained in this hour. The answers to the quiz that follows can be found in Appendix A, "Answers to Quizzes."

Quiz

1. How are tags created for a canvas item?
2. What is the command to delete all the tags in a canvas?
3. Fill in the blank. Binding scripts are executed in _____ scope.
4. What tag name is automatically added when the mouse enters an item in the canvas?
5. How do you remove binding on an item?

Exercises

Solutions to the exercises are on the CD-ROM that accompanies this book.

1. Write a script to reflect the polygonal item, L-plate shown in Figure 16.8. Attach a tag binding so that the L-plate is reflected about the vertical axis shown in the figure.

FIGURE 16.8

Reflecting a polygonal item about the vertical.

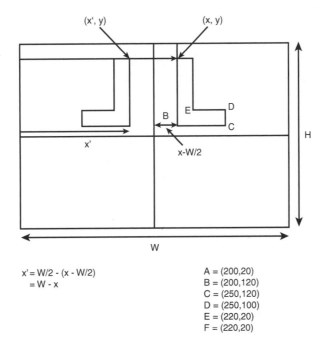

$x' = W/2 - (x - W/2)$
$\quad = W - x$

A = (200,20)
B = (200,120)
C = (250,120)
D = (250,100)
E = (220,20)
F = (220,20)

16

2. Write a script to display a horizontal line with the following functionality: When the mouse enters one of the end points, stretch the line as the mouse pointer moves but keep the other end point fixed. See Figure 16.9 which follows.

FIGURE 16.9

Resizing a line.

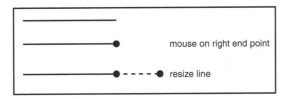

mouse on right end point

resize line

HOUR 17

Working with Images in the Canvas

This is the last of the three hours we are allocating to learn about the Tk canvas widget. In Hour 15, "Getting Started with the Canvas," you learned about creating canvas items, canvas commands, and the canvas coordinate system. In the last hour, "Using Canvas Commands," you learned how to group canvas items into higher order structures using the tag mechanism and then how to manipulate such items as a single entity. You also learned canvas-specific action subcommands that operate using item identifiers as well as tags. It remains for you to learn the remaining Tk canvas widget's advanced utilities such as incorporating images and other widgets in a canvas. You of course will also learn how to use the canvas Postscript command.

In this hour, you will learn

- How to use Tk image commands
- How to display images in a canvas
- How to interact with an image in a canvas

- How to create and use embedded widgets in a canvas
- How to generate a hard copy of the contents of a canvas

Tk Images

The Tk canvas supports two types of images: *bitmap* and *photo*. Bitmaps are displayed with two colors, one for the foreground and another for the background. Photo images, on the other hand, are full color images, which can also include transparency. You can use built-in bitmaps that have the .bmp extension, or you can use any bitmap created by other bitmap generating applications such as xpaint. You can use GIF, PPM, and PGM formats with photo images.

Or, you can supply photo image data from a C code! This gives you a hint, quite rightly, that there are Tk image commands. In fact, Tk provides you with utilities to create, delete, copy, query, and manipulate images. You can use these utilities to include a true color image in your Tk application or even include an image created with your own image data format by providing the data and data format handlers to Tk. In this hour, we will keep to a modest objective of using photo images in GIF format but will strive to understand the built-in utilities to include such images in the canvas.

You can add your own photo image format beside the PPM, GIF, and PGM that Tk supports. You do this by defining a data format handler and using the Tk C library routine Tk_CreatePhotoImageFormat. You will, of course, need to know how to use C and Tcl/Tk together. That subject is covered in Hour 18, "Using C with Tcl/Tk." Refer to the online pages of Tcl/Tk when you want to use these advanced utilities.

Creating Tk Images

The Tk built-in command image action-command ?option value? is used to create, delete, and query images. The form of this command is dependent on the action and Table 17.1 gives a gist of the image commands.

TABLE 17.1 Subset of Image Commands—I

Command	Action
image create type ?option value?	An image of the specified type is created. The command returns the name of the image.
image delete name ?name?	Deletes named images.
image height name	Returns the height of the named image in screen units.
image names	Returns a list all existing images.
image type name	Returns the type of the image.
image types	Returns a list of all the valid image types.
image width name	Returns the width of the named image in screen units.

There is another layer of built-in image commands that you can have with Tk. Whenever an image is created, Tk automatically creates an associated command whose name is the same as that of the image it is associated with. These commands take the form `imageName action-subcommand ?option value?`. Table 17.2 gives a list of this second set of image commands.

TABLE 17.2 Subset of Image Commands—II

Command	Action
imageName cget *option*	Retrieves the current value of the option.
imageName configure ?option value?	Queries or modifies the option specified.
imageName copy source ?option value?	Copies the source image to the image named by imageName. See online manual pages for the full list of valid options.
imageName get x y	Returns the r, g, b values of the image at the pixel position (x,y).

Embedding Images in Canvas

The Tk image utilites are useful for creating, deleting, and manipulating images in canvas and text widgets. In Hour 15, "Getting Started with the Canvas," you learned about the structured graphic items you can create in a canvas. You can also create two types of image items in canvas. The `command pathName create imageType x y ?option value?` creates an imageType image at position (x, y). By default, the center of the image is positioned at (x, y).

By now, you are becoming quite familiar with options. Whenever you want to know the options that are available either for a widget or for a canvas item, use the configure action command with no options. The interpreter will return the list of all applicable options.

Whenever you wish to check the current value of an option, use the cget or itemcget action subcommand to query. These commands, as we have already seen frequently, take the form pathName cget option or pathName itemcget tagOrId option.

In the case of images, you have the special options -image file and -format formatName. Armed with all this information, let us experiment with some of these commands. Listing 17.1 illustrates the simplest use of image creation.

You must specify the correct directory path name to the image for this script. Make this change in line 4 of Listing 17.1. If you don't, the Tk interpreter will search for a subdirectory of images in your current working directory and look for image 50p.gif.

Note also that Listing 17.1 is an input script file that is "sourced." That is, the return values for individual commands are not included. You, too, can create a script file and source it rather than try each command interactively. Both methods are equivalent and educational.

INPUT   **LISTING 17.1**   Image Commands—I

```
 1: #read in an image
 2: wm title . "Image in a canvas"
 3:
 4: set im [image create photo -file ../images/50p.gif \
 5:         -height 450 -width 500]
 6: set w [image width $im]
 7: set h [image height $im]
 8:
 9: frame .f -bg yellow
10: pack .f
11:
12: # create canvas set the canvas big enough to hold the image
13: canvas .f.c -width [expr $w+50] -height [expr $h+50]
14: pack .f.c -side left
```

```
15:
16: # create an image item in the canvas
17: .f.c create image 0 0 -image $im -anchor nw  -tag 50pcoin
```

The command image create photo -file ./images/50p.gif -height 450 -width 500 creates an image of type photo from the file containing the GIF image 50p.gif and returns its identity. This identifier is assigned to the variable im. In lines 6 and 7, we use the image action commands to acquire the width and height of the image and assign these two values to the variables w and h. We use these values to determine which canvas we want to use to display the image.

We create a frame, .f, as the child of the main window and the canvas .f.c as the child of the frame. The canvas is packed in its parent master with the -side option set to left. In the script in line 17, we use the canvas create command to create and display the canvas item of type image made of the 50 pence coin. We also attach a tag called 50pcoin to this image canvas item.

Note that we have specified the coordinates x and y of the point at which we want the image to be displayed as 0 and 0. By default, this option will be interpreted to display the image in such a way that the center of the image will be at the point (0,0). Given that the canvas coordinate system has its origin at the top-left corner, this positioning would lose most of the image. We have also set the option -anchor to nw. This option will place the center of the top of the image at the positioning point. Voilá!We have our image correctly positioned at the top left of the canvas. Figure 17.1 shows the result.

17

FIGURE **17.1**

Image displayed with anchoring set to nw.

The Tk interpreter creates an image command when it creates the image. Besides, we have also associated a tag with the image item. We use the tag binding to illustrate the image command from Listing 17.2. Execute the script in Listing 17.1 from a wish shell. When the coin image is displayed, type the script in Listing 17.2 at the command line of the wish shell.

INPUT   **LISTING 17.2**   Image Commands—II

```
1: #continuation of Listing 17.1. Type this at wish
2: #command prompt or appnd to the script file containing
3: #Listing 17.1.
4: .f.c bind 50pcoin <Button-1> { puts [$im get %x %y] }
```

ANALYSIS   You have now defined a tag binding for the event sequence Button-1. The event handler script for this binding executes the image action subcommand imageName get %x %y to return the RGB values of the pixel at the current cursor location. Note that you can use the script to get and examine the current value, apply some algorithm to modify it, and use the put action to modify the RGB values at the given pixel.

It is essential to understand the positioning of the image in a canvas using the x, y coordinates of position and the -anchor option. Note that it is mandatory to specify the position. As we stated before, by default, the center of the image is placed at the positioning point. The script in Listing 17.3 allows you to explore the anchoring interactively.

> Observe again that this listing is only what you input to the interpreter. The return value from the execution of each command is not included.

INPUT   **LISTING 17.3**   Image Anchoring

```
1: #read in an image
2: set im [image create photo -file ../images/50p2.gif \
3:         -height 450 -width 500]
4: set w [image width $im]
5: set h [image height $im]
6: frame .f -bg yellow
7: pack .f
8: canvas .f.compas -relief groove -bd 2 -width 1.6i -height 1.6i
9:
10: # create canvas set the canvas big enough to hold the image in im
11: canvas .f.c -width [expr $w+50] -height [expr $h+50]
12: pack .f.compas .f.c -side left
13: set data   { 0.8i 0.8i c 1.55i 0.8i e 0.05i 0.8i w \
```

```
14:                 0.8i 0.05i n 0.85i 1.6i s 0.05i 0.05i nw \
15:                 1.6i 0.05i ne 1.6i 1.6i se 0.05i 1.6i sw }
16: foreach {x y d} $data {
17:     .f.compas create text $x $y -text [string toupper $d] \
18:             -font {Courier 14 bold}\
19:             -anchor $d -tags $d
20: }
21: # create an image item in the canvas
22: .f.c create image 0 0 -image $im -anchor nw  -tag 50pcoin
23: foreach t {c n e s w ne se sw nw} {
24:     .f.compas bind $t <Button-1> {updateAnchor .f.compas $im }
25: }
26:
27: proc updateAnchor { w imag} {
28:     set direction  [lindex [$w gettags current] 0]
29:     puts "direction: $direction"
30:     .f.c delete 50pcoin
31:     set xpos 0; set ypos 0
32:     .f.c create image $xpos $ypos -image $imag \
33:             -anchor $direction  -tag 50pcoin
33: }
```

17

ANALYSIS Our purpose is to explore the effect of anchoring an image. To do this, we want
to create a simplistic compass. We do this by creating another canvas widget,
.f.compas. This canvas and our image canvas .f.c are packed in the frame .f with the
-side option set to left. In lines 13–15, we define a data list consisting of a series of
triplets: Each of which gives the x and y positions and an admissible value for the
-anchor option.

The foreach loop in lines 16–20 creates four text items at the given (x,y) position in the
canvas widget, .f.compas. Note that we have used the anchor value for the text label as
well by converting the letter to uppercase and giving it a larger font. We have also used
the value of the anchor option to set a tag for each text item that reflects its direction.

Lines 21–25 are the same as those in Listing 17.2. The application layout is shown in
Figure 17.2.

This script places the center of the image at the default position (0,0) and
varies the anchoring to illustrate the effect of anchoring. Try setting the
image position to (256,256) by setting xpos and ypos to *256* and *256* (in line
31) and run the example through all the anchoring.

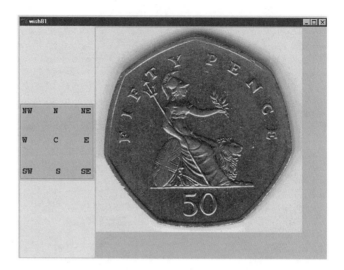

Lines 27–33 define the procedure updateAnchor. It takes two input arguments, the name of the canvas widget, and the image name. When one of the directions is selected, the built-in tag current is automatically attached to it. We use this tag to retrieve all the tags associated with the item with current tag. Because tagging, as applied by Tk, is ordered, the lindex command retrieves the first tag, the anchoring direction tag of the item. We delete the old instance of the image and recreate another instance with the new anchoring.

This script does introduce you to image command and canvas commands associated with images. However, one of our purposes is to understand the effect of anchoring. Figure 17.3 shows a schematic diagram of the relationship between positioning and anchoring. The image on the left shows the placement of the image at any (x, y), with default anchoring placing the center of the image at that point (x, y). The image on the right shows the effect of selecting s for anchoring and default position which is (0, 0). When you select a direction, the tag binding associated with that item re-places the image accordingly. You need to remember that the value given to the anchoring places the center of the corresponding edge of the image at the positioning point. Note that the anchoring set to s, shown in the right diagram, makes the translation shift of the center of the image and places the bottom of the image in line with (0,y).

Executing the script in Listing 17.3 gives you an application to try the positioning of images.

FIGURE 17.3

Schematic diagram to show anchoring of images.

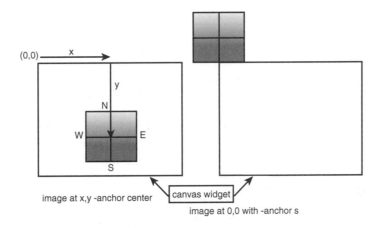

image at x,y -anchor center

canvas widget

image at 0,0 with -anchor s

17

Manipulating Images

Tk provides a set of useful image manipulation utilities. For instance, you can copy to and from an image or shrink or expand an image, although you can't scale it in the same sense as other canvas items we have been dealing with. You already know that when an image is created, Tk creates an associated image command. You also learned about associating tags and tag bindings to images. In addition, you also know that you can attach bindings to the canvas widget itself. Let us bring all these utilities together in an application to explore the image manipulation commands and how to use them.

Image names, similar to widget names, are not in the global scope. Only tags are placed automatically in the global scope. Because bindings are executed in the global scope, it is very easy to mistake that image and widget names are in the global scope. This means that image names and widget names that are needed in any procedure must be passed as input arguments to the procedure (unless the event-handler accesses the widget it is acting on). You can, of course, assign variables to hold image names, making this variable and its value, the image name, available in global scope.

Listing 17.4 creates a photo image of one of our favorite stamps that is in a 1:2 ratio of its original. We then reduce it by half and again by half. The reduced images are displayed one below another as shown in Figure 17.4.

We also introduce some tag bindings to the canvas as well as the image to produce behavior such as moving the image around. The purpose is to illustrate how you can manipulate images both in content as well as an item in a canvas. It is our hope, after we have illustrated the building blocks, that you, the interested reader, will be able to develop your applications imaginatively to create, for example, interactive catalogs or photo albums.

FIGURE 17.4

Manipulating images using image commands.

LISTING 17.4   Image Manipulation Commands

```
 1: wm title . "The Royal Scot"
 2: set royalscot [image create photo -file "[pwd]/images/royalscot.gif" ]
 3: pack [canvas .c -bg white]
 4:
 5: .c create image 0 0 -image $royalscot -anchor nw -tags royalscot
 6: pack [canvas .c2 -bg violet]
 7:
 8: set RShalf [image create photo]
 9: $RShalf copy $royalscot -shrink -subsample 2 2 ;# every other pixel
10: .c2 create image 0 0 -image $RShalf -anchor nw
11:
12: set RSqtr [image create photo]
13: $RSqtr copy $royalscot -shrink -subsample 4 4
14: .c2 create image 0 145 -image $RSqtr -anchor nw -tag stamp
15: .c2 bind stamp <Button-1> {.c2 move stamp 10 0}
```

```
16: .c2 bind stamp <Button-3> {.c2 move stamp -10 0}
17:
18: bind .c2  <Key-Up> {.c2 move stamp 0 -10}
19: bind .c2  <Key-Down> {.c2 move stamp 0 +10}
20: focus .c2
```

ANALYSIS Let us begin with our customary scripting of a title for our application in line 1. We then use the command `image create photo -file "[pwd]/images/royalscot.gif"` in line 2 to create a photo image and assign the returned image identifier to the variable `royalscot`.

> The image file path we have given is relative rather than absolute. It is based on the assumption that you have placed your images in a top-level directory above your current working directory. Change this to give the appropriate relative or absolute pathname.

Line 3 uses the widget creation command to create a canvas `.c` with a white background. The output from this widget creation command execution is then piped to the `pack` command for visual management. Recall from Hour 2, "Getting Started with Tcl," that this is command substituition in Tcl/Tk. You will encounter this style of scripting so often, it is worth your while to get accustomed to it.

In line 5, we create an image canvas item in the canvas `.c` using our `royalscot` photo image. This image item is quite large. So, let us have another canvas for our reduced images. We create this second canvas `.c2` with a `violet` background and pack it as before. Note that the default packing side is `top`.

Lines 8–10 are interesting. We first create a blank image of type photo to hold the new image data when we are ready to give it. We assign the variable `RShalf` to this holder-image. In line 9, the command `imageName copy sourceName -shrink -subsample x y` is used to copy every xth and yth pixel in X and Y directions respectively. In our case, the destination is our newly created holder-image `RShalf` and the source image is `royalscot`. We have sampled every second pixel in both X and Y directions. As a result, `RShalf` is half the size of `royalscot`. In line 10, we create an image type canvas item using `RShalf` in canvas `.c2`. This image canvas item is positioned at (0,0) with `nw` anchoring.

In lines 12–14, we deploy the similar script to create an image item `RSqrt` that is a quarter of the size of the `royalscot`. We also attach a tag `stamp`. In lines 15–19, we define a set of bindings, the first two of which are tag bindings associating the tag stamp to the event sequences Button-1 and Button-3. The second set of bindings is for the canvas widget `.c2` itself. These attach the up and down arrows to the `.c2`. The event-handlers for all the four bindings move the quarter-sized image `RSqtr` with the tag `stamp` to move left, right, up, and down. The command focus `.c2` ensures that keyboard input is rerouted to the canvas `.c2` so that the arrow key events can be responded to.

> You can indeed overlap the images in `.c2`, illustrating the stacking ordering for traversal and drawing.

Embedding Other Widgets

Until now in this hour, you learned about the image creation, deletion, query, and manipulation commands provided by Tk. There might be application contexts in which graphical information needs to be presented to the user selectively under his interactive control. For instance, one possible application is an interactive stamp catalogue. You might want to present a list of thumbnail images of stamps. Selecting an image presents a full size image with associated information in a text window.

In Hour 14, "Doing More with Text Widget," you learned about embedding other widgets in text windows. Tk extends the facility for embedding other interactive controls to the canvas widget too. This means that you can create interesting applications which present graphical and textual information selectively and elicit input and feedback from the user via intuitive interactive control widgets. The goal is to use the most appropriate widget for the information presentation and interaction.

Embedding a widget in canvas is made straightforward. You create the widget to be embedded using the widget creation command. Then you create a canvas item of the type window with `-window` option set to the widget you want to embed. The execution of this command assigns the management of the embedded widget to the canvas widget's internal geometry manager.

In Listing 17.5, which follows, we provide a compact application that illustrates how to embed and use other widgets in canvas. Figure 17.5 shows the result of executing such an application.

Figure 17.5

An application with embedded widgets.

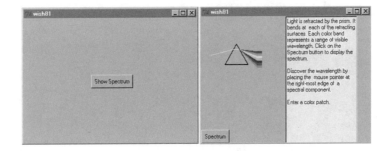

Listing 17.5 Embedded Widgets

```
 1: # Embedded widget in a canvas
 2: #    example of visible light spectrum
 3: #    button, text, label
 4: wm title . "Embedded widgets"
 5:
 6: # store wavelengths
 7: #
 8: set WAVELENGTHS(red)      {780-630 nm}
 9: set WAVELENGTHS(orange)   {630-600 nm}
10: set WAVELENGTHS(yellow)   {600-570 nm}
11: set WAVELENGTHS(green)    {570-520 nm}
12: set WAVELENGTHS(blue)     {520-450 nm}
13: set WAVELENGTHS(#8944fd)  {450-400 nm}
14: set WAVELENGTHS(violet)   {400-380 nm}
15:
16: pack [canvas .c]
17:
18: # start with a single button in the middle
19: button .b -text {Show Spectrum} -command showCB
20: set midX [expr [.c cget -width]/2]
21: set midY [expr [.c cget -height]/2]
22: .c create window $midX $midY -window .b -anchor center -tags showButton
23:
24: proc showCB {} {
25:     .c delete showButton
26:     drawPrism .c
27: }
28:
29: proc drawPrism { w } {
30:     global A B C h
31:     # place the drawing, text, button in w
32:     set th [expr acos(-1)/3]
33:     set h [expr 100 - 50*sin($th)]
34:     set A {50 100}
35:     set B {100 100}
36:     set C "75 $h"
```

continues

17

LISTING 17.5 continued

```
37:
38:     eval $w create line $A $B -width 2 -tags { prism }
39:     eval $w create line $A $C -width 2 -tags { prism }
40:     eval $w create line $B $C -width 2 -tags { prism }
41:     button .bspec -text {Spectrum} -command displayBeam
42:     $w create window 0 [$w cget -height] -window .bspec \
43:             -anchor sw -tags specButton
44:     # text widget
45:     text .notes -width 25 -height 20 -wrap word
46:     $w create window 180 0 -window .notes -anchor nw -tags textWidget
47:     placeNotes
48:
49: }
50:
51: proc placeNotes {} {
52:     # Insert some text
53:     #  use double quotes to interpret the new line
54:     set notes "Light is refracted by the prism. It bends at \
55:             each of the refracting surfaces. Each color\
56:             band represents a range of visible wavelength.\
57:             Click on the Spectrum button to display the spectrum."
58:     .notes insert end "$notes \n\n"
59:     .notes insert end "Discover the wavelength by placing the \
60:             mouse pointer at the right-most edge of \
61:             a spectral component. \n\n"
62: }
63:
64:
65: proc displayBeam {} {
66:     global A B C h x2 y2
67:     set t 0.75
68:     set x [expr 50*(1-$t)+75*$t]
69:     set y [expr 100*(1-$t)+$h*$t]
70:     eval .c create line 20 80 $x $y -tags { beam1 }
71:     # a point on the line BC
72:     set x2 [expr 100*(1-$t)+75*$t]
73:     set y2 [expr 100*(1-$t)+$h*$t]
74:     eval .c create line $x $y $x2 $y2 -tags { beam2 }
75:     .c itemconfig beam1 -fill white
76:     .c itemconfig beam2 -fill white
77:
78:     showSpectrum
79:
80: }
81:
82: proc showSpectrum {} {
83:     global A B C h x2 y2 WAVELENGTHS
84:     set indigo #8944fd
85:     set colors "red orange yellow green blue $indigo violet"
86:     set w 10; set depth 5
87:     set x0 120; set y0 72
```

```
 88:     foreach c $colors {
 89:         set x1 [expr $x0+$w]; set y1 [expr $y0+$depth]
 90:         .c create rectangle $x0 $y0 $x1 $y1 -fill $c \
 91:                 -outline {} -tag "tg$c"
 92:         .c create polygon $x2 $y2 $x0 $y0 $x0 $y1 -fill $c
 93:         set x0 120; set y0 $y1
 94:     }
 95:     # put a simple binding on the colors of the spectrum
 96:     #    to show their wavelength
 97:     set waveInfo {Enter a color patch.}
 98:     .notes insert end "$waveInfo \n" {tgWaveInfo}
 99:
100:     foreach c $colors {
101:         .c bind tg$c <Enter> "updateWaveInfo $c"
102:         .c bind tg$c <Leave> "updateWaveInfo {Enter }"
103:     }
104: }
105:
106: proc updateWaveInfo { c } {
107:
108:     global WAVELENGTHS
109:
110:     # use a simple condition to decide the text to display
111:     eval .notes delete [.notes tag ranges tgWaveInfo ]
112:     if { [regexp {^[roygb\#v].*} $c] } {
113:         .notes insert end \
114:             "Wavelength of $c color is $WAVELENGTHS($c) \n" {tgWaveInfo}
115:     } else {
116:         .notes insert end "Place the mouse pointer ... \n" {tgWaveInfo}
117:     }
118: }
```

17

ANALYSIS Rather long code, wouldn't you say? Let us take a deep breath and analyze this together. This is a simple application to demonstrate the diffraction of light through a prism into its spectral components. Note that the incident and diffraction angles are only approximate because we do not include a full model using refractive index.

We start with an associative array, WAVELENGTHS, to hold the wavelengths of the spectrum. Recall from Hour 6, "Exploring Arrays," the syntax and semantics of associative arrays. Note that the fields are indexed using the symbolic names of the spectral colors except for indigo, which is referred to using its hexadecimal code. The values stored are the wavelengths in manometers.

Note that variable WAVELENGTHS in the interpreter is in the global scope and available to all the procedures where declared as such.

On the graphical user interface side, we create and manage a default canvas in line 16. We then create a button widget .b with the -text option set to Show Spectrum and the -command option set to invoke the callback procedure showCB. We find the coordinates midX and midY of the center of our canvas by invoking the canvas widget action subcommand cget -width and cget -height.

> You can set the background color of the canvas to a color of your choice. This will show the embedded widgets in contrast. However, make prudent use of background colors. Individual color preferences vary, and a neutral background makes a safe choice. This also ensures that users of your application with visual impediments are not put at a disadvantage.

In line 22, we use the canvas action subcommand canvasName create itemType ?args? ?option value? to create a canvas item of type window. In our present instance, the canvas is .c, the itemType is window, and args is set to the x and y coordinates midX and midY of the point for positioning the window item. The window item is specified with the option -window set to the button .b. In addition, we have set the -anchor option to center so that the widget might be positioned with its center at the positioning point. Finally, we have attached the tag showButton to this window item using the -tags option.

Lines 24–27 define the procedure showCB that consists of just two commands. The first line of script deletes the window item using the canvas command canvasName delete tagOrId. The second line of script invokes the execution of the procedure drawPrism, passing the canvas widget name .c as input argument.

Lines 29–49 of Listing 17.5 define the procedure drawPrism, which takes a canvas widget as its input argument. We declare the variables with global scope to be available within this procedure. The next task is to define a two dimensional representation of our prism. We want to draw an isosceles triangle. The angle th between any two sides of this triangle is 60°, and we specify this value by executing [expr acos(-1)/3] to ensure the machine dependent precision. The height h is similarly computed by executing the command [expr 100 - 50*sin($th)], where the length of the base is 50 in arbitrary units.

So the three vertices A, B, and C of the prism is given by {50 100}, {100 100}, and "75 $h", where each is a list consisting of two elements each of which is the x and y coordinates of the point. We then create our prism in lines 38–40 as a set of three line items using the canvas widget creation command canvasName create itemType ?args? ?option value?.

Your script is more readable if you specify points as a list of two elements, each of which gives the value of a coordinate for that point. The line item create action command, in contrast, expects the coordinates of the two defining points to be specified directly as x1, y1, x2, and y2. Because you have specified a list, you need to apply the eval command to force the reevaluation of the coordinate lists to extract the information and the correct execution of the line item create command.

You have already encountered this necessary style of script development in this book, and you will also encounter this style in almost all the Tcl/Tk code you come across. It is our hope that you are developing an appreciation for it and that you are acquiring this necessary skill yourself.

17

The sides of the prism are now drawn as line items of 2 pixel width and with the common tag prism.

The next step is to provide some basic information to the user about the application and provide the user with an interactive control to display the spectrum if she chooses to see it. To accomplish this, we embed a text widget and a button in the canvas. The mechanism of creating and embedding these two widgets in our canvas is similar to that of the window showButton described in lines 19–22. In line 41, we create the button .bspec and attach the procedure displayBeam as its callback script. We then create a window item using the canvas widget command, specifying the position (0, height of canvas) with a sw anchoring so that the button will appear at the bottom left corner.

Notice again how the canvas coordinate system with its origin at the top-left with y increasing down the canvas and x increasing left to right is being exploited to specify pixel positions.

The tag attached to this window item is specButton, which can be used to access this window item should you require it.

You could have reused the button window item that was created using .b for the button window item that was created using .bspec. In such a case, you need to reposition the widget using the item configuration command and also to replace its -command option to invoke the script in displayBeam. In fact, reusing widgets, for instance, to toggle between on and off or start and stop is more desirable than delete and recreate widgets.

In line 45, we create the text widget .notes that is 25 characters wide and 20 lines long with word wrapping enabled. In line 46, we execute the canvas widget creation command once again to create a embedded window item of our text widget and call it .notes. Note that the positioning of embedded windows in canvas needs to be specified in terms of screen units; whereas in text widgets, you place embedded windows in terms of character positions. The last script in this procedure makes a call to the procedure placeNotes.

The procedure displayBeam is defined in lines 65–80. We start with declaring globally scoped variables. This procedure needs to create an incident and a reflected ray as line items in the canvas. The coordinates x and y of the point of incidence of the incoming ray on the side AC of the prism is calculated using linear interpolation in lines 68 and 69.

Similarly, the coordinates of the point of intersection of the refracted ray on the side BC are calculated in lines 72 and 73. To compute the linear interpolation, we use the parameter t, which is assigned an arbitrary value between 0.0 and 1.0 in line 67. We once again execute the canvas widget action command create to draw the two rays. Note that we force a further round of evaluation to unpack the coordinates. We assign the tags beam1 and beam2 to refer to these two rays later. We reconfigure the -fill option for our rays and set them to white. The last command of this procedure invokes the script showSpectrum.

Lines 82–104 define the procedure showSpectrum. The task of this procedure is to draw the spectral regions as canvas items. Each spectral region consists of a rectangle and a polygon, with tag bindings attached to the rectangular ends alone. The gut of this procedure is perhaps the computation of the coordinates of the polygons and rectangles that make up the spectral regions. For this purpose, we define a list of colors. Note the efficiency that the foreach loop offers for us to cycle through colors to create the spectral region and to assign a dynamically computed tag name. We take care to alter the coordinates of each spectral region within this loop.

We insert an instruction in .notes informing the user that moving the mouse cursor over the rectangular tail region of each spectral patch will display the wavelength of that patch in the text widget. It is important to note that when we insert the wavelength information in the text widget, we attach a tag to that line of text. This tag enables us to retrieve and update that line, without having to either scan the text widget contents or clear it completely and reinsert all the text again and again.

The last step is to define the tag bindings for the Enter and Leave events for the spectral tags. The event callback for both these bindings for each spectral tag is the same procedure, updateWaveInfo. It takes one input argument, which is a string. In the case of Enter callback, the string is the color name and in the case of the Leave callback, the string is the word "Enter". Note that it could have been any word including NULL string.

Phew, we are getting there! The last stage is to define the procedure updateWaveInfo, which is done in lines 106–118. The function of this procedure is to update the wavelength information in the text widget .notes. This is achieved by using a regular expression pattern matching. Because no two spectral colors begin with the same letter nor do they share the same first letter with the string Enter, we anchor the pattern to the first character. So the regexp command will succeed if the first letter of the input argument is one of v, #, b, g, y, o, and r. It will fail for all others.

If the pattern matching is successful—that is the input is a color name—the wavelength is extracted from the associative array WAVELENGTHS using the color name as the index— the message "Wavelength of $c color is $WAVELENGTHS($c) \n" is computed and inserted in .notes. Otherwise, the message "Place the mouse pointer ... \n" is inserted at the same position. The tag tgWaveInfo is attached to the message string in both cases. The purpose of this tag, as we noted already, is to enable us to access this message and update it.

Note that this is done in line 111. In that line, we retrieve the range of the message line using the tag and then execute the text widget command delete. Recall from Hour 13, "Using the Tk Text Widget," the syntax and usage of action subcommands such as range and delete will show that you need to force a reevaluation to unpack the list output from range to apply delete.

The image on the left-hand side of Figure 17.5 shows the initial window, and the right-hand image shows the spectrum and the embedded text window.

Postscript

This, we promise, is as short as a postscript! You will perhaps want to print the contents of the canvas or save it to a file. Tk provides the canvas widget action subcommand postscript to dump the canvas items to a postscript file. Listing 17.6 shows how to achieve this. Note that only canvas items other than the embedded windows are dumped to the postscript file.

It is equally useful to create a Tcl script that will create a Tcl script file whose contents reproduce your canvas. Showing how to do this will far exceed the scope of this hour. We refer you to http://www.tcltk.com/tclets/impress, and *Effective Tcl/Tk Programming* by Harrison and McLennan.

You can use the action command dump with a text widget to print its contents. Consult Tk manual pages for more information on valid options.

Note that the code in Listing 17.6 below is a continuation of Listing 17.5. We only list the appended code in Listing 17.6 to focus our analysis.

INPUT   **LISTING 17.6**   Creating Postscript

```
1: focus .c ;# to get the keyboard events
2: bind .c <Control-p> {generatePostscript}
3: proc generatePostscript {} {
4:     .c postscript -file spectrum.ps
5:     puts "Output written to spectrum.ps"
6: }
```

ANALYSIS   In Listing 17.6, we implement a simple script as a keyboard event binding to the canvas. We already know that because no default binding is provided for the canvases, we need to explicitly specify each binding. For keyboard events, the starting point of this specification is to assign the keyboard focus to the canvas widget .c.

In line 2, we specify the binding of the keyboard event <Control-p> to .c. Pressing the key p while holding down the Control key will invoke the canvas widget action postscript to dump the line drawings to a file named spectrum.ps in your current working directory.

You could of course attach a menubar to this application with a pull-down File menu exactly as we did in Hour 12, "Understanding Intercommunication Commands." The File menu item save will provide a more visible hint to the user that the postscript and save options are available and also allow the files to be output according to a user's choice. For instance, he might route the output to a printer directly.

Do	Don't
Do set the focus of the keyboard in the canvas for binding keyboard events to it.	**Don't** forget to create images with image commands before creating image items in canvas.
Do use image command to manipulate the contents of an image.	**Don't** forget that embedded windows always remain on top and will obscure any other drawing item on the canvas drawn at that position.
	Don't forget that you can attach tags to images and embedded windows when they are created as canvas items.

17

Summary

This is the last of the three hours you have spent learning about the Tk canvas widget and associated utilities.

This hour also concludes our coverage of essential Tcl/Tk usage. Beginning with the next hour, "Using C with Tcl/Tk," you will be learning advanced applications and usage of Tcl/Tk. We hope that the last 17 hours have given you the foundation required to tackle these varied but useful applications.

Q&A

Q What is the difference between embedding widgets in a text widget and a canvas widget?

A One of the essential differences is the positioning of the embedded widget in the text or canvas. In a text widget, the specification of the position location is line/character oriented, whereas in a canvas, it is pixel oriented. That is, in the canvas, you specify the location for an embedded widget as a pixel position.

The second difference is that the geometry management of the embedded widgets in a canvas is assigned to the internal geometry manager of the canvas. In a text widget, the embedded widget has to be either a descendant of the text widget or a descendant of its parent so that the geometry management is handled globally by the application.

Q **Scaling an image item in the canvas is doing peculiar things. Sometimes it appears to work, and sometimes nothing happens. What is going on?**

A Let us say we have an image placed at (0,0), and it is tagged with the name `pic`. Now, if we try the canvas command `.c scale pic 0 0 2 2`, nothing happens. Recall that the canvas scale command changes the distance of an item from `xOrigin, yOrigin` (0,0 in our example) by a factor of `xScale, yScale` (2,2 in this example), respectively.

An image item has just one positioning point associated with it. If you happen to choose that position to be (0,0), using the `scale` command will produce no effect. Nothing happens because the 0 multiplied by the scale factor results in zero. On the other hand, if you have placed the image at any position other than the origin, the image will be relocated to the new position.

You probably expect the entire image to be scaled by the given factor too. After all, the other canvas items scaled up or down by the scaling factor, did they not? However, the contents of the image are not affected by the `scale` command. Why not? The reason is that these commands are implemented in such a way that the content of an image is left to be manipulated at pixel level by the image commands.

Workshop

The following quiz section is designed to provide you with an opportunity to recall some of the important concepts introduced in this hour. These might be commands, command syntax, common mistakes, usage, and so on. The exercises section following the quiz section helps you consolidate the material you learned via an example of practical value. Our aim is that these two sections should reinforce the knowledge you have gained in this hour. The answers to the quiz that follows can be found in Appendix A, "Answers to Quizzes."

Quiz

1. What is an image command?
2. What are the image types that canvas supports?
3. What is the difference between bitmap and photo?
4. What is the command to create a full-color image?
5. What is the command to place an image item in the canvas?
6. How do you move an embedded window in a canvas?

Exercises

Solutions to the exercises are on the CD-ROM that accompanies this book.

1. Use your own image and place it in the canvas. Set up a tag binding to display the rgb values of a pixel where the mouse pointer is clicked. (Hint: Use *imageName* get %x %y to obtain the rgb values.)

2. Place a photo image in the canvas. Create a tag binding to display a magnified portion of the image where <Button-1> is clicked.

17

PART III

Advanced Applications

Hour

HOUR 18

Using C with Tcl/Tk

Hour 17, "Working with Images in Canvas," completes the fundamentals you need to learn on the core functionality of both Tcl and Tk. If you have not yet asked the question "But how do I hook up my own application with specialist functionality?" you might ask it quite soon. The genius of Tcl is its extensible architecture. The Tcl and Tk C libraries provide comprehensive access to the scripting environment, allowing you to create new commands to invoke your own specialist application functions and to extend Tcl and Tk with new data types, image types, graphic items, I/O channels, and widgets.

From complete libraries of extensions and add-ons to GUI hooks for legacy, applications can be developed. It is straightforward to carry out these types of developments, after you have grasped the basic underlying principles and the mechanics. Beginning this hour, the rest of this book covers such advanced aspects.

This hour focuses on using the C language with Tcl. In this hour, you will learn how

- To create new Tcl commands
- To create and load your own libraries of your new Tcl commands
- To access and update variable values between your C application and Tcl

You need not be a proficient C programmer to understand the concepts introduced in this hour, but familiarity with C will help. All the code examples are explained, so novices can pick it up. An important aspect to note is that you can customize and reuse the example templates.

Creating Your Own Tcl Commands

The built-in commands and functionality provided by Tcl/Tk are rich. You can build medium to large-scale applications without having to stray outside the Tcl/Tk core. Even though Tcl/Tk is an interpreted language, given the computing power of modern computers, you might not encounter serious performance issues for such applications either. However, as we noted already, you might want to provide some special functionality not available in Tcl/Tk as such. For large applications, performance might also become an issue because a command implemented in C is more efficient than an equivalent Tcl procedure. It is for these reasons that you might want to write your application's special functionalities in C, register them as Tcl commands, and use them from your Tcl scripts as you would any other core Tcl command.

You use the Tcl C library extensively to implement your new commands. You use the Tk C libraries to create new widgets.

There are two alternate ways to create your own Tcl commands. The first is to create a stand-alone C application that can be run as a separate process by using the Tcl exec command, a non-integrated approach. The second method is to embed the Tcl interpreter in your C application - after all the interpreter and all the Tcl/Tk commands are C libraries. This method is useful if you require most of the code to be developed in C with a small portion of Tcl/Tk to control your application and provide it with a GUI. The functionality supported by Tcl/Tk is so rich that you should think twice before undertaking such a verbose lower level implementation.

There are two ways to integrate your commands with the Tcl interpreter. The newest, simplest, and most straightforward method is to create a loadable package that you can load into tclsh, wish, or your application. This is the method we will adopt here. The second method is to use the basic Tcl application structure by calling Tcl_Main or Tk_Main.

> The examples in this section require you to compile the code using a C compiler. In UNIX systems, the command which cc will show you whether or not you have access to a C compiler. On a PC, you are likely to have interactive application builders and compilers such as Visual C++ Builder or Borland compiler. Consult the online manual pages on how to compile a shared object library of these examples. It is a simple process; it just needs learning carefully. This hour essentially gives you the template for extending Tcl with your own C application code.

Your First Tcl Command

The original Tcl/Tk was entirely string based, necessitating conversion to internal data type formats for processing. From Tcl/Tk 8.0 onwards, the interface to Tcl commands has become object based. Each of these dual-ported objects has one port allocated to the original string representation, whereas the other stored the object in the native representation of that data. In the new interface, the commands, their arguments, the variable values, and Tcl scripts all are defined as dual-ported objects. Conversion to string representation is made only on demand.

In Listing 18.1, we use the object method. The string interface is similar, but we recommend that you upgrade to the latest version of Tcl/Tk. The purpose of the following application is to demonstrate how to pass arguments from your Tcl script to the C routine and make available the computed result from C to the Tcl script layer. We do this with the simplest command that takes a number and returns its value cubed. We call this command cubed. Let us see how we can do this.

LISTING 18.1   A Simple Command Implemented in C

```
1: #include <stdio.h>
2: #include <math.h>
3: #include "tcl.h"
4: #include "tclDecls.h"
5:
6: int CubedObjCmdProc (ClientData cdata, Tcl_Interp *interp,
7:            int objc, Tcl_Obj *CONST objv[])
8: {
9: int error;
```

continues

LISTING 18.1   continued

```
10: Tcl_Obj *resultPtr;
11: double   num, cube;
12:
13: if (objc < 2 ) {
14:     Tcl_WrongNumArgs(interp, 1, objv, "usage: cube ?input?");
15:     return TCL_ERROR;
16:     }
17: if (objc ==2) {
18:     error = Tcl_GetDoubleFromObj (interp, objv[1], &num);
19:     if (error != TCL_OK)
20:         return error;
21:     }
22: cube = (double) pow (num, 3);
23: resultPtr = Tcl_GetObjResult(interp);
24: Tcl_SetDoubleObj(resultPtr, cube);
25:
26: return TCL_OK;
27: }
28:
29: int Cubed_Init (Tcl_Interp *interp)
30: {
31: Tcl_CreateObjCommand (interp, "cubed", CubedObjCmdProc,
32:                 (ClientData)NULL, (Tcl_CmdDeleteProc *)NULL);
33: Tcl_PkgProvide(interp, "Cubed", "1.0");
34: return TCL_OK;
35: }
```

ANALYSIS   The first four lines of the preceding code include the necessary header files. The Tcl header files contain the definition of all the object types we need to use for this command. Lines 6–27 define the C command procedure. The Tcl C library defines a function prototype Tcl_ObjCmdProc, which has a predefined input and output argument list as explained in the following.

The Tcl command procedures always return an integer value, which is the error condition TCL_OK or TCL_ERROR. The other values are TCL_BREAK and TCL_CONTINUE. It can also return application-specific code. The input arguments for a Tcl command procedure are ClientData, a pointer to the Tcl interpreter interp, objc, an integer giving the count of arguments, and a list of input arguments to the command that this procedure implements. ClientData is a pointer to the Tcl object of this action or command. objc gives the number of command-line arguments including the name of the command. So the count will be one more than the number of input that the command requires. That is, if your command is called mycommand and takes one input argument, then objc will be 2. objv[] is an array of the command-line arguments—each of which is of the type Tcl_Obj, the first of which is the command itself (for example, mycommand). The ClientData is useful if you want to overload the operator/command. We do not make use of the ClientData in the examples in this book. Consult "Tcl/Tk for Programmers with Solved Exercises that Work with Unix and Windows" by A. Zimmer (IEEE Press, 1998) for more details on how to use ClientData.

Following the preceding convention, we define the command procedure CubedObjCmdProc in lines 6–7. Note that objv is an array of Tcl objects. In lines 9–11, we declare a few local variables. Note that in line 10, we declare resultPtr as a pointer to an element of the type Tcl_Obj.

Objects are always declared as pointers. Use a Tcl C library procedure that returns a Tcl_Obj to assign a value to your object variable before you do anything with them. This assigns the required memory and—depending on the library routine you used to create the instance—the type of the object. Figure 18.1 gives a schematic diagram of the Tcl object creating and manipulation functions.

18

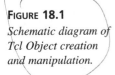

FIGURE **18.1**
Schematic diagram of Tcl Object creation and manipulation.

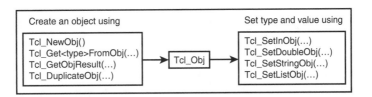

Create an object using		Set type and value using
Tcl_NewObj() Tcl_Get<type>FromObj(...) Tcl_GetObjResult(...) Tcl_DuplicateObj(...)	→ Tcl_Obj →	Tcl_SetInObj(...) Tcl_SetDoubleObj(...) Tcl_SetStringObj(...) Tcl_SetListObj(...)

In lines 13–16, we invoke the Tcl library procedure Tcl_WrongNumArgs to generate and send an error message to the interpreter interp if the number of arguments is less than 2. If the number of arguments is exactly 2, we invoke a call to the Tcl_GetDoubleFromObj library function to retrieve the input argument to our command and assign it to the variable num. Note that you need to pass the address of num as an argument to this function call. You also pass the interp so that any error message can be directed to it. If you provide NULL, the error message will be suppressed. If the returned value is not TCL_OK, the process will terminate. In line 22, we call the built-in mathematical library function pow to compute the cubed value of our input num. We cast it to the type double before assigning the value to the variable cube.

As we noted earlier, all Tcl C command procedures are prototyped to return the error condition, an integer value in any case. So we need another mechanism to return the value of the command to the Tcl layer. When you start a tclsh or a wish session, Tcl keeps track of the state of that interpreter using the global data structure defined as Tcl_Interp in the header file tcl.h. When a Tcl command is executed, the result field of this data structure is pointing to the variable to hold the result returned from the command. In line 23, we use the Tcl C library call Tcl_GetObjResult, with interp as input, and assign it to our resultPtr. This corresponds to one case on the left side of Tcl_Obj in Figure 18.1.

> Note how we are accomplishing the required memory allocation to hold our returned result as well as passing the return value to the Tcl layer in this one statement.

In line 24, we follow our advice on the right side of Tcl_Obj in Figure 18.1. The Tcl C library procedure Tcl_SetDoubleObj enables us to assign the value of cube to the resultPtr.

We already said that we want to extend the Tcl interpreter; that is, extend the number of commands we can use with the tclsh with our own by creating our own commands as a loadable package. When you load a package into tclsh or wish, they invoke the Tcl library function package_Init, where package is the name of the package you want to load. So our next task is to define this function for our package. Lines 29–35 do this. Within this function/procedure call, our first task is to register our command so that the Tcl interpreter knows which procedure call to invoke to execute our command. We do this via a call to the library procedure Tcl_CreateObjCommand. The first argument to this function is the Tcl_Interp structure. Then we give it cubed, the name by which our command will be invoked in the Tcl layer. The third parameter is the Tcl command procedure, CubedObjCmdProc, associated with this cubed command. The fourth parameter ClientData is NULL in this case. The last input parameter to Tcl_CreateObjCommand is the name of the Tcl_CmdDeleteProcedure. This is used to deregister our command. In this case, this is also NULL.

The procedure Tcl_PkgProvide is called in Cubed_Init to register version 1.0 of the package Cubed. The procedure also makes sure that Cubed is available to the interpreter for loading when the command package require Cubed is executed by the Tcl interpreter. The last line returns TCL_OK.

> Package names must begin with capital letters.

Loading the Package

Having created the source code for our cubed command, we want to extend our Tcl with this command. We will use the dynamic load method. This involves the following very simple steps:

1. Create a dynamic shared object library of the code. For UNIX systems, this would involve creating a shared object file cubed.so. For PCs, it would involve creating a dynamic loadable library cubed.dll. Consult your system manuals on how to achieve this. On PCs, you might have high-level Builder tools to do this interactively. On most UNIX systems, executing the compilation command `cc -o cubed.so -G cubed.c -I${TCLTK}/include` at the shell prompt will create a shared object library. Note that TCLTK is the environment variable that points to the directory which Tcl/Tk installed in your system. You need to set this.

   Alternatively, you can include the full path to your Tcl library. Also note that the compilation command (given in the last paragraph) is an example tested on various Solaris systems. Please check the appropriate options for your compiler.

2. Change to the directory in which your shared object library cubed.dll or cubed.so resides.

3. Start up a tclsh application session.

4. Execute the command `lappend auto_path DIRECTORY_WHERE_THE_SHARED_LIBRARY_<cubed.so¦cubed.dll>_IS`.

5. Execute the command `pkg_mkIndex DIRECTORY_WHERE_THE_SHARED_LIBRARY_<cubed.so¦cubed.dll>_is _<cubed.so¦cubed.dll>`.

6. Execute the command `package require Cubed`.

Let us quickly go through what we have done in the preceding steps. We first created a dynamically loadable library in binary code. We need to tell the Tcl interpreter where to find this shared object library. We append this path to the paths pointed to by the auto_path environment variable that Tcl uses to search for loading required libraries.

The command `pkg_mkIndex ?dir ?pattern pattern ...?` creates index files that allow packages to be loaded automatically when `package require ?-exact? package` commands are executed. Remember to give absolute pathnames for dir. You can index binary files such as cubed.so as well as Tcl script files with .tcl extensions.

18

Remember to substitute the correct directory path for your set up when executing `auto_path` and `pkg_mkIndex` commands.

Script files must contain the `package provide` command to declare the package and version number just as binary files must contain a call to `Tcl_PkgProvide`.

Executing `pkg_mkIndex` command will create a *pkgIndex.tcl* script file in that directory. This script file for our `cubed` command should look like the following code.

```
pkgIndex.tcl for Cubed command.
package ifneeded Cubed 1.0 [list tclPkgSetup $dir Cubed 1.0 {{cubed.so load
➡cubed}}].
```

Having created the index, you then tell the Tcl interpreter that your script requires the package by executing the command `package require ?-exact? package ?version?`. The `-exact` option loads the exact version of the package if several versions are available. If this command succeeds, it returns the version number of the loaded package.

When you have created the package index, from that time on, you only need to repeat step 4 and step 6 to have your cubed command available to you. In Hour 22, "Adding Tcl/Tk Extensions," we will see how to automate this process.

In Listing 18.2, you can see a sample session of loading and using our Cubed package. Start a `tclsh` application and execute the commands interactively to see the return values. Please note, once again that we have used two environment variables—TCLTK and STYTCLTK. The first points to where Tcl/Tk is installed on your system. The second variable, STYTCLTK, points to where you are creating and executing these example script files.

LISTING 18.2   Loading and Executing the Cubed Command

```
 1: %lappend auto_path $STYTCLTK/ch18
 2: $TCLTK/src/tcl8.1.1/library $TCLTK/src/tcl8.1.1 $TCLTK/solaris/bin \
 3: $TCLTK/solaris/lib $STYTCLTK/ch18
 4: %pkg_mkIndex $STYTCLTK cubed.so
 5: %package require Cubed
 6: 1.0
 7: % cubed 3.0
 8: 27.0
 9: % cubed 27
10: 19683.0
```

ANALYSIS The preceding code goes through the steps described previously for our cubed command. Note that all directory pathnames need to be customized for your system.

Your Second Command

In Listing 18.1, our command returned a single result. You can essentially use it as a template to return a string or an integer, making sure that you made all the suitable changes such as `Tcl_Set<type>Obj()`, for instance. However, you are more likely to want to return more than a single value from a command. You have time and again come across the core Tcl commands that return lists. What is more natural than to implement your own command that does the same? In Listing 18.3, we implement a simple command that illustrates how to return a list from a command. This simple command `quad` takes three arguments, the coefficients a, b, and c of a quadratic equation of the form $ax^2+bx+c = 0$ and returns the two roots in a list.

 The algorithm to solve the quadratic equation needs additional care for production level code. For example, line 39 can suffer from loss of precision.

18

Let us explore how to implement this command. An important aspect we want you to take note of is the use of the `Tcl_Obj`s in this implementation.

LISTING 18.3 Command Returning a List

```
 1: #include <stdio.h>
 2: #include <math.h>
 3: #include "tcl.h"
 4: #include "tclDecls.h"
 5:
 6: int QuadObjCmdProc (ClientData clientData, Tcl_Interp *interp,
 7:             int objc, Tcl_Obj *CONST objv[])
 8: {
 9: int error;
10: Tcl_Obj *resultPtr, *p1, *p2;
11: double a,b,c;
12: char v[20];
13: double disc, sdisc;
14: double root1,root2;
15:
16: p1 = Tcl_NewObj();
17: p2 = Tcl_NewObj();
```

continues

LISTING 18.3   continued

```
18:
19: if (objc < 4 ) {
20:     Tcl_WrongNumArgs(interp, 1, objv, "usage: quad ?input? ?input ?input?");
21:     return TCL_ERROR;
22:     }
23: if (objc == 4) {
24:     error = Tcl_GetDoubleFromObj (interp, objv[1], &a);
25:     if (error == TCL_OK){
26:         error = Tcl_GetDoubleFromObj (interp, objv[2], &b);
27:         if (error == TCL_OK)
28:             error = Tcl_GetDoubleFromObj (interp, objv[3], &c);
29:         }
30:         if (error !=TCL_OK)
31:         return error;
32: }
33:
34: disc = (b*b - 4.0*a*c);
35: if ( disc >= 0.0 )
36:         {
37:            sdisc = sqrt( disc );
38:            root1 = ( -b + sdisc )/(2.0*a);
39:            root2 = ( -b - sdisc )/(2.0*a);
40:         Tcl_SetDoubleObj(p1,root1);
41:            Tcl_SetDoubleObj(p2,root2);
42:         }
43:    else
44:         {
45:            sdisc = sqrt( -disc );
46:            root1 = ( -b/(2.0*a) );
47:            root2 = ( sdisc/(2.0*a) );
48:         sprintf(v,"%lf+i%lf",root1,root2);
49:         Tcl_SetStringObj(p1,v, (int)strlen(v));
50:         sprintf(v,"%lf-i%lf",root1,root2);
51:         Tcl_SetStringObj(p2,v, (int)strlen(v));
52:         }
53:
54: resultPtr = Tcl_GetObjResult(interp);
55: Tcl_ListObjAppendElement(interp,resultPtr,p1);
56: Tcl_ListObjAppendElement(interp,resultPtr,p2);
57: Tcl_DecrRefCount(p1);
58: Tcl_DecrRefCount(p2);
59:
60: return TCL_OK;
61: }
62:
63: int Quad_Init (Tcl_Interp *interp)
64: {
65: Tcl_CreateObjCommand (interp, "quad", QuadObjCmdProc,
```

```
66:         (ClientData)NULL,(Tcl_CmdDeleteProc *)NULL);
67: Tcl_PkgProvide(interp, "Quad", "1.0");
68:
69: return TCL_OK;
70: }
```

ANALYSIS The analysis of much of the previous code is the same as for Listing 18.2. We will only analyze the new concepts. In this example, we have introduced two new Tcl_Obj pointers p1 and p2 to hold the roots root1 and root2. Recall that we need to initialize these pointers and allocate memory. In lines 16 and 17, we use the Tcl C library function Tcl_NewObj to do that. This command has three input arguments, and hence the value of objc. The total number of input objects is four because it includes the command name. If this condition is satisfied, we repeatedly use the Tcl C library function Tcl_GetDoubleFromObj to retrieve and assign the input coefficients to the variables a, b, and c.

Note that objv is an array of Tcl_Objs and objc provides the count. Note the similarity with argv and argc variables in C.

18

In order to compute the roots, we first compute the discriminant disc. If this value is greater than zero, the equation has real roots that are given by (-b+sqrt(b²-4ac))/2a and (-b-sqrt(b²-4ac))/2a. In lines 38 and 39, we use the Tcl C routine Tcl_SetDoubleObj to assign these values to p1 and p2, respectively. If disc is negative, the roots are given by (-b+i*sqrt(-b²+4ac))/2a and (-b-i*sqrt(-b²+4ac))/2a, where i is sqrt(-1). The real and imaginary parts of the roots are stored in root1 and root2, respectively. We create strings of the forms root1+iroot2 and root1-iroot2 and assign these to p1 and p2. Note how we are dynamically able to assign the type of p1 and p2 by using Tcl_SetStringObj in lines 49 and 51. Once again, Tcl_GetObjResult(interp) is called to allocate the object resultPtr in line 54. Tcl_ListObjAppendElement allows us to append p1 and p2 to resultPtr, converting the resultPtr data type to a list automatically in that process.

For each Tcl_Obj, Tcl keeps a reference counter that keeps track of the number of references made to this object by increasing the counter. It is the programmer's responsibility to increase and decrease this counter for each object when these are used in his C code because Tcl will not know of this usage. This is done using the calls Tcl_IncrRefCount(Tcl_Obj *obj) and Tcl_DecrRefCount(Tcl_Obj *obj), respectively. If the Tcl_Obj is a local variable, as in our case, you never need to use Tcl_IncrRefCount(Tcl_Obj *obj), but you need to use Tcl_DecrRefCount(Tcl_Obj *obj) to free the allocated memory at the end. Lines 57 and 58 do this.

The procedure Quad_Init is almost identical to Cubed_Init and is self-explanatory. In Listing 18.4, we once again go through steps described earlier to load this package and illustrate the usage of the quad command.

Listing 18.4 Packaging the Quad Command

```
% lappend auto_path $STYTCLTk/ch18
$TCLTK/src/tcl8.1.1/library $TCLTK/src/tcl8.1.1 \
    $TCLTK/bin $TCLTK/lib $STYTCLTK/ch18
 1: % pkg_mkIndex $STYTCLTK/ch18 quad.so
 2: % package require Quad
 3: 1.0
 4: % set x [quad 1 -3 2]
 5: 2.0 1.0
 6: % set x [quad 1 0 4]
 7: -0.000000+i2.000000 -0.000000-i2.000000
 8: % llength $x
 9: 2
10: % set x [quad 1 2 3]
11: -1.000000+i1.414214 -1.000000-i1.414214
12: % lindex $x 1
13: -1.000000-i1.414214
```

ANALYSIS   Listing 18.4 repeats the steps of loading a package and extending Tcl commands with your own quad command.

You can format each element of the returned list from quad as you see fit. For instance, you might want to insert blank spaces between the real and imaginary parts of the root, the + and - signs, and the imaginary unit i, to make the result more readable. Make sure that you protect each element by {} or "" in such cases. This will return a list of lists.

Accessing Tcl Variables from Your C Code

There might be occasions when you require accessing and updating variables from your application's Tcl layer from your C code. For instance, you might want to keep track and to display a counter for the number of floating point operations being carried out by the many commands implemented in C for a computationally intensive application. It is not worthwhile to pass this counter as an input argument to every computational C command. Tcl C library also provides library routines that enable you to access and update Tcl variables. Listing 18.5 provides a simple example that keeps track of the floating point operations counter for our cubed command.

Despite the changed name, Listing 18.5 is almost identical to the cubed command. The changes are bolded.

LISTING 18.5 Accessing and Updating Tcl Variables

```
 1: #include <stdio.h>
 2: #include <math.h>
 3: #include "tcl.h"
 4: #include "tclDecls.h"
 5:
 6: int CubedObjCmdProc (ClientData clientData, Tcl_Interp *interp,
 7:             int objc, Tcl_Obj *CONST objv[])
 8: {
 9:
10: int error;
11: Tcl_Obj *resultPtr;
12: double  num, cube;
13: int fc;
14: char *str, s[10];
15:
16: if (objc < 2 ) {
17:     Tcl_WrongNumArgs(interp, 1, objv, "usage: cube ?input?");
18:     return TCL_ERROR;
19:     }
20: if (objc ==2) {
21:     error = Tcl_GetDoubleFromObj (interp, objv[1], &num);
22:     if (error != TCL_OK)
23:         return error;
24:     }
25:
26: cube = (double) pow (num, 3);
27:
28: str = (char *) Tcl_GetVar2(interp, "flopcount",
29:             (char *)NULL,TCL_LEAVE_ERR_MSG);
30: fc = atoi(str);
31: fc++;
32: sprintf(s,"%d",fc);
33: str= (char *)Tcl_SetVar2(interp, "flopcount",
34:     (char *)NULL, (char *)s,TCL_LEAVE_ERR_MSG);
35: resultPtr = Tcl_GetObjResult(interp);
36: Tcl_SetDoubleObj(resultPtr, cube);
37: return TCL_OK;
38: }
39:
40: int Cubed_Init (Tcl_Interp *interp)
41: {
```

continues

18

LISTING 18.5 continued

```
42: Tcl_CreateObjCommand (interp, "cubed", CubedObjCmdProc, (ClientData)NULL,
43:             (Tcl_CmdDeleteProc *)NULL);
44: Tcl_PkgProvide(interp, "Cubed", "1.1");
45: return TCL_OK;
46: }
```

ANALYSIS As we mentioned already, we want to keep a counter called flopcount in our Tcl layer, query its value in the CubedObjCmdProc, and update it by one whenever a floating point operation takes place. In line 28, we make a call to the Tcl C library routine Tcl_GetVar2 to query the current value of flopcount. If the third input argument to this routine is NULL, it treats the second argument to be the name of a scalar variable or a complete name including both variable name and index. If the third argument is non-NULL, the second argument is treated as the name of an array and the third argument indicates the index of that array. The first argument to Tcl_GetVar2 is the interpreter to send the result and error to and the fourth argument is the OR-ed combination of bits providing additional information. Refer to the online manual pages for all the valid flags. Here we always set the flag to return the error message.

Tcl_GetVar2 returns the value of flopcount as a string str. So, we need to make a call to the C math library function atoi to retrieve the current value of flopcount and assign it to fc. When we compute the cube of the number, we increment fc by one. The C library utility sprintf is given the string variable s, a format specified by "%d" and the value of fc to be substituted in the string under that format. sprintf returns the new value of fc as a string. Tcl_SetVar2 is used in line 32 to assign this new value to flopcount.

You can see that using Tcl_GetVar2 and Tcl_SetVar2 is less efficient. Use the corresponding—almost identical—Obj versions instead. For more details, see the Tcl/Tk online manual pages.

We have upgraded our package to version 1.1 by changing the input argument for the version parameter to the function call Tcl_PkgProvide in line 44. You can now decide to load whichever version of your cubed command with the -exact option by executing package require -exact Cubed in your interpreter. You can have two different versions of the same package running in different Tcl interpreters.

Listing 18.6 illustrates the use of `flopcount` in an interactive `tclsh` session.

LISTING 18.6   Counter for Floating Point Operations

```
 1: % lappend auto_path $STYTCLTK/ch18
 2: $TCLTK/src/tcl8.1.1/library $TCLTK/src/tcl8.1.1
 3:    $TCLTK/solaris/bin $TCLTK/solaris/lib $STYTCLTK/ch18
 4: % pkg_mkIndex $STYTCLTK/ch18 cubed.so
 5: %package require Cubed
 6: 1.1
 7: % set flopcount 0
 8: 0
 9: %  cubed 6.0
10: 216.0
11: %  set flopcount
12: 1
13: % cubed 4
14: 64.0
15: %  set flopcount
16: 2
```

Do	**DON'T**
Do remember that the package name should begin with a capital letter.	**Don't** use `Tcl_ConvertToType` unless you are creating a new type of object. Use `Tcl_Set type`.
Do ensure that your `auto_path` includes the directory in which your own command packages reside.	**Don't** forget to include the package require packageName command in your `tclsh`, `wish`, or application script.
Do implement new commands only for complex application specific functionality. Doing so will provide significantly improved performance compared to a corresponding Tcl procedure. The effort is worth it, however, only if you need to implement computationally intensive code or want to create new widgets.	**Don't** create one package for each command you want to implement. You can create as many commands as you want in a single package.

18

Summary

In this hour, you learned how to extend the Tcl interpreter to include your own commands. This might be required to provide special application functionalities currently not available in core Tcl/Tk. You learned how to implement and load these as packages modules into your Tcl interpreter. You also learned how to access and update Tcl variables from your C code.

In Hour 20, "Understanding Object-Oriented Programming with Tcl/Tk", you will learn to use one such packaged module that extends Tcl to support even higher-level productivity for application development.

In Hour 19, "Creating Tcl/Tk Interfaces to Legacy Applications," you will learn how to use Tcl/Tk with externally running applications. It will illustrate the use of pipes and asynchronous execution. Using these enables you to preserve essential, proven legacy software while improving its user interface.

Q&A

Q How do I load more than one of my own packages or commands in my Tcl interpreter?

A You can load as many shared object libraries and Tcl scripts as you want using the `pkg_mkIndex` command. The following code shows an interactive session in which we have loaded both the Cubed and Quad packages. However, do not create one package for each command. Create a whole load of them as one shared object library.

```
 1: %  pkg_mkIndex /u/ls/book/chapters/ch18 cubed.so quad.so
 2: % more pkgIndex.tcl
 3: # Tcl package index file, version 1.1
 4: # This file is generated by the "pkg_mkIndex" command
 5: # and sourced either when an application starts up or
 6: # by a "package unknown" script.  It invokes the
 7: # "package ifneeded" command to set up package-related
 8: # information so that packages will be loaded automatically
 9: # in response to "package require" commands.  When this
10: # script is sourced, the variable $dir must contain the
11: # full path name of this file's directory.
12:
13: package ifneeded Cubed 1.1 [list tclPkgSetup $dir
14: Cubed 1.0 {{cubeD.so load cubed}}]
15: package ifneeded Quad 1.0 [list tclPkgSetup $dir
16: Quad 1.0 {{quad.so load quad}}]
18: % lappend auto_path $STYTCLTK/ch18
19: $TCLTK/tcl8.1.1/library $TCLTK/src/tcl8.1.1
20:                  $TCLTK/bin $TclTk/lib $STYTCLTK/ch18
21: %  package require Quad
22:1.0
```

Note that you will need to change line 1 for your system. After you have created an index for your package, you must ensure that auto_path knows the location of the directory which contains the package and the index script pkgIndex.tcl. Line 18 ensures that to be the case. For your own application packages, use this mechanism. If you have created and tested a complete suite of extensions that a lot of other people will want to use, then see the next question on how to achieve this.

Q How do I automate the loading of packages I want to add into `tclsh`, `wish`, and application scripts for site-wide use?

A The environment variable *`tcl_pkgPath`* is set up to point to a site-wide packages directory. Place each package under a subdirectory of this directory. It is necessary that you have proper access rights to this directory. Run the `pkg_mkIndex` command in this directory to create all the indices required. Auto_path will automatically point to the *`tcl_pkgPath`* and make the required packages available. See the last part of the preceding code (lines 18–21).

Workshop

The following quiz section is designed to provide you with an opportunity to recall some of the important concepts introduced in this hour. These might be commands, command syntax, common mistakes, usage, and so on. Our aim is that these two sections should reinforce the knowledge you have gained in this hour. The answers to the quiz that follows can be found in Appendix A, "Answers to Quizzes."

The exercises section following the quiz section should really be called a *practical*, in that you have to do them at your machine.

18

Quiz

1. What does the Tcl C library provide?
2. What are the advantages of implementing commands in C?
3. What does `pkg_mkIndex` do?
4. What are the commands to bring the packages into the Tcl interpreter?
5. What is the command to retrieve a command line argument that is passed to your C routine as a Tcl_Obj?

Exercises

Solutions to the exercises are on the CD-ROM that accompanies this book.

1. Implement the commands `cubed` and `quad` on your machine. Run them in interactive `tclsh` sessions as described in Listings 18.2, 18.4, and so on to verify.
2. Change the command `cubed` to a new command called `mycbrt`. This should use the built-in math library `cbrt` that computes the cube root of a given number (that is, `mycbrt` is the inverse of `cubed`).
3. Write an extension that will retrieve a string variable defined at the Tcl level and append it with a `Hello` and return it. Check that this is done when the new command is executed.

Hour **19**

Creating Tcl/Tk Interfaces to Legacy Applications

In the last hour, you have learned to define your own commands for use in the Tcl interpreter. This approach enables you to define a set of building blocks for a larger application. Another approach for developing GUIs to legacy code is to develop GUI front ends using Tcl/Tk. This approach preserves the past investment and increases the usability of the software. It is assumed that you have a basic working knowledge of programming in FORTRAN.

In this hour, you will learn

- To develop simple GUI front ends to legacy code in FORTRAN 77 or FORTRAN 90
- To execute an external program by opening it as a UNIX pipe
- To execute programs by connecting an input data file

There are two approaches to executing external programs. One way is to treat them as "black boxes," meaning you don't know much about the internal workings of the program except for the type of inputs that are required and the output it generated. The other approach is to treat them as "white boxes," in which you have complete access to the source code of the program. In this hour, we will consider the external programs as "black boxes."

The basic principle is to use shared data file between the GUI front end and the external program. This approach works equally well for a program written in any language. What you do is simply collect all the data that is required by the program from the front end, write it to a file, and then invoke the external program. The external executable writes its results to a file. The GUI reads the output and displays the results into a text widget.

External program can be invoked in several ways:

- Open the executable as a UNIX pipe.

- Using exec *executableFile* with synchronous execution. Returns to the Tcl prompt only after the program has finished.

- Using exec *executableFile* & with asynchronous or background execution. Returns to the Tcl prompt immediately.

A Simple FORTRAN Program

Consider a simple example to illustrate the mechanics of the process. Our task here is to develop a GUI front end to a FORTRAN program that sums numbers from 1 to a specified limit. This limit is read from the user. The FORTRAN program sum.f is shown in Listing 19.1.

LISTING 19.1 A FORTRAN Program That Sums Numbers from 1 to n

```
 1: c      sum.f
 2: c      sum upto ntop numbers starting from 1
 3: c
 4:        real*8 sum
 5:        integer i, ntops
 6: c
 7:        print*,'Input ntops'
 8:        read*, ntops
 9: c
10:        sum = 0.0D0
11:        do 10 i = 1, ntops
12:           sum = sum + dble( i )
13:    10  continue
14:        print*,' Sum upto ',ntops, ' is : ', sum
15:        stop
16:        end
```

ANALYSIS The FORTRAN program reads an integer from the standard input, goes away and does its sums, and prints the result to the standard output. The program is compiled using the command `f77 -o sum sum.f`. Note that the executable is stored in the file `sum`. (An equivalent program `sumupton.c`, written in C, is supplied on the CDROM for experimentation.)

A typical session at the UNIX terminal is shown in Listing 19.2.

LISTING 19.2   Running the Executable of `sum.f` at the UNIX Prompt

```
1: neuman% ./sum
2:   Input ntops
3: 10
4:    Sum upto   10 is :     55.000000000000
5: neuman%
```

ANALYSIS The executable is invoked in line 1, which prints the prompt string shown in line 2. The user supplies a number in line 3. The program returns the text containing the answer. For example, the sum of the first 10 numbers is 55 and is printed with additional annotation. All we know about this black box is that it wants a number, and that it returns a string such as the one in line 4.

Now let us develop a simple GUI to illustrate the basic idea. The front end collects the required input to the FORTRAN program from an entry widget. When the user hits return in the entry widget, we invoke a procedure that in turn talks to the FORTRAN program, gets the result, and updates the GUI elements as appropriate. The complete listing is shown in Listing 19.3 and the generated interface is shown in Figure 19.1.

19

LISTING 19.3   The GUI Front End to `sum.f`

```
 1: #!/usr/local1/bin/wish -f
 2: wm title . "gui_sum"
 3: frame .f
 4: pack .f -padx 5 -ipadx 5
 5:
 6: label .f.la -text "Sum up to first "
 7: entry .f.e   -relief sunken -width 5
 8: label .f.la2 -text "integers is : "
 9: label .f.la3 -width 15 -bg yellow
10:
11: pack .f.la .f.e .f.la2 .f.la3 -side left -padx 3 -pady 2 -ipadx 2 -ipady 2
12:
13: bind .f.e <Return> {
14:   invokeSum [.f.e get]
```

continues

Listing 19.3 continued

```
15: }
16:
17: proc invokeSum ntops {
18:     set f [open |./sum r+]   ;# useful to specify the path
19:     puts $f $ntops
20:     flush $f             ;# you can only flush after
21:                          ;# you have written to the pipe
22:     gets $f in_prompt ;# from sum
23:     gets $f answer    ;# we want that
24:     close $f          ;# close the pipe other wise
25:                       ;# a broken pipe will be left
26:     regsub {Sum.*:} $answer "" nanswer
27:     .f.la3 configure -text $nanswer
28: }
29:
30: frame .bf -bd 2 -relief groove
31: pack .bf -padx 5 -ipadx 5 -fill x
32: set infoMsg {Enter n and <Return>.}
33: label .bf.info -textvar infoMsg  \
34:             -font {courier 10 bold}
35: button .bf.quit -text Quit -command {exit}
36: button .bf.clear -text Clear \
37:             -command {.f.e delete 0 end; .f.la3 configure -text {} }
38: pack .bf.info -side left
39: pack .bf.quit .bf.clear -side right -padx 2 -pady 2 -ipadx 3 -ipady 3
40: focus .f.e    ;# set focus to the entry widget
41: #
42: # some info messages
43: #  enter events
44: bind .f.e <Enter> {set infoMsg {Enter n and <Return>.}}
45: bind .bf.clear <Enter> {set infoMsg {Clears input and result.}}
46: bind .bf.quit <Enter> {set infoMsg {Quits gui_sum.}}
47: # Leave events
48: foreach w {.f.e .bf.clear .bf.quit} {
49:     bind $w <Leave> { set infoMsg {}}
50: }
```

ANALYSIS Let us skip the explanation of GUI layout, which should be familiar to you by now. If not, consult Hour 10, "Getting Started with Tk," for a quick recap and come back here. The important procedure invokeSum is defined in lines 17–26. How do we talk to the FORTRAN executable? As mentioned before, this can be achieved in several ways. In this example, we open it as a UNIX pipe to illustrate the concept.

UNIX pipes are opened with the Tcl command open. When this command sees the vertical bar |, the file is opened as a pipe. In line 18, we open it for reading and writing. Why? We want to write the input collected from the GUI and to read the answer the pipe has generated. Specifying the access mode as r+ in line 18 does this. Now, we write the input data to the pipe in line 19. We want to read the result and update our GUI. The data sitting in the file handle is usually buffered and is released when it is full. Because we have finished our task, we flush it and then read it.

When reading from this pipe, remember that the prompt string comes out first (line 21), and then comes the answer (line 22). Now that we are done with our job, we close the pipe as in line 23. We extract the numerical result using a simple regular expression in line 24 and reconfigure the label widget's -text attribute to display our result. That is all there is to it.

Note that for simple tasks such as these, opening a UNIX pipe is overkill and is used here as an example. A more generic approach is to store the input data in a file and connect it to the executable which is discussed next.

FIGURE 19.1

GUI front end to sum up to n numbers.

In the example, the FORTRAN executable is called sum, which also happens to be a UNIX command for printing the check sum and block count for a file. The precise path of the program (dot for the current directory) ./sum makes sure that we use our FORTRAN executable and not the UNIX program.

19

Another useful method of executing the external program is to store the data required by sum in an input data file and to use the I/O redirection commands. This approach is illustrated in Listing 19.4. You may wish to store the following lines in a file and source them in the interpreter.

LISTING 19.4 Catching Errors or Results

```
1: %if { [catch {exec ./sum <sum-input.dat >results} msg] } {
2:          puts "Problem executing ./sum. The error message is $msg"
3:       } else {
4:          puts "Results are in the file results."
5:       }
6: Results are in the file results.
7: % if { [catch {exec ./sum <inp.dat >results} msg] } {
8:          puts "Problem executing ./sum. The error message is $msg"
```

continues

LISTING 19.4   continued

```
 9:          } else {
10:              puts "Results are in the file results"
11:          }
12: Problem executing ./sum. The error message is couldn't [ccc]
13:  file "inp.dat": no such file or directory

14: %
```

ANALYSIS The code fragment in lines 1–5, uses the catch command to report any problems with execution. First the input data is stored in the file sum-input.dat. Next, we use the I/O redirection operators < to pre-connect the input and > to write results to the file results. If exec is successful, catch returns 0, and hence we get the message from the else branch saying where the results are written (line 4). Lines 6–10 demonstrate what happens, when we supply a nonexisting input data file.

Note that the program sum in Listing 19.4 is executed synchronously and is suitable for programs with smaller execution times. For computationally demanding programs, it is better to run the programs in the background or asynchronously. The distinction between these two modes of execution is illustrated in Listing 19.5.

LISTING 19.5   The Difference Between Synchronous and Asynchronous Execution

```
 1: % exec ./sum
 2: 6
 3:  Input ntops
 4:   Sum upto   6 is :     21.000000000000
 5: % exec ./sum &
 6: 19313
 7: %  Input ntops
 8: 7
 9:   Sum upto   7 is :     28.000000000000
10:
11: %
```

Here, sum is the name of an executable FORTRAN program. The command exec sum, in line 1, will return immediately and will be waiting for you to supply the data. If there are any prompt strings printed by the FORTRAN program, they will not appear at this point. After supplying the data, the program will print all the text. When you run the program in the background, as in line 5, the exec command returns the process ID, and the control returns to Tcl. Note the order of prompt string (line 3 and line 7) in respective approaches. Note also that you need to press the Return key (line 10) to get back to the Tcl prompt.

Do	Don't
Do remember to close the opened pipes. **Do** make sure that you have specified the paths of your executable file correctly, and that you are not inadvertently using some other (system) program.	**Don't** try and open interactive programs such as Matlab, telnet, or ftp as pipes and try to talk to them. This kind of interaction requires additional functions to manage the process.

Summary

In this hour, we looked at a simple way of generating GUI front ends to legacy code written in languages such as FORTRAN. The basic idea is to open the program as a pipe, which is illustrated with a simple example. This approach can be applied to several situations.

Executing intensive applications requires a slightly different tack. The input data required by the executable is gathered from the user interface and written to a file, and the external executable is invoked using I/O redirection and executing the program as a background process.

Simulation programs that write data at regular intervals to a file need to be handled differently altogether, and is a subject beyond the scope of this book. Such applications can be handled by the `fileevent` command.

Q&A

Q **I have an input data file and want to pass that to the executable file. How do I do that?**

A A simple way is to use the input/output redirection commands, < or >. See online manual under `exec`. For example, if your executable is `sample`, you issue the command

```
exec sample <input.dat >results
```

which will take the data in `input.dat` and write the output to the file `results`. This is another popular way of generating GUI front ends. You simply collect the data from the GUI and write it to a file, execute the external FORTRAN program and display the results by dumping the text in the `results` file in a text widget.

19

Q I need to link my code with other library software to create the executable. How do I do that?

A You need to compile the code together with the library software. Let us say, your source file is called `sample.f` and you want to link in the NAG Library (a commercial numerical library for scientific computations). (See `http://www.nag.co.uk`.) The following Tcl code fragment illustrates a typical way of achieving this.

```
set fn sample.f
regsub {.f} $fn {} execFile ;# generate a name for executable file
if { [catch {exec /usr/bin/f77 -o $execFile $fn -lnag} msg] } {
    puts "Problem compiling $fn. Check compile command."
    puts "Message from compile command: $msg"
}
```

Q Is there a way to collect the compiler generated error messages?

A Yes. Normally the compiler writes its error messages to the logical unit called `stderr` on UNIX platforms. Messages written to this unit can be redirected to a file when invoking the `exec` command. For example, compiling a nonexistent file is an error. We can store this error in a file as shown in the dialogue below.

```
exec f77 a.f 2> err.msg
```

Here it is assumed that the file <u>a.f</u> does not exist in your directory. A typical error message reported by the compiler is shown below.

```
a.f:
Error: Cannot open file a.f
```

For additional information on controlling flow of input and output, see online manual under `exec`.

Workshop

The following "Quiz" section is designed to provide you with an opportunity to recall some of the important concepts introduced in this hour. These might be commands, command syntax, common mistakes, usage, and so on. The "Exercises" section following the "Quiz" section helps you consolidate the material you learned via an example of practical value. Our aim is that these two sections should reinforce the knowledge you have gained in this hour. The answers to the quiz that follows can be found in Appendix A, "Answers to Quizzes."

Quiz

1. How do you execute an external program?
2. What is the command to read from and write to a pipe?
3. What is the command to execute a program asynchronously or in the background?

4. How do you open a pipe for reading and writing?

5. How do you collect any errors that might be reported by the external executable?

Exercises

Solutions to the exercises are on the CD-ROM that accompanies this book.

1. Develop a GUI front end to your own FORTRAN program, which requires a single input. You might use Listing 19.3 as a model.

2. Develop a GUI front end to solve a quadratic equation for its roots. The FORTRAN source program is shown in Listing 19.6. A sample GUI layout is shown in Figure 19.2. The output strings from the FORTRAN executable differ, depending on whether roots are real or complex. Handle both cases. Do check to see that all the entries are not empty. A typical session with the FORTRAN executable is shown in the following:

```
neuman% quads2
 Input the coefficients a,b,c
 1 0 -4
 DISC :     16.000000000000
 IFLAG =    0
 ROOTS ARE REAL
 x1 =     2.0000000000000   x2 =     -2.0000000000000
neuman% quads2
 Input the coefficients a,b,c
 1 0 4
 DISC :    -16.000000000000
 IFLAG =    1
 ROOTS ARE COMPLEX — (RealPart, ImagPart) = (x1,x2)
 x1 =   0.   x2 =     2.0000000000000
neuman%
```

19

FIGURE 19.2

GUI front end to quadratic solver.

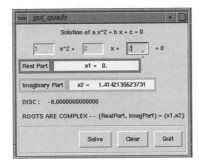

LISTING 19.6   The FORTRAN Program quads.f

```
 1: C
 2: CThis program solves the quadratic equation
 3: C          2
 4: C     a x  + b x + c = 0
 5: C
 6:       INTEGER IFLAG
 7:       DOUBLE PRECISION A,B,C,X1,X2
 8:       EXTERNAL QSOLVE
 9:       COMMON IFLAG
10:
11:       PRINT *,'Input the coefficients a,b,c'
12:       READ *,A,B,C
13:       CALL QSOLVE(A,B,C,X1,X2)
14:       IF (IFLAG.EQ.0) THEN
15:           PRINT *,'IFLAG = ',IFLAG
16:           PRINT *,'ROOTS ARE REAL'
17:       ELSE
18:           PRINT *,'IFLAG = ',IFLAG
19:           PRINT *,'ROOTS ARE COMPLEX — (RealPart, ImagPart) = (x1,x2)'
20:       END IF
21:       WRITE (UNIT=6,FMT=*) 'x1 = ',X1,'  ','x2 = ',X2
22:       END
23:       SUBROUTINE QSOLVE(A,B,C,X1,X2)
24: C---subroutine QSOLVE
25: C    solves the quadratic equation
26: C    input parameters   a,b,c  (DOUBLEPRECISION)
27: C
28:       DOUBLE PRECISION A,B,C,X1,X2
29:       INTEGER IFLAG
30:       DOUBLE PRECISION DISC
31:       INTRINSIC SQRT
32:       COMMON IFLAG
33: C
34:       DISC = (B*B-4*A*C)
35:       PRINT *,'DISC : ',DISC
36:       IF (DISC.GE.0) THEN
37:           X1 = (-B+SQRT(DISC))/ (2.0*A)
38:           X2 = (-B-SQRT(DISC))/ (2.0*A)
39:           IFLAG = 0
40:       ELSE
41:           IFLAG = 1
42:           X1 = -B/ (2*A)
43:           X2 = SQRT(-DISC)/ (2*A)
44:       END IF
45:       RETURN
46:       END
```

Hour **20**

Understanding Object-Oriented Programming with Tcl/Tk

The Tk widgets support the concept of objects, hierarchy of objects, and objects inheriting attributes from other objects and methods. In Hour 18, "Using C with Tcl/Tk," we even saw that with Tcl/Tk 8.0 the notion of objects is attached to every Tcl/Tk construct. However, this notion does not fully contribute to creating data structures and procedure components in a reusable way that more rigorous object-oriented programming approaches allow. It is, therefore, understandable that Tcl/Tk has been extended to provide powerful object-oriented programming functionality.

There are two ways of incorporating object-orientation in your Tcl/Tk applications. The first is to implement your own Tcl commands in an object-oriented language such as C++ and register them with the Tcl interpreter. This is done much the same way as you learned how to implement your own commands using C in Hour 18.

The other way is to exploit the power and the functionality of [incr Tcl] and [incr Tk] developed by Michael McLennan and his team at DSC Communications. [incr Tcl] brings object technology to the scripting level, providing powerful structures but without the verbosity of C++. In this hour, you will learn how to adopt this strategy. In particular, you will learn how

- To define simple classes using [incr Tcl]
- To use [incr Tcl] class definitions with Tk
- To use [incr Tk] mega-widgets in your applications

It is beyond the scope of this book to cover the power and functionality supported by [incr Tcl] and [incr Tk]. Instead, we aim to provide you the basic flavor of both. The aim is to guide your first step towards exploring and exploiting these tools within the scope of this book, whose focus is Tcl/Tk. For a full treatment of this elegant extension to Tcl/Tk, we recommend the sample code and manuals at http://www.tcltk.com/itcl. References to books by McLennan and his team are included in Appendix B. This hour does not cover object-oriented programming. You can find excellent literature elsewhere on that.

The examples in this hour require you to execute them in itclsh and itkwish interpreters. These are the extensions of tclsh and wish to include the [incr Tcl] and [incr Tk] commands. In addition, you should also download and install the [incr Widgets] package. All these are available from http://www.tcltk.com/itcl. Lucid installation instructions are given, and the process of installation is straightforward.

Integrating Object-Orientated Programming with Tcl/Tk

The [incr Tcl] class is an extension of Tcl to support object-oriented programming. In the words of its creator Michael McLennan, "[incr Tcl] borrows some familiar concepts from C++...but while it resembles C++, it is written to be consistent with the Tcl language." It is this particular aspect, the capability to integrate structured programming via object-orientation at the Tcl scripting level, mixing it with regular Tcl commands, that influenced our choice to use [incr Tcl] in this book.

The principal aspect of object-oriented programming is the capability to define a new class of objects that encapsulates the data describing the objects that belong to that class and the methods that manipulate that data. An object is a particular instance of its class with a specific value set for the data. For instance, if you have a screw-driver class, the size and type can be considered as two kinds of data associated with it and a small screw-driver or a Phillips screw-driver can be thought of as two objects belonging to this class. Each class has *instance variables* or *data members* to represent such data.

Equally important is the capability to derive another class of objects that inherit attributes and methods from an existing class and add or modify its own on top. Encapsulation ensures that the attributes or data variables are not directly accessed and modified by any external program. Methods are the only disciplined mechanism to change the variables, unless you have specifically decided against such a protection. As a first step, [incr Tcl] enables you to define new classes and use inheritance and encapsulation at the scripting level. Besides the style of [incr Tcl] is closer to Tcl, making it easier to learn. Let us explore this with a very simple example, given in Listing 20.1.

Topics such as multiple inheritance, the capability to derive one class from more than one parent class, are well beyond the scope of this book.

LISTING 20.1   A Simple Class Definition

```
 1: # A simple example to create a
 2: #   task bar with a message
 3:
 4: class TaskBar {
 5:     variable name
 6:     variable canvas
 7:
 8:     constructor {c {n "TaskName"}} {
 9:     set canvas $c
10:     set name $n
11:     }
12:
13:     destructor {
14:     erase
15:     }
16:
17:     method erase {} {
18:     $canvas delete $this
19:     }
20:
21:     method delObj {} {
22:      delete object $this
23:     }
24:
25:     method draw {x y  } {
26:     $canvas create line $x $y [expr $x+50] $y -tags $this
27:     $canvas create text [expr $x+5] [expr $y-5] -text $name \
```

continues

20

LISTING 20.1   continued

```
28:                           -anchor w -tags $this
29:     }
30: }
31:
32: pack [canvas .c]
33: set counter 0
34:
35: # create some task bars
36: bind .c <Button-1> {
37:     set t "tb$counter"
38:      set tn [TaskBar $t .c $t ]
39:      incr counter
40:     $tn draw %x %y
41: }
42:
43: bind .c <Button-3> {
44:     # get the instance name of the object
45:     # to invoke its delObj method
46:
47:     set x [lindex [.c gettags current] 0]
48:     $x delObj
49:
50: }
```

ANALYSIS In line 4, we use the [incr Tcl] built-in command class to create a new class of objects. We call this class TaskBar. We follow the principle of encapsulation and define the data and methods that describe a generic object belonging to this class next. The class has two *instance variables*, name and canvas. The name points to the name of an instance of this class and canvas holds the name of the canvas widget in which this object will be displayed. The class has five methods, a constructor, a destructor, and three other methods called erase, delObj, and draw.

> Note that constructor, destructor, and method are [incr Tcl] keywords.

The constructor and the destructor are special methods that are automatically called when you try to create an instance of an object of this class, and they are optional. The input arguments of the constructor are passed as command-line arguments when an object is created. Note that you cannot pass arguments to the destructor.

When an object of a class is created, [incr Tcl] also creates a special variable called this that holds the name of the object. Compare this with the current tag for the canvas items.

All the [incr Tcl] methods, including the constructor and destructor, are like Tcl procedures having a name, an optional argument list where applicable (note that a destructor doesn't take arguments), and a body with syntax similar to Tcl procedures. There is one crucial difference. The methods of an object have access to all the variables of that object, without the need for explicit argument passing. See how the variable name is available to all the methods within TaskBar without having to be passed as an argument. The special variable this is also available for manipulating the data. Similarly, within one method of a class, the other methods of the class can be used as commands. For instance, the destructor calls the erase method.

If you want to delete (destroy) an object, you need to remove the object reference and resources from the object's database. This needs to be done explicitly and is done by the delObj method. We free the allocated memory by executing the delObj method. The body of this method contains the single [incr Tcl] action command delete object objName ?objName?. When the object is destroyed, its destructor method is automatically invoked, which invokes erase in turn.

The erase method executes the canvas action subcommand delete to remove the graphical items with *tagOrId* that is held in this.

The last method of this class is draw. It takes the current mouse cursor position in the canvas when the mouse Button-1 event is generated. It executes the canvas action subcommand to create a line item and a text item. The text is the name of the object. Both the line and the text items are tagged with the object's name.

Having defined our TaskBar class, we want to exercise its use. We want to create an instance of the TaskBar class at the mouse position whenever the left mouse button is pressed in a canvas. We want to delete the currently selected items when the right mouse button is pressed.

In line 32, we create a canvas and pack it. We set a counter at 0. We want to use this counter to generate object names in the form tb$counter. The binding for the Button-1 event creates the object using the [incr Tcl] object creation command className objName ?arg?, where args are the input arguments to the constructor. In this example, this object creation command happens to be TaskBar tb$counter .c tb$counter. We use command substitution in line 38 to assign the variable tn the identity of the TaskBar tb$counter when it is created. For convenience, we have used the same name for the object and its tag.

In lines 43–50, we define a binding for the event sequence <Button-3>. This uses the current tag to retrieve the tag name, which is also the object name. We then execute the [incr Tcl] command objectName method ?arg arg? to erase and delete the object reference and free the resource allocation.

20

Inheritance

We noted earlier that one of the powerful features of object-oriented programming is inheritance. Neither Tcl nor Tk provide support for inheritance, even though Tk is object based. For instance, you can bundle a hierarchy of Tk widgets as a small module and reuse it, but you cannot encapsulate data and methods into this "made up" hierarchy of components. Neither can you apply the Tk widget commands such as configure and cget. [incr Tcl] allows you to inherit classes to create derived classes. Listing 20.2 illustrates this functionality.

LISTING 20.2   Inherit Command

```
 1: # A simple example of inheritance
 2:
 3: class TaskBar {
 4:     variable name
 5:     variable canvas
 6:
 7:     constructor {c {n "TaskName"}} {
 8:       set canvas $c
 9:       set name $n
10:       }
11:
12:     destructor {
13:       erase
14:       }
15:
16:     method erase {} {
17:       $canvas delete $this
18:       }
19:     method delObj {} {
20:       delete object $this
21:       }
22:
23:     method draw {x y  } {
24:       $canvas create line $x $y [expr $x+50] $y -tags $this
25:       $canvas create text $x [expr $y-5] \
26:           -text $name -tags $this -anchor w
27:       }
28: }
29:
30: class ButtLine {
31:     inherit TaskBar
32:     constructor {c {n "BTask"}} {
33:       TaskBar::constructor $c $n
34:       } { }
35:     method draw {x y } {
36:       $canvas create line $x $y [expr $x+50] $y -tags $this
```

```
37:    $canvas create line $x [expr $y-5] $x [expr $y +5] -tags $this
38:    $canvas create line [expr $x+50] [expr $y-5] \
39:        [expr $x+50] [expr $y +5] -tags $this
40:    }
41: }
42: pack [canvas .c]
```

ANALYSIS   Lines 3–28 define the TaskBar class exactly as in Listing 20.1. In the definition of ButtLine in line 30, we have used the [incr Tcl] command inherit className to specify that the class ButtLine inherits the variables and methods of TaskBar. In [incr Tcl], object construction starts from the least-specific class construction to the most-specific class. Therefore, each base class gets fully constructed before the derived class constructor is executed.

In view of this, we pass the arguments for the base class TaskBar constructor in the constructor for ButtLine. We have qualified the scope of the base class constructor using ::. Namespace and scope are explained in Hour 22, "Adding Tcl/Tk Extensions." Now all the variables and the methods of the base class TaskBar are available to ButtLine class. We can now add new variables, new methods that are specific to ButtLine. In addition, we can also choose to override any method of the base class with a new definition, as shown in lines 35–39.

Listing 20.3 shows an interactive itkwish to demonstrate this inheritance. Figure 20.1 shows the end product.

LISTING 20.3   Illustration of Inheritance

```
 1: % source listing2.itcl
 2: % ButtLine bl1 .c bl1
 3: bl1
 4: % ButtLine bl2 .c bl2
 5: bl2
 6: % ButtLine bl3 .c bl3
 7: bl3
 8: % itcl::find objects
 9: bl2 bl3 bl1
10: % bl2 draw 80 80
11: 3
12: % bl1 draw 40 40
13: 6
14: % bl3 draw 120 150
15: 9
16: % itcl::find objects
17: bl2 bl3 bl1
18: % bl3 delObj
19: % itcl::find objects
20: bl2 bl1
```

20

ANALYSIS We first source listing2.itcl. Then we create three instances of the class ButtLine in
lines 2, 4, and 6. Note that the constructor returns the name of the object. In line 8,
we execute the [incr Tcl] command `itcl::find objects` to retrieve the list of the
objects. The rest of the code is self-explanatory.

FIGURE 20.1

*Illustration of class
inheritance using
[incr Tcl].*

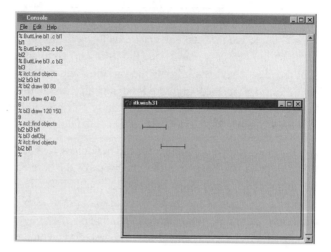

Using Mega-widgets

As you start developing large Tk applications, you will find yourself bundling a few Tk
widgets together to create a super structure of some GUI component. This is useful but
restrictive. For instance, you cannot apply the Tk framework commands `configure` and
`cget` to the newly created superstructure as a whole. If you, on the other hand, want to
create new Tk widgets, you have to do so in C. [incr Tk] uses [incr Tcl] classes to inherit
Tk widget classes to create new widgets. So by using [incr Tk], you can create new widgets from Tk widgets without writing either in C code.

In addition, you can encapsulate data and methods as if this super or mega-widget is a
single entity. At the same time, it preserves the access to and functionality of the individual components. [incr Widgets] is a collection of widgets created with [incr Tk]. See the
[incr Tcl] documentation for the complete set of [incr Widgets]. In Listing 20.4, we illustrate how to use one of these widgets, namely the tabset.

A tabset is a [incr Widgets] attached to another window such as canvas or text, and it
contains a set of tab buttons. When a tab button is selected, an appropriate section of
contents can be displayed in the attached widget. The task here is to display a classified
collection of items in a canvas widget. The names of your collection are shown as tab

labels. When a particular label is selected, the relevant item(s) is shown in the canvas. Listing 20.4 shows the code required.

> The package [incr Widgets] is not automatically loaded into your [incr Tcl] interpreter. You need to use the built-in Tcl command package require Iwidgets to make it available. Use the command namespace import iwidgets::*, so that all the commands of this package are available to you. If you do not execute the second command, you will be required to use iwidgets::tabset in line 45 below. Recall the description of including packages and extensions into the core interpreter from Hour 18, "Using C with Tcl/Tk." Hour 22, "Adding Tcl/Tk Extensions," covers automating package loading in detail.

LISTING 20.4   A Tabbed Canvas

```
1: pack [canvas .c]
2:
3: proc showShapes {} {
4:     .c delete all
5:     .c create line 40 10 10 10 40 60 10 60 40 10  \
6:         -width 4 -tags { pline }
7:     .c create oval 60 10 110 60 -fill yellow -tags { disc1 }
8:     .c create oval 70 20 120 70 -fill red -tags { disc2 }
9:     .c bind disc1 <Button-1> { .c raise disc1 }
10:     .c bind disc2 <Button-1> { .c raise disc2 }
11: }
12:
13: proc showStamps {} {
14:     .c delete all
15:     .c create text 10 20 -text "My Stamp Collection" -anchor w
16:     # just show one stamp
17:     set RS [image create photo -file ./royalscot.gif]
18:     set RShalf [image create photo]
19:     $RShalf copy $RS -shrink -subsample 2 2
20:     .c create image 155 108 -image $RShalf -anchor c
21: }
22:
23: proc showCoins {} {
24:     .c delete all
25:     .c create text 10 20 -text "My purse is empty." -anchor w
26: }
27:
28: proc showQuotes {} {
29:     .c delete all
```

20

continues

LISTING 20.4   continued

```
30:    .c create text 50 50 -text \
31:        "A mind is like a parachute - it only works when it's open. -Anon." \
32:            -width 160 -anchor w
33: }
34:
35: proc displayTabItem {num } {
36:     switch — $num {
37:     0 { showShapes }
38:     1 { showStamps }
39:     2 { showCoins }
40:     3 { showQuotes }
41:     default { .c create 10 20 -text {None...} }
42:     }
43: }
44:
45: tabset .tbw -angle 25 -bevelamount 2 -command displayTabItem
46: pack .tbw -fill x
47:
48: foreach item {Shapes Stamps Coins Quotes} {
49:     .tbw add -label $item
50: }
51:
52: .tbw select 0
53: frame .bf -bg lightblue -bd 2 -relief groove
54: pack .bf -fill x
55: button .bf.qb -text Quit -command {exit}
56: pack .bf.qb -side right
```

ANALYSIS   Most of the preceding code is plain Tcl/Tk and should be familiar to you by now. In line 45, we introduce the [incr Widgets] tabset. Note the similarity between Tk and [incr Widgets] widget creation command.

The options we have used here are -angle, -bevelamount, and -command. The option -angle specifies the slope of the edge of the tab, whereas -bevelamount controls the roundness of its corners. The tabset automatically appends the index of the selected tab button to the callback attached to the -command option. The callback procedure is displayTabItem, which uses the tab index as an argument to a switch command. Each case invokes a procedure to display appropriate items in the canvas. Figure 20.2 shows the stamp collection.

FIGURE 20.2
*[incr Widgets] tabset
with second tab
selected.*

Do	Don't
Do declare variables public if you want to access them from outside the class.	**Don't** forget to execute the command package and require the packageName before using optional extensions.
Do fully qualify the methods when defining derived classes.	**Don't** forget to pass constructor arguments at the time of object creation.

Summary

In this hour, you learned how to use the power of object-oriented programming in Tcl/Tk. [incr Tcl], [incr Tk], and [incr Widgets] provide you the ability to exploit object-oriented programming at the scripting level. You can incorporate extensions such as [incr Tcl] together with other extensions and your own applications using the Tcl namespace and package utility commands. In the next hour, "Programming with Perl/Tk," you will learn how to exploit the popular scripting language Perl with Tk.

20

Q&A

Q **How do I query and configure instance variables?**

A In [incr Tcl] terminology, instance variables declared as public are treated as attributes that can be queried and manipulated using the `configure` and `cget` methods. This is similar to Tk widget options. Each class in [incr Tcl] also has the built-in `configure` and `cget` methods. For instance, insert the [incr Tcl] keyword `public` in front of the instance variables `canvas` and `name`. You will then be able to query `tb0` `cget -canvas`.

Q **I can't use [incr Widgets] and run the examples. Why?**

A [incr Widgets] are no longer automatically loaded into your [incr Tcl] interpreter. You need to issue the package require Iwidgets command. For more detailed information on namespace and packages, refer to Hour 22, "Adding Tcl/Tk Extensions."

Q **Are there other object-oriented extensions to Tcl/Tk and other super-widgets?**

A Yes, there are. For example, the package STOOOP (Simple Tcl Only Object Oriented Package) can be found at `http://www.multimania.com/jfontain/stooop.htm`.

Workshop

The following quiz section is designed to provide you with an opportunity to recall some of the important concepts introduced in this hour. These might be commands, command syntax, common mistakes, usage, and so on. Our aim is that these two sections should reinforce the knowledge you have gained in this hour. The exercises are designed to help you explore the object-oriented programming supported by [incr Tcl]. Download the latest version of [incr Tcl] (Version 3.0.0), if you do not already have it, and try the examples and exercises. The answers to the quiz that follows can be found in Appendix A, "Answers to Quizzes."

Quiz

1. How do you define a class?
2. How is a class method defined?
3. How do you access class variables and methods outside the definition of a class?
4. What is the difference between Tk attributes and class variables?
5. What is the command to create an instance of a class?
6. When is the destructor invoked?

Exercises

Solutions to the exercises are on the CD-ROM that accompanies this book.

1. Modify the procedure showCoins in Listing 20.4 to display the image of a coin.

2. Use [incr Widgets] combobox to create a list of font names. Attach the combobox to a text widget. Associate a callback to the combobox for a font selection event. The callback should change the font of the displayed text.

Hour 21

Programming with Perl/Tk

In the last hour, we studied one of the popular extensions called [incr Tcl] to exploit object-oriented methods. A somewhat closely related topic is a Perl module called Tk that offers facilities to develop graphical user interfaces (GUIs) for the Perl programmer.

This hour is primarily aimed at those who have some exposure to Perl, but never ventured into the wonderful world of GUIs. This hour might equally appeal to those Tcl programmers who not only want to exploit a fairly extensive collection of Perl modules in their GUIs, but also want to retain their knowledge of Tk.

In this hour, you will learn

- The basics of Perl objects
- The basics of GUI programming
- To create Tk widgets using Perl
- To create GUIs using other Perl modules

Why Perl/Tk?

What is Perl? If you haven't already heard about it, here is what it is. Perl is an acronym for Practical Extraction and Reporting Language, designed by Larry Wall. Perl is very popular among CGI, database, and system programmers. Perl offers powerful pattern matching tools, and there is a wealth of programming tools developed purely in Perl. These user contributed Perl programs are usually developed as modules. With the arrival of Tk widgets, there is a Perl module, which offers GUI components based on Tk widgets to the Perl programmer. Now, the Perl programmers can add a neat user interface to their scripts.

Why should Perl/Tk be of any interest? Well, for the Perl programmer, he need not learn another scripting language; and he gets the added benefit of neatly wrapping his application in a GUI. This might also be of interest to a Tcl programmer, who wants a specific Perl module, but wants to retain his knowledge of Tk. In either case, here it is.

A Very Brief Overview of Perl Objects

What are Perl objects? In a nutshell, a Perl object is a reference. That is too abstract. For practical purposes, think of it as a bundle of data and subroutines called methods that define the behavior of the object. In programming terms, all the related information pertaining to an object is stored as a reference to a memory location. You can think of them as a kind of *derived types* in C or *records* in Pascal.

This paradigm fits neatly with GUI programming, where each widget (for example, Button) is defined as a method (more accurately as a class method) of a root window. Each widget has attributes and associated values. For example, the button widget has a `text` attribute that specifies the label that should appear on the button.

The behavior of a widget is defined as a *subroutine*. For example, a generic method that all widgets share is called `configure(...)`, which alters a specific attribute of the widget. Widgets also have specific methods. For example, a button can be made to `flash()` or `invoke()` a specific procedure. We will illustrate these concepts with examples in the following sections, after a quick recap on the basics of event-driven programming.

The Essence of GUI Programming

There are three simple steps in developing GUIs:

1. Create a widget specifying the attribute you require. The remaining attributes assume their default values.

2. Render the widget using the `pack(...)` method.

3. Add behavior. That is, specify what to do when some interesting event happens. This is normally written as a subroutine.

We will explain these steps with an example in the next section.

Getting Started with the Perl/Tk Module

Before starting with the examples, make sure that you have Perl software installed on your platform that has Tk module. Normally, any version greater than 5.0 should be fine. If not, obtain the software and install it. (http://www.perl.com is a good starting point.) The examples in this hour are run on a UNIX platform using 5.004 on Sun Solaris workstations, and explanations regarding Perl syntax are kept to a minimum.

Using the Tk Module

The Tk module provides all the standard Tk widgets: Button, Radiobutton, Checkbutton, Listbox, Scrollbar, Entry, Canvas, Frame, Scale, Menu, and Menubutton. Additional widgets such as Axis are also available, but they are specific to the Perl/Tk module. For extensive details of their attributes and default values, check either the Perl/Tk documentation or the Tcl/Tk documentation. First, we start with a simple example.

The task is to create a button that displays Hello.... When pressed, it changes the text to Hello from Tk/Perl and also reconfigures itself to quit the application, when pressed further. We know it might sound a bit daunting. Believe us, it is simpler to do than it sounds! The complete code is shown in Listing 21.1.

LISTING 21.1   Creating a Simple Button in Perl/Tk

```
 1: #!/usr/local1/bin/perl
 2:
 3: # a simple Tk Perl demo
 4:
 5: use Tk;
 6:
 7: $top = MainWindow->new();
 8: $top -> title("Simple Demo");
 9: $b = $top->Button(text    => 'Hello ...',
10:                     command => sub{ $b->configure([ccc]
                                           text => 'Hello from Tk/Perl',
11:                                        command => sub{ exit } );}
12:                 );
13: $b->pack();
14: MainLoop();
```

21

ANALYSIS The first line is a special comment. When the UNIX shell sees an exclamation mark after the # sign, the remaining text is understood as the path of the executable to use to interpret the following commands. In this example, we are saying that we want to use Perl. You might need to change this line depending on your local installation. You also need to set the execute permission. For example, on UNIX platforms a command such as chmod +x *fileName* will do the job. For registering file extensions on NT platforms, see Perl documentation.

In line 5, we invoke the Tk module. This enables us to access all the available Tk widgets and associated methods. We create an instance of a toplevel window with the method new associated with the class MainWindow. The reference returned by Perl is stored in the variable $top to refer to this object later.

One of the properties or attributes of a MainWindow is the title. To set this property, we invoke the object method as seen in line 8. Note the use of the object reference we have stored in $top. Next, we want to create a simple button with a label Hello..., which when pressed does something.

Such actions are referred to as callbacks in event-driven programming. All the callbacks are written as Perl subroutines. In this example, we want to be somewhat adventurous and do two things. When the user presses the button, first we change the label for the button to read Hello from Tk/Perl. Second, we want to change the call back to exit the program itself. This requirement is expressed in lines 9–12.

Note that we can specify as many attribute-value pairs as are applicable at the time of widget creation. Next, we pack the button ($b) we have thus created in line 13. Now, we ask the program to sit in a big loop processing user events, with the command MainLoop(). That is all. The results of our efforts are shown in Figure 21.1 and Figure 21.2.

FIGURE 21.1

Hello program in Perl/Tk—initial state.

FIGURE 21.2

Hello program in Perl/Tk—after pressing the button. This time if you press the button, the program exits itself.

Binding Tk Events

What is an event? An *event* is an action triggered by the user interacting with the GUI you have created. For example, the user placing the mouse pointer on the button is an event. In fact, this is what the subroutine MainLoop does—tracking and responding to these events generated by a user's actions.

For an extensive list of Tk events, see Table 11.2 in Hour 11, "Adding Behavior to Your Widgets." You specify a script or subroutine to be executed whenever an interesting event occurs. Such a subroutine is called a *callback*. We will illustrate these concepts with a short example.

The task is to raise a number a to a given exponent b and to display the result. We want to add a button to exit this application. Well, what type of widgets do we need? It is convenient to use entry widgets for entering the numbers and to use a label to display the answer. An additional label is used to provide the context of the application. Finally, a simple button is used to exit the application. See Figure 21.3 for a sneak preview of the interface.

Now, let us consider the type of functionality we want to provide. When the user modifies the number in either of the entry of widgets and hits a return key, we want to take that latest information from those widgets, compute a^b, and update the result. So, how do we do that? We attach a subroutine as a call back to the <Return> event in the entry widgets. The magic of updating the result is achieved with the -textvariable property of the label. The complete code is shown in Listing 21.2.

> Properties or attributes of a widget can be specified either with a leading dash or without it. For example, the width of a button can be specified as width => 4 or -width => 4.

LISTING 21.2   Entry Widgets with Bindings to the <Return> Event

```
1: #!/usr/local1/bin/perl
2:
3: # compute power in  Tk Perl
4: # using sub as callback
5: #
6: use Tk;
7:
8: $top = MainWindow->new();
9: $top -> title("Simple Demo");
```

21

continues

Listing 21.2 continued

```
10: $baseVal = 2;
11: $base = $top->Entry(width => 5,
12:                      relief => 'sunken',
13:                      textvariable => \$baseVal);
14: $lab1 = $top->Label(text => 'to the power');
15: $expVal = 5;
16: $exp = $top->Entry(width => 4,
17:                     relief => 'sunken',
18:                     textvariable => \$expVal);
19: $result = $top->Label(width => 15,
20:                        textvariable => \$resultVal);
21: $qb = $top->Button(text=>'Quit',
22:                     command => sub { exit } );
23: $base-> bind("<Return>", \&computePower );
24: $exp-> bind("<Return>", \&computePower );
25: $base->pack(-side => 'left');
26: $lab1->pack(-side => 'left');
27: $exp->pack(-side => 'left');
28: $result->pack(-side => 'left');
29: $qb -> pack(-side => 'left');
30: MainLoop();
31:
32: sub computePower {
33:     $b = $base->get();
34:     $e = $exp->get();
35:     $resultVal = $b ** $e;
36: }
```

ANALYSIS   Creating the entry widgets `$base` (line 11), `$exp` (line 16), the label widgets `$lab1` (line 14), `$result` (line 19), and the button widget `$qb` (line 21) is fairly straightforward. We will focus on the important attribute `-textvariable`. This attribute stores the value associated with a widget in the named variable. If the variable changes, it is immediately reflected in the widget.

For example, in line 10, we define a variable called `$baseVal` and use that variable reference in specifying the `textvariable` attribute for the entry widget `$base` (line 13). Note that we need to give the reference to the variable `$baseVal`, and therefore the backslash in `\$baseVal`. Refer to your favorite book on Perl for further information.

Now, what does it mean? In practical terms, when the GUI is fired up, you have the entry widget already filled with the number 2 as a result of lines 10–13. Similarly, the other entry widget `$exp` is filled with the number 5 (lines 15–18). This is convenient, you might say. Wait until we come to displaying the answer to appreciate the beauty of this mechanism. In lines 19–20, we define `$result` to display our computed answer. At the moment, we haven't said anything about the value for `$resultVal`.

Lines 21–22 define a button to quit the application. Its callback is the exit command. Now for the callbacks in the entry widgets. These are defined in lines 23–24 using the bind(event,sub) method. It is convenient to define a sub for this task as shown in lines 32–36. Note that when specifying the value for the callback, we need to give the reference to the subroutine computePower. This subroutine gets the current value in the entry widgets (lines 33–34) and computes the required exponentiation (line 35).

Now comes the magic. We store the answer in the variable $resultVal, which is the variable named in-textvariable property for the $result label widget (line 19). So, when the value for $resultVal changes, it is immediately updated in the label. That completes our task. For comparison, the corresponding Tcl/Tk code is shown in Listing 21.3. For an explanation of widgets and binding events, see Hour 10, "Getting Started with Tk," and Hour 11, "Adding Behavior to Your Widgets," respectively.

LISTING 21.3 Equivalent Tcl/Tk Script for the Interface Shown in Figure 21.3

```
 1: #!/usr/local/bin/wish -f
 2: set base 2
 3: entry .base -width 4 -relief sunken -textvariable base
 4: label .label1 -text "to the power"
 5: set power 5
 6: entry .power -width 4 -relief sunken -textvariable power
 7: label .label2 -text "is"
 8: set result 32.0
 9: label .result -width 15 -textvariable result
10: pack .base .label1 .power .label2 .result -side left
11: button .b -text Quit -command exit
12: pack .b
13:
14: # bind Return event
15:
16: bind .base <Return> {set result [expr pow($base,$power)] }
17: bind .power <Return> {set result [expr pow($base,$power)] }
```

FIGURE 21.3

Computing a^b *(a to the power* b*), where* a *and* b *are numbers. Modify either number and* press Return *in the entry widgets to display the answer.*

Variable Precision Arithmetic: An Application

We round out this hour with an example that might appeal to both Tcl and Perl program-mers. In Tcl all the arithmetic is restricted to finite precision. Let us say that you want to work with arbitrary precision integer arithmetic for generating hard-to-break passwords. Perl provides two very useful modules BigInt and BigFloat that perform variable preci-sion arithmetic. A simple application of using these modules, together with Tk module, is illustrated next.

The task is to compute the factorial of a number to arbitrary precision. Note that the default arithmetic represents the answer as a floating-point approximation, as soon as the integer overflow occurs. To keep the interface simple, we use an entry widget for enter-ing and modifying the number whose factorial we want to compute.

How shall we display the answer? A label would be disastrous because our answer is potentially a long string. A text widget would be a reasonable compromise. In fact, we should make it scrollable to accommodate very long strings. We settle for a simple text widget. You can make the additional improvements after you understand the basic princi-ple. As for functionality, we trigger the computation of factorial when the user presses Return in the entry widget. The GUI is shown in Figure 21.4, and the complete code is given in Listing 21.4.

LISTING 21.4 Computing Factorial of a Number to Arbitrary Precision

```
 1: #!/usr/local1/bin/perl
 2: # Factorial of a number in arbitrary precision
 3:
 4: use Tk;
 5:
 6: $top = MainWindow->new();
 7: $top -> title("Factorial of a number - BigInt");
 8: $ent = $top->Entry(-width => 5,
 9:                     -relief => 'sunken',
10:                     -textvariable => \$number);
11: $text = $top->Text(-width => 25,
12:                     -height => 10);
13: $qb =  $top->Button(-text => 'Quit',
14:                     -command => sub { exit });
15:
16: $ent -> pack();
17: $text -> pack();
18: # insert some instructions in the text widget.
19: $text->insert('end',"Enter a number and hit return in the entry widget.");
20: $qb -> pack('-fill'=>'x');
21: # bind Return in the entry
```

```
22: $ent->bind("<Return>", \&factorial );
23:
24: sub factorial {
25:     use Math::BigInt;
26:     my ($temp) = $ent->get();
27:     my $n = $temp;  # n is essentially descent integer, not necessarily big
28:
29:     $x = Math::BigInt->new($temp);  # convert to BigInt
30:     print "x: ", $x, "\n";
31:     while ($n > 1) {
32:         $x = $x*($n-1);
33:         $n--;
34:     }
35:     # put the result in the text widget
36:     # delete any previous stuff which might be there
37:     $text->delete('1.0', 'end');
38:     $text->insert('end', "Factorial of $temp is \n");
39:     $text->insert('end',"\n");
40:     $text->insert('end', $x);
41:
42: }
43:
44: MainLoop();
```

ANALYSIS The entry, text, and button widgets are created in lines 8–10, 11–12, and 13–14, respectively. They are all packed using the default options, and thus appear stacked one below the other. We pack the quit button by specifying the -fill x attribute. This makes the button occupy the available horizontal space. For an additional explanation of how the pack geometry manager works, consult Hour 10.

> More complex arrangements can be achieved using Frame as a container. See the examples in Hour 10.

We place some text into the text widget using the insert(*position, string*) method as in line 19. Note that 'end' is a symbolic name that is tracked by the text widget. For more information on specifying the *position*, either see Hour 13, "Using the Tk Text Widget," or refer to the documentation for the Perl Tk module. We define a binding in the entry widget for the <Return> event, which is the subroutine factorial (line 22).

The callback is defined in lines 24–42. The required module Math::BigInt is brought into the subroutine in line 25. We get the user supplied number from the entry widget $ent and store it as *my* variable because the variable is not required outside the scope of the subroutine. (Refer to David Till, *Teach Yourself Perl 5 in 21 Days,* for further

21

information regarding the scope of variables.) We keep a copy of it in $n for further reference as in line 27.

Now, we proceed to compute the factorial. We need a variable to store the big integers. This is done by creating an instance of BigInt as in line 29. We go through a simple while loop to compute the factorial in lines 31–34. Note that $n is a normal integer. (We are not particularly interested in computing factorials of big integers, even though that can be done.) The variable $x is an instance of a big integer.

The big integers are stored in a specific internal format for which all the basic arithmetic operations are defined as methods. Because $x is a big integer, the computation in line 32 is stored without any loss of precision. When we exit the while loop, we get our answer in $x. All we have to do is to display it in the text widget, and it is shown in lines 37–40. We take care to remove any previous text in the text widget using the delete(*from, to*) method for the widget (line 37).

Listing 21.4 is reasonably quick for the computation of factorial of integers up to 1,000. For larger numbers, the computation will require a significant amount of CPU time to complete the task.

FIGURE 21.4

Arithmetic with integers can be performed using variable precision module BigInt.

Do	**Don't**
Do remember to pack(...) the widgets you have created. Without applying this method, you won't see anything on the screen.	**Don't** forget to use the references when assigning Perl variables as values to widget attributes.
Do invoke the MainLoop() to process the Tk events.	**Don't** forget the references while defining callbacks.

Summary

In this hour, you have learned how to exploit the Perl Tk module for creating GUIs. The Tk module contains all the standard widgets that are provided in Tcl-based Tk, plus additional widgets such as Axis for plotting. The Tk module is written as an object-oriented program. In this style of programming, all the data and associated functions that operate on them are bundled into objects. Objects have attributes and methods that describe the behavior of the object. This style of programming is quite convenient for developing GUI programs.

GUI components are created as children of the MainWindow specifying the required attributes. These children widgets are rendered by using the pack(...) method of the object. The Tk events are specified using the bind(...) method, which are handled by the MainLoop() command.

This has been a very demanding hour syntactically. Depending on the application at hand, use your judgment in order to choose the appropriate scripting language for developing the GUIs. The undeniable fact is that Tk widgets are very powerful. This power is exploited in myriad ways by building application specific extensions, which we will explore in the next two hours.

Q&A

Q My widgets aren't appearing the way I intended. What is going on?

A Let us clarify with a code fragment. Let us say that you want to keep two entry widgets next to each other and a quit button below them. You create a frame to hold the two entry widgets and the button as a descendent of the main window as shown in the following:

```
use Tk;

$top = MainWindow->new();
$f = $top->Frame(); # $top is the main window
$f->pack(-side => 'top', -fill => 'x');
$ent1 = $f->Entry()->pack(-side => 'left');
$ent2 = $f->Entry()->pack(-side => 'left');
# now for the button in the main window
$qb = $top->Button(-text=>'Quit', -command => sub{ exit } );
$qb->pack(-side => 'top', -fill => 'x');
MainLoop();
```

Newly created widgets are packed in the parent window using the pack method. Packing algorithm works analogous to packing a suitcase with books. By default, the packer uses the top side. In this example, we pack the widgets using the left

21

side of the suitcase. As mentioned in this hour, for a detailed explanation of the packer algorithm and examples, see Hour 10.

Q Can I have more than one MainWindow?

A Yes. Create as many as you like with the command `MainWindow->new();`. Be careful while creating their children.

Workshop

The following "Quiz" section is designed to provide you with an opportunity to recall some of the important concepts introduced in this hour. These might be commands, command syntax, common mistakes, usage, and so on. The "Exercises" section following the quiz section helps you consolidate the material you learned via an example of practical value. Our aim is that these two sections should reinforce the knowledge you have gained in this hour. The answers to the quiz that follows can be found in Appendix A, "Answers to Quizzes."

Quiz

1. How is a button created?
2. How do you define callback to a button?
3. How do you make a widget appear on the screen?
4. How do you trigger the event loop?
5. How do you delete the entire contents of a text widget?

Exercises

Solutions to the exercises are on the CD-ROM that accompanies this book.

1. Modify the code in Listing 21.4 to display the square root of a number to an arbitrary precision.
2. One of the additional widgets provided in Perl Tk is a widget called `Axis` for creating line plots. Read the documentation on `Axis` and write a simple program to display a line. You need the module `Axis.pm` for this exercise. Visit `http://www.perl.com` for further details.

HOUR 22

Adding Tcl/Tk Extensions

There are many useful Tcl/Tk components, tools, and applications that you can download and use to develop your applications. Many of these *extensions* are robust, well documented, maintained, and supported by their developers and the users in the Tcl/Tk community. Using these extensions significantly reduces application development time.

Tcl/Tk commands and utilities such as namespace and packages allow you to include extensions in your tclsh and wish applications and use them as an integral part of Tcl/Tk for application development. These utilities also allow you to create your own Tcl/Tk libraries and extensions. You have already learned about extending Tcl/Tk with your own commands in Hour 18, "Using C with Tcl/Tk," and how to use an extension on a standalone basis in Hour 20, "Understanding Object-Oriented Programming with Tcl/Tk."

In this hour, you will learn

- About Tcl/Tk namespace, package utilities, and commands
- How to automatically load the extension that you require for your applications
- How to extend the Tcl interpreter to include extensions using the compile and link method

Namespace

You have already come across the Tcl namespace command in Hour 20 when you started the itcl or itkwish application and executed the command namespace import iwidgets::* so that the [incr widgets] extension is available to you for the example. Now you will learn a little more detail about this command. We will borrow the definition of a namespace from the online manual: "A namespace is a collection of commands and variables. It encapsulates the commands and variables to ensure that they won't interfere with the commands and variables of other namespaces."

Tcl's global namespace holds all global variables and procedures. Under this global namespace, you can nest other namespaces or your own namespaces. The global namespace is an empty string, whereas all others are textual strings. You use the symbol :: to fully qualify a variable or procedure for unambiguous specification in much the same way that you specify absolute or relative pathnames for files. For instance, ::cubed refers to our cubed command from Hour 18, whereas ::iwidgets::tabset .tb -option value refers to a widget command in the extension package IWidgets to configure an option. In general, all Tcl/Tk variables and commands support namespaces.

The Tcl/Tk namespace commands let you create and manipulate namespace contexts for commands and variables. There are over a dozen namespace commands that are described in detail in the online manual. These can be classified into those needed for creating and deleting namespaces. The other namespace commands are used to import and use the namespace utilities and commands in your current application context. For instance, the command namespace eval namespaceName arg ?arg...? allows you to create a new namespace called namespaceName.

If namespaceName already exists, this command activates it and evaluates the given command in that context. For this hour, it is sufficient to understand that the command namespace import namespaceName::* allows you to import the exported commands of namespaceName into the current context in which you are working and thereby eliminate the tedious need to fully qualify frequently used commands in that context. This is exactly what we did in Hour 20.

Table 22.1 gives you a snapshot of namespace commands from the manual pages. Consult the online manual for details.

TABLE 22.1 Tcl Namespace Commands Summary

Command	Description
namespace child ?ns? ?patt?	Returns a list of nested namespaces of namespace ns.
namespace code *script*	Executes the script later.
namespace current	Returns the fully-qualified name for the current namespace.
namespace delete ?ns?	Deletes each namespace ns.
namespace eval *ns* ?arg?	Creates or activates namespace ns.
namespace export ?-clear? ?*pat*?	Specifies commands to be exported from a namespace.
namespace forget ?*pat*?	Deletes the loaded namespace variables and procedures.
namespace import ?-force? ?pat?	Imports the variables and procedures into current namespace.
namespace inscope *ns* ?arg?	Executes script within the scope of ns.
namespace origin *command*	Returns a fully qualified name of a command.
namespace parent ?ns?	Returns a fully qualified name of the parent namespace of ns.
namespace qualifiers *string*	Returns namespace qualifiers of string.
namespace tail *string*	Returns a string without qualifiers.
namespace which ?-com? ?-var? *n*	Returns a type of n: command or variable.

Namespace commands are most useful when you are using third-party packages and extensions, and you want to execute the procedures from those packages within your application, that is, within the current scope. You might also use namespaces when you want to protect or contain the scope of a variable. Let us see two very simple examples of these two uses.

In Listings 22.1 and 22.2, we create a namespace called bumpIt and check how we can pass or protect variable values within the bumpIt namespace and the current namespace. Start a tclsh or wish application and try these examples interactively.

INPUT/
OUTPUT   **LISTING 22.1** Namespace Commands (Version 1)

```
1: % set x 1
2: 1
3: % namespace current
4: ::
5: % namespace eval bumpIt {
6: > namespace export bumpit
```

continues

LISTING 22.1   continued

```
 7: > proc bumpit {} {
 8: >      set x [uplevel {expr $x + 5}]
 9: >      puts "value of x in bumpIt is $x"
10: >   }
11: > }
12: % bumpit
13: invalid command name "bumpit"
14: % namespace children
15: ::bumpIt ::tcl
16: % namespace current
17: ::
18: % namespace origin bumpit
19: ::bumpIt::bumpit
20: % ::bumpIt::bumpit
21: Value of x in bumpIt is 6
22: % puts "Value of x in current namespace is $x"
23: Value of x in current namespace is 1
24: % namespace import bumpIt::*
25: % bumpit
26: Value of x in bumpIt is 6
27: % puts "Value of x in current namespace is $x"
28: Value of x in current namespace is 1
```

ANALYSIS   The above listing shows an interactive session in a wish application. In line 1, you set the value of the variable x to 1. In line 3, you inquire the current namespace using the command namespace current. Note that the name of the current namespace is ::, the global namespace. This is returned in line 4.

You then define your namespace bumpIt in lines 5–11. The command namespace eval namespaceName script evaluates the script, if the namespace namespaceName already exists; otherwise it creates namespaceName (as it does in this case). bumpIt is a simple namespace. It contains a single procedure, bumpit, which is defined in lines 7–10. In line 6, bumpIt declares that it is exporting bumpit so that other namespaces can import bumpit using the command namespace import ::bumpIt::* or ::bumpIt::bumpit.

The procedure bumpit simply adds five to the value of the variable x. Note the use of uplevel in line 8. Calling uplevel ensures that the expr command is executed in the current namespace in which the value of x is set. Within bumpit, in line 8, you set the value of x to its bumped up value and print it in line 9. Having defined your namespace bumpIt and exported the procedure bumpit from within that namespace, it is tempting to execute bumpit in the current namespace. You try this in line 12, only to get the error message that it is an invalid command in line 13.

You check for the children of the current (global) namespace in line 14. They are ::bumpIt and ::tcl, as they should be, as shown in line 15. You then inquire the origin of bumpit. Line 19 shows it to be ::bumpIt::bumpit. In line 20, you call bumpit, this time taking care to specify its full qualifier. This automatically executes bumpit within the namespace ::bumpIt and in line 21 the message "Value of x in bumpIt is 6" is displayed.

You can check what effect bumping up the value of x within the namespace bumpIt has in the current namespace. In Line 22, you execute a simple puts command to inquire the value of x in current (global) namespace ::. The value of x remains unaltered in ::! This shows clearly how you can protect the values of variables within different namespaces.

If you are using a big package, such as [incr Widgets], it is rather awkward to keep referring to each [incr Widget] command by its full qualifiers each time you want to use it. It is easier to import all the commands exported by [incr Widgets] into your current namespace. You can import exported commands from a namespace namespaceName using the command namespace import namespaceName::* as shown in line 24 for your command bumpit. You can now call bumpit without any qualifiers, as shown in line 25. This time, you get the right response and not the error message. Note how the value of x in bumpIt is still 6 and not 11! Execute the simple puts command in the global scope once again, as shown in line 27. You can see from line 28, the value of x in :: is 1 and not 6. The variable scope is very much in action both within bumpIt and in ::.

In Listing 22.2, you try essentially the same steps, but this time you ensure that whenever bumpit changes the value of x, the change is reflected in the global scope.

LISTING 22.2 Namespace Commands (Version 2)

```
 1: % set x 1
 2: 1
 3: % namespace eval bumpIt {
 4: > namespace export bumpit
 5: > proc bumpit {} {
 6: > global x
 7: > set x [uplevel {expr $x+5}]
 8: > puts "x in namespace bumpIt is $x\n"
 9: > }
10: >  }
11: % namespace import ::bumpIt::*
12: % bumpit
13: x in namespace bumpIt is 6
14: % puts "Value of x in :: is $x"
15: Value of x in :: is 6
16: % bumpit
17: x in namespace bumpIt is 11
18: % puts "Value of x in :: is $x"
19: Value of x in :: is 11
```

ANALYSIS In line 6 the variable x is declared to be global. As a result, calling `bumpit` in line 12 increases the value of x by five, not only within `bumpIt` but in `::`, as well, as seen in line 15. Calling `bumpit` the second time increases the value once again by five to make it 11, both within `bumpIt` (as seen in line 17) and in `::`, as shown in line 19.

Package

The Tcl package commands provide facilities for package loading with precise version control if required. These commands are related to namespace commands in the sense that both are used in the context of extensions. There are two distinct contexts for the use of the package commands—one for the creation of packages and the other for using these packages. We will try to distinguish these two aspects throughout. Table 22.2 gives you a snapshot of Tcl package commands from the manual pages.

TABLE 22.2 Snapshot of Tcl Package Commands

Command	Description
`package forget p`	Removes the package from current context.
`package ifneeded p version ?script?`	Makes package p of version available.
`package names`	Returns a list of all packages in current interpreter.
`package present ?-exact? p ?version?`	Checks for the package p.
`package provide package ?version?`	Makes package p, version version available for the current interpreter.
`package require ?-exact? p ?version?`	Requires package p of specified version in current interpreter.

Dynamic Loading Method

You have already learned that the statement `Tcl_PkgProvide (interp, "Cubed", "1.0")` in Listing 18.2 from Hour 18 is included to indicate that version 1.0 of our package—a simple command, "cubed"—is available for loading in the current interpreter. The Tcl script level command that is equivalent is `package provide package ?version?`. The following are the steps to creating and/or using a dynamically loaded library:

1. Create a package out of your binary shared object file(s). They must have been compiled as shared library extensions (.dll or .so files), and they must contain the `Tcl_PkgProvide` statement. All Tcl/Tk script files of a package similarly must contain the package provide command to declare the package and version number.

2. It is advisable to put each package under a subdirectory of its own under a parent *packages* directory. For each package, again it is worthwhile putting all the shared

object libraries in one subdirectory, the scripts under a second, data such as images into a third, and so on.

3. You can add the packages directory to your TCLLIBPATH environment variable. If you do that, the Tcl global environment variable `auto_path` is automatically initialized to take account of the packages directory. Alternatively, you can also set the environment variable `tcl_pkgPath` to point to the packages directory. As a last resort, you can also dynamically add the packages directory to `auto_path` by executing the command `lappend auto_path` *dir_of_packages*. The principle is to ensure that the auto-loader and the package loader know the directory or directories of the packages you want to use.

> Step 3 is needed whether you are a creator or user of packages.

4. If you are creating and installing your own packages, you need to ensure that you create an index for your package in the packages database. To do this, execute the `pkg_mkIndex ?-direct? ?-load pkgPat? ?-verbose dir ?pattern pattern ...?` in the top directory of each of your packages, making sure that you give the absolute pathname for `dir`. This creates a pkgIndex.tcl script file in that directory. This script typically contains the `package ifneeded package version ?script?` command. The script is the command to auto-load the package.

5. After the package has been installed in an appropriate directory, with all the dynamic shared library extensions, scripts, and other data together with an index in the packages database, you can invoke the package in your Tcl interpreter by executing the `package require -exact packageName` command.

6. If you are using some commands of a loaded package frequently, use the namespace `import namespace::*` to skip the tedium of fully qualifying commands. Note that this might generate an error message if there is a conflict with an existing command. You can add a `-force` option to override this, but be cautious of what you are doing.

Listing 22.3 is a very simple example to show you how to dynamically load the BLT package you will be using in Hour 23, "Using Tcl/Tk Extensions." The example shows the input and output of an interactive session carried out on a PC running NT. The method is similar on UNIX platforms, except that the `type` command should be replaced with the `more` command. You will need the BLT package to try this listing. BLT is an advanced graphing package which can be downloaded from `http://www.tcltk.com/blt`. It can be used with Tcl/Tk 8.0 and 8.1.

> If you are using a UNIX system, you can build it from scratch using the
> instructions that accompany the package. You can then use it as a stand-
> alone package or use the compile and link method described below to
> include it within your standard Tcl/Tk interpreter. If you are using a PC, you
> can download precompiled dynamic loadable libraries (BLT24.dll), install it
> on your system, and follow the instructions below to use it.

Start up a `tclsh` application in the directory in which you have installed the BLT
dynamic link library BLT24.dll.

LISTING 22.3   Dynamic Loading of the BLT Package

```
 1: % pkg_mkIndex -verbose -load Tk  E:/Blt/Tcl/bin/*.dll
 2: loaded   Tk
 3: processed BLT24.dll
 4: % pwd
 5: E:/Blt/Tcl/bin
 6: % type pkgIndex.tcl
 7: # Tcl package index file, version 1.1
 8: # This file is generated by the "pkg_mkIndex -load Tk" command
 9: # and sourced either when an application starts up or
10: # by a "package unknown" script.  It invokes the
11: # "package ifneeded" command to set up package-related
12: # information so that packages will be loaded automatically
13: # in response to "package require" commands.  When this
14: # script is sourced, the variable $dir must contain the
15: # full path name of this file's directory.
16:
17: package ifneeded BLT 2.4 [list tclPkgSetup $dir BLT 2.4 {{BLT24.dll load
{::blt::barchart ::blt::beep ::blt::bgexec ::blt::bitmap ::blt::bltdebug
18: ::blt::busy ::blt::drag&drop ::blt::graph ::blt::hierbox ::blt::htext
19: ::blt::printer ::blt::spline ::blt::stripchart ::blt::table ::blt::tabset
20: ::blt::vector ::blt::watch ::blt::winop}}}]
21: %cd E:book/Chapter22
22: %lappend auto_path E:/Blt/Tcl/bin
23: E:/TclTk81/Tcl/lib/tcl8.1 E:/TclTk81/Tcl/lib E:/TclTk81/Tcl/lib/tk8.1
24: E:/Blt/Tcl/bin
25: % package require BLT
26: 2.4
27: % namespace children
28: ::auto_mkindex_parser ::blt ::tcl
29: % namespace import ::blt::*
```

ANALYSIS   The preceding listing shows you how to dynamically load the Tcl/Tk extension
BLT. We have downloaded and installed the dynamic link library BLT24.dll. This
package depends on the Tk package. So in executing the `pkg_mkIndex`, you use the

-load option to specify that the system requires Tk. The -verbose option provides you the feedback on the loading process, as shown in lines 2 and 3. In line 4, you check the current working directory, which in this case is E:Blt/Tcl/bin. The result of executing pkg_mkIndex is the creation of a script file pkgIndex.tcl in the current directory.

Note that the Tcl interpreter enables you to execute your system command type (or more in the case of UNIX) to check the contents of pkgIndex.tcl. After you go past the comments in lines 7–15, pkgIndex.tcl is shown to contain a single Tcl command that specifies the BLT shared object library that will be made available in response to a package require command from your Tcl script. It also shows all the BLT commands that are exported from the namespace BLT.

The option -textvariable associates a global variable to some textual value of the widget for which this option is specified. The value is dependent on the widget's class. The utility of this option is that whenever the value changes, the new value can be retrieved from the global variable associated with it. In this case our button's -textvariable is set to tn. The value changes every time you click mouse button 1 on .b and this value is assigned to tn. The second configure action results in the background color of the button being set to red. The result is shown in the right-hand image of Figure 11.1.

In line 22, you execute the command lappend auto_path E:/Blt/Tcl/bin to include this directory in the search path of the auto package loader. This command returns the list of all package directories that will be searched when the command package require is executed.

In line 25, you execute the command package require BLT. When the package is loaded, the version number 2.4 is returned by the interpreter in line 26. You check the namespaces of all the children in line 27 and find ::blt to be in the list in line 28. In line 29, the command namespace import ::blt::* is executed so that you can execute any of the BLT commands in your current interpreter (global namespace) without having to fully qualify each of them every time.

Compile and Link Method

This section assumes that you have some familiarity with C. All instructions are described, so you should be able to follow the statements, compile, and run the example. This shows how to embed BLT and other user-defined commands in your interpreter and create a new extended Tcl interpreter for your application.

The Tcl/Tk source distribution contains the files tclAppInit.c and tkAppInit.c. In most extensions, you will find equivalents to these files. The tkAppInit.c is essentially the same as tclAppInit.c except that it creates an application main window to parent all the internal windows, returning a handle to it. You use one of these files to compile and link an extended version of the Tcl interpreter. A modified version of the tkAppInit.c, supplied with the source distribution of Tcl/Tk, is given in Listing 22.4.

LISTING 22.4   A Modified tkAppInit.c

```
 1: #include "tk.h"
 2: #include "locale.h"
 3: #include "tclDecls.h"
 4: #include <stdio.h>
 5: #include <math.h>
 6:  int CubedObjCmdProc(ClientData clientData, Tcl_Interp *interp,
 7:             int objc, Tcl_Obj *CONST objv[]) {
 8: int error;
 9: Tcl_Obj *resultPtr;
10: double  num, cube;
11: if (objc < 2 ) {
12:     Tcl_WrongNumArgs(interp, 1, objv, "usage: cube ?input?");
13:     return TCL_ERROR;
14:     }
15: if (objc ==2) {
16:     error = Tcl_GetDoubleFromObj (interp, objv[1], &num);
17:     if (error != TCL_OK)
18:         return error;
19:     }
20: cube = (double) pow (num, 3);
21: resultPtr = Tcl_GetObjResult(interp);
22: Tcl_SetDoubleObj(resultPtr, cube);23: return TCL_OK;
24:
25: }
26:
27: int main(int argc, char **argv){
28:     Tk_Main(argc, argv, Tcl_AppInit);
29:     return 0;
30: }
31:
32: int Tcl_AppInit(Tcl_Interp *interp) {
33:     if (Tcl_Init(interp) == TCL_ERROR) {
34:     return TCL_ERROR;
35:     }
36:     if (Tk_Init(interp) == TCL_ERROR) {
37:     return TCL_ERROR;
38:     }
39:     if (Blt_Init(interp) != TCL_OK) {
40:             return TCL_ERROR;
41:         }
42:     Tcl_StaticPackage(interp, "Tk", Tk_Init, Tk_SafeInit);
```

```
43:
44: /* Call Tcl_CreateCommand for application-specific commands*/
45:  Tcl_CreateObjCommand (interp, "cubed", CubedObjCmdProc, (
46:        ClientData)NULL, (Tcl_CmdDeleteProc *)NULL);
47:
48:      Tcl_SetVar(interp, "tcl_rcFileName", "~/.swishrc", TCL_GLOBAL_ONLY);
49:      return TCL_OK;
50: }
```

ANALYSIS Lines 6–25 contain the same code that you learned in Hour 18. It defines the cubed command procedure. You will notice that lines 27–30 contain a main program that does nothing more than make a call to Tk_Main (line 28), which creates the application main window (or wish if you prefer) and a Tcl interpreter. This makes the entire core Tcl available.

Tk_Main also stores any command line arguments in the Tcl variables argc and argv. Tk_Main then invokes Tcl_AppInit, passing it a handle for the interpreter. Tcl_AppInit, lines 32–50, initializes all the packages the application uses. In this case, you want to include the BLT extension beside Tcl and Tk commands. So in line 39, you include and initialize BLT_Init. Tcl_AppInit also calls Tcl_Init to set up the script library facility (line 33). In line 36, it initializes Tk and makes Tk commands available.

Tcl_AppInit then initializes all application specific commands. In this case, you want cubed to be included. You make a call to the Tcl_CreateObjCommand in lines 45–46. This is how you compile and link your application-specific commands as an integral part of your own Tcl interpreter. If you don't want the BLT package, omit that line.

> You can use tclAppInit.c if you only want to extend Tcl commands. You will need to retain line 36 if you want to use Tk widgets.

Finally in line 48, Tcl_AppInit defines an application start-up script: a tcl_RcFileName to be used for interactive execution of the application. In this case, the start-up script is called .swishrc.

To compile and link this, you need to copy it into your current working directory. An example makefile is given in Listing 22.5. This is a minimal version which gives you a template for UNIX systems. This is tested on a Solaris operating system. You might need to customize it for your system. If you want to use Builder tools such as Visual C++ Builder in a PC, consult the appropriate manual. Please note that you need to customize the directory path of TCLTK and XPATH for your system. Also note that the initial spacing in lines 11 and 13 should be tabs and not spaces. You will get a fatal error if you use spaces.

LISTING 22.5   Makefile for `tkAppinit.c`

```
 1: TCLTK = /u/ls/tcltk/solaris
 2: XPATH = /usr/local/openwin
 3: BLT_LIB = $(TCLTK)/blt/lib/libBLT.a
 4: INCS = -I$(XPATH)/include -I$(TCLTK)/include \
 5: -I$(TCLTK)/blt/include
 6: LIBS = -L$(TCLTK)/lib -ltcl8.1 -ltk8.1 -lX11 -lm
 7:
 8: CFLAGS = -g -Xc $(INCS)
 9:
10: .c.o:
11:     $(CC)  -c $(CFLAGS)    $*.c
12: swish: tkAppInit.o
13:     $(CC) -o swish tkAppInit.o $(BLT_LIB) $(LIBS)
```

You need to have downloaded and installed BLT.

The `*_Init` must be in this form, with a capital I used for the `Init` part. The first letter of the prefix should be capitalized, too.

Do	**Don't**
Do remember that commands and variable names are resolved by searching first in the current namespace and then in the global namespace. A search for a namespace is restricted to the current namespace. **Do** prefix your own commands/extensions/packages with a suitable name beginning with a capital letter and trailing lowercase letters.	**Don't** forget that `::` is not allowed in command and variable names, except in the context of qualifying these. **Don't** forget to use `package require packageName` and `package forget packageName` when you want to use or discontinue the use of a named package, if you are dynamically loading these into your Tcl session. **Don't** forget that `namespace import namespaceName::*` will import only those commands that `namespaceName` has exported using the `namespace export ?pattern?` command.

22

Summary

In this hour, you learned the Tcl namespace and package commands. Namespace commands enable you to create, to access, and to manipulate variables and commands in Tcl/Tk extension libraries and packages without conflict. Namespaces encapsulate the variables and commands of each namespace within that namespace. The package commands enable you to dynamically load and use Tcl/Tk extensions in your current interpreter and make the variables and procedures of these packages available to your applications. You also learned how to extend the Tcl interpreter using the compile and link method. This method allows you to embed a Tcl interpreter in your application. You will want to compile and link when your application code is the major portion of your code, with Tcl/Tk used as a GUI interface to your application commands.

For most applications, you will not need to adopt this compile and link method. Most Tcl/Tk extensions are now available as precompiled shared object libraries that you can download and install. This means you can use the package commands and dynamically load these. The examples in this hour taught you how to do this for the package BLT, which you will use in the next hour, "Using Tcl/Tk Extensions."

Q&A

Q When do I use the compile and link method?

A The dynamic loading of packages and extensions using the Tcl package commands has largely eliminated the need to extend the Tcl interpreter using the compile and link method. However, if your application draws heavily on application-specific source code, and you are only using Tcl/Tk to provide a GUI and a scripting interface, you might want to embed the Tcl interpreter in your application. If, for some reason, your system does not support the creation and use of dynamic or shared object libraries (.dll and .so files), you might have to resort to the compile and link method.

Q What is the difference between the load method and the compile and link method?

A Very little in practice. In both cases, you are instructing the Tcl interpreter to recognize and execute new commands. All commands, including the interpreter itself, are specified in source code form, which is translated into binary code using compilation and linking. In the load method, you specify that the extension is available to the interpreter as dynamic or shared object libraries. In the compile and link method, this binary code is part of the interpreter.

Q Do I create packages only if I am developing commands in C or C++?

A No, you can create extensions or packages of any reusable component consisting of binary modules as well as pure Tcl/Tk scripts.

Workshop

The following "Quiz" section is designed to provide you with an opportunity to recall some of the important concepts introduced in this hour. These might be commands, command syntax, common mistakes, usage, and so on. The "Exercises" section helps you consolidate the material you learned via an example of practical value, especially because you will be using the two popular extensions BLT and Expect in Hour 23, "Using Tcl/Tk Extensions." The answers to the quiz that follows can be found in Appendix A, "Answers to Quizzes."

Quiz

1. What is a namespace?
2. What do the namespace commands do?
3. What does the command namespace import `namespaceName::*` do?
4. What environment variables can you set to get the auto-loader and package-loader to search for your extensions.
5. What does the command package `require -exact packageName` do?
6. What does the command package `provide packageName ?version` do?

Exercises

Solutions to the exercises are on the CD-ROM that accompanies this book.

1. Download the latest versions of Expect5.30, and BLT2.4 and install them. Note that Expect is version incompatible with Tcl/Tk 8.1 as of the writing of this book. Try the dynamic loading method to use this package with Tcl/Tk 8.0.

2. Optional: Build the compile and link example of extending the Tcl interpreter with BLT 2.4.

3. Download the [incr Tcl], [incr Tk], and [incr Widgets] extensions. These are available as .dll for PC platforms. The UNIX installation is well-documented and straightforward. Start a itkwish3.0 application. Execute the command package require `::Iwidgets` to load the [incr Iwidgets] package into the itkwish interpreter. Execute the command namespace import `iwidgets::*` to import all the exported [incr Iwidgets] commands.

HOUR 23

Using Tcl/Tk Extensions

In the last hour, "Adding Tcl/Tk Extensions," you learned about adding extensions to the Tcl/Tk interpreter. In this hour, you will learn to use some of these valuable extensions. We chose the two extensions to be discussed based on their utility. The first one is BLT, which contains several useful widgets for graphing and creating simple hyper-text–based applications. The second extension is called Expect. It helps you automate interactions with an interactive program such as ftp and telnet.

In this hour, you will learn

- Graphing with BLT
- Talking to Matlab using Expect
- Developing simple applications using these extensions

What Is BLT?

BLT, developed by George Howlett, is one of the popular extensions to Tcl/Tk. It introduces several convenient widgets that produce plots for data visualization, a vector object for manipulating a set of numbers as a single entity, a simple hypertext type widget, and more. BLT is not an acronym for anything. In its author's own words it can be, "Whatever you want it to." (*Bacon, Lettuce, and Tomato* has been suggested!)

We cannot do full justice to the topic in only one hour. However, we can look at a typical application that exploits some of the important features of BLT. We will focus mainly on the graph widget and only touch on vector objects for manipulating sets of real numbers.

The Graph Widget

The graph widget is developed in the spirit of a Tk widget. You have a command to create the widget (optionally specifying several attribute-value pairs), and associated widget action subcommands. The graph widget introduces one additional layer called *components* for manipulating entities such as axes, curves, and so on. The eight components are shown in Figure 23.1.

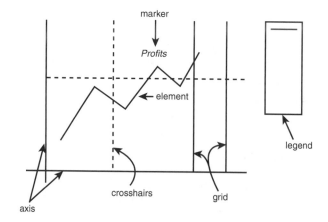

FIGURE 23.1

Components of a graph widget. The pen and postscript components are not shown.

The action subcommands are attached to the components of a graph widget and are invoked in the same way as any Tk widget. The structure of a graph widget command is shown in Listing 23.1.

LISTING 23.1 The Structure of a Graph Widget Command: `w` `component`
`actionSubCommand Option Value`

```
pack [graph .g]
.g element create c1 -xdata {1 2 3} -ydata {1 4 9}
.g axis config x -majorticks {1 2 3}
.g element config c1 -pixels 3 ;# marker size
.g grid config -hide no          ;# show grid
```

23

All action subcommands associated with a component can be listed at the
interpreter. For example, if g is the name of the graph widget, the command
`.g element` will list all the available action subcommands for the component
`element`.

Developing an Application for Data Visualization

To illustrate the power of BLT, consider the data set consisting of the mean temperatures
of central England since 1659 (available at `http://www.meto.gov.uk/sec5/CR_div/`
`UK_Climate/index.html`). The data is arranged as a table. Column 1 denotes the year,
columns 2–12 are average temperatures for the month, and column 13 shows the average
for the year. The temperature data is available for the past 341 years, making this the
longest-kept temperature record since instrumental recording of data started. You want to
build a simple visualization tool to peruse the data.

For this example, define your task as follows: Display all the years in a scrollable list
box. For a selected year, display 10 contiguous years' data to provide a quick comparison. Next, display the legend and make it sensitive. That means when the user clicks on
an item in the legend, the corresponding curve is highlighted to distinguish it from the
clutter. The code is shown in Listing 23.2, and the corresponding graph, together with the
GUI, is shown in Figure 23.2.

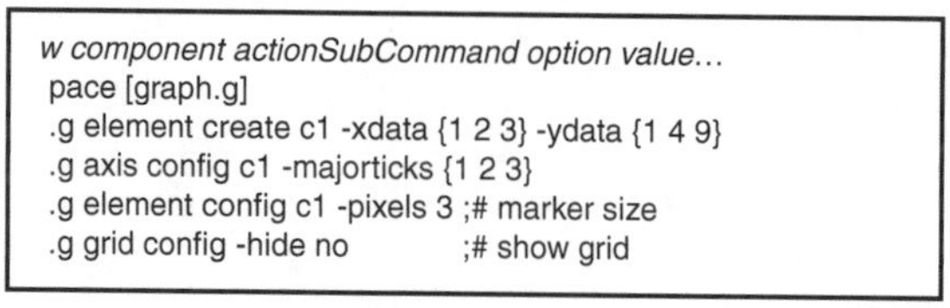

FIGURE 23.2

Visualization of average monthly temperature data.

```
w component actionSubCommand option value...
pace [graph.g]
.g element create c1 -xdata {1 2 3} -ydata {1 4 9}
.g axis config c1 -majorticks {1 2 3}
.g element config c1 -pixels 3 ;# marker size
.g grid config -hide no          ;# show grid
```

LISTING 23.2   Visualizing Monthly Temperature Data

```
 1: # Plot temperature data 1659-1999
 2: # data courtesy
 3: # http://www.meto.gov.uk/sec5/CR_div/UK_Climate/index.html
 4: # read the file
 5: set fh [open ./mly_cet_ext.txt]
 6:
 7: gets $fh titleLine
 8: # just skip next 8 lines
 9:
10: for {set i 1} {$i<=8} {incr i} {
11:     gets $fh skipLine
12: }
13: # ... now comes the data
14: #     put it in an array DATA(year) { val1    .... val13 }
15: #     val13 is the annual average
16:
17: while { [gets $fh dataLine]>=0 } {
18:     set year [lindex $dataLine 0]
19:     set DATA($year) [lrange $dataLine 1 end] ;# include the average as well
20: }
21:
22: close $fh
23:
24: # now create some widgets
25: frame .f
26: listbox .f.lb -width 6 \
27:        -yscrollcommand ".f.sb set"
28: scrollbar .f.sb -orient vertical -command ".f.lb yview"
29: pack .f.sb .f.lb -side left -fill y
30: pack .f
31:
32: set g [graph .f.g -title $titleLine]
33: pack $g -side left
34: # button frame
35: #
36: frame .bf -bd 2 -background lightblue
37: button .bf.qb -text Quit -command { exit }
38: label .bf.info -bg lightblue \
39:        -text {Click on a legend item to display the annual mean.} \
40:        -textvariable meanInfo
41: pack .bf.qb -side right
42: pack .bf.info -side left
```

```
43: pack .bf -fill x
44:
45: # fill the list box with years
46: #    you need to sort them, otherwise they will appear
47: #    in a peculiar order
48: foreach n [lsort [array names DATA]] {
49:     .f.lb insert end $n
50: }
51: # plot data starting from a given year
52:
53: proc plotData { g y0 } {
54:     global DATA
55:     # pick ten years from the base year y0
56:     set years {}
57:     for {set y $y0} {$y<[expr $y0+10]} {incr y} {
58:        if { $y > 1999 } {
59:            break
60:        } else {
61:            lappend years $y
62:        }
63:     }
64:     # delete any previous elements
65:     #
66:     foreach e [$g element names] {
67:        $g element delete $e
68:     }
69:
70:     # we use $y itself for the element label.
71:     #   that is what is used in the legend.
72:     #
73:     set months {1 2 3 4 5 6 7 8 9 10 11 12}
74:     foreach y $years {
75:        set tVals $DATA($y)
76:        $g element create $y -xdata $months -ydata $tVals
77:        $g element configure $y -pixels 3
78:     }
79:     # configure axisNames
80:     # by default we get x and y
81:     $g axis config x -majorticks $months
82:     $g axis config y -majorticks {0 5 10 15 20}
83:     $g grid configure -hide no
84: }
85:
86: plotData $g 1980
87:
88:
89: # use the BLT library procedures for zooming etc.
90: Blt_Crosshairs $g
91: Blt_ActiveLegend $g
```

continues

LISTING 23.2   continued

```
92: Blt_ZoomStack $g
93: Blt_ClosestPoint $g
94:
95: # provide a binding to display the mean
96:
97: proc dispMean { n } {
98:     global DATA meanInfo
99:     # compute the mean for the year
100:    set yVals [set DATA($n)]
101:    regsub -all — {-99.[9]+} $yVals {} yVals
102:    vector yy ;# define a temporary vector item
103:    vector ans ;# to hold the standard deviation
104:               ;# needs to be a vector object
105:    yy set $yVals
106:    set m [set yy(mean)]
107:    ans expr sdev(yy)
108:    set std $ans(0)
109:    # now we are done with it, destroy it.
110:    vector destroy yy
111:    vector destroy ans
112:    set meanInfo "Year: $n Mean: $m Std: $std"
113: }
114:
115: # link up legend and meanInfo
116:
117: proc activeLegend { graph } {
118:    $graph legend bind all <Enter> [list blt::ActivateLegend $graph]
119:    $graph legend bind all <Leave> [list blt::DeactivateLegend $graph]
120:    $graph legend bind all <Button-1> [list showMean $graph]
121:    $graph legend bind all <ButtonRelease-1> [list restore $graph]
122: }
123:
124: proc showMean { graph } {
125:    set elt [$graph legend get current]
126:    $graph element config $elt -color red
127:    dispMean $elt
128: }
129:
130: proc restore { graph } {
131:    set elt [$graph legend get current]
132:    $graph element config $elt -color #000080
133: }
134:
135: activeLegend $g
```

ANALYSIS You need to make sure that BLT is loaded into the interpreter. You can check this with the command package names or info loaded. After BLT is loaded, you import the BLT namespace with the command namespace import blt::*, and then type source list23_01.tcl in the interpreter. Note that if you are using the interpreter that comes with the BLT distribution, the package is loaded. You only import the namespace. For further details on package and namespace commands, see Hour 22, "Adding Tcl/Tk Extensions."

In lines 5–22, you read the data file and store the required values in an array DATA. The layout of the interface is defined in lines 25–43. In line 32, you create the graph widget. The listbox is filled with data in lines 48–50. For convenience, define a procedure plotData, which takes the graph widget's name and the base year. In lines 56–63, you collect the years you are interested in. Care is taken, in lines 58–62, to collect only those years for which the data is available.

Now focus on the graph widget's action subcommands. A curve is displayed using the component element and the action subcommand create. For example, line 76 draws a curve in the plotting area, using the data specified in -xdata and -ydata. Each element is also given a name for future reference. In this example, you use the year itself as the name of the element ($y). The default size, used by BLT for data points, is somewhat large. Change it, in line 77, using the option -pixels. Repeat this process for all the curves you are interested in, using a foreach loop (lines 74–78). Additional customization is shown in lines 81–83. Finally, invoke your procedure plotData in line 86, using the year 1980 as your base year. That is all. You will take care of curve highlighting later.

BLT provides some useful utility procedures (found under the Tcl/lib/blt2.4 subdirectory of where BLT is installed), and these are demonstrated in lines 90–93. The procedures are fairly self-explanatory, and we now move on to learn about vector objects.

A *vector* in BLT is a set of numbers that are indexed using integers and can be manipulated as a single entity. To illustrate some of the operations using BLT vectors, extend the previous example a bit further. You want to display the mean and standard deviation of the data for a given year. Typically, when the user clicks on an item in the agenda, you want to display that year's mean and standard deviation. While doing that, you can also change the color of the curve for the duration the <Button-1> is pressed. The procedures showMean and dispMean do this job. How do you compute mean? You create a vector object yy (line 102) and populate it with required data (line 105).

The mean is computed in two ways in BLT—using a special index or using the action subcommand expr. Line 106 uses the special index mean to get the mean of the data in yy. Standard deviation is computed using the expr action subcommand in line 107. Some of these action subcommands have a nasty habit of storing the result in the vector itself (if you try yy expr sdev(yy)), thus destroying the original vector components. For this purpose, you can use an auxiliary vector, ans, (line 103) to store your standard deviation. Now you can destroy the vector objects (lines 110–111). You pass the mean and standard deviation to your interface through the -textvariable meanInfo of the label (line 40).

You must now make the legend sensitive. This is achieved with the help of BLT utilities in lines 118–119. You hook up the procedures showMean and restore as callbacks to the tag bindings of the legend component of the graph widget $g. Note that the <Button-1> event triggers the procedure showMean, which also changes the color of the curve. <ButtonRelease-1> invokes the restore procedure. You can see that, apart from this additional layer of the component, the graph widget is just like any other Tk widget.

What Is Expect?

Expect, developed by Don Libes, is a program to control interactive applications. It is one of the earliest extensions to Tcl/Tk. Using Expect, you can automate interactive programs such as ftp and telnet. We cannot explore the full potential of Expect in these few pages. However, a few examples will give you some idea of this extension. Consult the book *Exploring Expect,* by Don Libes, for an excellent exposition of the topic.

To illustrate Expect,, we will use the popular interactive program, Matlab (http://www.mathworks.com). Matlab is widely used for scientific computing and is ideal for problems that involve matrix manipulations, which includes practically every engineering discipline.

> There are other ways of embedding Matlab into Tcl/Tk. If you are serious about embedding Matlab functionality into your GUI, consider using Swig (Simplified Wrapper and Interface Generator, http://www.swig.org) developed by David M. Beazley.

The Expect program offers two shells—expect (similar to tclsh) and expectk (analogous to wish). First, look at a simple interactive session with Expect. All the examples in this section are run on a Unix platform. The dialogue is shown in Listing 23.3.

LISTING 23.3 An Interactive Session Using Expect

```
1: neuman% expect
2: expect1.1> spawn matlab
3: spawn matlab
4: 4950
5: expect1.2> expect -re ">>"
6:
```

```
 7:                        < M A T L A B >
 8:            Copyright 1984-1999 The MathWorks, Inc.
 9:                     Version 5.3.0.10183 (R11)
10:                          Jan 21 1999
11:
12:
13: This version of MATLAB, SIMULINK and all the proprietary toolboxes, are
14: licensed under an educational licence and as such are subject to the
    ➥following restriction on use: ....some material deleted.....
15:
16:
17: >> expect1.3> exp_send "a = rand(3,3) \r"
18: expect1.4> expect -re ">>"
19: a = rand(3,3)
20:
21: a =
22:
23:     0.9501    0.4860    0.4565
24:     0.2311    0.8913    0.0185
25:     0.6068    0.7621    0.8214
26:
27: >> expect1.5> exp_send "eig( rand(4,4) ) \r"
28: expect1.6> expect -re ">>"
```

ANALYSIS   At the Unix prompt, invoke the `Expect` program (line 1). Be sure you have the correct paths for your environment. At the Expect prompt, invoke the interactive program. In this example, you are invoking `Matlab` (line 2). The `spawn` command returns the process ID for the `Matlab`. You can use this number to kill the process later. Matlab uses the >> prompt to accept commands. So, tell Expect to wait for this prompt in line 5. When the Expect program receives this (regular expression) pattern, the output from the Matlab program is echoed back to the standard output. In line 17, you send a command to the Matlab interpreter and wait for it. You absolutely must include the return \r at the end of the command in line 8. If you don't, nothing is executed by Matlab until it receives \r. You can continue the dialog in this way.

It is more interesting to run this as a script file. In the interactive use, the Expect program times itself out after a certain period, if it gets no response from the other program. When running this as a script, it is useful to override the timeout and wait until you get a response. You must also learn how to retrieve the results from the other program. The process of collecting output by pattern matching is illustrated in Listing 23.4.

LISTING 23.4   An Expect Script to Work with Matlab

```
 1: #!/usr/local1/bin/expectk
 2: # simple example
 3:
 4: set timeout -1
 5: set mid [spawn matlab]
 6: expect -re "(.*)"
 7: expect -re ">>"
 8: exp_send "a = \[1 -1;2 1\]; \r"
 9: expect -re ">>"
10: exp_send "ai = inv(a) \r"
11: expect -re ">>"
12: expect -re "\n(.*)\n"
13: set result $expect_out(0,string)
14: # process the result string
15: regexp "ai =\r(.*)" $result ma aa
16: puts "Inverse of matrix a is "
17: puts $result
18: puts $aa
19: # now kill matlab
20: exec kill $mid
21: exit
```

ANALYSIS   For this script to work, you must override the `timeout` as shown in line 4. In this example, you want to send a matrix to Matlab for finding its inverse. You first collect the initial header from Matlab as in line 6 and then wait for the prompt as in line 7. Send the matrix and the command to invert the matrix in lines 8–11, and wait for the prompt. Expect stores the recently matched pattern in a Tcl array `expect_out`. In this case, the string matching `\n(.*)\n` is stored in `expect_out(0,string)`. The regular expression matches a typical output from Matlab. (Subpatterns are stored in `1, string`, and so forth.) Now, you can process the result to extract the information you want for further processing in Expect.

This example can be wrapped up in a GUI (see Figure 23.3). The code is shown in Listing 23.5.

FIGURE 23.3
Talking to Matlab via
the Tk interface.

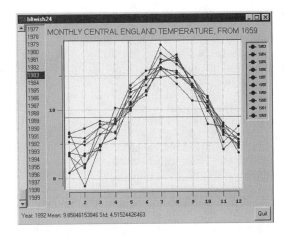

23

LISTING 23.5   Wrapping Matlab Interaction in a GUI

```
 1: #!/usr/local1/bin/expectk
 2: frame .f
 3: pack .f
 4: label .f.la -text "Enter matrix"
 5: entry .f.e  -width 15
 6: pack .f.la .f.e -side left
 7: bind .f.e <Return> sendToMatlab
 8: text .t -width 20 -height 20
 9: pack .t -fill x
10: frame .bf -bd 2 -bg lightblue
11: pack .bf -fill x
12: button .bf.matlab -text StartMatlab -command initMatlab
13: button .bf.quit -text Quit -command exit
14: pack .bf.matlab -side left
15: pack .bf.quit -side right
16:
17: proc initMatlab {} {
18:         # start matlab
19:         global matSID
20:         set timeout -1
21:         set mid [spawn matlab]
22:         expect -re "(.*)\r\n"      ;# header info
23:         expect -re ">>"
24:         .t insert end "$expect_out(0,string) \n"
25:         .bf.matlab config -text ExitMatlab -command "exec kill $mid"
26: }
27:
28: proc sendToMatlab {} {
29:         global matSID
30:         set timeout -1
31:         set spawn_id $matSID
```

continues

LISTING 23.5   continued

```
32:        set m [.f.e get]
33:        exp_send "mInv = inv($m) \r" ;# don't suppress output by using ;
34:        expect -re "\n(.*)\n"
35:        .t delete 1.0 end
36:        set result $expect_out(0,string)
37:        # process the result string
38:        regexp "mInv =\r(.*)" $result ma aa
39:        regsub -all "\r" $aa {} a2
40:        puts "Inverse of matrix a is "
41:        .t insert end "Inverse of the matrix is: \n"
42:        .t insert end "$a2 \n"
43: }
```

ANALYSIS   The guts of the program are very similar to that of Listing 23.4, except for the additional widgets and a couple of procedures. The only important point is that the scope of the variables `timeout` and `spawn_id` is local. When you are sending some command to Matlab from a `proc`, be sure of the value of `spawn_id`.

Do	**DON'T**
Do remember that graph widget has components.	**Don't** forget to kill the processes you have spawned.
Do remember that arithmetic on vector objects is performed using the action subcommand `expr`.	
Do use the `timeout` variable when interacting with programs that might take some time.	

Summary

In this hour, you looked at two extensions, namely BLT and Expect. BLT is an ideal extension for graphing applications. It also adds dozens of other valuable widgets, which were not fully covered here. The other important widget (or object) BLT introduces is a `vector` object. A `vector` object is useful when dealing with a large array of numbers, typically on the order of thousands. The online documentation contains a good introduction to BLT widgets. It can be found under `Directory-where-BLT-is-installed/Tcl/lib/blt2.4/html`.

The other extension briefly illustrated was Expect. This extension is useful while automating interactions with interactive programs. As stated in the beginning, we can only give you a taste of these extensions. For a more detailed exposure to these valuable extensions, consult the documentation that comes with the software.

After this lesson, you should be fully aware of what can be done using Tcl/Tk extensions. A topic of current interest is how to work with the Web in a seamless fashion. What about publishing your code on the Web? That is your task in the next hour, "Building Web-Based Applications with Tcl/Tk."

23

Q&A

Q Can I run Expect on NT machines?

A Yes. There is a version available at `http://bmrc.berkeley.edu/people/ chaffee/expectnt.html`. Note that this version works with Tcl/Tk 8.0 only.

Q Are there other alternatives to talking to programs on PCs?

A One useful alternative to Expect on PC platforms is the package `dde`. It stands for Dynamic Data Exchange and is distributed with Tcl/Tk. You can use this package to send and retrieve data from programs running on the PCs. To give you a flavor of the package, you can try the following lines at the Tcl interpreter to talk to, say, Matlab. Make sure that Matlab is running before typing these lines.

```
dde execute MATLAB Engine {a = rand(3,3)}
dde execute MATLAB Engine "aInv = inv($a)"
set result [dde request MATLAB Engine {mInv}]
```

The `dde` command requires a service name and a topic name. For Matlab, these are shown in the previous code. You can use this package to talk to other programs such as Word, Excel, and so on. Refer to the documentation regarding service and topic names.

Another powerful alternative is the client-server approach using sockets. This approach can be implemented using the Tcl `socket` command. It offers a considerable amount of flexibility.

Workshop

The "Quiz" section is designed to provide you with an opportunity to recall some of the important concepts introduced in this hour. These may be commands, command syntax, common mistakes, usage, and so on. The "Exercises" section helps you consolidate the material you learned via an example of practical value. Our aim is that these two sections should reinforce the knowledge you have gained in this hour. The answers to the quiz that follows can be found in Appendix A, "Answers to Quizzes."

Quiz

1. What are the components of a graph widget?

2. How do you display the available action subcommands of a graph widget's components?

3. How do you define a vector object whose elements are 1 0 1 in BLT?

4. If x is a vector with elements 1 2 3, what does the command
   `set m [set x(mean)]` return?

5. How do you submit a command to a spawned process?

Exercises

Solutions to the exercises are on the CD-ROM that accompanies this book.

1. Using the graph widget, plot the graphs of `sin(x)` and `cos(x)` for x varying between $-\pi$ to π, and show them as red and green curves, respectively.

2. Modify Listing 23.2 so that when the user-selected year in the list box is used as the base year, temperatures for the following nine years are collected and shown in the graph widget.

3. Interact with the Unix program bc (arbitrary-precision arithmetic language) using Expect.

Hour **24**

Building Web-Based Applications with Tcl/Tk

The World Wide Web (WWW or the Web) has become an integral part of the desktop, providing a common interface for accessing information distributed on servers across the world. The Web has also rapidly established itself as a powerful mass communication medium for application developers and users. This has been achieved via the *applet* mechanism. An applet is an application that is embedded within a Web page, and, on request, it will be downloaded and executed within your Web browser such as Netscape Navigator, provided it can support such an execution.

Plug-ins are the general mechanisms that the browsers employ to provide this support, especially for specialized applications and data in special formats. When the browser encounters an embedded special word or key, it invokes the associated plug-in to process the embedded directive, usually by executing an application within the browser or displaying some data. There are plug-ins for all sorts of things, and yes, you guessed it; there is a plug-in for Tcl/Tk too! The Tcl/Tk applets, quite aptly, are called *tclets* (pronounced ticklets).

Another way of exploiting the power of Tcl in the context of Web-based applications is to use it for developing *Common Gateway Interface (CGI)* scripts. CGI scripts are scripts that enable you to create Web pages dynamically. CGI scripts process data received from a Web client as a string and create customized Web pages in response.

In this hour, you will learn

- The reasons for using Tcl/Tk with the Web
- The requirements for embedding tclets and the schematics of their execution
- How to create tclets
- How to pass additional parameters to the embedded application
- An overview of CGI
- How to use Tcl as CGI

Tcl/Tk and the Web

Languages such as Java and JavaScript have been specially designed to provide scripting facilities to be used with the Web. So a natural concern will be the benefits of using Tcl and Tk with the Web. To be honest, it is primarily a question of your choice, the language you are familiar with, and the development specification of your application. However, if you have the option to make the choice, it is worth noting that

- tclets don't require the precompilation that Java requires, thereby rendering them customizable and dynamic.
- Tcl/Tk is much easier and quicker to learn.
- The Tk widgets provide a wider range of powerful GUI components than the Java toolkit AWT.
- You can opt to add digital signatures to your tclet. This allows you to use the full range of Tcl/Tk commands in your tclet. The end user is given the opportunity to note the signature and make the decision to trust your application and run it.

If your choice is to develop a tclet, or to use Tcl as a CGI scripting language, the rest of this hour illustrates the basics.

Using Tcl/Tk Plug-in

The Tcl plug-in is very special in that it contains a full implementation of Tcl and Tk and therefore is *programmable*. As a result, you can embed applications based on core Tcl/Tk, barring certain commands in your Web page.

When you request to view a Web page with an embedded tclet, the Web reference provides the browser with information on the source for the Tcl/Tk application as well as the height and width requirements for the execution of the application within the browser. Additional data can also be passed. The browser downloads both the Web page requested and the tclet. The MIME type *application/x-tcl* returned with the HTML and the tclet enables the browser to delegate the execution of the tclet to the Tcl plug-in. When invoked, the plug-in Tcl interpreter starts a slave interpreter to execute the Tcl application.

Figure 24.1 shows the schematic diagram of this operation. The slave interpreter operates on a restricted environment. The exclusion of certain commands for this slave interpreter guarantees that the execution does not cause any security violation.

> Several security policies can be implemented. Refer to the documentation available at http://www.scriptics.com/products/tcltk/plugin/faq.html.

24

FIGURE 24.1
A schematic diagram of your Web browser and a tclet.

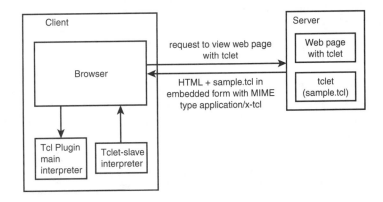

> You can check whether you have the Tcl Plug-in by using the Help menu of your browser and selecting About Plugins. Popular browsers such as Netscape and Internet Explorer automatically prompt whether you want a plug-in, in case you do not have it installed already. Consult the preceding URL for more information.

Embedding tclets

Embedding tclets in your Web page is quite straightforward. You can create an HTML document with an *embed* tag. The embed tag specifies the complete path of a tclet *source* and two other parameters, a *height* and a *width*. When the client browser requests to view this HTML page, your server will dispatch this HTML document and the tclet source.

The browser will recognize the MIME type, and—assuming that you have the plug-in—the browser will invoke the plug-in to interpret the tclet. At this point, the interpreter will use the parameters *height* and *width* to embed the root window of your tclet (the Tcl application) within the Web page. You can learn these rudimentary steps via the example in Listings 24.1 and 24.2.

LISTING 24.1   A Hello World tclet—HTML

```
1: <html> <head>
2: <title>My First Tclet ...</title>
3: </head>
4: <body>
5: <h1>A button with a smile</h1>
6: <embed src=list1.tcl width=80 height=30> </embed>
7: </body> </html>
```

ANALYSIS   This is an HTML file with its familiar syntax. In the unlikely chance that you might be unfamiliar with this syntax, let us reassure you that it is easy to follow this analysis and mimic the syntax for the present. We will perform a quick run-through of the HTML for the purpose of making this analysis self-contained.

Web pages are written using HTML. It allows you to associate special tags to markup textual strings to indicate some structure or special formatting. It is immediately obvious that the tag terminology and usage are not dissimilar to their use with the Tk canvas items and text widget contents. The general syntax of an HTML tag is <tagName parameters>text string</tagName>. Tags are not case sensitive and come in pairs. The open tag might have parameters; for instance, the anchor tag A has the parameter REF, which refers to a URL (uniform resource locator). The close tag has a / before the tag name. It is up to your browser to parse the HTML.

Line 1 identifies the start of the HTML syntax with the <html> tag and follows it with the <head> tag. This tag ensures that the title "My first tclet" will appear on the root window title bar of your browser when you view this Web page. At the end of line 2, we close the title tag with </title> and do the same for the </head> tag.

No, we haven't finished with tags yet! Within the <body> in line 4 and </body> in line 7, we define the simplest Web page you can think of. It has just two instructions. The first defines a level one heading, "A button with a smile", for the page itself within <h1> and </h1>. Line 6 is of particular interest to us. As we noted earlier, the embed tag identifies the source for the tclet. In this case, the script file list1.tcl happens to reside within the same machine, in the same directory. In fact, the tclet can be in any server anywhere in the world.

We want the root window of our first tclet to be fully embedded within the browser, occupying an area of 80 pixels by 30 pixels. The top image in Figure 24.2 shows the result. Click on that button, and you will see its label change to "Smile!" as shown in the bottom image of Figure 24.2.

Our next task is to define our simple tclet. Listing 24.2 does just that.

LISTING 24.2   A Hello World tclet—Tcl

```
1: # list1.tcl
2: # button with a smile
3: button .b -text {Hello World!} \
4:     -command {.b config -text {Smile!}}
5: pack .b
```

24

ANALYSIS   The preceding code creates a simple button with the -text option set to "Hello World!" and the -command option set to reconfigure the -text option to "Smile!" In line 5, the button is packed.

FIGURE 24.2

A tclet in Netscape browser.

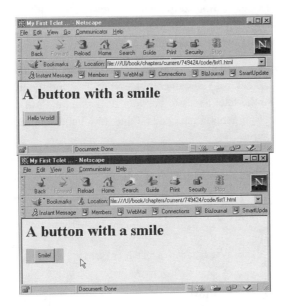

Instead of the embed tag, if you specify the tclet with the A tag, the browser will still invoke the plug-in to execute the tclet. However, in this case, the entire browser will be used as the root window of the tclet.

Embedded Input Arguments

It is great that you can turn almost all your Tcl scripts into tclets, and we actively encourage you to do so. All you need to do is to slightly modify Listing 24.1 to provide new source, width, and height.

Some restrictions exist. Refer to the Q&A section to learn more about them.

We stated that you could embed most Tcl scripts as tclets. It is likely that you might want to create Web pages that embed someone else's tclets. For instance, you might have come across a Tk based visualization script that can be used to display your experimental data without having to develop this script yourself. If access to use the script is available, you can insert the full URL of the script in its original site.

There is no requirement that your Web page and the tclet have to be on the same machine or even on the same server. You can combine your data and the third-party tclet to create your Web page. So the tclet needs to get your data as input. You can pass this by embedding user-defined arguments. Listings 24.3 and 24.4 list a very simple application that illustrates this facility.

LISTING 24.3   Embedded Arguments—HTML

```
 1: <html> <head>
 2: <title>Embedded arguments</title>
 3: </head>
 4: <body>
 5: <h1>How do I display embedded arguments?</h1>
 6: <hr>
 7: <center>
 8: <embed src=list2.tcl width=300 height=150 myword="This is an example"
 9: dob="11-11-11" expiry_date="12-12-99">
10: </center>
11: <hr>
12: </body> </html>
```

ANALYSIS We will skip the explanation of the HTML tags, which are self-explanatory. We will focus on the embed tag in lines 8–9. The embed tag points to the source list2.tcl, which is located in the same directory and on the same server as the HTML file.

When the browser calls the plug-in, it creates an associative array called *embed_args*, which contains the argument value pairs of source, width, height, and any other name-value pair. It is from this array that the Tcl script gets and sets the dimensions of its main window. The embed-args in fact will hold the name value pairs enclosed in the embed tag. This is the mechanism you exploit to provide user supplied data. Listing 24.4 illustrates the use of this array.

LISTING 24.4   Embedded Arguments—Tcl

```
1: pack [text .t]
2: # display the embedded arguments in the text widget
3:
4: foreach n [array names embed_args] {
5:     .t insert end "name: $n \t its value is: $embed_args($n) \n"
6: }
```

24

ANALYSIS The purpose of this script is to display the name value pairs of the embedded input arguments. These values are simply displayed in a text widget .t using default options. Line 1 creates and packs the text widget .t. Lines 4–6 use the foreach loop to retrieve the name value pairs and append these at the end of current text in .t.

Note that in line 4, the action command array names retrieves the first half—that is, the name—in each name value pair of the associative array embed_args. To recall our earlier discussion of array commands, refer to Hour 6, "Exploring Arrays." We then use the retrieved name to index into the second half of the name value pair. Figure 24.3 shows the result of this tclet.

 Please read through the information available at the Sunscript Web site on the usage and customization of the Tcl Plug-in with both Netscape Communicator and Internet Explorer. In the examples here, we have used the Communicator. You can get the latest version of the Tcl plug-in from the resource section of the Scriptics Web site, http://www.scriptics.com.

FIGURE 24.3

*Embedded name value
arguments.*

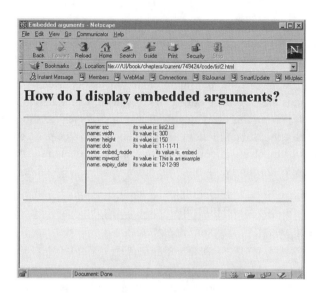

The Common Gateway Interface

You learned in the introduction to this hour that a CGI is a program to compute dynamic
Web pages. Most Web pages provide static or fixed information irrespective of how
many times they are viewed. In contrast, there are occasions when you are required to
create Web pages whose contents are created dynamically to provide up-to-date information. From the typical stocks and shares information applications to the multi-user,
multimedia distributed social applications of Microsoft Research (http://
vworlds.research.microsoft.com) are classic examples of dynamic Web pages.

> The term "dynamic" is not applied from a graphics or animation context.

Just as in the case of the plug-in, here you have a script to process a user's input and the
associated Web pages. Usually you create a Web page with some form to collect input
from the user. When the user submits this input, the browser collates the input into a single string and invokes the CGI script referred to under the action tag. It also passes the
user input to the script.

The CGI standard defines how the input is formatted by the browser and therefore how
the input is interpreted by the CGI script. The CGI program simply writes the results
to the standard output. It is the responsibility of the Web server to deliver the output to

the Web client. The standard also defines how to send, and therefore identify, images and plain or specially formatted text in the result that the CGI returns.

> For further information on using Tcl for CGI scripting, see Don Libes's paper "Writing CGI Scripts in Tcl" at http://expect.nist.gov/cgi.tcl (see under Documentation).

Let us explore a simple example here for you to understand how to create a Tcl CGI script. Listing 24.5 and Listing 24.6 provide the necessary code on a UNIX platform. The specifics of how to link up your CGI script to your site Web server is server dependent and is something your Web site administrator has to set up for you. Contact that person. She will set up a subdirectory for you under the CGI directory for the site.

24

LISTING 24.5   CGI—the HTML

```
 1: <html> <head>
 2: <title>A simple example using CGI</title>
 3: </head>
 4:
 5: <body>
 6: <h1>STY Tcl/Tk in 24 Hours - Feedback</h1>
 7: Please fill in the information requested below:<BR>
 8:
 9: <form action="http://neuman/cgi-bin/vs/stytcltk.tcl" method="POST">
10: <hr>
11: <CENTER>
12: <TABLE WIDTH="75%">
13: <TR><TD ALIGN=RIGHT>Name:<TD><input name="userName" size="20"><BR>
14: <TR><TD ALIGN=RIGHT>e-mail:<TD><input name="emailAddress" size="20"><BR>
15: <TR><TD ALIGN=RIGHT VALIGN=TOP>Comments:<TD>
16: <textarea name="comments" rows=4 cols=40>
17: </textarea>
18: </TABLE>
19:
20: <input type="SUBMIT" value="submit"><input type="RESET" value="reset">
21: </CENTER>
22: </form>
23:
24: <hr>
25: <address></address>
26: <!-- hhmts start -->
27: Last modified: Mon Aug 23 08:15:36 1999
28: <!-- hhmts end -->
29: </body> </html>
```

The Web page defined in this HTML solicits your name and email address and your comments on the *STY Tcl/Tk in 24 Hours*. We, the authors, have provided you with a free sample as a service! Let us focus on the salient lines of this code. The title "A simple example using CGI" will appear on the top window border of your Web browser. The Web page itself has a level 1 header telling you that this is the "STY Tcl/Tk in 24 Hours Feedback". A request to fill out the form below will be displayed in ordinary text font. Line 9 is where the specifics start. This line starts with the *form* tag. The parameter for this tag is *action*. It specifies the full URL for the CGI script to be invoked when the user submits the completed form.

You need to change the pathname in this example. list3.tcl is normally kept in your cgi-bin directory allocated by your Webmaster.

The METHOD parameter specifies how the input is passed to the CGI script as defined by the CGI standard. There are two options, POST and GET. In both cases, the name=value pairs are concatenated with special characters and + signs for blank spaces. With GET, this string gets appended to the URL and passed to the Web server. In the POST method, the string is placed in the standard input. It is up to the CGI script to read it.

The browsers support simple user interface (UI) components such as entry, button, and text widgets within a form. Note that these are not Tk widgets. In our simple form, we create two UI components of the type *input*, one for the name and another for email. We also create a UI component of type *textarea* that is four rows long and 40 columns wide. Comments are entered in the text area. We have created this user interface in a table element that occupies 75% of the width of your browser and is centered. First column entries are right aligned for additional visual appeal. The result is shown in Figure 24.4.

In line 20, we define two more input components, with built-in parameter types *SUMBIT* and *RESET* and values set to submit and reset. The syntax is fixed and carries special meaning. These input types define two UI buttons with labels *SUBMIT* and *RESET*, respectively. The value parameter has the effect of invoking the action submit or reset, depending on which button is pressed. The action is predefined within the browser. For *submit*, it generates the input string and invokes the CGI script specified as the value for the action parameter in line 9. We close the form in line 22. We have added some useful information at the end that indicates when the HTML file was last modified. The CGI script is listed in Listing 24.6.

FIGURE 24.4
CGI HTML page for
user input.

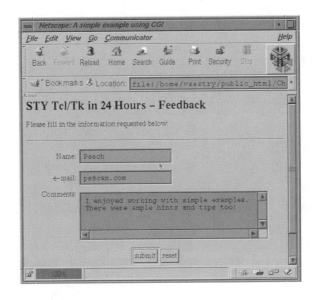

LISTING 24.6 CGI—the Script

```
 1: #!/usr/local/bin/tclsh
 2: # say what type of stuff is coming
 3:
 4: puts "Content-type: text/html\n"
 5: puts "\n"
 6: puts "<HTML>"
 7: puts "<HEAD>"
 8: puts "<TITLE>A Simple example of using Tcl for CGI scripting</TITLE>"
 9: puts "</HEAD>"
10:
11: puts "<BODY>"
12: puts "<H1>You entered ...</H1>"
13:
14: # get the data and process it
15:
16: if { [string compare $env(REQUEST_METHOD) "POST"] == 0 } {
17:     set formData [split [read stdin $env(CONTENT_LENGTH)] &]
18: } else {
19:     set formData [split $env(QUERY_STRING) &]
20: }
21:
22: #
23: foreach p $formData {
24:     regexp (.*)=(.*) $p match name value
25:     # replace + by spacee
```

continues

LISTING 24.6   continued

```
26:        regsub -all {\+} $value { } value
27:        # replace line delimiters by \n
28:        regsub -all {\%0D\%0A} $value "\n" value
29:        # prepare to process all %-escapes
30:        regsub -all {%([A-F0-9][A-F0-9])} $value {[format %c 0x\1]} value
31:        # now process %-escapes
32:        set value [subst $value]
33:        # store them in an array for further reference later
34:        set DATA($name) "$value"
35: }
36:
37: puts "<br><hr>"
38: foreach {n v} [array get DATA] {
39:        puts "DATA($n) \t = $v <br>"
40: }
41:
42: puts "Thank you $DATA(userName) for filling the form.<br>"
43:
44: puts "The time is : [clock format [clock seconds]]\n"
45: puts "<hr>"
46: puts "</BODY></HTML>"
```

ANALYSIS   A CGI program writes its results directly to the standard output. The primary task of the CGI is to generate an HTML document to acknowledge or confirm user input or display the results of some computation. The Web server handles the CGI's output to standard output and passes it to the client browser. The format tells the client browser how to handle the received result.

In Listing 24.6, our CGI script generates an HTML document. The first line starts up a Tcl session on a Unix platform where the tclsh is installed under /usr/local/bin. If you are using a UNIX platform and your tclsh is located elsewhere, provide the correct pathname. If you are using other platforms, remove this line as it is not applicable. Line 2 is a comment. Note that line 3 is an empty line because it is important that a blank line be output after the content header and before any other output from the CGI script. This is important. The server needs to send an empty line before the hypertext protocol. Line 4 tells the browser what type of data is being sent. Note that lines 1–12 are nothing more than a series of puts statements where the arguments are strings in HTML syntax. Each string will generate a formatted line of text in your browser.

Lines 16–20 read in the input. From the analysis of Listing 24.5, recall that the browser "POST"ed the input. That is, the input was sent to the standard input. Also recall that the browser formats the input with special characters when it concatenates all the input. The input is passed in HEX code. The Tcl global variable env holds the input parameters and their values.

The first task is to retrieve the environment variable REQUEST_METHOD and check its value. If it is POST, as shown in line 16, our second task is to execute the command read stdin $env(CONTENT_LENGTH) to read the input from stdin. For our third task, we use the embedded separator character & to split each name value pair and store them in formData. If the REQUEST_METHOD matches GET, our fourth task is to retrieve the contents of QUERY_STRING and use the split action command to split using & as the delimiter and store the resulting data in formData.

> The environment variables CONTENT_LENGTH, REQUEST_METHOD, and QUERY_STRING are defined by the CGI automatically for you when the browser acts upon submit. For additional environment variables, refer to any of the books on CGI listed in Appendix B.

The list formData consists of three elements:

```
userName=Peach
emailAddress=ps%40cam.com
andcomments=I+enjoyed+working+with+simple+examples.%0D%0AThere+were+
ample+hints+and+tips+too%21
```

The next task for the CGI is to process the formData list to extract each input item. Because each name value pair is of the format name=value, we exploit the Tcl regular expression pattern matching (line 24) to do this task. Our next task is to clean the strings stored in the variable value and replace any HEX code by its equivalent ASCII. Remember that the browser embeds the HEX symbols before passing the input to the server. Note that the special HEX coding embedded by the browser are %40 for @, %0D for \r, and %0A for \n. Blank spaces are replaced by +. The foreach loop defined between lines 23–35 achieves the translation of the HEX symbols back into ASCII, and stores the name-value pairs in an associative array DATA.

In lines 37–42, we generate some more puts statements to create the acknowledgement in HTML syntax. We are essentially repeating user's input and then appending a personalized thank you. Line 44 time-stamps the transaction. The remaining lines close the HTML tags. The resulting HTML page is shown in Figure 24.5.

Remember that you will need to have your own CGI facility set up to be able to run this example. Contact your system administrator. Also remember to execute your CGI script by executing the tclsh for your platform. The example here is tested on a UNIX platform. Ensure that you include the correct CGI source for the action parameter.

FIGURE 24.5

HTML created by CGI script in Listing 24.6.

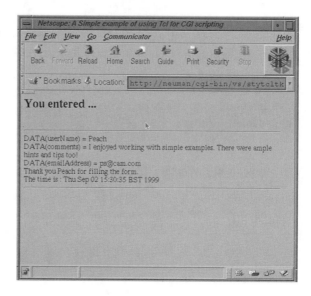

Form input is a potential security risk and needs to be checked thoroughly. In particular, do not take a form input and pass it as a parameter to any exec command. The input might contain embedded commands that either remove your files or copy some secure datafiles to the user's mailbox. In the Listing 24.6 example, we didn't check for any malicious input because it is used to illustrate the basic principle. You need to ensure that you do check for malicious input.

Do	**Don't**
Do remember that you need the Tcl Plug-in for using tclets.	**Don't** forget to get a cgi-bin subdirectory set up for you.
Do check the availability of the plug-in from your browser's Help menu and then About Plugins.	**Don't** pass user input directly to system commands, such as exec, in your CGI script.
Do remember that there are normally restrictions on what Tcl/Tk functions are used in tclets. Only core functions can be used.	

Summary

The World Wide Web has become the de facto medium of mass publication. In this hour, you learned how to embed your Tcl/Tk application in the Web using the Tcl Plug-in. You also learned how to use Tcl for developing the Common Gateway Interface. This allows you to create dynamic Web pages, especially in response to user input.

Learn about security policies and how to configure your plug-in without risking security. Adrian Zimmer's book, *Tcl/Tk for Programmers*, has a good chapter on this.

Also read the paper by Don Libes mentioned earlier in this hour.

This completes your essential learning of Tcl/Tk and its usage. We hope that you are by now a confident "tikkler" ready to join the 300,000 or so Tcl/Tk users out there! Good Luck!!

24

Q&A

Q How do I make use of the full power of Tcl/Tk in my tclets?

A The Tcl Plug-in is designed to protect your file system and privacy. A tclet cannot, in general, access your file system—even the file system of the server it came from—because it cannot connect to any other computer. It cannot create TCP/IP connections or send email. Each such restriction is known as a security policy. The script that executes and controls your Tcl Plug-in makes use of a set of configuration files, one for each set of security policies. You can customize these configuration files to allow greater access but be mindful of the security risk.

If you are a tclet developer who is keen to provide the full power of Tcl/Tk to your application, you can consider attaching a digital signature to your tclet. This allows the user to make an informed choice whether to allow greater access to your tclet. Scriptics Web site mentioned earlier and Adrian Zimmer's book, *Tcl/Tk for Programmers*, contain more information.

Q My Tcl script uses data files such as images. How do I turn it into a tclet without changing the plug-in security policies?

A For most applications, requiring a change in the Plug-in's security policy is unnecessary. Embed the contents of the data files in the script. For instance, the word scramble game you learned in Hour 11, "Adding Behavior to Your Widgets," is given here, with a sample of words from the word9.dat file included as an array. You can now use this as a tclet. If you want to include images, there are image data converters that can read your image files and generate the data string that make up that image. You can include that data string in your tclet as static data and use the Tcl image commands (Hour 17, "Working with Images in the Canvas") to dynamically recreate the image.

```
#The HTML
<html> <head>
<title>Unscramble the nine letter word</title>
</head>

<body>
<h1>Unscramble word</h1>

Unscramble the nine letter word. If you want a hint ... well, go ahead!

<hr>
<center>
<embed src=jumble.tcl width=280 height=150>
</center>

# jumble.tcl - as plugin
# see Chap. 11

label .la -text {Unscramble the nine letter word} \
    -justify left
proc getWord {} {
    set WORDS {
    accession acclimate accordion pageantry palladium
    paperback parachute paralysis patriotic pecuniary
    extrovert exquisite expensive excellent euphemism
    sagacious satellite scapegoat sclerosis segregant
    }
    set n [llength $WORDS]
    set i [expr (round(100*rand()) % $n)]
    return [lindex $WORDS $i]
}


proc jumble { word } {
    set chars [split $word {}]
    ;# get a number between 1 to 9
    ;# take care to avoid repetitions
    set jumbledWord {}
    ;# produce a list of length 9 of ints (0-8)
    ;# without repetitions
    set lind {}
    while { [llength $lind] < 9 } {
    set i [expr ( round(10*rand()) % 9 )]
    if { [lsearch -exact $lind $i] >= 0 } {
        ;# we already have the element
        continue
    } else {
        ;# we haven't got this, so ...
        lappend lind $i
    }
    }
```

```
    foreach k $lind {
    lappend jumbledWord [lindex $chars $k]
    }

    return $jumbledWord
}

label .word \
    -font {Helvetica -36 bold} \
    -bg lightblue \
    -relief groove

pack .la -anchor w
pack .word -anchor w
entry .e -width 9 -font {Helvetica -24 bold}
pack .e -anchor e
# you need the borderwidth to see the groove
frame .f -borderwidth 4 -relief groove
button .f.q -text Quit -command exit
button .f.n -text New  -command getNewWord
button .f.h -text Hint -command {giveHint $newWord}
label  .f.m -width 25  ;# to show a hint

pack .f.q .f.h .f.n -side right
pack .f.m -side right
pack .f -padx 2 -ipadx 2 -pady 2 -ipady 2 -fill x

proc getNewWord { } {
    ;# assume the file is opened
    global newWord
    .e delete 0 end
    .f.m configure -text {}
    .la configure -text {Unscramble the  nine letter word}
    set newWord [getWord]
    .word configure -text [jumble $newWord]

}

getNewWord
global newWord


bind .e <Return> {
    global newWord
    checkIt $newWord
}

proc giveHint { wrd } {
    ;# display just the first letter
    set hstr [lindex [.f.m configure -text] 4]
```

```
;# if hits string is 0, there is no hint at all
;# display hint incrementally
if { [string length $hstr] == 0 } {
set firstChar [string index $wrd 0]
.f.m configure -text "Begins with ... $firstChar"
} else {
;# there is some stuff there. Determine how many chars are there
;# and add one more to it
;# get the text after the ...
regexp {\.\.\. ([a-z]+)} $hstr ma1 ma2
;# ma2 contains the current help, find its length
set len [string length $ma2]
set nextChar [string index $wrd $len]
set new ${ma2}${nextChar}
#    puts "From giveHint: $new"
.f.m configure -text "Begins with ... $new"
}
}

proc checkIt { w  } {
set ans [.e get]
#    puts "Checking $ans ..."
if { [string compare $ans $w] == 0 } {
.la config -text Congratulations!
} else {
.la config -text "Hard luck, try again..."
}
}
```

Q **The input translation and parsing in the CGI scripts look messy. Do I have to recreate many such scripts for developing CGIs in Tcl?**

A Listing 24.6 is pretty much a template that you can reuse. Also, a number of Tcl procedures can make working with HTML easier. These are kept in the script file cgilib.tcl, which can be downloaded from the Scriptics Web site mentioned previously.

Q **Can I access Web servers to embed additional third-party scripts and applications in my CGIs?**

A For developing powerful ways of embedding Web servers in applications, see TclHttpd, which is written in pure Tcl. Further details can be found at http://www.scriptics.com/products/tclhttpd. A whole chapter on this topic is included in the forthcoming 3rd edition of Brent Welch's book *Practical Programming in Tcl and Tk*.

Q **What are the differences between a Tcl Plug-in and a CGI in Tcl?**

A The Tcl Plug-in executes the tclet in the client machine; the CGI executes the tclet in the server. If your application requires special hardware, software, or more powerful resources that are available at your site, it is better to use CGI. But, beware of demand load: the number of people accessing and using your resources and application at the same time. Tclet is embedded in a Web page. CGI creates a dynamic Web page. In creating the dynamic Web page, the CGI can gather user input from the client. The tclet executes at the client side. Any user input via Tk widgets in the tclet are processed internally within the Plug-in's slave interpreter. In both methods, you can embed third-party applications and scripts, and the source of your application remains inaccessible.

Workshop

The following quiz section is designed to provide you with an opportunity to recall some of the important concepts introduced in this hour. These might be commands, command syntax, common mistakes, usage, and so on.

The exercises section following the quiz section should really be called a *practical*, in that you have to do them. This hour has provided a basic template that is quite invariant, and all you need to do is to get the right environment set up and to try examples that are relevant for you. Our aim is that these two sections should reinforce the knowledge you have gained in this hour. The answers to the quiz that follows can be found in Appendix A, "Answers to Quizzes."

Quiz

1. What is a tclet?
2. How do you create a tclet?
3. What are security policies?
4. What is a CGI?
5. Where does the output from a CGI go?

Exercises

Solutions to the exercises are on the CD-ROM that accompanies this book.

1. Check whether your browser has Tcl Plug-in. If not, download it from the Scriptics Web site and install it. It is easy and well documented.
2. Get your CGI access set up and try simple examples.
3. Write a Tcl plug-in which displays the elapsed time since last activated. Use one button as a Start/Stop button and use a label to show the elapsed time. Remember to reconfigure the callbacks to the button as appropriate.
4. Modify Listing 24.6 to return a HTML containing an embedded button. Pressing this button should display "Thank you".

PART IV
Appendices

APPENDIX A

Answers to Quizzes

 Solutions to the exercises are on the CD-ROM that accompanies this book.

Hour 1 Quiz

1. What is an interpreter?

   An interpreter reads the commands typed at the prompt, and the results are returned. This is in contrast to compiled languages, where the source code is translated into machine code in several stages.

2. What is the difference between `tclsh` and `wish`?

   The program `tclsh` understands and interprets Tcl commands only. The program `wish` understands both Tcl and Tk commands. It helps to think of it as `windowing shell`.

3. What is the default Tcl prompt?

   A `%` sign.

4. How do you execute a script file directly in the interpreter?

   At the Tcl prompt, you use the `source` command, For example, if the file `exam-ple.tcl` contains the commands, issuing `source example.tcl` at the Tcl prompt will execute the commands in the file.

5. What are typical events?

   Typical events include a keypress, a button click on the mouse, hitting a return key, moving the pointer, and closing a window.

Hour 2 Quiz

1. What is a Tcl command?

   A Tcl command is group of words and the words are separated by one or more whitespace characters.

2. What is meant by variable substitution?

   It is the process of referring to the value of a variable, and it is normally performed by preceding the name of the variable with a dollar sign.

3. What is command substitution?

   The return value from the command is used. For example, `set now [clock seconds]`, the return value from `clock second`, is used when evaluating the `set` command.

4. When do you use curly braces?

   Curly braces are used to group blank separated words.

5. When do you use double quotes?

   When you want the embedded variables and commands to be evaluated.

6. Are the commands inside curly braces evaluated?

   No, command evaluation takes place inside curly braces.

7. Given the commands
   ```
   1: set i 0
   2: set y[set i] 1.3
   ```

   what is the name of the variable in Line 2?

   The variable name in Line 2 is y0. Command substitution takes place on the variable name as well.

8. What is wrong with the command `puts "Airfare: $250"`?

   $250 is treated as a name of the variable. (Assume that there is no such variable defined.) If you intend to include the dollar sign as part of annotation text, you must escape it as `\$`.

9. What is the command to list all the available Tcl commands that begin with p?

Use info commands p*.

10. What is the value of the variable y in the following code?

```
1: % set x 5
2: 5
3: % incr x
4: 6
5: % set y $x
```

The value of y is 6.

Hour 3 Quiz

1. What is the value of y in the following dialogue?

```
% set x 5
5
% set y [expr ($x % 2 == 0 ) ? 1 : 0]
```

Zero. Because x is 5, the logical test fails, and the result of the expression is the false branch of the ternary operator.

2. What are regular expressions used for?

Regular expressions are used for searching for patterns in text strings.

3. What is the regular expression to find the three letter words in a string?

A word can be described as one or more blanks followed by any three letters, followed by one or more blanks. Thus the pattern is

```
set p {[ ]+[a-zA-Z]{3,3}[ ]+}
```

See the manual page for regexp command for further details on specifying bounds.

4. What is the command to generate random integers in the range 1 through 6?

```
set r [expr round( 10*rand() )%6+ 1]
```

5. What is returned by expr 1/4?

Zero. The arguments to expr are integers, and hence the division results in integer. If you expected a decimal number, you must use include a decimal point in one of the numbers as expr 1./4.

6. Given the following procedure, what does the command guessWhat 4 return?

```
1: % proc guessWhat x {
2: >    set y [expr $x * $x / 2]
3: > }
4: % guessWhat 4
```

The return value of a procedure is the value of the last command. Thus, line 4 returns 8.

7. What is the regular expression to pick Tcl comment lines?

```
set p {[\t ]*#(.*)}.
```

A Tcl comment line begins with a hash mark and can be preceded by zero or more tabs or blanks. You can anchor the pattern at the beginning as `set p {^[\t ]*#(.*)}`, but you will miss in-line comments. Note the use of zero or more in the pattern. Using + instead of * will be restrictive.

8. What does `set errorInfo` do?

It displays the most recent error message.

Hour 4 Quiz

1. What is the syntax for an `if...elseif...else` command in Tcl?

```
if {test1} { body1 } elseif {test2} { body2 }
```

2. What are the arguments for the `switch` command?

The `switch` command takes a variable, and series of pattern, action pairs as its arguments.

3. Why do you need to indicate termination of the options for `switch`?

If you don't terminate the options with `--`, there is room for confusion, when either the variable's value or a pattern begins with a dash, `-`.

4. What is wrong with this script:

```
switch -- $answer {
        yes: { puts Ok }
        no:  { puts NotOK } }
```

The colons (:) are part of the pattern and are not required by the syntax (as in C) of the `switch` command.

5. What are the differences between the `switch` and `if....elseif....else` commands?

There are two notable differences. First, a `switch` command is used to evaluate one of several scripts depending on a given value. Secondly, the choice of the script to be executed can be made using powerful pattern matching. Note that a `switch` command can be emulated using an `if...elseif...else` block.

6. What are the admissible options for `switch` command?

Answer. `-exact`, `-glob`, `-regexp` and `--`. Did you miss `--`?

7. What is the command to print a message if you are not using the latest version of Tcl?

```
if {![info tclversion] > 8.0} {
        puts "I have got old version. Update!"}
```

8. Can I write an `if..elseif...else` command in a single line?

Yes. Here is an example.

```
if {$x==1} {puts OK} else {puts NotOK}
```

9. What happens when you use a `-` for specifying an action for a pattern in a switch command?

When a pattern is associated with action `-`, the action for the following pattern is used.

Hour 5 Quiz

1. What is the length of the list set `la {Marks List {Phil 75}}`?

The last element is a sublist.

2. What is the length of the list set `la {a b\ c\ d end}`?

The whitespace character is escaped.

3. What is the command to extract the second element in the list set `la {Fruits: {pears mangoes apples}}`?

```
lindex $la 1
```

4. What is the command to extract the last element of the list set `makes {Ford Toyota Saab Audi}`?

```
lindex $makes end
```

5. What is the command to sort the numbers set `nums {-5 1 7 12 3}`?

```
lsort -integer $nums
```

6. What is the default sorting order for `lsort`?

ASCII collating sequence.

7. What is the command to replace 12 by 36 in the list set `nums {-5 1 7 12 3}`?

```
lreplace $nums 3 3 36
```

Hour 6 Quiz

1. What is an associative array?

An array that uses any character string as an index to store some value(s) in an array.

2. What is the size of the array `FRUITS` defined by the command

```
array set FRUITS {Juicy Mango Fleshy Pear Crunchy Apple}?
```

Here the array is defined as name-value pairs. The size of the array is three. You can confirm this with `array size FRUITS` command.

A

3. Given the array MODELS defined in the following code, what is the command to list Ford models?

```
% set MODELS(Ford90) {Fiesta Escort Modeo Ka}
Fiesta Escort Modeo Ka
% set MODELS(Citroen85) {Xantia Zx Bx}
Xantia Zx Bx
% set mfr Ford
Ford
```

The solution is to make up the required element name as in puts "Ford models are : $MODELS(${mfr}90)". Use an extra pair of curly braces to obtain the required name. (Refer to Hour 2, "Getting Started with Tcl," the section on Variable Substitution.)

4. Write a foreach loop to extract all occurrences of the bottom left coordinates from the array COORDS defined in the following code:

```
1: % set COORDS(BottomLeft1) {1.0 2.0}
2: 1.0 2.0
3: % set COORDS(TopRight1) {10 20}
4: 10 20
5: % set COORDS(BottomLeft2) {3 4}
6: 3 4
7: % set COORDS(TopRight2) {30 40}
8: 30 40
```

You need to be careful in choosing the correct pattern. The pattern Left* will not work because there are no names that begin with Left. You need a more general pattern, such as *Left*, as shown in the following code:

```
1: % foreach n [array names COORDS *Left*] {
2:      puts " All left coords: $n \t $COORDS($n) " }
3:  All left coords: BottomLeft1    1.0 2.0
4:  All left coords: BottomLeft2    3 4
```

5. How do you set the array variable env(MYHOME) to point to a suitable directory path and print the contents of the array env?

Set env(MYHOME) {C:\Tcl\WorkingDir}. Remember to use curly braces to protect the DOS path separators. Print the contents of the array with parray env.

Hour 7 Quiz

1. Can I have zero arguments for a proc?

Yes. If a procedure has no arguments, you must still indicate their absence by a pair of braces. For example, proc empty {} { ... }.

2. What is the constraint on specifying default values for input arguments for a proc?

Arguments with default values must appear at the end of the argument list.

3. What is the purpose of the special argument `args`?

   To pass a variable number of input arguments. If specified, it must be the last argument in the argument list. If the parameter named `args` is not the last argument, it is treated as a normal argument accepting a single value.

4. What is the scope of the variables defined inside a procedure?

   Any variables defined inside a procedure are local and are not visible outside, unless declared as a global variable.

5. What is the command to inspect the global variables?

   The command `info global` returns all the global variables currently defined.

6. How are arguments passed to a procedure?

   Arguments to a procedure are passed by value.

7. What Tcl command enables you to implement call-by-name method of argument processing?

   The command is `upvar`.

8. What is the command to time a Tcl script?

   The command is `time script ?count?`.

9. What does the variable `auto_path` contain?

   A list of directory path names that contain Tcl script libraries.

10. Can I declare an array as a global?

    Yes. In fact, this is the best way to keep your code neat and tidy. Put all the initialization information into an array. Any modifications or additional information can be added with the least amount of disruption. Here is a sample to give you an idea:

```
proc initMyApp {} {
   global INIT
   set INIT(homedir) ...
   set INIT(editor) ...
   set INIT(appTitle)
   set INIT(version) 1.1.0
   ...
}
```

Hour 8 Quiz

1. What is returned by
```
set s {Hello World}
string index $s [expr [string length $s ]-1]
```

   The letter d.

2. What is the result of the command `string compare C A`?

   The result is 1 because the letter C comes after A in the ASCII collating sequence.

3. In the command `regexp {([0-9]+)-.*-([0-9]+)} {The card expires on: 30-Aug-2001} ma A B`, what is stored in the variable B?

   2001. The pattern matches the string `30-Aug-2001` and the variable A stores `30`. Note the use of dashes in the pattern specification.

4. Write a regular expression to match the two integers in the string `set msg {He is aged 12 and weighs 55 Kg.}`

   The regular expression is `regexp {([0-9]+)[^0-9]+([0-9]+)} $msg match age weight`. Note the pattern for matching the intervening text between the two integers. You will not get the right numbers using `.*`.

5. Why doesn't the command `if {[string compare OK OK]} {puts Fine}` work as intended?

   The string command returns zero, if the strings are equal. You need to amend the conditional as `if {[string compare OK OK] == 0} {puts Fine}` to get the intended behavior.

6. What is returned by the command `string match {[Yy]*} yes` ?

   `1`. The command found a successful match. Remember that the curly braces are essential.

Hour 9 Quiz

1. How do you open a file for writing?

   You need to use the access mode `w` for writing. Use the command `open fileName w`. You can also use `r+` or `a` or `a+`. See online manual pages for further details.

2. Does `gets $fh` read blank lines in a file?

   Yes. It returns zero for the number of characters read.

3. What does `gets $fileHandle Line` return?

   The number of characters read from `fileHandle`.

4. What is stored in the variable `msg` after executing the following sequence of commands?

   ```
   set x 2
   catch {incr x} msg
   ```

   The variable `msg` contains 3. Note also that the variable `x` has value 3. The command `incr x` succeeds, and hence the catch command returns zero, and the result of the `incr x` command is stored in the variable `msg`.

5. A file contains a single character followed by a return character. What is the size of the file?

The file size is platform dependent. On Windows, the file size is 3 bytes, one byte for the character, one byte for return (\r) and another byte for newline (\n). On a UNIX platform, the file size is 2 bytes, one for the character and another for newline. (Create the file on respective platforms to check the file size.)

Hour 10 Quiz

1. What does widget hierarchy mean?

   A widget hierarchy is a tree-like structure of nested widgets, starting from a single, unique root or main window. Figure 10.4 shows a typical widget hierarchy for an application. Widgets in a hierarchy inherit common attributes from their parents. The hierarchy also allows the geometry management of the children as a group.

2. What is the name of the toplevel widget when you start a `wish` shell?

   The name . refers to the toplevel widget. Note that this . is unique for each Tk application, regardless of how many of them are running simultaneously.

3. How do you inquire the children of the toplevel widget?

   Use the command `winfo children windowName`.

4. How do you add a title to your application?

   Use the command `wm title windowName titlestring`. Note that if you do not provide an explicit title, the name of the application's executable is used by the window manager to decorate the title bar.

5. How do you delete a widget?

   Use the command `destroy pathName`. Note that if you supply . as argument for `destroy`, the application will terminate. Destroying a node destroys all its descendants as well.

6. What are `frame` widgets used for?

   `Frames` are used as containers for a collection of widgets.

7. How many geometry managers are there in Tk?

   There are four geometry managers, namely the Grid, the Placer, the Packer and the internal structured geometry manager for the Tk canvas widget.

8. What are the main differences between the Grid, the Placer and the Packer?

   The Packer provides more powerful dynamic geometry management in comparison to the placer and grid geometry managers. You can specify policy such as expand, fill, or anchor to the Packer. These dictate how the slaves are laid out when their master is changed.

A

9. Where is the widget .f.b packed by default?

   Each slave is packed in its parent master by default, in this case, .f. If you want to pack the slave in another widget, use the -in option. Note that if the master is not the slave's parent, it has to be a descendant of the slave's parent.

10. What is the default side for the pack command?

    The default value for -side is top.

11. How do you unpack slaves?

    Use the command pack forget pathName.

12. How will you find the default minimum size of your application's main window?

    Use the command wm minsize.

Hour 11 Quiz

1. What is a widget command?

   When Tk creates a widget, it also creates a command specific to that particular widget, known as widget command. A widget and its command share their names. The widget command is used to query and alter a widget's configuration options, as well as to invoke other actions in the widget.

2. What are the widget actions or subcommands that are common across all Tk widget classes?

   The action subcommands configure and cget are common to all widget classes. The configure subcommand is used to set values of options, that is configure the options of a widget at times other than when it is created. The cget action subcommand retrieves the current value of a specified option. More complex widgets support more actions to provide more complex behavior.

3. What does the action subcommand pathName cget option do?

   It gets the current value of the specified option.

4. What is the syntax of the bind command?

   It is one of the following:

   bind tag

   bind tag <eventsequence>

   bind tag <eventsequence> script

   bind tag <eventsequence> +script

5. What is the syntax of the event sequence for a bind command?

   <?modifier??modifier?Type-qualifier>. Note that the qualifier is prefixed with -.

6. How will you find out if a binding is defined for a widget?

   Use the command `bind tag`. It will return a list of all the currently defined bindings for `tag`.

7. What is the command to examine the action script associated with a particular binding of a widget?

   Use the command `bind tag <eventsequence>`.

8. What is the difference between the `-command` option and a widget binding?

   The `bind` command provides greater flexibility by enabling you to associate any particular event sequence with a Tcl script and bind these two to any particular widget. In general, the `-command` option is applied to predefined event sequences and for particular widget classes.

9. Why are intercommunication commands used?

   Intercommunication commands are used to make widgets/windows to communicate with other widgets/windows within the same application or with widgets/windows of other applications on the same or remote display. They are also used to communicate with application data objects. The goal is to provide meaningful response to user interactions and help the user to achieve his tasks.

10. What does the `grab set` command do?

    The `grab set` command takes a window as an input argument and confines all keyboard and mouse input to that particular window/widget and its descendants.

Hour 12 Quiz

1. Why are intercommunication commands used?

   Intercommunication commands are used to communicate between widgets within the same application, with widgets of other applications on the same or remote display. and also to communicate with application data objects.

2. What does the `grab set` command do?

   The `grab set` command takes a window as an input argument and confines all keyboard and mouse input to that particular window/widget and its descendants.

3. Why doesn't the Tcl/Tk interpreter return a widget or path name when you execute a command of the type menu add `entryType ?option value??`

   Menu entries are not button widgets. So no path name is specified when these are added to the menu to be returned by the interpreter.

4. What are the types of entries can you use for a menu?

   Command, checkbutton, radiobutton, cascade, and separator.

5. Can I use a menubutton to spawn a submenu?

No, you can't. Use a cascadebutton entry.

6. What are the differences between option menus and lists?

Option menus have fixed number of predefined choices and allow a one-of-many choice. Lists allow both single and multiple choices, but option menus don't.

7. What are the built-in Tk message icons and types?

The icons are warning, question, information, and error. The types are ok, yesno, yesnocancel, retrycancel, and abortretrycancel.

8. What is a modal dialog?

A modal dialog is one that requires the user to respond definitely before further execution of an application can take place.

Hour 13 Quiz

1. Where will the following command insert text in the text widget: .t insert "end - 5 chars"?

The text will be inserted after the fourth character from the last newline character.

2. What is the syntax of index?

The syntax for index is a base followed by any number of optional modifiers. The base specifies a starting point and the optional modifiers adjust the index from this starting point.

3. What is the command to determine the number of lines displayed in a text widget?

.t index end

4. What is the command to insert some text at the point where the mouse is clicked?

.t insert insert "Some inserted text"

5. How do you create a mark called lastbutone to mark the start of the second last line of text?

.t mark set lastbutone "end - 1lines"

6. How do you find the current position of a mark?

.t index markName

7. How do you list a range of characters using a mark?

.t get markName

8. How would you configure a tag for overstrike display style?

.t tag configure tagName -overstrike on

9. What is the command to attach a tag to a text string?

.t insert index {text string} tagName

Hour 14 Quiz

1. What is the use of text tags?

   Tags are used to alter configuring display styles of the associated text. They are also used for binding mouse-pointer events over the tagged characters. When such events happen, an associated script is executed.

2. What happens to a tag when the characters or words associated with the tag disappear?

   The tag disappears as well. Recall that this characteristic does not apply to marks.

3. Is this code correct?

   ```
   eval .t delete [.t tag range newTxt]; .t tag remove newTxt 1.0 end
   ```

   Not really. The first command deletes all the text associated with the tag newTxt; this will automatically removes the tag. The second command is redundant and does nothing.

4. Explain the need for Line 20 in Listing 14.1.

   The newTxt tag is removed when all the associated text is removed by the eraseTxt procedure call. You must reconfigure the tag.

5. How many characters does an embedded window or image take in the text widget's index space?

   Both take only one character of index space.

6. Can two embedded windows have the same name?

   No. They must have uniquely identifiable names and should have the text window either as its parent or as a descendant of its parent.

7. What is the naming convention for embedded images?

   If the name option is not specified, the value of the image option is taken for the name. If more than one instance of the same image is used, the name is appended with a number of the form #nn by default.

8. What geometry management rules apply for embedded windows?

   Embedded windows must have the text window either as a parent or as a descendant of a parent. So both are managed together by the geometry manager. When the text around an embedded window changes or when it is scrolled, the text window automatically updates the position of the embedded window.

A

9. What is the scope of variables in tag bindings and binding callbacks?

Tag bindings and binding callbacks have the same variable scope mechanism as normal procedures and their callers. When writing scripts for binding callbacks, you must remember that the variables defined in the main program are not available inside the procedure (unless passed as a procedure argument). Also, any variable defined in the callback will be known to the calling program only if you return that value from the callback procedure.

Hour 15 Quiz

1. What are the canvas items you can have?

Arc, bitmap, image, line, oval, polygon, rectangle, text, and windows are the items you can use in canvas widget.

2. What do the input arguments x1, y1, x2, and y2 refer to in the creation of canvas item rectangle in the command `pathName create rectangle x1 y1 x2 y2 option ?value??`

The arguments x1, y1, x2, and y2 give the coordinates of the two diagonally opposite corners of the rectangle. The resultant rectangle will include its upper and left edges, but not its lower or right edges.

3. What styles of arcs can you have with Tk?

Chord, arc, and piestyle.

4. What do the options `-extent`, `-start` mean for the canvas item arc?

`-extent` (set to a value in degrees) specifies the size of the angular range occupied by the arc. `-start`, whose value (specified in degrees) sets the beginning of the angular range occupied by the arc. The value can be positive or negative.

5. What does setting `-scrollregion` do?

It sets the boundary for information display for the canvas.

6. What does `-xscrollcommand` option in a canvas do?

It takes a script argument which is the widget command set for the associated scrollbar of the canvas and invokes the scrollbar to set its initial position in the specified proportion of the contents of the canvas.

7. What is the syntax for binding an event sequence to a canvas item?

`pathName bind tagOrId <event sequence> {script}`.

8. What does the command `pathName find enclosed x1, y1, x2, y2` do?

It returns a list of all the items that are completely enclosed within the specified bounds.

9. What does the command `pathName find overlapping x1, y1, x2, y2` do?

   It returns a list of all the items that overlap or are completely enclosed within the specified bounds.

10. What is the difference between the commands `pathName bbox tagOrId` and `pathName coords tagOrId`?

    `pathName bbox tagOrId` returns a list of four elements, x1, y1, x2, y2 that give the bounds of an approximate bounding box for `tagOrId` where x1 is on the left, x2 is on the right, y1 is on the top, and y2 is on the bottom of the bounding box of the drawn area of item. `pathName coords tagOrId` returns the actual coordinates of the item given by `tagOrId`.

Hour 16 Quiz

1. How are tags created for a canvas item?

   Tag names are specified using `-tags` option at the time of creation or added subsequently with the command `canvas addtag tagOrId tagName`.

2. What is the command to delete all the tags in a canvas?

   The command `canvas delete all`. The symbolic tag name `all` can be used to refer to all the items in a canvas.

3. Fill the blank. Binding scripts are executed in _____ scope.

   Binding scripts are executed in global scope.

4. What tag name is automatically added when the mouse enters an item in the canvas?

   The tag name `current` is added to the list of tag names for the item.

5. How do you remove binding on an item?

   Set the binding to null script. For example, `.c bind mytag <Enter> {}`. A similar mechanism equally applies to bindings in canvas widget as well.

Hour 17 Quiz

1. What is an image command?

   An `image` command is used to create, delete, query, and manipulate images. An image command is also associated with each image created. You can use the image specific command to invoke actions on the image.

2. What are the image types that canvas supports?

   Canvas supports two types of images called bitmaps and photo.

A

3. What is the difference between bitmap and photo?

Bitmaps are displayed with two colors: one for the foreground and another for background. Photo images, on the other hand, are full-color images, which can also include transparency.

4. What is the command to create a full-color image?

A full-color image is created with the command `image create photo` *name*.

5. What is the command to place an image item in the canvas?

The command `.c image` *x y* `-image` *imageName*

6. How do you move an embedded window in a canvas?

Attach a tag to the window item when it is created using the canvas action create. Then add a tag binding.

```
.c create window -window .mybutton -tags mybutton
.c move mybutton xinc yinc
```

Hour 18 Quiz

1. What does the Tcl C library provide?

The Tcl and Tk C libraries provide comprehensive access to the scripting environment, enabling you to create new commands.

2. What are the advantages of implementing commands in C?

You can implement your own version of a command. Commands implemented in C run faster than a Tcl procedure.

3. What does `pkg_mkIndex` do?

The command `pkg_mkIndex` builds an index for the automatic loading of packages.

4. What are the commands to bring the packages into the Tcl interpreter?

Append the packages directory to `auto_path` variable. If a package index has not yet been created, execute the command `pkg_mkIndex` to create it. Execute `package require packageName`.

5. What is the command to retrieve a command line argument that is passed to your C routine as a `Tcl_Obj`?

The command is error = `Tcl_Get<Type>FromObj(interp,objv[n],&var)`, where `Type` might be one of `Int`, `Double`, `String`, and so on, and *n* refers to the number of the argument.

Hour 19 Quiz

1. How do you execute an external program?

    You can use `exec` or open it as a pipe.

2. What is the command to read from and write to a pipe?

    Use `gets $fh` and `puts $fh` where `fh` is the file handle to the pipe.

3. What is the command to execute a program asynchronously or in the background?

    Use the command `exec prog &`.

4. How do you open a pipe for reading and writing?

    Use the command `[open "¦prog" r+]`.

5. How do you collect any errors that might be reported by the external executable?

    Wrap the exec command inside `catch` as `catch {exec prog} msg`. If there is a problem executing the program, the error message is stored in the variable `msg`. If there is no error, the results from `prog` are stored in `msg`. This is a compact way of trapping errors.

Hour 20 Quiz

1. How do you define a class?

    Use the `[incr Tcl] command class className {....}`, which defines a new class.

2. How is a class method defined?

    Use method `methodName ?args args ? {body}` inside class definition.

3. How do you access class variables and methods outside the definition of a class?

    Declare them as public. The default is private.

4. What is the difference between Tk attributes and class variables?

    The general commands to query and reconfigure attributes are available to all Tk widget attributes. These are applicable to class variables only if they are public.

5. What is the command to create an instance of a class?

    `className objectName ?arg arg?`

6. When is the destructor invoked?

    When the object is deleted. You cannot pass input arguments to a destructor method.

A

Hour 21 Quiz

1. How is a button created?

   Use the class method for the `toplevel` window. For example, `$t = MainWindow->new()`; then `$b = $t->Button(text =>'Hi There', -command => sub { exit } )` will give you a reference to an instance of a button.

2. How do you define a callback to a button?

   Use the command attribute of the button. You define the value of this attribute either as a subroutine (`sub`) or as a reference to a subroutine `\&buttonCB`.

3. How do you make a widget appear on the screen?

   Use the `pack(...)` with any required options specified. For example, `$b->pack()` will render the button on the screen in the `MainWindow`.

4. How do you trigger the event loop?

   Use the command `MainLoop` in your program. This will process all the Tk events.

5. How do you delete the entire contents of a text widget?

   Use the delete method of the text widget. For example, `$t->delete('1.0', 'end')`; where `$t` is an instance of a text widget.

Hour 22 Quiz

1. What is a namespace?

   A namespace is a collection of procedures and variables. You use namespaces to encapsulate the variables and procedures so that they do not interfere with variables and procedures of the same name defined in other namespaces.

2. What do the namespace commands do?

   They create and manipulate the namespace contexts.

3. What does the command namespace import `namespaceName::*` do?

   It imports the exported commands of `namespaceName` available within the current namespace context.

4. What environment variables can you set to get the auto-loader and package-loader to search for your extensions?

   `TCLLIBPATH` and/or `tcl_pkgPath`. Note that `tcl_pkgPath` is an environment variable set by Tcl/Tk. If you are an end user with no system administrative privileges, you should not directly alter `tcl_pkgPath`. Instead, use `lappend auto_path ?dir?`. `TCLLIBPATH`, a system environment variable that you can set in your start up files.

5. What does the command package `require` `-exact` `packageName` do?

   It specifies the packages that need to be loaded. The `-exact` option indicates the exact version of the package to be loaded in the event that more than one version of the same package is available in the same directory. It is used in Tcl scripts or at the prompt level in interactive sessions.

6. What does the command package `provide` `packageName` `?version` do?

   It indicates that version `version` of `packageName` is now available for the interpreter.

Hour 23 Quiz

1. What are the components of a graph widget?

   The components are `axis`, `crosshairs`, `element`, `grid`, `legend`, `marker`, `pen`, and `postscript`.

2. How do you display the available action subcommands of a graph widget's components?

   If `.g` is the name of the graph widget, the command `.g` `componentName` returns all the available commands. Note that this list can not be captured into a variable.

3. How do you define a vector object whose elements are `1` `0` `1` in BLT?

   First create a vector object as `vector` `x`. This creates a command by the same name. Then use the action subcommand `x` `set` `{1 0 1}`.

4. If `x` is a vector with elements `1` `2` `3`, what does the command `set` `m` `[set x(mean)]` return?

   The command returns the mean of the numbers in the vector. Here the variable `m` has value `2.0`.

5. How do you submit a command to a spawned process?

   Use the command `exp_send` `"command \r"`. The return at the end of the command is important. Without that, the other program will do nothing.

Hour 24 Quiz

1. What is a tclet?

   A tclet is a Tcl/Tk application that is embedded in a Web page. Its root window is your browser's window.

2. How do you create a tclet?

   Create the Web page. Use the embed tag to include the URL for the tclet.

3. What are security policies?

The Tcl plug-in starts a slave Tcl interpreter to execute your tclet. It is run on your local machine. The plug-in imposes restrictions on what commands can be executed by the slave interpreter to protect your file system and so on. These are the security policies and are defined in the plug-in configuration files.

4. What is a CGI?

A CGI is a program script that creates dynamic Web pages.

5. Where does the output from a CGI go?

To standard output. The Web server routes this to the client Web browser.

APPENDIX B

Useful Tcl/Tk Resources

What next? Now that you have a firm grasp of the essentials of programming in Tcl/Tk, the next step is to apply your skills. Because this book is aimed at beginners, we will not cover some topics in great detail. This Appendix is aimed at filling this gap by pointing you in the right direction for your next step. This Appendix contains a list of books (annotated where appropriate) and some useful resources on the Web.

Books

Ball, Steve. *Web Tcl Complete*. McGraw-Hill, 1999. ISBN: 0-07-913713-X. A good resource for developing Web-based applications using Tcl/Tk.

December, John and Mark Ginsburg. *HTML3.2 & CGI Unleashed*. SAMS Net, 1996. An excellent coverage of all topics concerned with HTML and CGI. Contains lots of practical information.

Flynt, Clif. *Tcl/Tk for Real Programmers*. Academic Press, 1998. ISBN: 0-12-261205-1. Comes with an interactive tutor developed in, you guessed it, Tcl/Tk. Accompanying CD-ROM contains a useful collection of case studies from real-world applications.

Foster-Johnson, Eric. *Graphical Applications with Tcl and Tk*. M&T Books, 1997. ISBN: 1-55851-569-0. The second edition contains a chapter on CGI and Plugin applications.

Gundavaram, Shishir. *CGI Programming with Perl*. O'Reilly, 1999. ISBN: 1-56592-419-3. A good introduction to CGI. Most examples use Perl. A very short discussion using Tcl for CGI programming.

Harrison, Mark. *Tcl/Tk Tools*. O'Reilly, 1997. ISBN: 1-56592-218-2. Includes discussion of several extensions including [incr tcl] and its cousins, TclX, BLT, Tcl-DP, Expect, and so on. Also contains a useful chapter on recording and playing back your favorite applications.

Harrison, Mark and Michael McLennan. *Effective Tcl/Tk Programming (Writing Better Programs with Tcl and Tk)*. Addison-Wesley, 1997. ISBN: 0-201-63474-0. The main focus of this book is on developing medium-to-large applications in the field. Advanced concepts such as building client/server applications are introduced from the ground level up.

Libes, Don. *Exploring Expect*. O'Reilly, 1995. ISBN: 1-56592-090-2. A very powerful and popular extension to Tcl. An excellent introduction that contains a host of applications applying to system administration tasks.

Ousterhout, John K. *Tcl and the Tk Toolkit*. Addison-Wesley, 1994. ISBN: 0-201-637-X. The seminal book on the subject by its creator. Though somewhat dated, it contains plenty of valuable information. Explanations are succinct and to the point. If you are serious about Tcl/Tk, this book is a must-read.

Raines, Paul. *Tcl/Tk Pocket Reference*. O'Reilly, 1998. ISBN: 1-56592-498-3. A very useful and neatly laid out reference to have on your desk.

Raines, Paul and Jeff Tranter. *Tcl/Tk in a Nutshell: A Desktop Quick Reference*. O'Reilly, 1999. ISBN: 1-56592-433-9. A handy desk reference. Includes references to popular extensions—Expect, [incr Tcl] and [incr Tk], Tix, TclX, BLT, Oratcl, SybTcl, and Tclodbc.

Schroeder, Hattie and Mike Doyle. *Interactive WEB Applications with Tcl/Tk*. Academic Press, 1998. ISBN: 0-12-221540-0. Contains lots of examples for developing Web-based applications. It uses the authors' own extended version of the plugin (Spynergy plugin).

Till, David. *Teach Yourself Perl 5 in 21 Days*. SAMS, 1996. ISBN:0-672-30894-0. An excellent introduction to Perl for beginners.

Welch, Brent B. *Practical Programming in Tcl and Tk*. Prentice-Hall, 1997. ISBN: 0-13-616830-2. This book is loaded with practical advice and is ideal for xintermediate-to-advanced users. (The third edition is currently under preparation.)

Zeltserman, Dave and Gerard Puoplo. *Building Network Management Tools with Tcl/Tk*. Prentice Hall, 1998. ISBN: 0-13080-727-3. A solid introduction to developing network management tools using Tcl/Tk. Examples are based on the commercial version of Scotty (a Tcl package that enables you to develop network management applications and supports several network protocols).

Zimmer, J. A. *Tcl/Tk for Programmers With Solved Exercises That Work With Unix and Windows*. IEEE Press, 1998. ISBN 0-8186-8515-8. Contains a collection of annotated examples, and explains how things work.

Internet Resources

Internet resources are invaluable, if only you know which ones are well maintained. Here is a list that we have benefited from. We hope you will find them equally useful.

Frequently Asked Questions. `http://www.tclfaq.wservice.com/tcl-faq/`

A well-maintained repository of frequently asked questions, collections of tutorials, books, articles, and so forth. From here, you will also find links to package-specific and platform-specific FAQs, and frequently-made mistakes. Be patient, and you will be amply rewarded.

Tcl/Tk Consortium. `http://www.tcltk.com`

Contains links to a variety of medium-to-large-scale applications.

Tcl/Tk Home. `http://www.scriptics.com`

A one-stop shop for Tcl/Tk related material. Contains links to user-contributed software, Tcl extensions, On-line manual collection, plugin software, and many useful articles.

News group. `comp.lang.tcl`

A very busy news group, catering to the programming needs at every level.

B

INDEX

The IT site
you asked for...

It's Here!

InformIT™

InformIT is a complete online library delivering
information, technology, reference, training, news
and opinion to IT professionals, students
and corporate users.

Find IT Solutions Here!

www.informit.com

Other Related Titles

Sams Teach Yourself Perl 5 in 21 Days, Second Edition
0-672-30894-0
David Till
$39.99 USA/$54.95 CAN

Red Hat Linux 6 Unleashed
0-672-31689-7
David Pitts, Bill Ball, et al.
$39.99 USA/$57.95 CAN

UNIX Unleashed, Third Edition
0-672-31411-8
Robin Burk and Salim M. Douba
$49.99 USA/$74.95 CAN

Sams Teach Yourself UNIX in 24 Hours, Second Edition
0-672-31480-0
James Armstrong, Jr.
$19.99 USA/$28.95 CAN

Sams Teach Yourself Linux in 24 Hours
0-672-31162-3
Bill Ball
$24.99 USA/$35.95 CAN

Sams Teach Yourself Shell Programming in 24 Hours
0-672-31481-9
David Horvath
19.99 USA/$28.95 CAN

Sams Teach Yourself KDE 1.1 in 24 Hours
0-672-31608-0
Nicholas D. Wells
$24.99 USA/$37.95 CAN

SAMS

www.samspublishing.com

All prices are subject to change.

Installation Instructions

Windows 95/98 NT 4

1. Insert the CD-ROM into your CD-ROM drive.

2. From the Windows desktop, double-click on the My Computer icon.

3. Double-click on the icon representing your CD-ROM drive.

4. Double-click on the icon titled START.EXE to run the multimedia user interface.

> If Windows 95/98 NT 4 is installed on your computer, and you have the AutoPlay feature enabled, the START.EXE program starts automatically whenever you insert the disc into your CD-ROM drive.

Multiplatform HTML View and Install Instructions

The disc is designed to be used with an HTML-based Web browser. Using a Web browser program, you can view information on Windows, Macintosh, Linux, and UNIX platforms concerning products and companies, and install programs with a few clicks of the mouse. You MUST have either a Web browser or another program that recognizes .HTML files in order to preview many of the files included on this CD-ROM.

Macintosh Installation Instructions

1. Insert the CD-ROM disc into your CD-ROM drive.

2. When an icon for the CD appears on your desktop, open the disc by double-clicking on its icon.

3. Double-click on the icon named Start, and use the Web browser that will appear.

Linux and UNIX

These installation instructions assume that you have a passing familiarity with UNIX commands and the basic setup of your machine. As UNIX has many flavors, only generic commands are used. If you have any problems with the commands, please consult the appropriate manual page or your system administrator.

1. Insert the CD-ROM in the CD drive.

   If you have a volume manager, mounting of the CD-ROM will be automatic. If you don't have a volume manager, you can mount the CD-ROM by typing

   ```
   Mount   -tiso9660   /dev/cdrom   /mnt/cdrom
   ```

   > /mnt/cdrom is just a mount point, but it must exist when you issue the mount command. You may also use any empty directory for a mount point if you don't want to use /mnt/cdrom.

2. After you've mounted the CD-ROM, you can install files from the tcltksoftware/linux or UNIX folders.

GNU GENERAL PUBLIC LICENSE

Version 2, June 1991

Preamble

The licenses for most software are designed to take away your freedom to share and change it. By contrast, the GNU General Public License is intended to guarantee your freedom to share and change free software—to make sure the software is free for all its users. This General Public License applies to most of the Free Software Foundation's software and to any other program whose authors commit to using it. (Some other Free Software Foundation software is covered by the GNU Library General Public License instead.) You can apply it to your programs, too.

When we speak of free software, we are referring to freedom, not price. Our General Public Licenses are designed to make sure that you have the freedom to distribute copies of free software (and charge for this service if you wish), that you receive source code or can get it if you want it, that you can change the software, or use pieces of it in new free programs, and that you know you can do these things.

To protect your rights, we need to make restrictions that forbid anyone to deny you these rights or to ask you to surrender the rights. These restrictions translate to certain responsibilities for you, if you distribute copies of the software, or if you modify it.

For example, if you distribute copies of such a program, whether gratis or for a fee, you must give the recipients all the rights that you have. You must make sure that they, too, receive or can get the source code. You must also show them these terms so they know their rights.

We protect your rights with two steps: (1) copyright the software, and (2) offer you this license which gives you legal permission to copy, distribute, and/or modify the software.

Also, for each author's protection and ours, we want to make certain that everyone understands that there is no warranty for this free software. If the software is modified by someone else and passed on, we want its recipients to know that what they have is not the original, so that any problems introduced by others will not reflect on the original authors' reputations.

Finally, any free program is threatened constantly by software patents. We want to avoid the danger that redistributors of a free program will individually obtain patent licenses, in effect making the program proprietary. To prevent this, we have made it clear that any patent must be licensed for everyone's free use or not licensed at all.

The precise terms and conditions for copying, distribution and modification follow.

GNU GENERAL PUBLIC LICENSE

TERMS AND CONDITIONS FOR COPYING, DISTRIBUTION AND

MODIFICATION

0. This License applies to any program or other work that contains a notice placed by the copyright holder saying it may be distributed under the terms of this General Public License. The "Program," below, refers to any such program or work, and a "work based on the Program" means either the Program or any derivative work under copyright law: that is to say, a work containing the Program or a portion of it, either verbatim or with modifications and/or translated into another language. (Hereinafter, translation is included without limitation in the term "modification.") Each licensee is addressed as "you."

Activities other than copying, distribution, and modification are not covered by this License; they are outside its scope. The act of running the Program is not restricted, and the output from the Program is covered only if its contents constitute a work based on the Program (independent of having been made by running the Program). Whether that is true depends on what the Program does.

1. You may copy and distribute verbatim copies of the Program's source code as you receive it, in any medium, provided that you conspicuously and appropriately publish on each copy an appropriate copyright notice and disclaimer of warranty; keep intact all the notices that refer to this License and to the absence of any warranty; and give any other recipients of the Program a copy of this License along with the Program.

   You may charge a fee for the physical act of transferring a copy, and you may, at your option, offer warranty protection in exchange for a fee.

2. You may modify your copy or copies of the Program or any portion of it, thus

forming a work based on the Program, and copy and distribute such modifications or work under the terms of Section 1 above, provided that you also meet all of these conditions:

a)You must cause the modified files to carry prominent notices stating that you changed the files and the date of any change.

b)You must cause any work that you distribute or publish, that in whole or in part contains or is derived from the Program or any part thereof, to be licensed as a whole at no charge to all third parties under the terms of this License.

c)If the modified program normally reads commands interactively when run, you must cause it, when started running for such interactive use in the most ordinary way, to print or display an announcement including an appropriate copyright notice and a notice that there is no warranty (or else, saying that you provide a warranty) and that users may redistribute the program under these conditions, and telling the user how to view a copy of this License. (Exception: if the Program itself is interactive but does not normally print such an announcement, your work based on the Program is not required to print an announcement.)

These requirements apply to the modified work as a whole. If identifiable sections of that work are not derived from the Program, and can be reasonably considered independent and separate works in themselves, then this License, and its terms, do not apply to those sections when you distribute them as separate works. But when you distribute the same sections as part of a whole which is a work based on the Program, the distribution of the whole must be on the terms of this License, whose permissions for other licensees extend to the entire whole, and thus to each and every part regardless of who wrote it.

Thus, it is not the intent of this section to claim rights or contest your rights to work written entirely by you; rather, the intent is to exercise the right to control the distribution of derivative or collective works based on the Program.

In addition, mere aggregation of another work not based on the Program with the Program (or with a work based on the Program) on a volume of a storage or distribution medium does not bring the other work under the scope of this License.

3. You may copy and distribute the Program (or a work based on it, under Section 2) in object code or executable form under the terms of Sections 1 and 2 above provided that you also do one of the following:

a)Accompany it with the complete corresponding machine-readable source code, which must be distributed under the terms of Sections 1 and 2 above on a medium customarily used for software interchange; or,

b)Accompany it with a written offer, valid for at least three years, to give any third

party, for a charge no more than your cost of physically performing source distribution, a complete machine-readable copy of the corresponding source code, to be
distributed under the terms of Sections 1 and 2 above on a medium customarily
used for software interchange; or,

c)Accompany it with the information you received as to the offer to distribute corresponding source code. (This alternative is allowed only for noncommercial distribution and only if you received the program in object code or executable form with
such an offer, in accord with Subsection b above.)

The source code for a work means the preferred form of the work for making modifications to it. For an executable work, complete source code means all the source
code for all modules it contains, plus any associated interface definition files, plus
the scripts used to control compilation and installation of the executable. However,
as a special exception, the source code distributed need not include anything that is
normally distributed (in either source or binary form) with the major components
(compiler, kernel, and so on) of the operating system on which the executable runs,
unless that component itself accompanies the executable.

If distribution of executable or object code is made by offering access to copy from
a designated place, then offering equivalent access to copy the source code from
the same place counts as distribution of the source code, even though third parties
are not compelled to copy the source along with the object code.

4. You may not copy, modify, sublicense, or distribute the Program except as
   expressly provided under this License. Any attempt otherwise to copy, modify, sublicense or distribute the Program is void, and will automatically terminate your
   rights under this License. However, parties who have received copies, or rights,
   from you under this License will not have their licenses terminated so long as such
   parties remain in full compliance.

5. You are not required to accept this License, since you have not signed it. However,
   nothing else grants you permission to modify or distribute the Program or its derivative works. These actions are prohibited by law if you do not accept this License.
   Therefore, by modifying or distributing the Program (or any work based on the
   Program), you indicate your acceptance of this License to do so, and all its terms
   and conditions for copying, distributing, or modifying the Program or works based
   on it.

6. Each time you redistribute the Program (or any work based on the Program), the
   recipient automatically receives a license from the original licensor to copy, distribute or modify the Program subject to these terms and conditions. You may not
   impose any further restrictions on the recipients' exercise of the rights granted

herein. You are not responsible for enforcing compliance by third parties to this License.

7. If, as a consequence of a court judgment or allegation of patent infringement or for any other reason (not limited to patent issues), conditions are imposed on you (whether by court order, agreement or otherwise) that contradict the conditions of this License, they do not excuse you from the conditions of this License. If you cannot distribute so as to satisfy simultaneously your obligations under this License and any other pertinent obligations, then as a consequence you may not distribute the Program at all. For example, if a patent license would not permit royalty-free redistribution of the Program by all those who receive copies directly or indirectly through you, then the only way you could satisfy both it and this License would be to refrain entirely from distribution of the Program.

If any portion of this section is held invalid or unenforceable under any particular circumstance, the balance of the section is intended to apply, and the section as a whole is intended to apply in other circumstances.

It is not the purpose of this section to induce you to infringe any patents or other property right claims or to contest validity of any such claims; this section has the sole purpose of protecting the integrity of the free software distribution system, which is implemented by public license practices. Many people have made generous contributions to the wide range of software distributed through that system in reliance on consistent application of that system; it is up to the author/donor to decide if he or she is willing to distribute software through any other system, and a licensee cannot impose that choice.

This section is intended to make thoroughly clear what is believed to be a consequence of the rest of this License.

8. If the distribution and/or use of the Program is restricted in certain countries either by patents or by copyrighted interfaces, the original copyright holder who places the Program under this License may add an explicit geographical distribution limitation excluding those countries, so that distribution is permitted only in or among countries not thus excluded. In such case, this License incorporates the limitation as if written in the body of this License.

9. The Free Software Foundation may publish revised and/or new versions of the General Public License from time to time. Such new versions will be similar in spirit to the present version, but may differ in detail to address new problems or concerns.

Each version is given a distinguishing version number. If the Program specifies a version number of this License which applies to it and "any later version." you have the option of following the terms and conditions either of that version or of any later version published by the Free Software Foundation. If the Program does not specify a version number of this License, you may choose any version ever published by the Free Software Foundation.

10 If you wish to incorporate parts of the Program into other free programs whose distribution conditions are different, write to the author to ask for permission. For software which is copyrighted by the Free Software Foundation, write to the Free Software Foundation; we sometimes make exceptions for this. Our decision will be guided by the two goals of preserving the free status of all derivatives of our free software and of promoting the sharing and reuse of software generally.

NO WARRANTY

11. BECAUSE THE PROGRAM IS LICENSED FREE OF CHARGE, THERE IS NO WARRANTY FOR THE PROGRAM, TO THE EXTENT PERMITTED BY APPLICABLE LAW. EXCEPT WHEN OTHERWISE STATED IN WRITING THE COPYRIGHT HOLDERS AND/OR OTHER PARTIES PROVIDE THE PROGRAM "AS IS" WITHOUT WARRANTY OF ANY KIND, EITHER EXPRESSED OR IMPLIED, INCLUDING, BUT NOT LIMITED TO, THE IMPLIED WARRANTIES OF MERCHANTABILITY AND FITNESS FOR A PARTICULAR PURPOSE. THE ENTIRE RISK AS TO THE QUALITY AND PERFORMANCE OF THE PROGRAM IS WITH YOU. SHOULD THE PROGRAM PROVE DEFECTIVE, YOU ASSUME THE COST OF ALL NECESSARY SERVICING, REPAIR OR CORRECTION.

12. IN NO EVENT, UNLESS REQUIRED BY APPLICABLE LAW OR AGREED TO IN WRITING, WILL ANY COPYRIGHT HOLDER, OR ANY OTHER PARTY WHO MAY MODIFY AND/OR REDISTRIBUTE THE PROGRAM AS PERMITTED ABOVE, BE LIABLE TO YOU FOR DAMAGES, INCLUDING ANY GENERAL, SPECIAL, INCIDENTAL, OR CONSEQUENTIAL DAMAGES ARISING OUT OF THE USE OR INABILITY TO USE THE PROGRAM (INCLUDING BUT NOT LIMITED TO LOSS OF DATA OR DATA BEING RENDERED INACCURATE OR LOSSES SUSTAINED BY YOU OR THIRD PARTIES OR A FAILURE OF THE PROGRAM TO OPERATE WITH ANY OTHER PROGRAMS), EVEN IF SUCH HOLDER OR OTHER PARTY HAS BEEN ADVISED OF THE POSSIBILITY OF SUCH DAMAGES.

END OF TERMS AND CONDITIONS

Linux and the GNU System

The GNU project started 12 years ago with the goal of developing a complete, free, UNIX-like operating system. "Free" refers to freedom, not price; it means you are free to run, copy, distribute, study, change, and improve the software.

A UNIX-like system consists of many different programs. We found some components already available as free software—for example, X Windows and TeX. We obtained other components by helping to convince their developers to make them free—for example, the Berkeley network utilities. Other components we wrote specifically for GNU—for example, GNU Emacs, the GNU C compiler, the GNU C library, Bash, and Ghostscript. The components in this last category are "GNU software."

The GNU system consists of all three categories together.

The GNU project is not just about developing and distributing free software. The heart of the GNU project is an idea: that software should be free, and that the users' freedom is worth defending. For if people have freedom but do not value it, they will not keep it for long. In order to make freedom last, we have to teach people to value it.

The GNU project's method is that free software and the idea of users' freedom support each other. We develop GNU software, and as people encounter GNU programs or the GNU system and start to use them, they also think about the GNU idea. The software shows that the idea can work in practice. People who come to agree with the idea are likely to write additional free software. Thus, the software embodies the idea, spreads the idea, and grows from the idea.

This method was working well—until someone combined the Linux kernel with the GNU system (which still lacked a kernel), and called the combination a "Linux system."

The Linux kernel is a free UNIX-compatible kernel written by Linus Torvalds. It was not written specifically for the GNU project, but the Linux kernel and the GNU system work together well. In fact, adding Linux to the GNU system brought the system to completion: it made a free UNIX-compatible operating system available for use.

But ironically, the practice of calling it a "Linux system" undermines our method of communicating the GNU idea. At first impression, a "Linux system" sounds like something completely distinct from the "GNU system." And that is what most users think it is.

Most introductions to the "Linux system" acknowledge the role played by the GNU software components. But they don't say that the system as a whole is more or less the same GNU system that the GNU project has been compiling for a decade. They don't say that the idea of a free UNIX-like system originates from the GNU project. So most users don't know these things.

This leads many of those users to identify themselves as a separate community of "Linux users," distinct from the GNU user community.

They use all the GNU software; in fact, they use almost all the GNU system; but they don't think of themselves as GNU users, and they may not think about the GNU idea.

It leads to other problems as well—even hampering cooperation on software maintenance. Normally, when users change a GNU program to make it work better on a particular system, they send the change to the maintainer of that program; then they work with the maintainer, explaining the change, arguing for it, and sometimes rewriting it, to get it installed.

But people who think of themselves as "Linux users" are more likely to release a forked "Linux-only" version of the GNU program, and consider the job done. We want each and every GNU program to work "out of the box" on Linux-based systems; but if the users do not help, that goal becomes much harder to achieve.

So how should the GNU project respond? What should we do now to spread the idea that freedom for computer users is important?

We should continue to talk about the freedom to share and change software—and to teach other users to value these freedoms. If we enjoy having a free operating system, it makes sense for us to think about preserving those freedoms for the long term. If we enjoy having a variety of free software, it makes sense for to think about encouraging others to write additional free software, instead of additional proprietary software.

We should not accept the splitting of the community in two. Instead we should spread the word that "Linux systems" are variant GNU systems—that users of these systems are GNU users, and that they ought to consider the GNU philosophy which brought these systems into existence.

This article is one way of doing that. Another way is to use the terms "Linux-based GNU system" (or "GNU/Linux system" or "Lignux" for short) to refer to the combination of the Linux kernel and the GNU system.

Copyright 1996 Richard Stallman

The FreeBSD Copyright

All the documentation and software included in the 4.4BSD and 4.4BSD-Lite Releases is copyrighted by The Regents of the University of California.

Copyright 1979, 1980, 1983, 1986, 1988, 1989, 1991, 1992, 1993, 1994 The Re

Redistribution and use in source and binary forms, with or without modification, are permitted provided that the following conditions are met:

1. Redistributions of source code must retain the above copyright notice, this list of conditions, and the following disclaimer.

2. Redistributions in binary form must reproduce the above copyright notice, this list of conditions and the following disclaimer in the documentation and/or other materials provided with the distribution.

3. All advertising materials mentioning features or use of this software must display the following acknowledgement:

   This product includes software developed by the University of California, Berkeley and its contributors.

4. Neither the name of the University nor the names of its contributors may be used to endorse or promote products derived from this software without specific prior written permission.

THIS SOFTWARE IS PROVIDED BY THE REGENTS AND CONTRIBUTORS "AS IS" AND ANY EXPRESS OR IMPLIED WARRANTIES, INCLUDING, BUT NOT LIMITED TO, THE IMPLIED WARRANTIES OF MERCHANTABILITY AND FITNESS FOR A PARTICULAR PURPOSE ARE DISCLAIMED. IN NO EVENT SHALL THE REGENTS OR CONTRIBUTORS BE LIABLE FOR ANY DIRECT, INDIRECT, INCIDENTAL, SPECIAL, EXEMPLARY, OR CONSEQUENTIAL DAMAGES (INCLUDING, BUT NOT LIMITED TO, PROCUREMENT OF SUBSTITUTE GOODS OR SERVICES; LOSS OF USE, DATA, OR PROFITS; OR BUSINESS INTERRUPTION) HOWEVER CAUSED AND ON ANY THEORY OF LIABILITY, WHETHER IN CONTRACT, STRICT LIABILITY, OR

TORT (INCLUDING NEGLIGENCE OR OTHERWISE) ARISING IN ANY WAY OUT OF THE USE OF THIS SOFTWARE, EVEN IF ADVISED OF THE POSSIBILITY OF SUCH DAMAGE.

The Institute of Electrical and Electronics Engineers and the American National Standards Committee X3, on Information Processing Systems have given us permission to reprint portions of their documentation.

In the following statement, the phrase ``this text'' refers to portions of the system documentation.

Portions of this text are reprinted and reproduced in electronic form in the second BSD Networking Software Release, from IEEE Std 1003.1-1988, IEEE Standard Portable Operating System Interface for Computer Environments (POSIX), copyright C 1988 by the Institute of Electrical and Electronics Engineers, Inc. In the event of any discrepancy between these versions and the original IEEE Standard, the original IEEE Standard is the referee document.

In the following statement, the phrase "This material" refers to portions of the system documentation.

This material is reproduced with permission from American National Standards Committee X3, on Information Processing Systems. Computer and Business Equipment Manufacturers Association (CBEMA), 311 First St., NW, Suite 500, Washington, DC 20001-2178. The developmental work of Programming Language C was completed by the X3J11 Technical Committee.

The views and conclusions contained in the software and documentation are those of the authors and should not be interpreted as representing official policies, either expressed or implied, of the Regents of the University of California.

www@FreeBSD.ORG

Date: 1997/07/01 03:52:05